Neuropsychology and the Dementias

Brain Damage, Behaviour and Cognition
Developments in Clinical Neuropsychology

Series editors: Chris Code, Scraptoft Campus, Leicester Polytechnic, and Dave Müller, Suffolk College of Higher and Further Education

Neuropsychology and the Dementias

Siobhan Hart
James M. Semple

Taylor & Francis

London · New York · Philadelphia
1990

UK   Taylor & Francis Ltd. 4 John St., London WC1N 2ET

USA   Taylor & Francis Inc., 1900 Frost Road, Suite 101, Bristol,
            PA 19007

First published 1990

British Library Cataloguing in Publication Data
Hart, Siobhan
  Neuropsychology and the dementias.
  1. Man. Dementia. Neuropsychological aspects
  I. Title II. Semple, James M.
  616.89

ISBN 0-85066-447-0 (cloth)
ISBN 0-85066-465-9 (paper)

Library of Congress Cataloging in Publication Data
Hart, Siobhan.
  Neuropsychology and the dementias/by Siobhan Hart and James
  Semple.
  p. cm.
  (Brain damage, behaviour, and cognition)
  Includes bibliographical references.
  Includes index.
  ISBN 0-85066-447-0 (cloth)
  ISBN 0-85066-465-9 (paper)
  1. Dementia. 2. Clinical neuropsychology. I. Semple, James, II.
  Title. III. Series.
  [DNLM: 1. Dementia. 2. Neuropsychology. WM 220 H326n]
  RC521.H37 1990
  616.8′ 4–dc20
  DNLM/DLC
  for Library of Congress   90-11188
                                                                 CIP
Typeset in 11/13 Bembo
by Chapterhouse, The Cloisters, Formby

*Printed in Great Britain by Burgess Science Press, Basingstoke
on paper which has a specified pH value on final paper
manufacture of not less than 7.5 and is therefore 'acid free'.*

Contents

Preface

Neuropsychology is a broad based scientific endeavour embracing the activities of researchers and practitioners in many academic disciplines. As such it has been at the forefront of the dramatic increase in knowledge about the dementias that has occurred in the last 15 or so years. This book aims to highlight some of the major advances that have been achieved and to consider their implications for future research and for the treatment and management of those afflicted by one or more of the devastating conditions that produce dementia. A second aim is to show how work from traditionally disparate disciplines is being integrated in an unprecedented way. In a very real sense the study of dementia has revolutionized neuropsychology.

In the first part neuropsychology is defined and some subdivisions are outlined. This part also introduces readers to the multifaceted problem of dementia; its costs in human and economic terms; issues related to definition of the dementia syndrome. Some of the many conditions that give rise to dementia are listed.

Part 2 is concerned with the pathological changes that take place in a number of key dementia-producing conditions, the changes in neurotransmitters that are associated with these and the first tentative steps towards rational symptomatic relief.

In Part 3 the clinical features of some of the major forms of dementia are outlined and diagnostic and differential diagnostic issues raised. The contributions and limitations of neuroimaging, electrophysiological and formal psychometric assessment procedures with respect to the resolution of differential diagnostic questions are also considered.

Investigations concerned with elucidating the psychological nature of the deficits shown by patients with dementia are considered in Part 4. The topics covered include memory, language and communication, attention, sensation and perception and finally praxis. The long-held view that, because of the generally diffuse nature of pathological changes in patients with dementia, such individuals are generally unsuitable for advancing our knowledge of brain-behaviour relationships is shown to be false. The advantages of comparative approaches are emphasised.

In the final part of the book we draw together some of the implications of the neuropsychological data that have been collected to date for the care and management of patients with dementia, as well as pointing towards those areas of investigation, e.g. molecular biology, which hold out much promise for the long-term goals of preventing, arresting or even reversing pathological changes.

Throughout this book there is a particular emphasis on Alzheimer's disease. We make no apology for this. Not only is Alzheimer's disease the most common cause of irreversible dementia, but in a very real sense it was the discovery of neurotransmitter changes in this condition that triggered much of the current scientific interest in dementia. It has also become very much a standard against which other conditions that give rise to dementia are compared.

The last 15 or so years have been tremendously exciting for those who are interested in dementia. The volume of literature has grown enormously with thousands of publications emerging in the last few years. The sheer volume of the data accrued is daunting for anyone new to the field, and even those who are experts in particular aspect(s) find it difficult to keep abreast of developments in other relevant areas outside their own particular niche. However dementia is in essence a multifaceted problem. No single discipline holds the key to its solution. It is only by bringing together information gleaned from different approaches that progress will be achieved. By taking a broad overview this book aims to provide newcomers to the field of dementia research with a summary of achievements to date and for those already actively engaged in relevant research and/or clinical practice it will provide an opportunity to examine the broader context into which their own work slots.

Acknowledgements

We would like to acknowledge all who helped us in the preparation of this book. Dr R. Doshi very generously provided us with the photographs of brain sections. Dr Mike Clark and Dr Chris Link read through and commented on the manuscript. Dr Chris Code was a constant source of encouragement. The DSM III and DSM III-R criteria for dementia are reproduced with the permission of the American Psychiatric Association. The NINCDS-ADRDA criteria for possible, probable and definite Alzheimer's disease are reproduced with consent from the authors and from the publishers of Neurology.

For Stephen

PART I

Chapter 1

Neuropsychology

Neuropsychology is that branch of science which seeks to elucidate the relationships between behaviour and the structure and function of the nervous system. In this context the term behaviour is interpreted in its broadest sense so that it encompasses not only observable motor acts but also cognition and affect. Over the years there has been a proliferation of prefixes reflecting the growing diversity of the field, the varied academic disciplines and training experiences via which the interests and skills of its practitioners have evolved (e.g. psychology, neurology, anatomy, speech pathology etc.), their specific goals and the methods they employ to achieve these. This trend will no doubt continue in the future.

However, the placement of boundaries within neuropsychology is somewhat arbitrary. There are many ways in which this broad field of scientific endeavour might be divided up. Moreover, the boundaries proposed are not static but rather fluid and evolving with considerable overlap between the subdisciplines. Furthermore, individual practitioners of neuropsychology may not be rigidly constrained to any one approach and may operate in various fields at the same or at different times. These caveats notwithstanding, we feel that a brief consideration of the various branches of neuropsychology will help the reader grasp the scope and diversity of the field.

Experimental Neuropsychology

Animal experimental neuropsychology seeks to determine the fundamental principles of brain function using infrahuman species. From the point of view of experimental design and control animal subjects offer many advantages. Lesions can be placed in specific regions of the brain and their extent carefully controlled. Recording and/or stimulating electrodes can similarly be placed in any desired area of the brain. Neurotransmitter systems can be manipulated by drug treatments in ways and/or to an extent not possible with human subjects. It is possible to exercise rigorous control over the subject's environment and thereby determine its developmental history. Accurate data on the nature and extent of the change(s) produced by experimental manipulations, in terms of histology and alterations in neurochemistry, are much more readily obtainable for animal subjects.

For some animal neuropsychologists the goal of elucidating brain-behaviour relationships in a given infrahuman species is an end in itself. Such limited goals inevitably raise questions concerning the definition of psychology and whether such individuals can claim to be psychologists. For most animal neuropsychologists, however, the ultimate aim is to foster understanding of human brain-behaviour relationships and animals are simply used as convenient models. The validity of such a comparative approach is problematic and has been highly controversial. The extent to which valid extrapolations can be made across species is difficult to determine but will undoubtedly depend upon the level of analysis involved. At molecular and physiological levels there is no good reason to suppose that there are significant differences between animals and humans. Thus, data obtained from animals on such basic mechanisms as the release of neurotransmitters, their effects upon the activity of neurons, the molecular mechanisms underlying such phenomena as synaptic plasticity should also apply directly to the human brain. However, cross-species comparisons of structural-functional relationships, the behavioural consequences of a lesion in a particular area of the brain or of manipulating neurotransmitter systems, are potentially more controversial.

At one extreme in this highly controversial debate has been the position adopted by writers such as Davison (1974: 6) who held that, 'With some few exceptions, it has not been possible to generalize from animal neuropsychology ... the range and complexity of human adaptive behaviours so far exceeds that of lower animals'. A very different view is expressed by Kolb and Wishaw (1980: 98) who argue that, 'it is not possible to study human neuropsychology without serious consideration of the neuropsychology of other mammals'. These authors contend (1980: 106) that the environment poses essentially similar basic problems for all mammals and that, despite differences in the details of their responses, the behavioural capacities to cope with these problems are 'class-common' and, 'are mediated by 'class-common' neural mechanisms sufficiently similar ... to permit valid generalizations across species'. Miller (1984a: 11), while conceding that, 'it is difficult, if not impossible, to make a straightforward extrapolation of detailed neuropsychological findings from animal to man and that the relevance of animal research is limited', advocates an eminently pragmatic approach to cross-species extrapolation. He holds that where information based solely on the study of humans is unavailable, inadequate or impossible to obtain, it is legitimate to turn to data obtained from research on animals to fill gaps and facilitate the formulation of hypotheses. Although the detailed results of such investigations will not give an exact indication of what might be expected in humans, they nevertheless point to general principles and possibilities.

Whatever one's views about the current contribution of animal neuropsychology to this very broad field of scientific endeavour, the historical importance of physiological and comparative psychologists in the development of the science of neuropsychology is beyond dispute. As Kolb and Wishaw (1980) point out, the term 'neuropsychology' was first alluded to by Hebb (1949) in a subtitle to his seminal book, *The Organization of Behaviour: A Neuropsychological Theory* when it was probably intended to represent a study that combined the neurologist's and physiological psychologist's common interests in brain function. When the term was used by Kluver (1957) in the preface to his book, *Behaviour Mechanisms in Monkeys* it seemed that, to use the words of Kolb and Wishaw (1980: 111), 'the term had become a recognized designation for a subfield of the neurosciences' but it received even greater publicity in 1960 with the bringing together of a collection of Lashley's writings concerned with studies of rats and monkeys under the title, *The Neuropsychology of Lashley*. Although the term neuropsychology was not used further or defined in the text, the studies presented were concerned with the relationship between brain and behaviour.

Much effort is currently being directed towards the developement of animal models of the cognitive dysfunction(s) experienced by victims of dementia. The goals are first, to increase our understanding of the contributions of the various brain structures and neurotransmitter systems affected in the dementias (see Chapters 3 and 4) to their clinical presentations and second, to produce assessment procedures in order to screen for compounds that may eventually serve as therapeutic agents. Excellent reviews of this research can be found in Iversen *et al.* (1988).

Another way in which animal neuropsychology has contributed to human neuropsychology is via the provision of assessment techniques. For example, the compound stimuli technique first developed by Konorski (1959) for research on animals has been adapted for use with human subjects and applied to the study of memory in epileptic patients before and after surgery (see Milner, 1964). There are a number of recent examples of the application of assessment procedures developed in the animal laboratory to the study of patients with dementia. These include the investigations of Flicker *et al.* (1984) into short-term spatial memory using a task developed for use with non-human primates and Irle *et al.* (1987) who employed a variety of memory and discrimination tasks originally developed for research using these species. Furthermore, Morris (1987a) has tested patients with dementia on a discrimination and reversal learning procedure of the type frequently used with rodents and Kesner *et al.* (1987) have investigated spatial memory in such patients using a task analogous to the radial arm maze so extensively employed in current research on rodent learning and memory ability. These workers have acknowledged that their paradigms were derived from those previously employed by physiological psychologists or animal neuropsychologists.

When Davison wrote the often quoted chapter in which he discussed issues similar to those under consideration here he stated that, 'Most of the research on experimental neuropsychology is performed on animals' (1974: 6). Even in the mid

1970s, however, human experimental neuropsychology was already clearly identifiable as a distinct subdivision of experimental neuropsychology. There was available a not insignificant body of knowledge derived from human subjects and concerned with the fundamental principles of brain-behaviour relationships without regard to their practical implications. In subsequent years, however, such experimental neuropsychological data have undoubtedly accumulated at an unprecedented rate. Ethical considerations clearly limit the sorts of experimental procedures that can be carried out on normal human subjects but this has not precluded the growth of a rich and diverse body of knowledge.

Techniques such as dichotic listening (Springer, 1986) and tachistoscopic presentation of stimuli (McKeever, 1986) have been employed extensively to explore hemispheric differences in the processing of information and the manner in which the activity of the two hemispheres is integrated. The electrophysiological correlates of information processing have been investigated using electroencephalography (EEG) and evoked potential procedures (Gevins, 1986). More recently, dramatic technical developments have led to the introduction of neuroimaging procedures such as Positron Emission Tomography (PET) and Single Photon Emission Computerized Tomography (SPECT) which have added a new dimension to the field of human experimental neuropsychological endeavour. These allow for the *in vivo* monitoring of regional physiological and biochemical processes such as blood flow and energy metabolism. Much psychopharmacological research could also be considered to fall within the bound of human experimental neuropsychology in that a compound is administered under controlled conditions and its effects upon cognition investigated systematically in order to throw light upon the mediating role of the neurotransmitter substance affected by the respective drug. In Chapter 5 the results of a number of investigations using drugs to manipulate brain cholinergic systems in young normal subjects will be considered in order to promote understanding of the functional significance of the transmitter deficits identified by biochemical investigations of patients with dementia and to assess the effects of augmenting the functional activity of the neurotransmitter acetylcholine.

Before going further it seems appropriate to remind readers that the subdivisions of neuropsychology as presented here (or indeed elsewhere) are arbitrary, as are the labels employed to designate particular subdisciplines. We consider it necessary to emphasize that the experimental method is not the sole prerogative of that group of neuropsychologists referred to above. A systematic scientific approach to research with emphasis on objectivity and experimental manipulation of variables is common to all branches of neuropsychology. Readers will appreciate that many of the techniques and paradigms employed with normal human subjects have also been used to investigate the victims of brain injury, although workers in this latter field are rather more constrained in terms of the variables they can manipulate and their goals are different (see below).

Cognitive Neuropsychology

Cognitive psychologists seek to develop models and theories concerning how people normally perform cognitive operations to represent and manipulate knowledge. It has long been recognized that patients with brain damage, in whom the processing of information is disrupted, can provide opportunities to test and extend the validity of these models and theories. In recent years such research has flourished and the term cognitive neuropsychology has thus been introduced.

A classic example of the use of data from a patient with brain damage to validate the models of cognitive psychology is provided by the case of HM who sustained bilateral damage to the hippocampi as a result of an operation to treat severe temporal lobe epilepsy. He has been the subject of intense investigation over several decades and his test results have had considerable impact on the development of theories of memory (Baddeley, 1982a; Markowitsch and Pritzel, 1985; Milner *et al.*, 1968). In particular, his differential performance on tests purported to measure short-term and long-term memory respectively has provided considerable support for the distinction between these two systems. Further support for this distinction comes from the performance of patients such as KF (Warrington and Shallice, 1969) who, following damage to the left inferior parietal lobe (Warrington, 1981), have exhibited the converse pattern of deficits. Such data have also been important in the debate concerning the interactions between short-term and long-term memory and, in particular, whether these systems operate in series or in parallel (see Shallice and Warrington, 1970). Another example of the way in which neuropsychological data can promote the development of cognitive theory is provided by work on the acquired dyslexias. Psycholinguistic studies of normal reading have led to the formulation of various dual-route models of reading aloud, postulating the existence of lexical and non-lexical procedures respectively, and these give rise to predictions concerning the types of reading disorder that might result from disruption of different processing stages in neurologically-impaired patients. The finding of a double dissociation of these two hypothetical procedures with some patients showing impairment of the non-lexical route while the lexical procedure is relatively spared (i.e. phonological dyslexia), and others showing impairment in the lexical route while the non-lexical procedure remains essentially intact (i.e. surface dyslexia), has provided evidence for the validity of dual-route models (see Coltheart, 1982).

Cognitive neuropsychologists have also sought to use the current theories of cognitive psychology as tools to increase our understanding of the deficits experienced by patients with brain damage. Recent examples of this in relation to dementia will be discussed in Chapter 8 concerning attempts to apply Baddeley's concept of working memory (and all its inherent subsystems) to the memory deficits of patients with dementia of Alzheimer type. The insight gained from such investigations may ultimately lead to the refinement of therapeutic approaches and perhaps even to the development of new methods of ameliorating the effects of the cognitive deficits consequent upon this and other degenerative disease processes. However, this is not generally the primary aim of the cognitive neuropsychologist.

Clinical Neuropsychology

Clinical neuropsychology also attempts to increase understanding of human brain-behaviour relationships, but its primary concern lies in the application of this knowledge to the clinical problems of patients with, or suspected of having, brain damage. It is concerned with assessment in order to identify, describe and measure changes in behaviour consequent upon brain dysfunction, whatever its cause, with a view to enhancing differential diagnosis, providing prognostic information and establishing baselines of performance against which change can be measured. More recently its practitioners have also sought to utilize such assessment data directly to guide the development and implementation of therapeutic programmes in order to ameliorate the detrimental consequences of neural damage.

It is not easy to distinguish between the applied discipline of clinical neuropsychology and that of clinical psychology. There is considerable overlap between the aims and interests of their practitioners. Traditionally, medical specialists, psychiatrists in particular, referred patients to clinical psychologists for psychometric assessment with reference to the gross differential diagnostic question of functional *vs* organic impairment. Such referrals were consistent with the view held by many clinical psychologists who, in accordance with the general philosophy of Lashley (1929) regarded 'organicity' as an essentially unitary concept. Hence, changes in behaviour following brain damage were thought to vary only in their degree, depending upon the extent and/or severity of the damage. Implicitly, even if not explicitly, most subscribed to the notion that all forms of brain damage led to essentially similar consequences. Thus differences in manifestation were considered to be in essence a quantitative variable, although one which might be influenced by idiosyncratic elements in the premorbid personalities of different patients.

Of course there were various psychologists whose knowledge of brain mechanisms was more sophisticated and who sought to apply this knowledge to clinical problems, taking into account many other variables likely to be important in determining the outcome of brain damage. These factors included the nature of the damage, its laterality and localization within a given cerebral hemisphere, the laterality of cerebral dominance in a particular patient, the age and sex of the patient, as well as age when the damage was sustained, and also the time that elapsed between the injury and the administration of tests.

The coexistence of such subgroups inevitably raised the question of whether they were distinct disciplines. Parsons (1970: 2) considered this moot point of whether a clinical neuropsychologist functions, 'in ways significantly different from a clinical psychologist so as to warrant his separate "specialized" identification' and, after surveying various lines of evidence (including training), concluded that the distinction was justified. His argument was bolstered most strongly by the acknowledgement that (1970 :3), 'it is no longer enough for the professional to have a general textbook familiarity with the central nervous system, as do most clinical psychologists. Rather, the clinical neuropsychologist must have appropriate education and training in modern biological aspects of behaviour before he can utilize neuropsychological data in a meaningful clinical or experimental fashion'. The contentious issue of training will be returned to later in this chapter. In the meantime it is important to emphasize that the evolution of the two disciplines has tended to blur the distinction between them at some levels of analysis while emphasizing it at others. We hope that this will become apparent to the reader in what follows.

The 1960s and 1970s marked a tremendous growth of awareness amongst clinical psychologists and a burgeoning of interest and endeavour in the application of diverse therapeutic techniques and procedures grounded in theoretical systems other than psychoanalysis, most notably application of principles derived from learning theories. Opposition to formal psychological testing of cognitive ability was expressed with varying degrees of vehemence by many clinical psychologists, and this at a time when clinical neuropsychologists were resolutely striving to extend the range and sophistication of their assessment procedures.

Detailed assessment of patients' cognitive ability has been and remains a fundamental aspect of clinical neuropsychology. The uses to which such data can be put are many and varied. Until comparatively recently one of the major goals of clinical neuropsychological assessment was localization of the site of damage and a contribution to the diagnostic process. With refinements in electrophysiological technology and the advent of neuroimaging techniques such as CT and MRI (see Chapter 7) this role has lost something of its former thrust. The emphasis has now shifted towards analysis of the functional consequences of injury with a view to providing a detailed description and quantification of cognitive and behavioural deficits and residual capacity. Clearly, such information can only be obtained by careful neuropsychological evaluation. The data obtained can be used to further our knowledge of the neural control of behaviour by examining its relationship to the site, aetiological nature and extent of the damage; to biochemical data on brain metabolism, neurotransmitter levels and turnover; and to histopathology if this becomes available. Detailed assessment is also the first step in the implementation of any therapeutic programme, whether this be 'physical' (e.g. drug treatment) or 'psychological' (e.g. training in the use of mnemonic strategies and external memory aids).

Amongst clinical neuropsychologists there is considerable individual variation in approaches to assessment. At one extreme of a continuum are those who routinely apply a fixed set of tests (such as the Halstead–Reitan battery) to all referrals.

Advocates of this approach argue that they thereby ensure that many aspects of cognition are tested so that subtle difficulties which may not be immediately obvious on superficial examination are not missed. Over the years a considerable body of data has been accumulated documenting the performance on standardized test batteries of normal individuals as well as those with various brain pathologies. The performance of any newly-referred subject can be compared against this data base for diagnostic and/or prognostic purposes. However, it could be argued that the goal of a comprehensive evaluation is illusory and impractical. Moreover, such an approach is very inefficient as it could expose the individual being assessed to unnecessary testing and still not provide information relevant to a particular referral question or to the difficulties encountered by that person as they confront the tasks of daily living.

An alternative, and more prevalent, approach involves the clinical neuropsychologist drawing from a pool of standardized tests as and when it is considered appropriate. This approach retains the potential for utilizing the validation data for each test employed but has the advantage of greater flexibility and more formally acknowledges the importance of the professional expertise of a practicing neuropsychologist in selecting the combination or series of tests to be administered. Promising lines of investigation can be followed up by more extensive testing to provide more data with respect to key questions. In such further assessment the neuropsychologist may again draw upon existing tests or devise procedures which will address the hypotheses entertained, hence verging towards the other extreme of the continuum, where lie those clinical neuropsychologists who favour single-case methodology. Such practitioners design tests for individual clients with specific referral questions in mind. The same tests may never be repeated in exactly the same format for any other individual. This approach shares much in common with another group of individuals interested in the clinical aspects of brain-behaviour relationships, namely behavioural neurologists. However, behavioural neurologists differ from clinical neuropsychologists in their emphasis on conceptual rather than operational definitions of behaviour and in their lack of concern for systematic and quantifiable behavioural observations.

It is only relatively recently that single-case experimental designs have begun to be accorded the acknowledgment they deserve as a means of advancing knowledge in clinical neuropsychology. In this chapter, where we must address the question of how clinical neuropsychology relates to clinical psychology, it seems appropriate to note that it is to representatives of the latter that we must accord credit for emphasizing the limitations of group data and directing attention to the potential of single-case methodology. In British clinical psychology, where a major proponent of the single-case investigation was Monte Shapiro, the emphasis was more on description and understanding of the patient's psychological problems than on direct treatment possibilities, while American workers were more concerned with the application of single-case experimental designs in therapeutic interventions. Hersen and Barlow's prestigious book, now in its second edition (Barlow and Hersen, 1984), leaves no doubt as to the importance of the contribution made by this approach in applied behaviour analysis and therapy. The methodology has been applied in both basic (e.g. Shallice, 1979) and applied (e.g. Gianutsos and Gianutsos, 1979; Wilson, 1987a) neuropsychological research, but most prolifically in the latter where an exciting development within clinical neuropsychology has been the growing emphasis on rehabilitation (Brooks, 1984; Meier *et al.*, 1987; Miller, 1984a; Powell, 1981; Uzzell and Gross, 1986; Wilson, 1987b). This is a novel field and it is not yet clear how far it can be advanced. However, the fact that neuropsychologists are giving serious consideration to rehabilitation is a welcome development in view of the therapeutic nihilism that has traditionally surrounded brain damage.

There are various approaches to rehabilitation, but these might be grouped into two broad classes. On the one hand are those which seek to accelerate, via appropriate stimulation, the process of spontaneous recovery or to promote and facilitate the assumption by an undamaged area of the brain of a function previously mediated by a damaged area: in effect a reorganization of the functional topography (see Buffery, 1977). The other broad framework for therapeutic intervention might be termed a 'strategic' approach as this seeks to devise ways of bypassing or avoiding problem areas by, for example, restructuring the environment, developing alternative means by which to achieve the same final goal, or making more efficient use of residual abilities (see Wilson, 1987b).

During the course of their work with brain-injured patients, and in particular their attempts at management and rehabilitation, clinical neuropsychologists have found it expedient to draw upon the therapeutic procedures devised by clinical psychologists for other patient groups. In this context, Horton (1979) has introduced the term 'behavioural neuropsychology' to draw attention to the interface between behaviour therapy and neuropsychology. Such developments inevitably resurrect questions concerning the status of clinical neuropsychology as a distinct discipline and whether the training and/or knowledge base of specific practitioners is sufficiently different so as to allow them to be assigned to one or other camp, or to be excluded from one.

Parsons (1970) placed considerable weight on the difference in knowledge base between clinical psychologists and clinical neuropsychologists respectively. Although the level of sophistication of knowledge regarding the biological aspects of behaviour is undoubtedly increasing amongst clinical psychologists, it still tends to fall far short of that required for an adequate holistic appreciation of the problems presented by neurologically-impaired patients. Moreover, extensive knowledge of cognitive psychology is undoubtedly a strong asset in promoting competent therapeutic interventions with this class of patients, and here too the level of sophistication required is not found typically in clinical psychologists except those who have chosen to specialize in neuropsychological applications.

It has to be said, however, that there are at present very few formal training programmes in clinical neuropsychology. Current practitioners have entered the field by a variety of routes, although many have received formal training in clinical psychology and for them it amounts to post-qualification specialization. The laying down of guidelines for the training and education of clinical neuropsychologists by the joint American Psychological Association/International Neuropsychological Society Task Force (see Noonberg and Page, 1982) and the recent establishment of the American Board of Clinical Neuropsychology with the express purpose of ensuring that practitioners possess adequately developed professional skills will no doubt stimulate the growth of formal training, at least in the USA (Bieliauskas and Matthews, 1987).

Concluding remarks: neuropsychology and the dementias

Until comparatively recently the dementias have been neglected by neuropsychologists, including clinical neuropsychologists. The global nature of the cognitive impairment characteristic of patients with dementia renders interpretation of their performance difficult and places severe limitations upon the sophistication of the experimental procedures in which they can reasonably be expected to cooperate. Moreover, the diffuse distribution of neural damage typical of dementia-producing conditions has made such patients unattractive to those whose models of brain-behaviour relationships are essentially anatomical. Patients with dementia have of course been the subject of many studies by clinical psychologists attempting to address the recurring problem presented to them, namely that of distinguishing between patients having functional psychiatric disorders and those with organic conditions. Such studies have for the most part been essentially quantitative in their approach with only marginal interest being shown in the underlying nature of the deficits found in such patients.

For reasons to be considered in the next chapter the past decade or so has seen a burgeoning of research interest in the hitherto neglected topic of dementia. This has become a major focus of endeavour for many scientific disciplines and is characterized by a high level of interchange of ideas between traditionally disparate branches of the neurosciences in a way that is perhaps unique. Neuropsychologists too have been drawn into these efforts and are not only advancing knowledge about the nature of the psychological deficits of patients with dementia but are interpreting the behavioural implications of advances made in other fields, including anatomy, biochemistry, molecular biology, neurology, pharmacology, speech pathology and radiology. The various academic disciplines whose work is relevant to the understanding of brain-behaviour relationships have for too long functioned in comparative isolation. This unsatisfactory state of affairs is being eroded with the growing recognition of the need for greater interdisciplinary communication and appreciation of the significance of the findings made by investigators from other neuroscientific disciplines (see Jeeves and Baumgartner, 1986). Workers researching the topic of dementia have been at the forefront of such integrative endeavours and this field is now marked by an unprecedented degree of interaction and cross-referencing among the various disciplines involved. Such developments are of course welcome, but nevertheless neuropsychologists must be aware of the danger of oversimplification of their concepts and methods in attempting to communicate and cooperate with other disciplines. It is our belief that as growing numbers of neuropsychologists are drawn towards research on the dementias in general, and Alzheimer's disease in particular, we are witnessing the first steps towards a new era in neuropsychological endeavour. This would encompass a more reductionist approach to brain function and therefore seek to relate cognitive and behavioural deficits not only at a macroscopic level to anatomical structure(s), but also at a microscopic level to forms and functions at cellular, subcellular and neurochemical levels. The task of investigating the neuropsychology of patients with dementia remains fraught with immense methodological difficulties but it is surely the mark of a mature discipline that problems are tackled because of their importance rather than eschewed because of their complexity.

Chapter 2

Multi-faceted problem of dementia

Developments in medical science have profoundly altered the demographic profile in developed countries, with greater protection against the ravages of disease, together with a lower birth rate, producing a proportional increase in the older age groups. The number of people in the UK over retirement age has increased substantially over the past 20 years so that already one in six of the population falls into this category (Central Statistical Office, 1984). However, it is the 'old elderly' (i.e. those who are 75 years old and over) who constitute the fastest growing group and it is estimated that their numbers will increase by some 30 per cent in the next 20 years. The 9.5 million retirement pensioners in the UK at the present time outnumber children of school age. The very high proportion of older people in the population, the vast majority of whom are no longer in full-time employment, clearly has profound implications for our society. Consequently dementia, the prevalence of which increases markedly with age, has become an increasingly important medical and social problem and has been described very appropriately as, 'the quiet epidemic' (Editorial British Medical Journal, 1978: 1), 'one of the most pervasive social health problems of our generation' (Royal College of Physicians Committee on Geriatrics, 1981: 143), and 'the disease of the century' (Thomas, 1981: 34). It is perhaps the most important single problem currently facing the health and social services (N. E. J. Wells, 1979). Quite apart from the economic consequences, the human cost is incalculable.

Economic Costs

The economic burden imposed by dementia has been examined in detail by Wells (1979). Although the figures he quotes are now somewhat out of date they provide a good starting point for consideration of the financial aspects of the problem posed by this condition.

In the financial year 1976–77 the total budget for Health and Personal Social Services in England (capital and revenue combined) was £6085 million. It has been estimated that some 35 per cent of this expenditure related to the treatment and care of individuals over the age of 65 years and a staggering 20 per cent of the total budget went on the treatment and care of those over 75 years old. The proportion of this which was spent on the care of individuals affected by dementia is difficult to determine, but Wells estimates that it was in the region of £300 million. Since Wells' analysis expenditure on the NHS has increased considerably, such that in 1984 it was of the order of £17 337 million. Assuming that the proportion of this spent on patients with dementia has not changed, the cost would be approximately £855 million. This figure is likely to be an underestimate since the number of patients with dementia will have increased.

A number of factors will profoundly influence the future economics of dementia. First, the number of sufferers is likely to increase given current demographic trends, particularly the growing number of 'old' elderly in whom prevalence is particularly high. Second, further developments in health care might serve to enhance the trend towards longer survival of patients with dementia. Third, there is a growing trend towards care in the community. Even at the time of the seminal Newcastle studies (Kay *et al.*, 1964) six out of every seven individuals with dementia were cared for by relatives and friends in the community but to date the financial contributions of such carers have not been included in official audits. The admittedly daunting task of measuring these must be addressed in the future. Community care does not necessarily equate to cheaper care than more traditional forms of provision, and indeed may be more expensive.

By way of comparison, it has been estimated that the cost of caring for patients with dementia in the USA is currently somewhere between $24 billion and $48 billion (Congress of the United States Office of Technology Assessment, 1987) and may rise to something of the order of $80 billion by the turn of the century. Medical costs alone have recently been estimated to be approximately $20 000 per affected individual per year (Hay and Ernst, 1987). Though seldom invoked, a number of states have passed so-called 'relatives' responsibility laws' which make not only spouses but also children and other more distant relatives (including grandchildren in some states) financially responsible for the costs incurred by demented patients maintained in nursing homes. Such laws raise many legal and ethical questions which are beyond the scope of this book but are considered by Gilhooly (1986) and by the report for Congress compiled by the Office of Technology Assessment (1987).

In conclusion, it is readily apparent that, even allowing for a margin of error, the economic cost of dementia is immense and is likely to increase further in the countries of the developed world as the current demographic trend continues and elderly people come to constitute an even higher proportion of the population.

Human Costs

Although the economic burden of dementia is immense, its cost in human terms is incalculable. This burden is borne primarily by the patients themselves and secondarily by those who care for them. At a tertiary level society in general suffers the loss of the accumulated wisdom and experience of the primary victims and of the energy of the secondary victims whose efforts might otherwise be directed elsewhere.

In the early stages of a progressive dementing condition patients may retain some degree of insight and must come to terms with the prospect of declining capacities and autonomy as they face what for many is a drawn-out terminal illness. Depression is a common reaction, although it may also be a feature intrinsic to some of the conditions which give rise to dementia. It is perhaps fortunate that increasing cognitive decline eventually robs patients of insight, although this need not render them immune to agitation and distress.

Some 80 per cent of patients with dementia are cared for in the community. In practice this means being cared for by relatives, a burden which is disproportionately borne by women. It has been estimated that currently there are more women in the community looking after elderly relatives than there are looking after children and it is not the case that those they care for are necessarily the less severely affected. The burden of care can prove very physically and emotionally demanding, as epitomized by such phrases as, 'the 36-hour day' and 'the funeral that never ends'. Research has shown that the burden of caring affects carers adversely in a number of ways (see Gilhooly, 1984; Gilleard, 1984; Mace, 1987). A significant proportion of carers rate their general health as being poorer than that of contemporaries. They report illnesses related to exhaustion and stress, as well as injuries resulting from the physical demands of caring. It has been found that those caring for individuals with dementia have three times as many stress-related symptoms as age-matched controls who are not engaged in a caring role. There are high levels of depression amongst carers, with many reporting feelings of anger, guilt and grief. They consume more sleeping tablets, tranquillizers, antidepressants and alcohohol than contemporaries. Carers report lower levels of life satisfaction. By virtue of their dependants' need for close supervision, they are deprived of opportunities to pursue leisure activities or engage in social interaction. Disturbed behaviour on the part of those affected by dementia may in various ways serve to exacerbate the social isolation of their carers. These secondary victims may have to give up work in order to fulfil their caring commitment with concomitant loss of career, financial status and social contacts. Caring for an individual with dementia may mean important alterations in living arrangements with one or other moving home. Some carers, particularly the children of elderly dementing parents, may have to cope with conflicting demands from the dependant *vis a vis* their spouse and/or children. The consequent family conflict can serve to increase the perceived burden of providing care.

Several studies have found that whether a patient remains in the community or enters an institiution is determined to a greater extent by the carer's morale and capacity to cope than by the physical, cognitive and functional status of the patient. In view of this, and the obvious need to reduce the strain on the supporters, much effort is being directed towards understanding the multidimensional nature of the burden of caring and providing the requisite physical and psychological support (Morris *et al.*, 1988b; Zarit, 1986).

Definition of Dementia

It must be recognized that the literature on dementia presents certain problems of terminology. Lishman (1987) has pointed out that the term 'dementia' has been employed in two different contexts. First, it has been used in a diagnostic or classificatory sense, referring to a specific disease or group of diseases characterized by chronic irreversible and progressive deterioration of higher intellectual functions based on primary neuronal disturbances. The second use of the term dementia is in a broad descriptive manner to refer to a general clinical syndrome characterized by chronic global impairment of mental status that may be caused by a wide variety of illnesses. Widespread use of the term in the first sense has given rise to an unjustified therapeutic nihilism when the diagnosis of dementia is considered. This is particularly unfortunate as a sizeable proportion of cases could benefit from existing forms of treatment if sufficiently thorough clinical investigations were pursued (Bradshaw *et al.*, 1983; Freemon, 1976; Marsden and Harrison, 1972; Smith and Kiloh, 1981). The second use of the term dementia in a broad descriptive sense, having neither aetiological nor prognostic implications, is becoming increasingly accepted and does seem preferable, although some would argue to the contrary (e.g. Isaacs, 1983). However, even amongst those who broadly agree that the term is descriptive of a clinical syndrome, the problem of definition remains and in the absence of a consensus of opinion diagnostic criteria vary.

Some of the more widely quoted definitions are as follows:

1 'The global disturbance of higher mental function in an alert patient'. (Marsden, 1978: 96)

2 'An acquired global impairment of intellect memory and personality but without impairment of consciousness'. (Lishman, 1987: 6)

3 'The global deterioration of the individual's intellectual, emotional and cognitive faculties in a state of unimpaired consciousness'. (Roth, 1980a: 24)

4 'The global impairment of higher cortical functions including memory, the capacity to solve problems of day-to-day living, the performance of learned perceptuomotor skills, the correct use of social skills and control of emotional reactions, in the absence of gross clouding of consciousness'. (Royal College of Physicians Committee on Geriatrics, 1981: 143)

5 The criteria outlined in the third edition of the Diagnostic and Statistical Manual (DSM III) of the American Psychiatric Association (1980: 111) are:

'A. A loss of intellectual abilities of sufficient severity to interfere with social or occupational functioning.

B. Memory impairment.

C. At least one of the following:

(i) impairment of abstract thinking, as manifest by concrete interpretation of proverbs, inability to find similarities and differences between related words, difficulty in defining words and concepts, and other similar tasks

(ii) impaired judgement

(iii) other disturbances of higher cortical function, such as aphasia (disorder of language due to brain dysfunction), apraxia (inability to carry out motor activities despite intact comprehension and motor function), agnosia (failure to recognize or identify objects despite intact sensory function), 'constructional difficulty' (e.g. inability to copy three-dimensional figures, assemble blocks or arrange sticks in specific designs)

(iv) personality change, i.e. alteration or accentuation of premorbid traits

D. State of consciousness not clouded (i.e. does not meet the criteria for Delirium or Intoxication, although these may be superimposed).

E. Either (i) or (ii):

(i) evidence from the history, physical examination, or laboratory tests, of a specific organic factor that is judged to be aetiologically related to the disturbance

(ii) in the absence of such evidence, an organic factor necessary for the development of the syndrome can be presumed if conditions other than Organic Mental Disorders have been reasonably excluded and if the behavioural change represents cognitive impairment in a variety of areas.'

6. 'An acquired persistent impairment of intellectual function with compromise in at least three of the following spheres of mental activity: language, memory, visuospatial skills, emotion or personality and cognition (abstraction, calculation, judgement etc.)'. (Cummings and Benson, 1983: 1).

Definitions such as those of Lishman, Marsden and Roth are comprehensive yet brief. However, while their simplicity is elegant and attractive for descriptive purposes, it leaves the clinician without practical guidelines, either qualitative or quantitative, as to what constitutes a global impairment. The definition offered by the Royal College of Physicians specifies further, at least in gross terms, the conditions necessary to conclude that impairment is global. However, like many other definitions of dementia, it fails to place due emphasis on the acquired nature of the impairment. This is important in view of the evidence that those with limited intellectual ability and/or little education are particularly likely to have the label dementia appended (Bergmann, 1979; Gurland, 1981).

Few of the definitions make explicit reference to the duration of impairment. In practice, however, most clinicians would not make the diagnosis if the process had

Table 2.1 DSM III-R Criteria for Diagnosis of Dementia

A. Demonstrable evidence of impairment in short- and long-term memory. Impairment in short-term memory (inability to learn new information) may be indicated by inability to remember three objects after 5 minutes. Long-term memory impairment (inability to remember information that was known in the past) may be indicated by inability to remember past personal information (e.g. what happened yesterday, birthplace, occupation) or facts of common knowledge (e.g. past Presidents, well-known dates).

B. At least one of the following:
   (i)   impairment in abstract thinking, as indicated by inability to find similarities and differences between related words, difficulty in defining words and concepts, and other similar tasks
   (ii) impaired judgement, as indicated by inability to make reasonable plans to deal with interpersonal, family and job-related problems and issues
   (iii) other disturbances of higher cortical function such as aphasia (disorder of language), apraxia (inability to carry out motor activities despite intact comprehension and motor function), agnosia (failure to recognize or identify objects despite intact sensory function) and 'constructional difficulty' (e.g. inability to copy three-dimensional figures, assemble blocks, or arrange sticks in specific designs)
   (iv) personality change, i.e. alteration or accentuation of premorbid traits

C. The disturbance in A and B significantly interferes with work or usual social activities or relationships with others.

D. Not occurring exclusively during the course of Delirium.

E. Either (i) or (ii):
   (i) there is evidence from the history, physical examination, or laboratory tests of a specific organic factor (or factors) judged to be aetiologically related to the disturbance
   (ii) in the absence of such evidence, an aetiologic organic factor can be presumed if the disturbance cannot be accounted for by any non-organic mental disorder, e.g. Major Depression accounting for cognitive impairment

Criteria for severity of Dementia:

Mild: although work or social activities are significantly impaired, the capacity for independent living remains, with adequate personal hygiene and relatively intact judgement.

Moderate: independent living is hazardous and some degree of supervision is necessary.

Severe: activities of daily living are so impaired that continual supervision is required, e.g. unable to maintain minimal personal hygiene; largely incoherent or mute.

lasted less than several weeks and some maintain that a period of 6 months or more in the symptomatic state is required before a diagnosis can be made (see Mahendra, 1984).

The DSM III definition of dementia has undoubtedly been one of the most widely used and does have a number of positive features. However, it too falls short of the required goal of providing operational criteria that would allow for diagnostic reliability. Jorm and Henderson (1985) provided an astute overview of the problems of implementing DSM III criteria and suggested a number of alterations to improve reliability and validity. The revised edition of the manual (DSM III-R 1987) appears to meet many of their criticisms (see Table 2.1) but it remains to be determined whether the changes introduced will improve the reliability and/or validity of the diagnosis of dementia. It is to be hoped that the tenth revision of the World Health Organization International Classification of Diseases (ICD 10), which will become effective in 1990, will herald further progress towards the achievement of a consistent definition of dementia.

Epidemiology of Dementia

A number of studies have investigated the prevalence of dementia in the elderly and this has been found to vary between 1 per cent and 9.1 per cent for severe cases and between 2.6 per cent and 15.1 per cent for milder forms (see Kay, 1972). The high degree of variation in these figures can be attributed in large part to differences in diagnostic criteria, as well as in sampling procedures and the intensity of case-finding efforts. Roth (1978, 1979) draws attention to what is undoubtedly another important factor hindering the establishment of accurate prevalence estimates, namely the difficulties of recognizing early cases of dementia, for which he cites evidence from the Newcastle-upon-Tyne Survey. In a follow-up study of 711 cases, aged 65 years and over, 30 subjects were found to have developed dementia during the 2–4 years since initial interview but in only six of these had the early stages of intellectual impairment been identified and progressive decline predicted when seen initially (Roth, 1979).

Unfortunately the early detection of mild dementia remains problematic. In a thoughtful overview of this issue Henderson and Huppert (1984) expressed their belief that neuropsychological evaluation had an invaluable part to play in enhancing the sensitivity of early screening procedures. They stated (1984: 6) that, 'the ascertainment of mild dementia can be made considerably more secure by psychometric tests of cognitive function' because, in contrast to the qualitative procedures often used in clinical assessment, psychometric tests yield quantitative data on a subject's level of ability and speed of responding. They are thus more sensitive to cognitive change and can provide evidence for a decline in performance more readily than a clinical interview. Henderson and Huppert recognize that there is at the present time no agreed rationale to guide investigators in the choice of cognitive functions to be assessed in screening for mild dementia or in the tests to be employed, although they appear to recommend sampling a wide representation of cognitive functions, and we would support this. Henderson and Huppert also point out quite rightly that cognitive impairment need not point to dementia and hence investigators must proceed further to address the question of the aetiology of the impairment detected by a screening instrument. These issues will be returned to in Chapter 7.

Another aspect of the problem with respect to identification of early cases is pointed out by Bergmann (1979), again using data from the Newcastle studies. Only 32 per cent of those subjects initially identified as potentially early cases subsequently developed dementia. At least some of those who did not deteriorate further, and continued to cope with environmental demands, may constitute examples of what Kral (1962, 1978) has termed 'benign senescent forgetfulness'. This emphasizes the need for follow-up of supposedly early cases. These data also highlight the need for research on normal ageing to go hand in hand with that on dementia in an attempt to establish sharper borderlines.

The UK estimates of prevalence obtained by Kay *et al.* in their Newcastle study (Kay *et al.*, 1964) are frequently quoted. Their findings suggested that dementia affects approximately 10 per cent of the population aged 65 years or over. More than 80 per cent of all cases were found to be resident in the community and in half of these cases the condition was severe. Prevalence increases markedly with age so that amongst those aged 80 years and over it rises to 22 per cent (Kay *et al.*, 1970). The prevalence of dementia in younger age groups is clearly lower and for this reason even more difficult to estimate accurately.

Not surprisingly, studies on the incidence of dementia have also yielded variable results (see Bergmann, 1985). Incidence rates of the order of five per 1000 per year have been reported using case index procedures. However, these rates are undoubtedly conservative and estimates based upon community surveys put the rate at 15 per 1000 per year. Estimates will of course vary according to the definition of dementia employed and the sensitivity of diagnostic procedures. Hence the issue of diagnostic reliability has important implications for descriptive epidemiology, for estimates of the number of individuals who have, or are likely to develop, the condition and hence for planning in terms of the level and breadth of services to be provided in order to care for such patients. More importantly, however, it is a necessary prerequisite for any attempt to draw inferences regarding causal mechanisms or potential risk factors. In attempting to proceed to the latter it will of course be necessary not only to achieve reliable diagnostic criteria for the dementia syndrome *per se* but also consistent differential diagnosis amongst the many and varied causes which can give rise to this clinical syndrome, but whose therapeutic and mangament implications are quite different.

Beyond the Diagnosis of Dementia

Table 2.2 lists some of the possible causes of dementia. Lists such as this abound in the literature, but it is worth noting that in many of these a distinction has been made between diseases which cause dementia and those which simulate it. However, there is an inherent illogicality in this distinction. If we accept that dementia is a clinical syndrome then any condition which produces the features necessary to satisfy the definition is a genuine cause. Use of words such as 'simulate' or the prefix 'pseudo-'

Table 2.2 Examples of Conditions which can give rise to a Dementia Syndrome

Primary degenerative diseases:
— Alzheimer's disease
— Pick's disease
— Parkinson's disease
— Progressive supranuclear palsy
— Huntington's disease

Vascular conditions:
— Multiple infarction
— Lacunar state
— Binswanger's disease

Metabolic and endocrine disorders:
— Hyper- and hypothyroidism
— Hyper- and hypocalcaemia
— Diabetes mellitus
— Hyperlipidaemia
— Hypopituitarism
— Hepatic failure
— Cushing's syndrome
— Addison's disease
— Wilson's disease

Infection:
— Creutzfeldt–Jakob disease
— Kuru
— Acquired immune deficiency
   syndrome
— Meningitis
— Encephalitis
— Neurosyphillis

Other causes:
— Normal pressure hydrocephalus
— Multiple sclerosis (some cases)
— Epilepsy (some cases)

Space-occupying lesions:
— Subdural haematoma
— Brain tumours (primary or secondary)

Toxicity:
— Alcohol
— Metal poisioning (e.g. lead, mercury,
   aluminium, arsenic)
— Organic insecticides
— Drugs (e.g. sedatives, hypnotics,
   anxiolytics, antipsychotics,
   antidepressants, antihypertensives,
   anti-arrhythmics, any drug having
   anti-cholinergic side-effects)

Anoxia:
— Cardiac arrest/failure
— Carbon monoxide

Trauma:
— Boxing (dementia pugilistica)
— Open and closed head injury

Psychiatric disorders:
— Depression
— Schizophrenia

Nutritional disorders:
— Pellagra (B3 deficiency)
— Wernicke–Korsakoff syndrome
   (thiamine deficiency)
— Folate deficiency
— Vitamin B12 deficiency

are inappropriate and belie use of the term dementia in the first sense outlined by Lishman, namely as a diagnostic category referring to a specific group of diseases characterized by chronic irreversible and progressive deterioration of higher intellectual functions based on primary neuronal disturbances. It would seem more appropriate to distinguish between dementia syndromes which are reversible, or at least open to significant amelioration, and those which to date remain irreversible pending the development of effective therapeutic interventions. However, as will become apparent in Chapter 7, one advantage of employing the term dementia in Lishman's first sense is that it allows for a certain economy of words and circumvents the need to employ linguistically cumbersome phrases when attempting to make explicit the specific conditions to which one is referring.

It would be virtually impossible to provide a full account of all of the conditions that can give rise to dementia. The strategy adopted in this book is to consider a small number of the dementia-producing conditions in some detail, namely Alzheimer's disease, Pick's disease, multi-infarct dementia, Parkinson's disease, Huntington's disease, progressive supranuclear palsy, Creutzfeldt–Jakob disease and alcoholic dementia. The rationale for this choice is outlined below.

Pathological studies (e.g. Jellinger 1976; Tomlinson *et al.*, 1970) have shown that irreversible dementia in old age is of two major types. These are primary degenerative dementia of the Alzheimer type and multi-infarct or vascular dementia. Together they account for approximately 80 per cent of all the dementias of old age. Other causes are considerably less frequent.

Traditionally Alzheimer's disease was considered to be a rather uncommon form of devastating presenile dementia, as the original observations were made on a 51-year-old woman. However, as is often pointed out (e.g. Mortimer, 1980; Roth, 1979), Alzheimer himself considered his case to represent a precocious form of senile dementia. It is now generally accepted that there is no clear difference between this primary degenerative dementia of early onset and that occurring in the senium (Hughes, 1970; Terry, 1976; Terry and Katzman, 1983). The neuropathological features of the two conditions (see Chapter 3) appear to be largely identical (Neumann and Cohn, 1953, 1978; Terry, 1978), although there is some evidence that the brains of younger patients may show more degeneration at autopsy (Constantinidis, 1978; Constantinidis *et al.*, 1978). There are also some suggestions in the literature that in younger patients the clinical features, although essentially identical, are more pervasive (see Lishman, 1987). Genetic differences have also been suggested (Heston *et al.*, 1981; Larsson *et al.*, 1963; Wright and Whalley, 1984). Although the nosological debate is by no means closed (see Seltzer and Sherwin, 1983), it remains true that the two conditions have been differentiated largely on the very dubious grounds of an arbitrarily fixed age, usually 65 years. Thus it is now generally accepted that these should be considered as a single disease entity (at least until such time as stronger evidence in favour of differentiation is produced). In the present book the term

Alzheimer's disease (AD) will be used irrespective of age at onset of the disease, provided the diagnosis has been confirmed histologically by biopsy or autopsy examination. In the case of clinically-diagnosed patients the term 'dementia of Alzheimer type' (DAT) will be employed. However, where it seems particularly appropriate to do so, the term 'senile dementia of Alzheimer type' (SDAT) or the description 'presenile' will be introduced.

The neuropathological evidence presented by Tomlinson *et al.* (1970) indicated that 50 per cent of demented patients coming to autopsy had a primary neuronal disorder of the Alzheimer type with no evidence of significant vascular involvement. In 12–18 per cent of cases the dementia was associated with vascular pathology (multiple infarcts) and a further 8–18 per cent showed characteristic features of both AD and multi-infarct dementia. Similar results have been obtained using an enlarged series of patients (Tomlinson, 1980) and also independently by Jellinger (1976) on the basis of a series of over 1000 autopsies carried out on patients with dementia, aged 55 years and over. Of course it must be recognized that hospitalized patients coming to autopsy may not constitute a totally representative sample of demented patients but this is the best data available to date. In the study of Tomlinson *et al.* (1970) Alzheimer pathology was more common in women while infarction was more common in men and of course in the older and more susceptible age groups females far outnumber males. These data indicate that AD, the most common of the presenile dementias, is also the major cause of dementia in the elderly. It is thus the most significant contributor to the considerable social and economic burden posed by the growing prevalence of dementia. Moreover, knowledge about many aspects of AD has increased remarkably in recent years so that it has come to occupy a key position and sets the pace for all research on the dementias. For these reasons it will be the major focus of this book.

Multi-infarct dementia is included because it is also a relatively common cause of dementia and its differentiation from DAT is therefore an important diagnostic task. Pick's disease is of interest because, although histologically distinct from AD, clinical differentiation of the two conditions is difficult, if not impossible. Although traditionally dementia was considered to result from widespread cortical dysfunction, it has now been recognized that syndromes of fairly global cognitive impairment may accompany neurological disorders in which the primary degeneration involves subcortical structures (Albert, 1978, 1981; Albert *et al.*, 1974; Bowen, 1976; Cummings, 1986; Cummings and Benson, 1983, 1984; McHugh and Folstein, 1975; Mayeux and Stern, 1983). Pathological evidence relating to this distinction will be reviewed critically in Chapter 3. However, various researchers have maintained that these 'subcortical dementias' can be distinguished clinically from the cortical dementias, of which the quintessential example is AD. It has been asserted that impairments of learning and memory in subcortical dementias are associated with disturbances of arousal and attention (marked by intellectual slowing, inertia, apathy and affective disturbance) but not with the disorders of perception, praxis and language which are typical of the cortical dementias. Parkinson's disease, Huntington's disease and progressive supranuclear palsy will be considered in this text, not only because they are interesting and important in their own right, but also because they represent examples of so-called subcortical dementias. This is a controversial distinction which will be considered at various points in subsequent chapters. A further reason for including Huntington's disease is that there exists a fairly substantial body of data concerning the nature of the memory deficits typically found in patients with this condition. Creutzfeldt–Jakob disease and Kuru are produced by infective agents with unusual properties and are of interest in relation to speculation that a similar agent may be involved in the aetiology of AD although we do not propose to dwell upon issues of aetiology in this text. Alcoholic dementia has been included as it shares certain pathological features with AD and of course alcoholism is common amongst elderly patients presenting to health and social services personnel, so that clinicians may be required to make a differential diagnosis between this and DAT.

Readers will probably be aware of the growing problem of dementia among those who suffer from the Acquired Immune Deficiency Syndrome (AIDS). Although recognizing the growing importance of the AIDS dementia complex, we do not propose to deal with it in this book since, like other aspects of AIDS (which is by no means a 'quiet' epidemic), it is being widely discussed by other authors. However, it is worth pointing out that many of the issues to be discussed in the subsequent chapters of this text are also relevant to AIDS and HIV infection.

PART II

In this part we overview the accumulating evidence on brain dysfunction, at microscopic as well as macroscopic levels, in patients with dementia and for the most part that of Alzheimer type. We recognize that for some readers the level of detail may seem daunting but we would urge such readers not to abandon this section too readily as it is to data at this level of analysis that neuropsychologists must ultimately seek to relate the cognitive and behavioural phenomena that constitute dementia. In order to help such readers appreciate the significance of the data reviewed we have included some background material. Furthermore, we would remind clinical neuropsychologists of Parsons' (1970) dictum that it is their appreciation of the modern biological aspects of behaviour that marks them as a distinct specialism.

PART II

Chapter 3

Neuropathology of Dementia

Understanding of the neuropathology of the dementias consequent upon primary neuronal degeneration has increased dramatically in recent years. As in the case of research on other aspects of dementia the pace has been set by investigations into AD for the reasons outlined in the previous chapter. Some awareness of the neuropathological changes found in various dementia syndromes is important for a number of reasons. First, while dementia is a clinical syndrome, some of the conditions which give rise to it, such as AD and Pick's disease, are ultimately defined in terms of neuropathological change and without histological evidence their differential diagnosis can only be tentative. Second, differences in terms of the nature and/or distribution of pathology between the various conditions giving rise to dementia can be exploited to further our understanding of brain-behaviour relationships through comparative studies. Third, many neuroscientists believe that a detailed understanding of neuropathological changes will help unravel the aetiology of certain types of dementia and, more importantly, open up new avenues for therapeutic intervention.

Alzheimer's Disease

On a gross macroscopic level AD is characterized by widespread cortical atrophy and enlargement of the ventricles (see Figure 3.1). However, considerable atrophy can also be found in the brains of non-dementing elderly subjects (Tomlinson et al., 1968). These post-mortem findings have been confirmed by the CT scan studies of Jacoby and Levy (1980) which indicate a 10–20 per cent overlap between the two populations. The situation with respect to brain weight is much the same (Terry and Katzman, 1983). Hence brain weights are of no significance as a criterion for the pathological diagnosis of dementia in old age (Tomlinson, 1980).

It has been widely accepted that AD is accompanied by loss of cortical neurons over and above that seen in normal ageing. Terry et al. (1981) reported considerable loss of the larger neurons in particular. These were reduced by about 40 per cent in the frontal cortex and 46 per cent in the temporal region. Similarly Bowen et al. (1979),

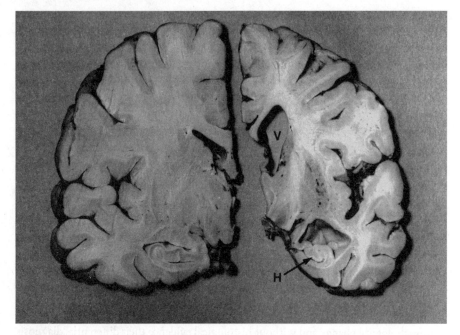

Figure 3.1   Coronal hemisections taken at the level of the mammillary bodies from a cognitively intact elderly subject (left) and a 75-year-old patient with AD who died after an estimated 5-year history of cognitive decline (right). Comparison of the sections reveals the gross cortical atrophy, dilation of the ventricles (V) and shrinkage of the hippocampus (H) typical of AD.

using biochemical markers, reported 26–36 per cent neuronal loss in the temporal lobe of AD patients. Another factor, besides neuronal fallout, which may be involved in cortical atrophy is a restriction of dendritic branching in the remaining nerve cells (Terry and Katzman, 1983), perhaps a consequence of metabolic disturbance within the cells or of deafferentation. This restriction of dendritic trees is in marked contrast to the pattern of net dendritic growth found in normal ageing (Buell and Coleman, 1981).

Given the considerable body of evidence suggesting that cholinergic dysfunction is an important feature of AD (see Chapter 4), the reports by Whitehouse *et al.* (1981, 1982) of marked cell loss (greater than 75 per cent) in the nucleus basalis of Meynert in the basal forebrain, the major source of cholinergic input to the cerebral cortex, have aroused much interest. However, less extensive reductions in cell count have been reported by Perry *et al.* (1982) and Candy *et al.* (1983) who studied SDAT patients as opposed to the mostly presenile cases included in the studies of Whitehouse *et al.* Moreover, Tagliavini and Pilleri (1983) reported negative correlations between percentage cell loss from this region and both age at onset and age at death. This is consistent with other evidence of more severe neuropathological and neurochemical changes in younger patients (e.g. Hubbard and Anderson, 1981; Mann *et al.*, 1984; Rossor *et al.*, 1984) who are perhaps less likely to die early in the course of the disease. Tagliavini and Pilleri (1983) also made a distinction between AD (of late or early onset) and 'simple senile dementia' (where memory and orientation problems predominate in the absence of aphasia, apraxia or agnosia) and they found that cell loss from the nucleus basalis of Meynert was not significant for the simple senile dementia group. Of course there is growing acceptance amongst continental workers of the more dominant view that these different forms do in fact constitute one disease process (see Constantinidis, 1978). Seen in this light the less pervasive clinical symptomatology and the lack of significant neuronal loss from the nucleus basalis of Meynert in some patients in the Tagliavini and Pilleri study may simply reflect a lesser degree of severity. This might be considered as evidence supporting the critical role of this nucleus in determining the clinical picture.

In addition to actual cell loss in the nucleus basalis of Meynert large numbers of neurofibrillary tangles (see below) are to be found in those parts of the nucleus projecting to cortical regions that also show pathological change (Arendt *et al.*, 1985). This suggests that the two are related, but it is still a matter of speculation as to whether changes in the cortex are secondary to those in the nucleus basalis of Meynert or *vice versa*.

Extensive pathological change is also to be found in regions of the brain mediating olfaction (see Pearson *et al.*, 1985), and in related structures such as the amygdala (Herzog and Kemper, 1980) and the hippocampus. Interestingly there is evidence of impaired olfactory discrimination in patients with DAT (Warner *et al.*, 1986) while damage to the amygdala may contribute to the changes in personality and emotional reactivity shown by such patients. The importance of pathological change in the hippocampus has been highlighted by Ball *et al.* (1985) who have gone so far as to assert that AD might be considered primarily as a syndrome of hippocampal damage.

Neuronal loss in the locus coeruleus, the source of noradrenergic projections to the cerebral cortex, has also been reported (Mann and Yates, 1986). Although cell loss from the raphe nucleus, the origin of cortical serotonergic input, seems slight in comparison, the presence of large numbers of neurofibrillary tangles and decreases in nucleolar volume (Mann and Yates, 1986) suggest that this region too is vulnerable to pathological change. These findings, together with the data on the nucleus basalis of Meynert, would tend to support Rossor's (1981) contention that AD is a disorder of the isodendritic core, that cluster of non-specialized cells running from the spinal cord to the basal forebrain, which display very extensive dendritic intermingling and which encompass parts of the reticular formation. However, they would also be consistent with the hypothesis of Appel (1981) that a loss of cortical neurotrophic factors, which exert their effect in a retrograde fashion, leads to degeneration of input pathways.

Microscopic examination of the brains of patients with AD reveals the presence of large numbers of neuritic plaques and neurofibrillary tangles, the features originally described by Alzheimer. In the hippocampus two additional changes are also found, namely granulovacuolar degeneration and Hirano-body formation.

Neuritic plaques (see Figure 3.2) are small spherical accumulations of cellular and extracellular debris consisting of amyloid cores surrounded by degenerating neural processes. Studies using antibodies indicate that the latter are the terminals of cholinergic and somatostatinergic neurons (Armstrong *et al.*, 1985, 1986). Considerable research effort is being directed towards determining the composition of the amyloid protein complex and the mechanism of its formation. An amino acid sequence has now been published (Masters *et al.*, 1985) and the techniques of molecular biology have allowed the gene responsible for coding this protein to be identified and its location traced to chromosome 21. This is of particular interest given the involvement of this chromosome in Down's syndrome, together with the reports of a higher than normal incidence of Down's syndrome in families affected by DAT and evidence of pronounced Alzheimer-type neuropathological changes in the brains of individuals with Down's syndrome older than 30 years of age approximately (Karlinsky, 1986; Oliver and Holland, 1986). It is of course difficult to determine whether these neuropathological changes are accompanied by intellectual decline in a group of individuals with low premorbid ability. Speculation on the origins of neuritic plaques has also been increased by recent findings of high concentrations of

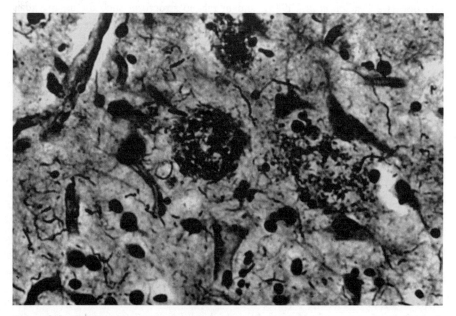

Figure 3.2   Neuritic plaque (large centre sphere) in the cerebral cortex of an individual with AD.

aluminosilicate complexes at the centre of plaque cores (Candy *et al.*, 1986). This has added a new twist to the long-standing debate as to whether aluminium toxicity plays any significant role in the aetiology of degenerative conditions such as AD (see Crapper McLachlan, 1986; Wisniewski *et al.*, 1986).

In patients with AD plaques are widely spread throughout the cortex and are found in all cortical layers (Tomlinson *et al.*, 1970). While similar plaques are to be found in the brains of normal elderly subjects they are generally less numerous and less widely distributed but there may be considerable overlap between the groups. Blessed *et al.* (1968) found a highly significant relationship between clinical measures of decline in old people and mean plaque count at autopsy, although there were a number of anomalous cases. Such instances of discrepancy are perhaps not surprising since plaque count alone can hardly be considered an adequate index of Alzheimer pathology. It must also be noted that the correlations between psychological and pathological measures were much less impressive when only demented subjects were considered, perhaps because there is a threshold point at which the degenerative process has already produced maximum damage in terms of measurable psychological function.

More recently, others have reported a more robust correlation between the number of neurofibrillary tangles and the presence and severity of dementia (Hubbard and Anderson, 1981; Wilcock and Esiri, 1982). Neurofibrillary tangles (see Figure 3.3) are thought to consist of paired helical filaments which develop in the neuronal

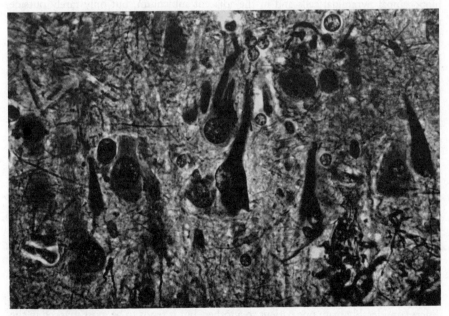

Figure 3.3   Cells in the cortex of a patient with AD. The darkly stained flame-like shapes are aggregations of neurofibrillary tangles.

cytoplasm, but despite intensive research effort over the past decade they remain enigmatic structures and their origin is obscure. Like plaques, they are not unique to AD, occurring with increasing frequency in the hippocampus and subiculum with normal ageing. However, in AD patients tangles are found in much greater numbers in these areas, and they are also widely distributed throughout the cortex. In normal elderly individuals, neurofibrillary tangles are rare in the neocortex (Tomlinson, 1980). Large numbers of neurofibrillary tangles are also to be found in a number of other degenerative conditions (see below).

Tomlinson (1982) cited evidence suggesting that parietal lobe symptomatology (aphasia-apraxia-agnosia) in elderly demented patients is related to the presence of numerous neocortical tangles, while demented patients who have only large numbers of neuritic plaques are relatively free of such symptomatology. Of course in presenile cases of AD neocortical tangles are invariably present, and parietal lobe signs are usually a prominent clinical feature. Similar data have been reported by Constantinidis (1978). Such observations may lend some support to the validity of a distinction between different subtypes of dementia in old age, sharing certain pathological features of AD (Roth, 1986).

Another important histopathological feature of AD is granulovacuolar degeneration, first described by Simkovich in 1912. This is marked by the presence within cell bodies of areas of degeneration consisting of silver staining granules surrounded by spaces or vacuoles. In AD granulovacuolar degeneration is found in hippocampal pyramidal cells and in the adjacent subiculum, but only rarely outside these areas. It is also found in the same areas in normal elderly subjects, albeit to a much lesser extent. To date little is known about the origin or significance of this pathological feature.

The other microscopic lesion which is essentially limited to the hippocampus is the occurrence of Hirano bodies. These are rod-like eosinophilic bodies found either in or near the cytoplasm of the pyramidal cells. Hirano bodies tend to be more numerous in elderly subjects with dementia than in intellectually well-preserved individuals although there can be considerable overlap between the groups.

Pick's Disease

The clinical and gross pathological features of this condition were first described by Arnold Pick in 1892, but its histological characteristics were only described later by Alzheimer in 1911. Although there may be generalized atrophy in Pick's disease, this condition, unlike AD, is typically characterized by more circumscribed shrinkage with deep sulci and knife-edged gyri in affected areas. The distribution of cortical atrophy differs considerably from one patient to another, but it tends to be most marked in the frontal and/or temporal lobes while significant involvement of the parietal lobes is unusual and occipital atrophy is extremely rare. There may be an abrupt transition between affected and unaffected areas. The ventricles are dilated and a variety of subcortical structures may also be affected including the amygdala, hippocampus, caudate nucleus, the thalamus and the nucleus basalis of Meynert (Munoz–Garcia and Ludwin, 1984; Rogers *et al.*, 1985). The two distinctive histopathological features of Pick's disease are first, the inclusion within the cytoplasm of 'Pick-bodies' comprising a mass of straight and twisted fibrils enmeshing a variety of cell organelles, and second, the presence of other inflated or swollen neurons that do not contain inclusion bodies.

There is controversy concerning the criteria for pathological diagnosis of Pick's disease in that not all patients showing typical changes at a macroscopic level have inflated cells or neurons with Pick bodies. Different types of Pick's disease have been postulated and while the nosological status of the variant without typical histological changes remains unresolved it is significant that the two forms are clinically indistinguishable. A variety of other pathological features may occur in Pick's disease including spongiform changes in severely affected cortical areas and when typical Pick cells are lacking on histological examination at autopsy the condition may be confused with Creutzfeldt–Jakob disease.

Vascular Dementias

Until comparatively recently most dementias were ascribed to 'hardening' of the cerebral blood vessels causing poor perfusion of the cortex. These views have been radically revised in the light of evidence that dementia due to vascular pathology is considerably rarer than first thought (Tomlinson *et al.*, 1970) and that its most likely cause is multiple occlusions of blood vessels, in effect a series of small strokes, resulting in focal areas of dead tissue (see Figure 3.4). To describe this form of pathological change Hachinski *et al.* (1974, 1975) introduced the term multi-infarct dementia. They concluded that most infarctions were secondary to disease of the heart and of extracranial blood vessels. Only in a minority of cases could cerebral softening be attributed to arteriosclerosis of the cerebral blood vessels themselves.

Vascular dementias can be classified in terms of the distribution of the infarcts and the size of the blood vessels involved. Occlusion of the small arteries leads to the development of two conditions, namely lacunar dementia and Binswanger's disease. Lacunes are small deep ischaemic infarcts located principally in the basal ganglia, thalamus and internal capsule. When ten or more are present the term lacunar state is applied (see Cummings and Benson, 1983). In many hypertensive patients deep lacunar lesions arc accompanied by superficial cortical infarction. Lacunar infarcts may also be present in patients with Binswanger's disease, but the most prominent feature of this condition is the presence of multiple infarcts in the white matter of the cerebral hemispheres. The posterior, temporal and occipital white matter is most vulnerable,

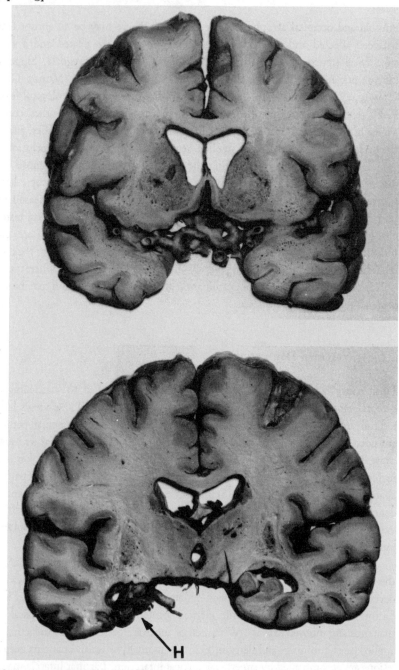

(i)

(ii)

H

Figure 3.4 Coronal sections from the brain of a 70-year-old patient with multi-infarct dementia and a 2-year history of cognitive decline. Note (i) the intense thickening of the major blood vessels at the base of the brain and (ii) the almost total destruction of the hippocampus (H) on one side.

but in some cases all white matter is affected. The nosological status of Binswanger's disease is controversial. Neumann (1947) suggested that it was a demyelinating condition rather than a vascular disorder. More recently, Roman (1987) has argued that Binswanger's disease and lacunar dementia are one and the same condition and Hachinski *et al.* (1986) proposed that the term Binswanger's disease should be abandoned in favour of the more general term leuko-araiosis which they introduced to describe all conditions resulting in a diminution of the density of representation of white matter on CT scan and MRI.

Cortical infarcts result from occlusion of the medium-sized intracranial arteries (anterior, middle and/or posterior and their associated branches) and the consequent pattern of neurological deficits depends upon the territory irrigated by the vessels involved (see Cummings and Benson, 1983). Of particular interest is the result of infarction in the tissue supplied by the posterior portion of the middle cerebral artery. This can give rise to a symptom complex termed the angular gyrus syndrome which may be difficult to distinguish clinically from AD. This condition will be returned to in Chapter 9 in relation to language impairment. Extracranial blockage of the large carotid vessels can also lead to widespread distribution of infarcts in the cerebral cortex.

Finally, it should be noted that in a sizeable proportion of individuals multiple infarcts coexist with the presence of Alzheimer-type pathological change. This condition is termed mixed dementia.

Parkinson's Disease

In Parkinson's disease there is a marked loss of pigmented cells from the zona compacta of the substantia nigra, reflecting a loss of dopaminergic neurons from the extrapyramidal nigrostriatal pathway. There is also loss of pigmented cells from other brainstem nuclei including the locus coeruleus, the origin of the majority of noradrenergic neurons in the brain. The ventral tegmentum and the hypothalamus can also be affected. Recent interest has focused on the nucleus basalis of Meynert where some workers have found cell loss to be in excess of that seen in older patients with AD (Candy *et al.*, 1983). Cortical atrophy, particularly in the frontal lobes, has also been reported (see Cummings and Benson, 1983) and this is of particular interest in view of the proposed classification of dementias into cortical and subcortical types with the dementia associated with Parkinson's disease being considered an example of the latter (see below).

Histologically, a notable feature of Parkinson's disease is the presence of so-called Lewy inclusion bodies in the remaining neurons of affected nuclei. These are round bodies with dense cores of closely packed filaments intermingled with granular material which are surrounded by a pale halo of loosely packed filaments.

The presence of Alzheimer-type neuritic plaques and neurofibrillary tangles has been reported in a proportion of patients with Parkinson's disease (Boller *et al.*, 1980; Hakim and Mathieson, 1978, 1979) and it has been hypothesized that the occurrence of dementia in patients with Parkinson's disease may represent the co-occurrence of the two diseases (Hakim and Mathieson, 1978, 1979). However, the presence of Alzheimer-type neuropathology does not appear to be a necessary condition for the development of dementia in patients with Parkinson's disease (Chui *et al.*, 1986).

Progressive Supranuclear Palsy

The pathological features of this rare condition, also referred to as the Steele-Richardson–Olszewski syndrome, include neurofibrillary degeneration, neuronal loss and gliosis in brainstem, diencephalic and cerebellar nuclei. The most affected areas are typically the globus pallidus, the subthalamic nucleus, substantia nigra, red nucleus, superior colliculi, cuneiform and subcuneiform nuclei, periaqueductal grey matter, pontine tegmentum and the dentate nucleus of the cerebellum (Steele *et al.*, 1964). More recently the nucleus basalis of Meynert has been implicated (Rogers *et al.*, 1985). Some granulovacuolar degeneration may be present (Steele *et al.*, 1964) but neurofibrillary degeneration is more prominent and is found more consistently. Electron microscopy reveals that the neurofibrillary tangles found in progressive supranuclear palsy differ morphologically from those found in AD, being composed of straight tubules rather than twisted filaments.

Huntington's Disease

The most prominent feature of this condition is a marked loss of neurons from the caudate nucleus, the putamen and, to a lesser extent, the globus pallidus. Hence there is dilation of the lateral ventricles (see Figure 3.5) and this is readily apparent on CT scanning. Many of the remaining neurons in these structures are shrunken. In addition, there is proliferation of glial cells in the affected regions. Other areas showing cell loss include a number of thalamic nuclei and indeed the cortex itself, in particular the frontal lobes, which is of note since Huntington's disease is also considered a subcortical dementia (see Cummings and Benson, 1983). The nucleus basalis of Meynert appears to be spared in this condition (Arendt *et al.*, 1983).

Creutzfeldt–Jakob Disease and Kuru

The principal features of Creutzfeldt–Jakob disease are neuronal loss, proliferation of astrocytes and frequently the development of a characteristic spongy appearance in the

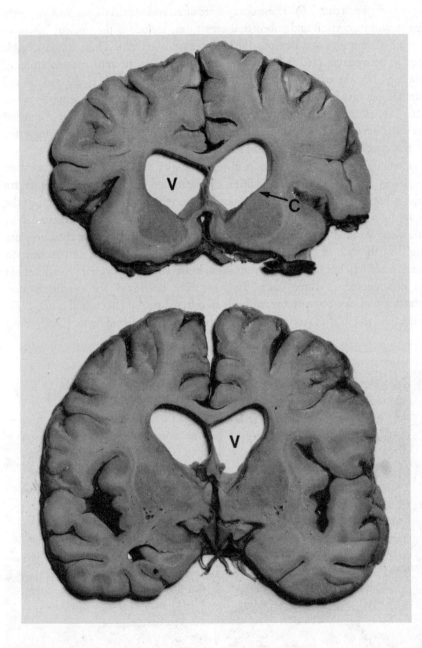

Figure 3.5   Two coronal sections from the brain of a 65-year-old patient with Huntington's disease who had dementia. Note the extreme dilation of the lateral ventricles (V) and shrinkage of the caudate nucleus (C) to a narrow strip along the ventricle floor.

grey matter (see Figure 3.6). These changes are often widespread throughout the brain being found in cortical and subcortical structures, including the nucleus basalis of Meynert (Cummings and Benson, 1983; Rogers *et al.*, 1985). There is considerable variation between affected individuals in terms of the extent and/or distribution of pathology, but the cortex is almost invariably involved. However, the parietal and occipital lobes may be relatively spared and likewise the hippocampus. Generally white matter is unaffected, although a number of cases with severe degeneration of cerebral fibre tracts have been reported (Shiraki and Mizutani, 1983) and it has been suggested that this condition may not be a single disease entity.

Creutzfeldt–Jakob disease shows histopathological similarities to Kuru, another spongiform encephalopathy. In addition to vacuolated tissue, amyloid plaques are found in both conditions, though it is not known whether these are identical to the plaques found in AD. Creutzfeldt–Jakob disease and Kuru are both transmissible. Little is known about the infective agents but it has been postulated that these are slow viruses. In the case of Creutzfeldt–Jakob disease the natural mode of transmission remains a mystery but iatrogenic transmission in the course of surgical procedures has been documented in three cases. Two of these developed the condition after implantation of electrodes recovered from an infected person (Bernouilli *et al.*, 1977) and the third did so after receipt of a corneal graft from an infected donor (Duffy *et al.*,

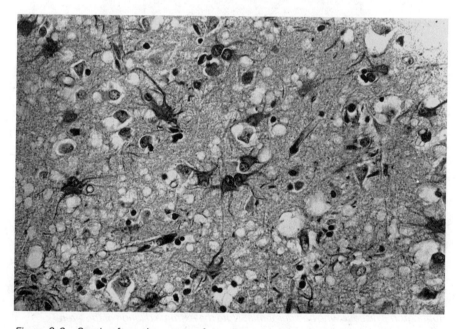

Figure 3.6   Section from the cortex of a patient with Creutzfeldt–Jakob disease showing spongy vacuoles and proliferation of astrocytes.

1974). More recently, it has been reported that individuals treated with human growth hormone may develop this condition (see Preece, 1986). Genetic factors may also be important in the expression of Creutzfeldt–Jakob disease as familial cases, demonstrating an autosomal dominant pattern of inheritance, account for some 6–9 per cent of the total (Brown *et al.*, 1979a; Cathala *et al.*, 1980; Will and Matthews, 1984). Kuru is essentially restricted to the Fore people of Papua New Guinea where it is believed to be transmitted by ritual cannabalism. The incidence is dwindling as this cultural practice becomes extinct.

Alcoholic Dementia

There are a number of neurological complications of chronic alcoholism. Among these are the Wernicke–Korsakoff syndrome and alcoholic dementia. Much research endeavour has focused on the former. It is characterized neuropathologically by symmetrical lesions of the periventricular parts of the thalamus, hypothalamus, the mammillary bodies, the periaqueductal grey and the floor of the fourth ventricle (see Figure 3.7). Korsakoff's psychosis, the chronic phase of the syndrome, is marked by

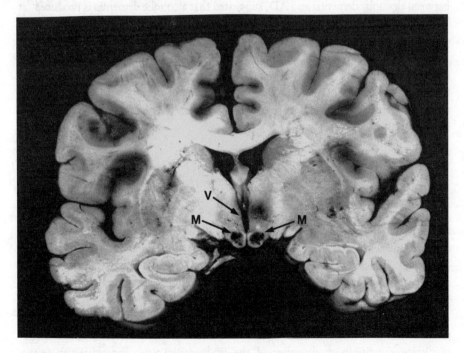

Figure 3.7   Coronal section of the brain of a 53-year-old patient with Korsakoff's syndrome and a long history of alcohol abuse. Note the multiple haemorrhages in the mammillary bodies (M) and the region adjacent to the fourth ventricle (V).

retrograde and anterograde amnesia with relative sparing of other aspects of cognition. Many alcoholics show more generalized intellectual impairments to which the label dementia can appropriately be appended. However, the nosological status of alcoholic dementia is controversial and attempts to clarify its underlying pathology have been confounded by associated and/or coincident conditions such as trauma, hepatic encephalopathy, anoxia, ischaemic infarction and indeed superimposed AD. CT scan studies have demonstrated a high incidence of cortical atrophy in chronic alcoholics (Ron, 1983). These observations are consistent with the results of autopsy examinations which indicate decreased brain weight and enlargement of the pericerebral space (Harper and Kril, 1985; Harper *et al.*, 1985). These cortical changes are thought to represent direct effects of alcohol toxicity as opposed to the subcortical changes of the Wernicke–Korsakoff syndrome which are caused by thiamine deficiency.

The relationship between these two conditions remains controversial. Torvik *et al.* (1982) have suggested that inactive Wernicke encephalopathy is the main underlying lesion in both alcoholic dementia and the Korsakoff syndrome, but that additional cortical lesions are present in the former, contributing to the overall clinical picture. More recently Lishman (1986), addressing the question of the similarity between alcoholic dementia and AD, suggested that alcoholic dementia is produced, at least in part, by the encroachment of Wernicke encephalopathy on key forebrain nuclei concerned with cholinergic function, including the nucleus basalis of Meynert. It seems likely that these two conditions associated with chronic alcoholism represent idealized extremes of a continuum with the majority of cognitively-impaired alcoholics falling somewhere in between and showing aspects of both conditions not only in terms of neuropathology, but also in terms of the nature and/or extent of cognitive impairment.

Concluding Remarks

A number of important points emerge from the foregoing review. It must be readily apparent that although there are differences between various dementia-producing conditions in terms of the nature and distribution of pathological changes there are also similarities. It is precisely this pattern of overlap and diversity which can be exploited to advantage in a comparative approach to the functional significance of the various morphological features.

Certain types of cell seem to be selectively vulnerable to pathological change. This point was emphasized by Rossor (1981) who characterized a variety of dementia-producing conditions as disorders of the isodendritic core. For whatever reason neurons whose cell bodies lie in the brainstem and midbrain and which have long projections to the cortex seem to be particularly at risk. However, it remains to be determined whether damage in these regions is primary or rather is secondary to cortical changes which lead to retrograde degeneration through loss of trophic factors (Appel, 1981; Hefti, 1983). Although there are a few notable exceptions (e.g. Huntington's disease), the cholinergic neurons of the nucleus basalis of Meynert appear to be particularly susceptible to degeneration in many dementia-producing conditions and it is widely believed that damage to this region is a significant factor in the genesis of cognitive impairment. Future studies must address the question of whether there are subpopulations of neurons within this nucleus which are preferentially affected in particular disease processes and whose degeneration can be correlated with specific clinical features.

A number of important points emerge with respect to the differential diagnosis and classification of dementia-producing conditions. Although diseases such as Alzheimer's and Pick's are defined in terms of neuropathology, and it is the goal of all serious researchers to have their clinical diagnoses validated by autopsy (or biopsy) examination, there is surprisingly little consensus among pathologists in terms of what are the critical features and the quantity and/or distribution of these necessary to justify diagnosis of a particular condition. Thus the supposedly gold standard for diagnosis is no more objectively or operationally defined than the clinical criteria. The neuropathological criteria need to be standardized, with agreement on minimal counts of particular morphological features required in specified areas of the brain. Such standards have been proposed for AD (Khachaturian, 1985) but are not in general use. The lack of well-defined and widely accepted criteria is clearly an impediment to research in this area. A second point concerns the distinction made by some authorities between so-called cortical and subcortical dementias. The term subcortical dementia was first introduced by Albert *et al.* (1974) with respect to the intellectual deterioration of patients with progressive supranuclear palsy. Later the term was also applied to the cognitive changes of Huntington's disease (McHugh and Folstein, 1975) and more recently to those of Parkinson's disease (Albert, 1978; Bowen, 1976; Mayeux and Stern, 1983) and indeed to the cognitive deficits produced by depression (Caine, 1981). Other conditions too, which are not being considered in this book, have been subsumed under this umbrella, for example Wilson's disease (Wilson, 1912). The consensus of opinion amongst advocates of this controversial distinction (see Cummings, 1986; Cummings and Benson, 1984) appears to be that in the subcortical dementias impairments of learning and memory are associated with disturbances of arousal and attention (marked by slowness of intellectual function, inertia, apathy and affective disturbance) but not with the disturbances of perception, praxis and language typical of the cortical dementias such as AD, Pick's disease and Creutzfeldt–Jakob disease. However, it must be readily apparent from the foregoing review in this chapter that whatever the merits in clinical terms of classifying the dementias into these broad categories, such a distinction cannot be upheld on strictly anatomical grounds as both cortical and subcortical damage, albeit to differing degrees, is the rule rather than the exception. Hence the anatomical label is certainly a misnomer. The question of whether the cortical/subcortical classification can be supported at other levels of analysis will be taken up again at various points throughout this book.

It is clear from the evidence reviewed above that the pathological changes occurring in dementia of Alzheimer type are not unique to this condition, but can be found also in the normal ageing brain. There is good evidence that, at a histological level, the difference between patients with AD and intellectually normal older subjects is quantitative rather than qualitative. Various authors (Roth, 1980a; Tomlinson, 1980; Tomlinson *et al.*, 1970) have maintained that there is considerable evidence favouring a threshold effect, with pathology in excess of a critical level being generally associated with dementia. It seems that in dementia of vascular aetiology a similar quantitative principle may govern the relationship between morphological change, expressed as post-mortem volume of softening (or infarction), and dementia during life (Tomlinson and Hendersen, 1976). This raises the possibility of an additive effect, with the functional consequences of Alzheimer-type pathology being potentiated by concomitant cerebral damage resulting from infarction, or indeed other cerebral insults. Likewise, the clinical expression of other disease processes might be precipitated by co-occurrence of less severe Alzheimer-type changes.

As discussed by Terry and Katzman (1983), each individual may well have a different threshold below which clinical symptoms do not appear, based upon his or her own reserve capacity. This reserve will depend on life experience in its broadest sense and the extent of redundancy in the neuronal circuitry, which is related to the number of active synapses subserving each cerebral function. The importance of psychosocial factors was long ago invoked by Rothschild in an attempt to account for the discrepancies he observed between clinical and pathological severity (Rothschild, 1937, 1942; Rothschild and Sharp, 1941). The question of 'premorbid endowment' in relation to time of presentation and clinical course will be taken up again in Chapter 6.

It has been considered by some (e.g. Drachman, 1983; Petit, 1982) that DAT may be an acceleration of the normal ageing process and the findings of quantitative rather than qualitative differences in neuropathology, as well as the concept of a threshold referred to above, might seem to lend support to this view. However, this is by no means a necessary conclusion (see Roth, 1980b; Tomlinson, 1980) and, as emphasized by Roth, the threshold point may reflect the entry of some qualitatively distinct process. The transition of pathological change from the subthreshold to the suprathreshold state might be under genetic control. Alternatively viral, immunological, environmental or other factors, or combinations thereof, might be responsible for precipitating the transition. The proposition that AD is a form of accelerated ageing remains contentious. Further consideration will be given to this topic in relation to biochemical data in Chapter 4.

It is of interest that the hippocampus seems particularly vulnerable in normal ageing, as in AD and certain other primary degenerative dementias, and indeed also in multi-infarct dementia, because of the nature of its vascular supply (Hachinski, 1979). This is the portion of the limbic system most often associated with learning and memory processes (Brierley, 1961; Milner, 1966; Penfield and Mathieson, 1974) and disturbance of these functions is a feature of both normal ageing and dementia, whatever its aetiology. Of course pathological similarities between AD and normal ageing, or between different dementing conditions, by no means prove that the processes are identical, and it is probably equally important to emphasize any differences which do occur. In the case of AD and normal ageing, it is worth pointing out that there are differences in the distribution of pathological changes within the hippocampus so that in AD the posterior region seems to be particularly vulnerable (Ball, 1976, 1977; Ball and Lo, 1977). Whether this difference in the distribution of pathological change can be related to differences in the nature of the memory impairment in these groups is a question that remains unanswered. Furthermore, it is clear that while hippocampal damage may be a sufficient reason for memory impairment it is unlikely to be a necessary one as damage to this region is slight in conditions such as Creutzfeldt–Jakob and Huntington's diseases. Comparative research on the nature of the memory impairment in patients affected by various dementia-producing conditions is clearly important for the development of knowledge of neuropsychology. Such investigations have begun and will be considered further in Part IV.

Not only are the neuropathological features of AD to be found in the brains of intellectually-intact elderly people but they also occur, either singly or in various combinations, in a number of other diseases (see Mortimer, 1980, in addition to the above review). The observation that one or another of the different pathological changes of AD can occur exclusively under certain conditions, together with the fact that their relative extent can vary considerably in individual patients with AD (see Terry *et al.*, 1987; Tomlinson, 1982), raises the possibility that a common aetiological mechanism may not exist for the different features. Of course an alternative explanation cannot be ruled out, namely that the independent occurrence of different neuropathological lesions arises from individual differences in response to a common aetiological factor. Although the aetiology of AD remains unknown, a number of theories have been suggested and the answer to this crucial question is being vigorously sought. We do not propose to dwell on these issues in this book but interested readers should consult sources such as Terry and Katzman (1983), Whitehouse (1986) and Wurtman (1985). In certain other conditions also (e.g. Pick's disease and Creutzfeldt–Jakob disease) there is variation in the extent to which different pathological features occur concurrently. As in the case of AD, it is believed by some that this variability has significance in relation to nosology and the pursuit of aetiological factors, although this remains to be demonstrated.

Chapter 4

Neurochemistry of Dementia

Although the neuropathological features of some dementia-producing conditions have long been recognized, research in the past two decades has added a new dimension to our understanding of these disorders by drawing attention to changes in neurotransmitter systems in the brains of afflicted patients. The number of putative neurotransmitter substances now exceeds 40, although the extent to which these have been investigated varies considerably. This chapter is not a comprehensive review. It is concerned only with the major transmitters which have been investigated in the brains of patients who have had dementia. As in the previous chapter the emphasis will be on AD as it is in relation to this condition that most attempts have been made to unravel the nature of the relationships between cognitive and behavioural disturbance and neurochemical dysfunction. Although patients with Parkinson's and Huntington's diseases have been the subject of many neurochemical investigations, most of these have focused upon neurotransmitter dysfunction *vis a vis* the movement disorders characteristic of these conditions rather than attempting to correlate biochemical markers with cognitive status *per se*.

In this chapter we will consider a number of transmitters in turn, providing some background information on each before reviewing its role in dementia-producing conditions. This is a highly active field of research in which knowledge has accumulated rapidly over recent years but there remain many gaps in our knowledge, especially concerning some of the rarer conditions because opportunities to carry out investigations are limited.

Acetylcholine

Acetylcholine (ACh) was the first of the neurotransmitters to be discovered. This is synthesized in nerve terminals from the precursors acetyl coenzyme A (acetyl-CoA) and choline (see Figure 4.1). Acetyl-CoA is a product of cellular metabolism and is always present in abundance. Choline, which is also a constituent of all cell membranes, is derived either directly from foods or from the breakdown of

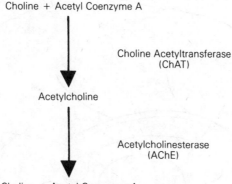

Figure 4.1   Synthesis and metabolism of acetylcholine.

phosphatidylcholine (lecithin). Lecithin itself can be obtained from the diet or synthesized by neurons. In the region of the nerve terminal choline enters the neuron via a high affinity uptake system, the activity of which is directly influenced by the rate of neural firing. The synthesis of ACh is catalyzed by the enzyme choline acetyltransferase (ChAT). This enzyme is stable and is localized to cholinergic neurons with a high degree of specificity. Hence ChAT has been extensively used as a marker for the integrity of the cholinergic system. The neurotransmitter ACh is stored in vesicles in the nerve terminal until released into the synaptic cleft where it binds to receptors. Several types of receptor have been identified. The division of these into 'muscarinic' and 'nicotinic' types is of long standing and is potentially significant in the context of the topic under consideration in the text. Since these two types of receptor mediate different functional effects in the autonomic and peripheral nervous systems they may also serve different functions in the central nervous system (CNS). Hence the behavioural consequences of alterations in their absolute or relative numbers, or levels of activity, may be of some significance regarding clinical manifestations. Muscarinic receptors are much more abundant than nicotinic receptors in the CNS and have been further subdivided (M1, M2, M3 and M4), although the status of certain subtypes is controversial. ACh is broken down very rapidly into acetyl-CoA and choline by the extremely active enzyme acetylcholinesterase (AChE) which is found both pre- and postsynaptically, and indeed is widely distributed in non-neural brain tissue. The high activity of this enzyme renders measurement of ACh levels in biopsy and necropsy samples technically very difficult.

A detailed description of the anatomy of cholinergic systems is beyond the scope of this book. For our present purposes it is sufficient to note that there are a number of major cholineric projections from cell bodies lying in the basal forebrain (see Figure 4.2). These include projections from the medial septum and the diagonal band of Broca

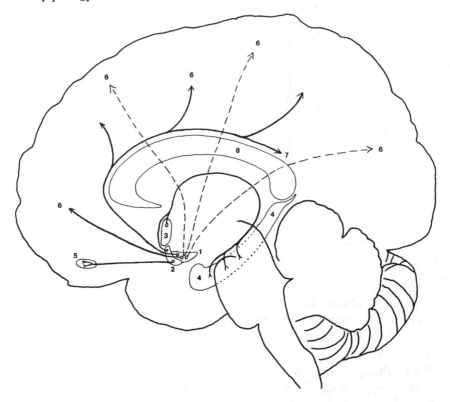

1 Nucleus basalis of Meynert   2 Nucleus of the diagonal band of Broca   3 Medial septal nucleus   4 Hippocampus   5 Olfactory bulb   6 Neocortex   7 Cingulate cortex
8 Corpus callosum

Figure 4.2   Major cholinergic pathways in the human brain.

to the hippocampus, from the diagonal band to the olfactory bulb and from the nucleus basalis to the cortex. In addition, there are cholinergic interneurons forming localized circuits in the striatum and in the cortex itself.

It has been established that the enzymes which synthesize and break down ACh, namely ChAT (e.g. Bowen, 1983; Bowen, D. M. *et al.*, 1976; Perry *et al.*, 1977a,b,c, 1981a; Rossor *et al.*, 1980a, 1984; White *et al.*, 1977) and AChE (Davies and Maloney, 1976; Perry *et al.*, 1978a) are significantly decreased in various brain regions in AD compared with normal brain tissue. The reported reductions of ChAT in AD are of the order of 60–90 per cent, being greatest in those brain regions in which morphological changes are most evident (e.g. the hippocampus and temporal neocortex) and less severe in areas which are structurally normal. There is some evidence that the cholinergic deficit may be more profound in patients who die at a 'younger' age (Bowen *et al.*, 1979; Davies, 1979; Rossor *et al.*, 1982a, 1984). Indeed, Rossor *et al.*

(1981) have reported that the cholinergic deficit in the frontal cortex of patients with SDAT is age dependent and Wilcock *et al.* (1982) present further evidence of a selectivity of the disease process for the temporal as opposed to the frontal lobe in very elderly patients with AD. These neurochemical findings regarding the extensiveness and distribution of pathology as a function of age are paralleled by the morphometric findings of Hubbard and Anderson (1981) on CT scanning.

The possible importance of the reduction in ChAT activity in AD was suggested by the negative correlation reported by Perry *et al.* (1978b) between neocortical ChAT activity and intellectual impairment, as measured by a brief test of orientation, memory and concentration (Blessed *et al.*, 1968). In this study ChAT activity was also found to correlate negatively with mean plaque count for the four cortical lobes combined, although Wilcock *et al.* (1982) failed to replicate this finding in single lobe comparisons. These latter workers did, however, find a significant correlation between the reduction in ChAT activity and the number of neurofibrillary tangles and they, like Perry *et al.* (1978b), reported a significant correlation between reduction in ChAT activity and severity of dementia.

A number of workers (Candy *et al.*, 1983; Perry *et al.*, 1982; Rossor *et al.*, 1982b) have reported that there are, in the brains of elderly patients with AD, significant losses of ChAT from the nucleus basalis of Meynert, the major source of cholinergic projections to the cerebral cortex. The data from the Newcastle team (Candy *et al.*, 1983; Perry *et al.*, 1982) indicate that, on a percentage basis, reductions in ChAT activity in the nucleus basalis are much greater than cell loss, though Henke and Lang (1983) failed to find reductions in ChAT activity in this brain region in their SDAT patients.

Since ChAT is far from saturated under normal circumstances (Haubrich and Chippendale, 1977), the functional significance of the reductions reported above comes into question. Hence it is of interest that Richter *et al.* (1980) were able to measure ACh itself in autopsy material from SDAT patients, and found significant reductions in its concentration in the temporal cortex but not in the caudate nucleus, results which agree with those for ChAT activity in these regions. Further evidence that the cholinergic system is functionally compromised in AD comes from the finding that there is a reduction both in uptake of choline and in synthesis of ACh in biopsy samples from frontal and temporal cortices (Sims *et al.*, 1983).

Decreases in ChAT activity have been reported in a number of other dementia-producing conditions (see Bowen and Davison, 1986; Mann and Yates, 1986). These include Creutzfeldt–Jakob disease, alcoholic dementia and Parkinson's disease. In view of the data cited above relating neuropathological and neurochemical indices in patients with AD to ChAT activity, and the question raised in the preceding chapter concerning the contribution of Alzheimer-type neuropathology to the genesis of dementia in Parkinson's disease, it is of interest that significant reductions of ChAT have been found in patients with Parkinson's disease who had dementia but who did not exhibit Alzheimer-type neuropathological changes (A. W. Clark *et al.*, 1986). These findings might be interpreted as further evidence for the functional significance of neurotransmitter abnormalities in relation to the clinical syndrome of dementia.

However, reduced cortical ChAT activity is not a necessary condition for the development of dementia. For example, ChAT activity is not significantly altered in the cortex in patients with Huntington's disease, although it is significantly reduced in the striatum. It has been presumed that diminished activity in this region of the brain relates to the motor dysfunction characteristic of Huntington's disease, but it might also be construed as support for the view that cognitive impairment in this condition is a consequence of subcortical dysfunction, and more specifically of cholinergic dysfunction. However, Kish *et al.* (1985) found ChAT activity to be normal in the brains of two patients with progressive supranuclear palsy who showed dementia, although in general ChAT activity is reduced in this condition (Agid *et al.*, 1986). The situation is somewhat confused in Pick's disease as Yates *et al.* (1980a) reported a significant decrease in ChAT activity in the frontal cortex of one patient but Wood *et al.* (1983) failed to confirm this in a larger series of four patients. Furthermore, Yates *et al.* (1980a) found ChAT activity to be unchanged in other brain regions which they sampled. Decreases in cholinergic activity in multi-infarct dementia tend to be much more circumscribed than those found in AD (Perry *et al.*, 1977a,c, 1978a,b), being of smaller magnitude and confined to the hippocampus, a structure in which ACh is an important neurotransmitter (Lewis and Shute, 1978) and which is particularly vulnerable because of its vascular anatomy (Hatchinski, 1979).

In contrast to the above evidence indicating significant decline in presynaptic cholinergic systems, a number of workers have found muscarinic receptor concentration to be essentially normal in patients with AD (Davies and Verth, 1978; Perry *et al.*, 1977a; White *et al.*, 1977). However, Reisine *et al.* (1978) did report a significant reduction in muscarinic receptors in the hippocampus, where neuropathological features are very marked and there is a severe reduction in ChAT activity. This has been confirmed by Rinne *et al.* (1984) whose findings also implicated other limbic areas. Several studies on muscarinic receptor subtypes have now been carried out but the results to date are somewhat contradictory. Mash *et al.* (1985) reported that, while binding to M1 receptors was unchanged, binding at M2 sites was significantly reduced. These authors accepted the view that M1 sites are located postsynaptically while M2 sites are presynaptic and therefore concluded that their finding of a decrease in M2 binding was consistent with other markers of presynaptic dysfunction (e.g. decreased ChAT activity). Similarly, Quirion *et al.* (1986) found no change in binding to M1 receptors in SDAT, but in their study reductions in M2 binding were found in only some patients. In contrast, Perry *et al.* (1986) found statistically significant decreases in binding to both M1 and M2 receptor subtypes in their AD patients, but they considered the magnitude of change to be modest and of little clinical significance.

The data from such binding studies has been widely interpreted as indicating that the postsynaptic muscarinic cholinergic system remains relatively intact in AD. This raises the possibility of pharmacological intervention, either by stimulating release of ACh from remaining neurons, by preventing its breakdown or by directly stimulating postsynaptic receptors. However an important caveat must be added, namely that it remains to be demonstrated that these receptors are functionally active.

Muscarinic receptor binding appears to be essentially unchanged in various other dementia-producing conditions such as chronic alcoholism, Huntington's disease, Parkinson's disease, as well as in aged individuals with Down's syndrome which is also characterized by the presence of Alzheimer-type neuropathology. However, reductions of muscarinic binding have been reported in Pick's disease (see Mann and Yates, 1986).

Interest in nicotinic receptors in dementia is relatively recent but a general concensus of opinion seems to be emerging that there is a decrease in nicotinic binding in at least a proportion of patients with AD (Flynn and Mash, 1986; Nordberg and Winblad, 1986; Perry *et al.*, 1986; Quirion *et al.*, 1986). It is of interest that one research group (Perry *et al.*, 1986) have reported finding increased concentrations of an apparently endogenous nicotinic inhibitor in the brains of their Alzheimer patients. These authors also reported that nicotinic binding was reduced in the brains of patients with Down's syndrome and Parkinson's disease (both with and without dementia), but not in those of patients with Huntington's disease or alcoholic dementia.

Dopamine

The neurotransmitter dopamine (DA) is synthesized in two steps from the amino acid precursor tyrosine (see Figure 4.3). The first (and rate limiting) step is the conversion of tyrosine to dihydroxyphenylalanine (L-DOPA) and this is catalyzed by the enzyme tyrosine hydroxylase. L-DOPA is then converted to DA by the enzyme DOPA-decarboxylase (also known as aromatic acid decarboxylase) and the transmitter is stored in vesicles to protect it from degradation. When released into the synaptic cleft DA binds to postsynaptic receptors and to other receptors located presynaptically on the releasing terminal, activation of which serves to halt the flow of transmitter release. Two major DA receptor subtypes have been identified and designated D1 and D2 respectively. The major mechanism for terminating the effects of released transmitter is reuptake into the presynaptic terminal. Metabolic degradation of DA is achieved via two major pathways involving the enzymes monoamine oxidase (MAO) and catechol-O-methyltransferase (COMT). The breakdown products include DOPAC (3,4-hydroxyphenylacetic acid) and HVA (homovanillic acid), both of which can be measured to yield information about transmitter turnover.

The development of histofluorescent procedures has allowed for the mapping of

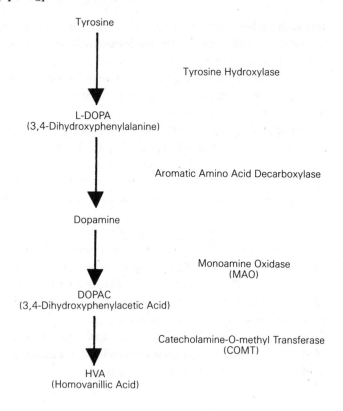

Tyrosine

Tyrosine Hydroxylase

L-DOPA
(3,4-Dihydroxyphenylalanine)

Aromatic Amino Acid Decarboxylase

Dopamine

Monoamine Oxidase
(MAO)

DOPAC
(3,4-Dihydroxyphenylacetic Acid)

Catecholamine-O-methyl Transferase
(COMT)

HVA
(Homovanillic Acid)

Figure 4.3   Synthesis and metabolism of dopamine.

monoaminergic transmitter systems in exquisite detail. Major dopaminergic pathways originate from cells located in the midbrain (see Figure 4.4). The fibres of the nigrostriatal pathway arise from cell groups A8 and A9 in the substantia nigra, join the medial forebrain bundle and run rostrally to the striatum (caudate nucleus and putamen) and the globus pallidus. Fibres arising from the A10 group of cells located more medially in the ventral tegmentum form the mesocorticolimbic pathway. These terminate in the nucleus accumbens, amygdala, olfactory tubercle and certain regions of the cortex. A third major pathway runs from cell group A12, located in the hypothalamus, to the median eminence of the pituitary gland.

The role of DA in AD is somewhat controversial. A number of studies (e.g. Cross *et al.*, 1983; Davies and Maloney, 1976; Ebinger *et al.*, 1987; Palmer *et al.*, 1987a; Yates *et al.*, 1979) have failed to find marked changes in a variety of indexes such as transmitter levels and concentration of the metabolites DOPAC and HVA. In contrast, other groups have reported changes in dopaminergic systems in AD (see Adolfsson *et al.*, 1979; Gottfries and Winblad, 1980). Sparks *et al.* (1986) found a decreased concentration of DA in the nucleus basalis of Meynert in their patients with

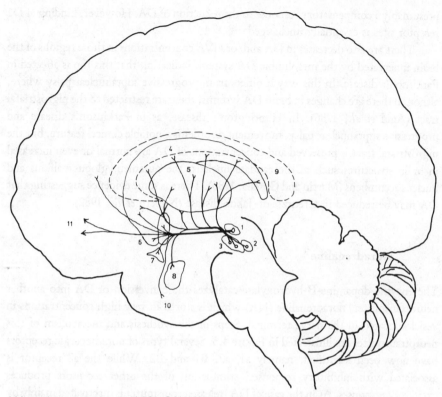

1 Ventral tegmental area (A10)   2 Nucleus parabrachialis pigmentosus (A8)
3 Substantia nigra (A9)   4 Caudate nucleus   5 Putamen   6 Nucleus accumbens   7
Olfactory tubercle   8 Amygdala   9 Corpus callosum   10 Entorhinal cortex   11 Frontal
cortex

Figure 4.4   Major dopaminergic pathways in the human brain.

AD, as well as reduced binding of the drug spiroperidol (spiperone) which labels both
dopaminergic and serotonergic receptors. Rinne *et al.* (1986a,b) found decreased
numbers of D1 and D2 receptors in a variety of brain sites in patients with AD, but
these were unchanged in multi-infarct dementia and in cases of mixed dementia,
although decreased concentrations of the metabolite HVA have been reported in the
cerebrospinal fluid (CSF) from such patients (Smirne *et al.*, 1985).

In Parkinson's disease, brain dopaminergic systems are undoubtedly severely
affected (see Hornykiewicz and Kish, 1986 for a recent review). The concentration of
the transmitter is reduced in all brain structures forming the nigrostriatal system, i.e.
the zona compacta of the substantia nigra, the caudate nucleus, the putamen and the
globus pallidus. Moreover, there are decreased concentrations of the major metabolites
of DA as well as a reduction in the activity of the synthetic enzymes. Binding studies
have indicated an increase in the number of D2 receptors in the striatum, which is

presumably a compensatory response to the reduction of DA. However, binding at D1 receptor sites is essentially unchanged.

There are also decreases in DA and/or HVA concentrations in those regions of the brain innervated by the mesolimbic DA system, indicating that this too is affected in Parkinson's disease. In this way it differs from progressive supranuclear palsy where, although there are changes in brain DA systems, these are restricted to the nigrostriatal tract (Agid *et al.*, 1986). In Huntington's disease, as in Parkinson's disease and progressive supranuclear palsy, movement disorder is a notable clinical feature, but the nigrostriatal tract is preserved and concentrations of DA are normal or even increased in brain structures such as the caudate nucleus, the putamen, globus pallidus and nucleus accumbens (Martin and Gusella, 1986). There is some evidence suggesting that DA may be reduced in Creutzfeldt–Jakob disease (Nyberg *et al.*, 1982).

Noradrenaline

The enzyme dopamine-B-hydroxylase catalyzes the conversion of DA into another neurotransmitter, noradrenaline (NA) which is stored in very high concentrations in vesicles located in the nerve terminal. Steps in the synthesis and metabolism of this neurotransmitter are illustrated in Figure 4.5. Several types of noradrenergic receptors have now been identified, namely a1, a2, B1 and B2. While the a2 receptor is associated with inhibitory responses, stimulation of the other receptors produces excitatory responses. As in the case of DA, released transmitter is inactivated mainly by reuptake into the presynaptic terminal via a specific transport mechanism. NA is degraded by the enzymes COMT and MAO and the metabolic product, 3-methoxy-4-hydroxyphenylglycol (MHPG), is a widely used marker of the activity of NA systems.

NA-containing terminals in the forebrain arise from groups of cells located in the pons and the medulla, principally from cell bodies lying in the locus coeruleus. Fibres projecting from this very small region of the brain terminate in the cortex, hippocampus, hypothalamus, basal forebrain and many parts of the limbic system (see Figure 4.6).

There is now a considerable body of evidence indicating that NA systems are altered in AD (see Mann and Yates, 1986, for a recent review). The concentration of NA is reduced, the activity of the synthetic enzyme dopamine-B-hydroxylase is decreased and the reuptake of NA is diminished in brain tissue obtained at autopsy. Finally some, although not all, studies (see Winblad *et al.*, 1986) have found reductions in the concentration of the metabolite MHPG. Postsynaptic binding of NA to all receptor subtypes in the cortex and hippocampus remains unchanged.

There is some disagreement concerning whether changes in noradrenergic systems in AD are an early or a late feature of the disease. Mann and Yates (1986)

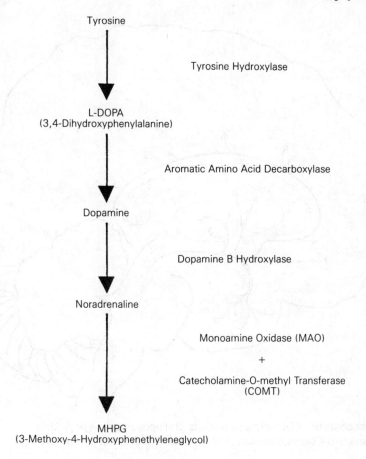

Tyrosine

Tyrosine Hydroxylase

L-DOPA
(3,4-Dihydroxyphenylalanine)

Aromatic Amino Acid Decarboxylase

Dopamine

Dopamine B Hydroxylase

Noradrenaline

Monoamine Oxidase (MAO)

+

Catecholamine-O-methyl Transferase
(COMT)

MHPG
(3-Methoxy-4-Hydroxyphenethyleneglycol)

Figure 4.5   Synthesis and metabolism of noradrenalin.

support the former position while the data of Perry *et al.* (1981a,b) led them to suggest that changes in this system occur late in the progression of AD and are possibly secondary to other pathological changes.

Widespread loss of NA is a feature of Parkinson's disease (Hornykiewicz and Kish, 1986), but not of progressive supranuclear palsy (Agid *et al.*, 1986). In Huntington's disease the concentration of NA may be increased in brain regions such as the caudate nucleus and the nucleus accumbens (see Bowen and Davison, 1986). In alcoholic dementia the level of NA may be reduced in a variety of structures, but the concentration of the metabolite MHPG may be normal or even slightly elevated (see Bowen and Davison, 1986), suggesting an increased turnover of this transmitter. Preliminary data reported by Nyberg *et al.* (1982) point to reduction of NA levels in a number of brain regions in Creutzfeldt–Jakob disease.

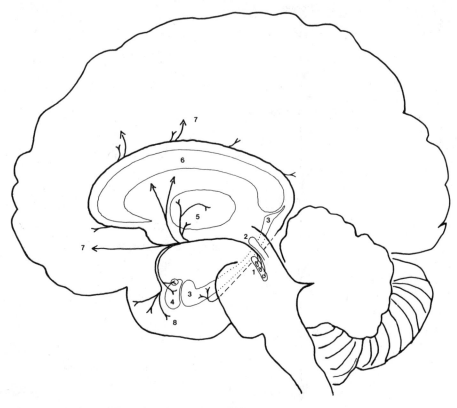

1 Locus coeruleus 2 Dorsal raphe nucleus 3 Hippocampus 4 Amygdala
5 Thalamus 6 Corpus callosum 7 Neocortex 8 Entorhinal cortex

Figure 4.6 Major noradrenergic pathways in the human brain.

Serotonin

The synthesis of serotin (5-hydroxytryptamine or 5-HT) is accomplished in two steps (see Figure 4.7). First, the enzyme tryptophan hydroxylase converts the amino acid precursor, tryptophan, to 5-hydroxytryptophan. The conversion of this to the transmitter 5-HT is then catalyzed by aromatic acid decarboxylase, an enzyme which is also involved in the synthesis of DA and NA. Metabolic degradation of the transmitter by MAO gives rise to 5-hydroxyindoleacetic acid (5-HIAA). However, the major mechanism by which the actions of 5-HT are terminated is reuptake into the presynaptic terminal. A variety of receptor types have now been identified (5-HT1a, 5-HT1b, 5-HT2 and most recently 5-HT3). The literature is somewhat complicated by the existence of an older nomenclature that distinguished between S1 and S2 receptors.

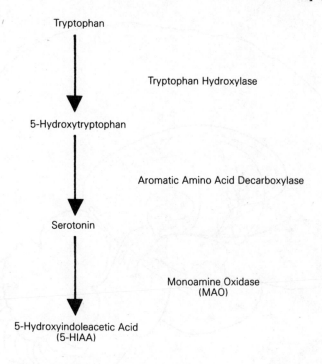

Figure 4.7   Synthesis and metabolism of serotonin.

Terminals containing 5-HT are widely distributed throughout the brain and are prominent in the frontal and cingulate cortices, the caudate nucleus, the nucleus accumbens, the hypothalamus, septum, amygdala and reticular formation. As in the case of the other monoamine neurotransmitters considered above the cell bodies giving rise to these terminals lie in the brain stem, particularly in the dorsal raphe nucleus (see Figure 4.8).

There is now considerable evidence pointing to deficiencies in 5-HT systems in AD, as reviewed in recent papers by Mann and Yates (1986), Whitford (1986) and Winblad *et al.* (1986). The concentration of 5-HT and of its metabolite 5-HIAA is reduced in tissue samples obtained at necropsy. Palmer *et al.* (1987b) have reported similar results using biopsy material. These workers also demonstrated a reduction in 5-HT uptake and in potassium-stimulated release of the transmitter. They concluded that changes in 5-HT systems were an early feature of AD but were unable to demonstrate a significant correlation between indexes of 5-HT activity and clinical severity, neuritic plaque count in the cortex, pyramidal cell loss from the cortex or decrease in ChAT activity. There was, however, a negative correlation between 5-HIAA concentration and neurofibrillary tangle count in the temporal cortex. Ligand binding studies point to a reduction in the number of 5-HT receptors, which is particularly marked for the 5-HT2 subtype.

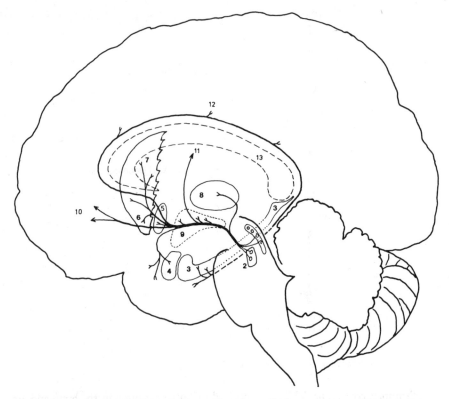

1 Dorsal raphe nucleus 2 Superior central nucleus 3 Hippocampus 4 Amygdala
5 Septum 6 Nucleus accumbens 7 Corpus striatum 8 Thalamus 9 Hypothalamus
10 Frontal cortex 11 Neocortex 12 Cingulate cortex 13 Corpus callosum

Figure 4.8   Major serotonergic pathways in the human brain.

Alterations in brain 5-HT systems are found not only in AD but also in a number
of other dementia-producing conditions. The concentration of the transmitter and of
its metabolite 5-HIAA is reduced in chronic alcoholics (see Bowen and Davison, 1986)
and in patients with Parkinson's disease (Hornykiewicz and Kish, 1986). Decreased
levels of 5-HIAA have also been observed in CSF obtained by lumbar puncture from
patients with Parkinson's disease, especially those who also show symptoms of
depression (Mayeux *et al.*, 1986). Furthermore, uptake of 5-HT may be reduced in
Parkinson's disease (Raisman *et al.*, 1986). In marked contrast, concentrations of both
5-HT and 5-HIAA are normal in the basal ganglia, hypothalmus and temporal cortex
of patients with progressive supranuclear palsy despite the clinical similarity of this
condition to Parkinson's disease (Kish *et al.*, 1985). In Huntington's disease too the
serotonergic transmitter system seems to be relatively spared. Cross *et al.* (1986) found
that binding to 5-HT uptake sites was marginally increased in the caudate nucleus but

unchanged in the putamen. It has also been reported that the concentration of 5-HIAA is diminished in the CSF of patients with multi-infarct dementia (Smirne *et al.*, 1985), but it is unclear whether this change reflects cell loss or persistent diffuse ischaemia.

Amino Acid and Peptide Neurotransmitters

Gamma-Aminobutyric Acid

Gamma-aminobutyric acid (GABA) is synthesized in the CNS from the precursor L-glutamic acid in a reaction which is catalyzed by L-glutamic acid decarboxylase (GAD). This enzyme has been used as a marker for the integrity of GABAergic systems. A number of receptor subtypes have been identified, but the actions of GABA are always inhibitory. It is widely distributed throughout the brain and constitutes the major inhibitory transmitter in the CNS. GABAergic nerve cells are generally interneurons involved in localized networks but longer projection pathways, e.g. from the caudate nucleus to the substantia nigra, have been mapped.

Perry *et al.* (1977b, 1978b) reported decreases in the activity of the synthetic enzyme GAD in patients with AD, but this change did not correlate with plaque density or with a gross clinical measure of impairment, namely a mental test score derived from questions tapping general information, memory and concentration (Blessed *et al.*, 1968). Moreover, it was not specific, being found also in other patient groups, and may therefore represent an artefact of the terminal state of the patient since Bowen (1980) reported no change in GAD activity in biopsy samples (cf. ChAT activity which is decreased in both biopsy and autopsy samples). Rossor *et al.* (1982a) failed to find significant reductions in GABA itself, except in the temporal cortex of patients with AD. However, more recent investigations (e.g. Ellison *et al.*, 1986) have pointed to widespread and significant reductions of the transmitter. Moreover, Hardy *et al.* (1987a) found a marked reduction in the uptake of GABA in brain tissue obtained from patients with this disease. They also concluded that something of the order of 70 per cent of GABA-containing terminals were lost from the cortex and the hippocampus in AD and it is of interest that reduced receptor binding of GABA in several brain regions has also been reported (Reisine *et al.*, 1978).

Data with respect to GABAergic systems in Parkinson's disease are conflicting (Hornykiewicz and Kish, 1986). Although the concentration of GABA is elevated in the striatum, it has been found that the activity of the synthetic enzyme GAD is decreased throughout the basal ganglia. The concentration of GABA is normal in many areas of the brain in patients with progressive supranuclear palsy (Kish *et al.*, 1985).

GABAergic systems are undoubtedly compromised in Huntington's disease with marked decreases in the concentration of transmitter in the striatum, globus pallidus and substantia nigra (see Martin and Gusella, 1986). It would be expected that damage to the striatonigral GABAergic tract would result in a disinhibition of the nigrostriatal dopaminergic pathway. This might account for the chorea-inducing effects of L-DOPA upon asymptomatic patients as well as the efficiency of dopaminergic antagonists in controlling the abnormal movements characteristic of Huntington's disease.

Glutamate

Glutamate is widely believed to be the neurotransmitter involved in a number of important pathways in the brain. These include corticocortical association fibres and corticofugal projections to such regions as the hippocampus and the nucleus basalis of Meynert. Its excitatory actions are mediated by a number of receptor subtypes. One of these, the NMDA receptor (defined by its sensitivity to the agonist N-methyl-D-aspartate) has been found to play an important role in synaptic plasticity and at least certain types of learning (Morris *et al.*, 1986).

In addition to its putative neurotransmitter functions, it has been shown that glutamate has neurotoxic properties. Consequently, it has been speculated that abnormality of glutaminergic neurons might play an important role in the genesis of a number of neurodegenerative conditions (Greenamyre, 1986; Maragos *et al.*, 1987) although to date there is little in the way of supporting evidence. The role of glutamate in the production of ischaemic damage is more firmly established (see Porsche-Weibking, 1989).

Investigation of this transmitter has been hampered by the lack of a specific enzyme marker for glutaminergic terminals. Moreover, as glutamate is involved in many metabolic functions, the amount of the amino acid which serves a neurotransmitter function is only a fraction of the total present in the CNS. However, there is evidence of glutaminergic dysfunction in AD. Ellison *et al.* (1986) reported reduced concentrations of glutamate in nine cortical regions in the brains of individuals with AD, although this decrease was only statistically significant for the inferior temporal region. Non-significant changes were also found in a variety of subcortical structures including the caudate, putamen, nucleus accumbens, hippocampus and the dorsomedial nucleus of the thalamus. In contrast, Sasaki *et al.* (1986) found significant reductions in cortical and subcortical areas of the brains of their patients with AD and Hyman *et al.* (1987) found an 83 per cent decrease in glutamate concentration in the perforant pathway (the major input to the hippocampus from the cortex) in their patient group. Smith *et al.* (1985) reported a significant correlation between severity of dementia and CSF levels of glutamate. Moreover, Hardy *et al.* (1987b) found a significant decrease in the uptake of a glutamate analogue in the hippocampus and in all cortical lobes of their patients with AD. On the basis of these results they estimated a loss of approximately 60 per cent of brain glutaminergic terminals. Similar reductions in analogue uptake have been reported by Cross *et al.* (1987). Loss of glutaminergic receptors from the cortex and hippocampus have also been reported (Greenamyre, 1986, but see also Geddes *et al.*, 1986). Somewhat paradoxically, however, release of glutamate from cortical prisms is not significantly reduced in AD (Smith *et al.*, 1983).

Greenamyre (1986) speculated that an abnormality of glutaminergic neurons played an important role in Huntington's disease. His argument was based on the similarity between the pathological changes seen in this condition and the effects of injections of the neurotoxin kianic acid, an analogue of glutamate, into the striatum of the rat. However, it has been reported that the concentration of glutamate in the striatum of patients with Huntington's disease is normal (see Martin and Gusella, 1986).

Somatostatin

The neuropeptide somatostatin is widely distributed in the brain. It is synthesized in the cell body and stored in granules which are transported to the nerve terminals. The most potent releasers of somatostatin are ACh, glutamate and vasointestinal polypeptide (VIP) while GABA is a potent inhibitor of release. Somatostatin has been reported to have both excitatory and inhibitory actions on the activity of neurons, but the apparent dual action may simply reflect an inverted U-shaped dose-response curve.

There are numerous reports of decreased levels of somatostatin-like immunoreactivity (SLI) in post-mortem tissue samples from patients with AD (e.g. Beal *et al.*, 1986a; Candy *et al.*, 1985; Davies *et al.*, 1980; Francis *et al.*, 1987; Perry *et al.*, 1981a; Rossor *et al.*, 1980b). In the cortex the decrease is most marked in the temporal region, although other areas can be affected. Cortical decreases of SLI are significantly correlated with reductions in ChAT activity (Davies *et al.*, 1982). SLI levels are also decreased in the hippocampus (Davies *et al.*, 1982) and the amygdala (Candy *et al.*, 1985), although other subcortical regions, including the nucleus basalis of Meynert, show little change (Beal *et al.*, 1986a; Candy *et al.*, 1985). Reductions in somatostatin receptor binding have also been reported (Beal *et al.*, 1985; Quirion *et al.*, 1986). Immunohistochemical investigations have revealed that while the density of somatostatin immunoreactive cells in the neocortex does not change in AD, many somatostatin-positive fibres are abnormally swollen, bulbous in shape and often observed within neuritic plaques (Nakamura and Vincent, 1986). Dawburn *et al.* (1986) reported significant correlations between the decrease in SLI and the density of neuritic plaques and of neurofibrillary tangles in the cortex, while Roberts *et al.* (1985) found tangles within somatostatin-positive cells. Performance on measures of intellectual ability (WAIS) and receptive language (Token Test) have been found to correlate with cortical SLI levels (Francis *et al.*, 1987).

CSF levels of SLI are also reduced in patients with AD (e.g. Beal *et al.*, 1986b;

Cramer *et al.*, 1985; Gomez *et al.*, 1986; Soininen *et al.*, 1988; Sunderland *et al.*, 1987; Tamminga *et al.*, 1987). Moreover, it has been reported by some investigators that these decreases correlate with the severity of cognitive impairment (Tamminga *et al.*, 1987; Soininen *et al.*, 1988; Sunderland *et al.*, 1987), although Gomez *et al.* (1986) failed to find significant correlations between CSF levels of SLI and either duration of illness or severity of dementia in their clinically diagnosed patients. The importance of somatostatin depletion in the genesis of cognitive impairment has also been questioned by Davies (1986) who reported finding very low levels of SLI in a group of elderly individuals who had performed well on neuropsychological testing a few months before death and autopsy examination. Moreover, Francis *et al.* (1987) found normal release of somatostatin from cortical samples obtained at biopsy from patients with AD.

Changes in SLI have also been observed in other dementia-producing conditions. Significant decreases were found in the CSF of patients with diagnoses of multi-infarct dementia (Beal *et al.*, 1986b), though Cramer *et al.* (1985) reported only moderate and non-significant reductions in this patient group. Normal cortical concentrations of SLI were observed in the brains of patients with Parkinson's disease who were not dementing, but reductions of up to 40 per cent were found in the frontal and temporal cortices of those patients who also showed evidence of dementia (Beal *et al.*, 1986a; Beal and Martin, 1986). Similarly, Jolkkonen *et al.* (1986) found that the reduction in CSF level in patients with Parkinson's disease was most marked when dementia was also present. Cramer *et al.* (1985) linked reductions in the CSF level of SLI in parkinsonian patients with impairments in concentration, akinesia, rigidity and autonomic disturbances.

A very different pattern of results is found in Huntington's disease. SLI concentrations are not significantly altered in the cortex and hippocampus, but there are three- to fivefold increases in the caudate, putamen and globus pallidus (Beal *et al.*, 1986b; Martin and Gusella, 1986). SLI concentration is unchanged in the cortex of patients with Pick's disease (Wood *et al.*, 1983).

Concluding Remarks

There can be no doubt that biochemical investigations have added a new dimension to our understanding of dementia. A rich and complex body of knowledge is rapidly accumulating (see Table 4.1), but the simple identification of transmitter abnormalities is in itself of only limited value. Some attempt must be made to relate the neurochemical alterations detected to the cognitive and behavioural deficits observed in patients.

The view that the cognitive deficits observed in patients with AD, and in particular the impairment of memory, are a consequence of an underlying cholinergic

Table 4.1 Summary of the neurochemical data reported in this chapter

	Alzheimer's disease	Pick's Disease	Multi-Infarct Dementia	Parkinson's Disease	Progressive Supranuclear Palsy	Huntington's Disease	Creutzfeldt-Jakob Disease	Alcoholic Dementia
Cholinergic Systems								
Choline acetyltransferase	↓	↓?	↓	↓?	↓?	—	↓	→
Acetylcholinesterase	↓→		↓		→↑	↓		←→?
Acetylcholine			—				↓	→
Muscarinic receptors	↓?					↑		↑→
Nicotinic receptors	↓ ↑?		→					
Dopaminergic Systems								
Dopamine	─ ↓			→→→↑(D1)		←		→↑←? ←
Homovanillic acid	→→→			→	─	─		
Receptors								
Noradrenergic Systems								
Dopamine β hydroxylase	─→→→			→	→→	←	←	
Noradrenaline								
MHPG				→				
Receptors	─→→→			→	─ ─			
Serotinergic Systems								
Serotonin	─↓?			→				
5HIAA	→→→			→→←		←→↑←? ←		
Receptors								
Amino Acid and Peptide Systems								
GAD								
GABA								
Glutamate								
Somatostatin								

dysfunction has come to occupy a central position in relation to research on this condition. The cholinergic hypothesis receives further support from pharmacological investigations which will be considered in the next chapter. Cholinergic deficits may also contribute to the cognitive deficits shown by patients with other conditions, for example those with Parkinson's disease (Ruberg and Agid, 1988) and alcoholic dementia (Lishman, 1986), but although a sufficient cause of cognitive impairment it is not a necessary one. Cognitive dysfunction is a feature of certain conditions in which cholinergic function is comparatively intact, such as Pick's disease and at least some patients with progressive supranuclear palsy. Only detailed neuropsychological investigations can reveal whether there are quantitative and/or qualitative differences in the nature of the cognitive deficits shown by different patient groups.

It must be abundantly clear from the foregoing review in this chapter that cholinergic dysfunction is not the only neurotransmitter abnormality in patients with AD. This is particularly true of younger victims of the disease, which lends some support to the notion that there may be distinct subtypes of the condition (Roth, 1986). However, at the present time there is some uncertainty concerning whether the changes in non-cholinergic systems are primary features of AD or secondary to cholinergic dysfunction.

Attempts to understand how these non-cholinergic changes might contribute to the cognitive impairments of patients with AD have scarcely begun, although as previously noted, it is recognized that the clinical features of younger patients, in whom neurotransmitter abnormalities affect a greater number of systems and are more severe and widespread, may differ in significant ways from those of older patients. The suggestion that the presence of receptive language dysfunction may be correlated with low levels of somatostatin is an interesting preliminary observation that should be pursued. It might also be of considerable value to explore possible relationships between neurotransmitter abnormalities and behavioural problems such as wandering, aggression and changes in personality and emotional reactivity, in addition to more detailed explorations of diverse aspects of cognition. However, it must be acknowledged that formidable methodological problems will have to be addressed in doing so.

Neurochemical investigations of patients with AD have produced data pertinent to the accelerated ageing hypothesis raised in Chapter 3. This question was considered in some detail by Rossor and Mountjoy (1986). They concluded that while neuronal degeneration and concomitant changes in neurotransmitter systems are a feature of both normal ageing and AD there are important differences. In normal ageing ChAT activity is only significantly reduced in the frontal cortex, whereas in AD decreases tend to be more widespread and are most marked in the temporal cortex. A similar pattern is seen with respect to GABA. In both normal ageing and AD there appears to be little evidence for cortical changes in DA concentration. Cortical levels of NA and 5HT show only modest declines in normal ageing, but these can be marked in AD.

Similarly, levels of the neuropeptide somatostatin appear to be unchanged during the course of normal ageing, but as we have seen there is quite an extensive body of data to suggest that they are abnormal in AD. It is difficult to dismiss the accelerated ageing hypothesis outright as it is always possible to argue that it would be supported by observations on the brains of still older controls, but the multi-faceted evidence accumulated to date (see Berg, 1985) would suggest that AD is distinct from normal ageing.

Biochemical investigations of Parkinson's and Huntington's diseases have been instrumental in the development of pharmacological treatments for the movement disorders associated with these conditions. In the next chapter we shall consider how pharmacological investigations have added to our knowledge of the mechanisms underlying cognitive impairment and how the first, albeit tentative steps are being taken towards amelioration of this.

Chapter 5

Pharmacological Investigations

In the previous chapter the major changes in neurotransmitters that accompany dementia-producing conditions were documented and the particular importance of brain cholinergic systems highlighted. In the present chapter we shall consider pharmacological investigations that have manipulated brain cholinergic systems with a view to gaining greater insight into the role played by ACh in cognitive processes as well as evaluating the potential of drugs which enhance cholinergic activity as therapeutic agents in dementia. Only passing reference will be made to other drug treatments. In reviewing first the human experimental results, followed by clinical psychopharmacological investigations, we shall be seeking to convey to readers an overall sense of the potential which such studies offer. We shall try not to refer repeatedly to the methodological shortcomings of the investigations to date. Rather, we shall withhold this critical overview until the final section of this chapter in which we will also highlight some of the challenges to neuropsychologists which are being generated by pharmacological research. The review of clinical studies will be restricted to those of patients with DAT as there has been a paucity of research into drug effects upon the cognition of patients with other dementia-producing conditions. Although precursor treatment of parkinsonian patients with L-DOPA to enhance dopaminergic activity has been hailed as revolutionary, it remains true that to date investigations of such patients have largely been directed at amelioration of the movement disorder characteristic of this condition, rather than at improvement of cognitive functioning *per se*. Similar considerations apply to other degenerative and dementia-producing conditions such as Huntington's disease.

Effects of Anticholinergic Drugs in Normal Subjects

There has long been anecdotal evidence that cholinergically active drugs have potent effects on memory and cognitive processes, ranging from ancient witchcraft ritual to the use of scopolamine in obstetric anaesthesia because of its ability to produce 'twilight sleep' with amnesia for painful experiences (Drachman, 1978; Dundee and

Pandit, 1972; Warburton, 1979). Over the course of the past two to three decades there has been systematic investigation into the nature and extent of the memory impairment induced in human subjects by anticholinergics such as scopolamine and atropine, both belladonna alkaloids which preferentially block muscarinic cholinergic receptors. Many of these studies have employed complicated designs and multiple tasks, the details of which defy succinct summary, and comparison between studies is rendered difficult by the lack of concensus with respect to the dose used, route of administration or the test material employed. It seems more profitable therefore to eschew where possible the details of specific studies and instead focus upon their overall conclusions.

Much of the review that follows will be concerned with the effects of drugs on various aspects of memory. In reporting their results investigators have often made reference to different components of cognitive psychological models. However, for the most part, such models have exerted only minimal influence upon the design of the experiments and the choice of the tasks to be employed. For this reason we consider that it would be unnecessarily diversionary to dwell upon the nature of memory in this chapter thereby detracting from the overall thrust. Hence, consideration of the details of the different models that have been proposed over the years, and the implications thereof, will be deferred until Chapter 8.

Scopolamine treatment produces marked deficits in the acquisition and storage of new material (e.g. Beatty *et al.*, 1986; Caine *et al.*, 1981; Crow and Grove-White, 1973; Drachman, 1977; Drachman and Leavitt, 1974; Frith *et al.*, 1984; Ghoneim and Mewaldt, 1975, 1977; Jones *et al.*, 1979; Liljequist and Mattila, 1979; Parrott, 1986, 1987; Petersen, 1977, 1979; Safer and Allen, 1971). There is only a slight effect upon ability to retrieve information acquired before drug treatment (Ghoneim and Mewaldt, 1975, 1977; Petersen, 1977; Safer and Allen, 1971). Beatty *et al.* (1986) found that scopolamine did not affect performance on semantically constrained word fluency tasks or on retrieval of words by first letter, although both Drachman and Leavitt (1974) and Caine *et al.* (1981), who used higher doses, reported significant impairment of the ability to retrieve material from familiar semantic categories in scopolamine-treated subjects. The latter authors also found decreased fluency in generating words beginning with a designated letter. Scopolamine has essentially no effect on relatively passive measures of short-term memory such as digit span (Drachman, 1977; Drachman and Leavitt, 1974), although it does disrupt performance on the Brown–Peterson distractor task (Beatty *et al.*, 1986; Caine *et al.*, 1981; Kopelman and Corn, 1988). Nissen *et al.* (1987) reported that scopolamine did not affect 'procedural' memory (see Chapter 8).

If the effects of scopolamine were the result of drowsiness then amphetamine, as a CNS stimulant, should be successful in reversing them, but if due to specific interference with the cholinergic system then an anticholinesterase such as physostigmine should be the more effective drug since it inhibits the breakdown enzyme acetylcholinesterase and so increases function at cholinergic synapses. It has been shown that the effects of scopolamine can indeed be reversed by physostigmine (Drachman, 1977; Liljequist and Mattila, 1979; Safer and Allen, 1971) and by the direct agonist arecholine (Sitaram *et al.*, 1978a; but cf. Ostfeld and Aruguete, 1962 who failed to so so). A partial reversal of scopolamine-induced effects has also been achieved by administration of the precursor choline (Mohs *et al.*, 1981). Drachman (1977) found that although *d*-amphetamine enhanced subjective and objective alertness in subjects treated with scopolamine, it failed to reverse (and indeed exacerbated) the scopolamine-induced deterioration in performance on a measure of learning and memory. Such results indicate that the detrimental effects of scopolamine upon learning and memory are a specific consequence of cholinergic blockade and not simply an artefact of drug-induced drowsiness.

Drachman and Leavitt (1974) drew attention to similarities between the performance profiles of normal elderly subjects and young normal subjects treated with scopolamine when these groups were assessed on the same battery of memory tests as well as on the Weschler Adult Intelligence Scale (WAIS). The two groups also performed similarly on a dichotic listening test (Drachman *et al.*, 1980). These workers interpreted their findings as support for the view that cholinergic systems play an important role in memory and cognition and, with the demonstration of marked cholinergic dysfunction in AD, their hypothesizing has clearly acquired a new dimension (see Drachman, 1983). Other workers, while acknowledging the similarities between the disruptive effects of scopolamine and the cognitive deficits seen in patients with AD, have emphasized that there are important differences (Beatty *et al.*, 1986; Kopelman, 1985). Even when pharmacological blocking studies on young normal subjects have investigated cognitive processes found to be deficient in patients with DAT, they have often employed different tests. Thus, while scopolamine blockade may produce a useful model of AD its utility has not been adequately tested to date, but it is unlikely that it will prove to be a perfect model for reasons outlined in the previous chapter.

A final point of interest may be the suggestion by a number of researchers that scopolamine treatment, and other manipulations of cholinergic activity, may affect attentional processes (see Parrott, 1986, 1987; Warburton, 1979; Warburton and Wesnes, 1984). Ostfeld and Aruguete (1962: 139) reported impaired ability to, 'maintain an attentive set' following scopolamine treatment and decreased performance on vigilance tasks has also been reported (Colquhoun, 1962; Safer and Allen, 1971; Wesnes and Warburton, 1983a) although this was not substantiated by Caine *et al.* (1981). Crow and Grove-White (1973) failed to find any effect on a visual scanning task. Drachman and Leavitt (1974) reported that, on a retrieval by category test, scopolamine-treated subjects tended to shift categories during the test and proceed to retrieve items from a different category. This would again suggest impaired ability to maintain an attentive set. In Petersen's (1977) study, subjects seemed to have difficulty concentrating on the task despite good motivation and effort as assessed by the investigator. Subjects themselves reported a tendency for their minds to wander.

Dunne and Hartley (1985) examined the effects of scopolamine on the performance of a dichotic listening task. Subjects were required to report the stimuli presented simultaneously to each ear, but were told before any given trial which ear they should attend to. Under placebo conditions the expected advantage of the attended ear was clearly demonstrated. Treatment with scopolamine did not have a significant effect upon the total number of items recalled, but it did produce a decrease in the number of items reported from the attended ear, together with a complementary increase in the number reported from the unattended ear. These results suggest that a major effect of scopolamine had been to disrupt the ability of subjects to allocate attentional resources appropriately. In another study these workers found that scopolamine decreased the detection of stimuli in high probability locations on a spatial display, but increased the detection of stimuli in low probability positions (Dunne and Hartley, 1986). These results too were interpreted as evidence of scopolamine-induced disruption of the optimal utilization of attentional resources.

Further support for an effect of scopolamine upon attention comes from evoked potential studies where drug treatment has been found to increase the latency and diminish the amplitude of the cognitive event related potential, P300, associated with the detection of rare auditory stimuli (Hammond *et al.*, 1987; Meador *et al.*, 1987). Scopolamine does not affect visual evoked responses to the reversal of a checker board pattern, but it does diminish the evoked response to a diffuse flash of light and this pattern of differential responding in the visual modality mimics that seen in patients with DAT (Bajalan *et al.*, 1986).

In summary, it would appear that treatment with anticholinergic compounds may produce widespread disruption of information processing operations. The results of studies which experimentally block the cholinergic transmitter system lend support to the view that depletion of ACh plays an important, though not necessarily exclusive, role in the genesis of cognitive dysfunction in patients with DAT.

Effects of Cholinomimetics in Normal Subjects

Given the evidence that memory and other cognitive functions can be impaired by anticholinergic drugs, the question arises as to whether cholinomimetics enhance performance. To date there is evidence to encourage the belief that such drugs may improve cognitive functioning under certain circumstances.

Davis *et al.* (1976) and Drachman and Leavitt (1974) failed to find a significant improvement in the performance of young normal subjects when treated with the anticholinesterase physostigmine. However, Davis *et al.* (1978), using a group of subjects who were pre-selected in order to avoid ceiling effects, demonstrated that infusion of physostigmine facilitated the acquisition of word lists presented according to the selective reminding procedure of Buschke (1973) and somewhat enhanced free recall of previously presented lists. Performance on the short-term memory tasks employed (digit span and a Sternberg memory scanning procedure) was unaffected by drug treatment. Sitaram *et al.* (1978a) demonstrated an improvement in serial learning of categorized word lists following treatment with the direct cholinergic agonist arecholine but the degree of improvement shown by individual subjects was related to their performance under placebo, with 'poor' performers showing greater improvement. Arecholine also facilitated the retrieval of categorized lists which had been learnt before drug administration (Weingartner *et al.*, 1979). Sitaram *et al.* (1978b) also found that acquisition of low imagery words was enhanced by the precursor choline so that the difference between recall of high and low imagery words found under placebo conditions was eliminated. Once again the degree of improvement was related to placebo performance. More recently, however, Davis *et al.* (1980) failed to find significant improvements in learning and memory following treatment with choline but they, like Mohs and Davis (1980), found a slight improvement in the performance of some subjects.

Overall the results of these studies suggest that the learning and memory performance of normal subjects may be enhanced by appropriate pharmacological manipulation of cholinergic systems. However, certain circumstances must prevail for the demonstration of beneficial effects. Dose level is a critical factor as there seems to be a narrow therapeutic window and benefits can be demonstrated most readily in subjects whose baseline performance is poor and when difficult test materials are employed.

Clinical Studies using Cholinomimetics

The driving force or momentum for studies of the effects of anticholinergic and, more specifically, cholinomimetic compounds on normal young adults was initially a desire to relate the psychological aspects of memory to the structure and function of the brain (Drachman, 1978; Drachman and Sahakian, 1979) but in recent years there has also been the strong hope of arriving at a treatment for AD in which central cholinergic functioning has been found to be impaired (see Chapter 4). Provided that receptor binding is relatively normal in patients with AD, as a number of studies seem to suggest, then the hope has been that it might be possible to improve memory functioning by increasing the availability of ACh at synapses or by direct stimulation of postsynaptic cholinergic receptors. With these considerations in mind a number of treatment strategies are currently being explored, namely: precursor loading to stimulate increased synthesis of ACh; preventing breakdown of ACh; enhancing release; direct stimulation of postsynaptic receptors; and, combinations of precursor loading with prevention of ACh breakdown or direct postsynaptic receptor stimulation or indeed with administration of other non-cholinergic compounds.

There have already been a number of studies of the effects of cholinomimetic drugs in patients with DAT, as well as in healthy elderly subjects with mild to moderate memory impairment. In reviewing these studies the above strategies shall each be considered in turn, with the exception of the combination approach which will be introduced as appropriate when considering the results obtained using other strategies.

Precursor loading. Mohs *et al.* (1979, 1980) found no improvement of learning and memory in healthy elderly subjects with mild memory impairment following treatment with the precursor choline. Ferris *et al.* (1979: 1040) also failed to find any beneficial effects of choline treatment in a group of, 'elderly outpatients suffering from mild to moderate cognitive impairment' and similar failures of oral choline therapy to produce significant enhancement of learning and memory in patients bearing diagnoses of DAT have also been reported (Bajada, 1982; Boyd *et al.*, 1977; Christie *et al.*, 1979; Smith *et al.*, 1978; Thal *et al.*, 1981), although a number of workers (Etienne *et al.*, 1978a; Fovall *et al.*, 1980; Signoret *et al.*, 1978) have found positive effects in at least some patients. The results reported by Fovall *et al.* (1980) are the most impressive to date, having been obtained in a double-blind study. In addition it should be noted that, while Boyd *et al.* (1977) and Smith *et al.* (1978) failed to find treatment effects on measures of learning and memory, both studies did suggest that choline had produced some improvement in awareness and general behavioural functioning. However, Renvoize and Jerram (1979) reported that daily treatment with choline over a 2-month period failed to improve either behaviour or communication skills in their sample of patients with DAT.

Lecithin, a naturally-occurring dietary constituent containing phosphatidylcholine, became a more popular source of precursor than choline itself on the grounds that its effects appeared to be more prolonged than an equivalent amount of choline base and the unpleasant fishy odour that can result from ingestion of choline was avoided (Etienne *et al.*, 1978b). As with choline itself, however, studies of patients with DAT have yielded both positive and negative results. Thus, although Etienne *et al.* (1978b) reported positive effects in an open study, a later and more extensive double-blind study carried out by these workers over 3 months failed to detect improvements on any of the measures employed (Etienne *et al.*, 1982). Other workers also reported essentially negative results (Brinkman *et al.*, 1982; Corser *et al.*, 1979; Dysken *et al.*, 1982; Fisman *et al.*, 1981; Heyman *et al.*, 1982; Weintraub *et al.*, 1983) but positive effects of lecithin treatment were obtained in some double-blind studies (Pomara *et al.*, 1983; Vroulis *et al.*, 1981). Sullivan *et al.* (1982) reported that, although their double-blind study failed to show significant effects of lecithin on objective measures of memory, relatives and caregivers noted behavioural improvements during the lecithin phase of the investigation. It has also been suggested that long-term treatment with lecithin slows the rate of cognitive decline in patients with DAT (Christie *et al.*, 1979; Levy *et al.*, 1983; Little *et al.*, 1985) and, although admittedly a much more modest achievement than the hoped for partial or complete reversal of deterioration, such findings, if confirmed, would represent a significant therapeutic advance.

The effects of combining precursor loading with the so-called 'nootropic' compound piracetam have also been examined. Despite some initially encouraging results (Ferris *et al.*, 1982; Serby *et al.*, 1983; Smith *et al.*, 1984) a recent investigation by Growdon *et al.* (1986) failed to show any beneficial effects of lecithin and piracetam, either alone or in combination.

The foregoing review indicates that, although treatment with choline or lecithin has produced improvement in some patients, the precursor loading approach has not on the whole been conspicuously successful. It has undoubtedly been less successful in the treatment of DAT than has the model on which this precursor approach was based, namely L-Dopa therapy for Parkinson's disease. The biochemical results of Marek *et al.* (1982) suggest one possible reason for the failure of the precursor loading approach in patients with DAT. These workers reported that cortical biopsy tissue obtained from a patient with AD was capable of synthesizing more ACh in the presence of extra choline, but they calculated that, for synthesis to occur at a normal rate in this tissue, the extracellular concentration of choline would have to be increased more than 50-fold. Needless to say, the possibility of achieving such an increase seems remote.

Moreover it is possible that although choline increases brain acetycholine concentration (Cohen and Wurtman, 1976; Haubrich *et al.*, 1975), it might not necessarily increase transmission at cholinergic synapses. Furthermore, choline may only increase ACh in brain regions not directly involved in memory processes (Eckernas *et al.*, 1977). However, it has to be acknowledged that, although one of the oldest questions addressed by psychology, our understanding of the nature of the engram and its 'localization' within the brain is still very far from complete. Deutsch (1971) proposed that memory consists of increased sensitivity of receptors to ACh at a specific set of memory synapses but Drachman *et al.* (see Drachman and Sahakian, 1979) have proposed a somewhat modified view. Rather than regarding the absolute ACh-sensitivity in a memory synapse as the critical factor that determines its response to cholinergic drugs, they would consider the difference in sensitivity between these synapses and alternate pathways, i.e. the signal-to-noise ratio, as a more likely determining factor. Thus in their view memories may be stored both by increasing sensitivity in certain synapses and decreasing it in others. The neural pathways representing stored memories are most likely, therefore, to be quite specific arrays of neurons and hence a general widespread increase in available and released ACh may not provide sufficiently selective facilitation of these pathways. If Drachman *et al.* are correct, then the most productive approach in attempting to facilitate memory might seem to be the use of anticholinesterases, which would prevent breakdown of the ACh released into synapses and thereby selectively potentiate the effect of existing signals. Of course, in the case of aged or dementing subjects it might also be necessary to supplement ACh stores by administration of precursors such as choline.

Preventing breakdown of ACh. Generally, encouraging results have indeed been obtained using anticholinesterases, principally physostigmine. Drachman and Sahakian (1980) reported that when physostigmine was administered subcutaneously to normal elderly volunteers, it produced consistent (although statistically insignificant) trends towards improvement. While some investigators have failed to find significant effects on measures of learning and memory in patients with DAT (Ashford *et al.*, 1981; Delwaide *et al.*, 1980; Gustafson *et al.*, 1987; Jotkowitz, 1983; Stern *et al.*, 1987), a number of other workers have reported significant improvement following treatment (Beller *et al.*, 1985; Christie *et al.*, 1981; Davis *et al.*, 1979; Johns *et al.*, 1985; Levin and Peters, 1982; Mohs and Davis, 1982; Schwartz and Kohlstaedt, 1986; Smith and Swash, 1979; Sullivan *et al.*, 1982). It is interesting that in one study (Rose and Moulthrop, 1986) physostigmine was found to facilitate recognition and recall of verbal material, but not of non-verbal materials, and the peptide ACTH produced the converse pattern of results. Modality-specific memory disorders following lesions in different parts of the brain have aroused much interest among neuropsychologists (Heilman and Valenstein, 1985; Ross, 1980, 1982) and the possibility now being raised that there might also be neurochemically-mediated modality-specific effects is intriguing. It is important to note that the facilitatory effects of physostigmine are not restricted to learning and memory. The drug has been found to improve the constructional ability of patients with DAT (Muramoto *et al.*, 1979, 1984; Sahakian *et al.*, 1987), to reduce their simple reaction time (Gustafson *et al.*, 1987), and to improve performance on some subtests of the WAIS (Stern *et al.*, 1987).

Davis *et al.* emphasized the importance of determining the optimal dose for each patient (e.g. Davis *et al.*, 1979; Davis and Mohs, 1982; Mohs and Davis, 1982). Furthermore, they maintained that when optimal doses were administered the beneficial effects obtained were consistent. However, this assertion has recently been disputed by Stern *et al.* (1987). Peters and Levin (1977) documented improvement of learning and memory in a case of herpes simplex encephalitis, a condition which primarily affects the limbic system, following treatment with a combination of lecithin and subcutaneously administered physostigmine. This combination was also reported to be effective in patients with DAT (Peters and Levin, 1979). There are now a number of reports suggesting that the combination of lecithin and physostigmine is also effective when both drugs are given orally (Peters and Levin, 1982; Thal and Fuld, 1983; Thal *et al.*, 1983, 1984), although Wettstein (1983) failed to find significant improvement using this combination. Similarly, Bajada (1982) failed to find a beneficial effect following oral treatment with physostigmine in combination with choline. When they administered physostigmine alone by the oral route Caltagirone *et al.*

(1982, 1983) failed to find beneficial effects, either when treatment was chronic or when optimal doses were administered acutely, optimal being defined in terms of effects on blood cholinesterase activity.

Enhancements of learning and memory have been reported following treatment with another anticholinesterase, tetrahydroaminoacridine (THA), both alone (Summers *et al.*, 1981) and in combination with lecithin (Kaye *et al.*, 1982). Considerable controversy has arisen following the recent claims by Summers *et al.* (1986) of spectacular efficacy for this compound. They reported that treatment with THA, generally in combination with lecithin, not only enhanced performance on laboratory tests of learning and memory, but also improved patients' ability to comply with the demands of everyday living. Consequent upon this report a large USA government-sponsored multicentre trial was initiated. This is still in progress and its results are eagerly awaited.

Enhancing release. Two studies have used the drug 4-aminopyridine to enhance release of ACh in patients with AD, but have produced conflicting results. Wesseling *et al.* (1984) reported positive effects in their study of 14 patients, but more recently Davidson *et al.* (1988) failed to demonstrate any beneficial effects of treatment. However, there were a number of methodological differences between the two studies which might have contributed to this discrepancy. For example, Davidson *et al.* investigated a somewhat younger patient group and employed a shorter treatment period.

Direct stimulation of postsynaptic receptors. As noted in Chapter 4 there is evidence that, despite extensive decreases in presynaptic markers of the cholinergic system, such as ChAT activity, muscarinic receptors appear for the most part to be spared. This suggests that it might be possible to bypass the damaged presynaptic components of the cholinergic system by directly stimulating the intact postsynaptic receptors. Data have now been published for a number of agonists.

Clinical studies of a number of muscarinic agents, namely arecoline (Christie *et al.*, 1981; Christie, 1982), bethanecol (Davous and Lamour, 1985; Harbaugh *et al.*, 1984; Penn *et al.*, 1988), oxotremorine (Davis *et al.*, 1987), pilocarpine (Caine, 1980) and RS86 (Bruno *et al.*, 1986; Hollander *et al.*, 1987; Wettstein and Spiegel, 1984) have now been carried out. By and large the results of these have been disappointing with only modest and generally clinically insignificant improvements. The incidence of undesirable side-effects appears to be high for many of these compounds, although admittedly few investigators have attempted to prevent the adverse effects of peripheral stimulation by concomitant administration of a quaternary anticholinergic with only poor penetration of the blood-brain barrier. Newhouse *et al.* (1988) reported that intravenous nicotine reduced the number of 'intrusion' errors (see Chapter 8) made by patients with DAT, but it also produced significant increases in anxiety and depression. More recently, Sahakian *et al.* (1989) found that nicotine enhanced the performance of patients with DAT on a number of tasks measuring attention and information processing ability. There is clearly a need for further investigations of the role of nicotinic cholinergic activity in cognition.

Bruno *et al.* (1986) raised important theoretical questions concerning the viability of any agonist treatment, pointing out that such treatments will result in the tonic activation of neural systems that might normally be expected to show only phasic activity. In order for an agonist approach to prove effective it will be necessary to develop new compounds that are CNS and possibly receptor subtype specific, and whose bioavailability could be strictly controlled so that they would augment the endogenous activity of residual cholinergic neurons rather than producing a generalized increase in stimulation which is not directed at any particular target neurons. The problem of generalized activation raised by Bruno *et al.* would be less critical if brain cholinergic systems were concerned with regulating the level and prolonged allocation of possessing resources rather than with the detailed processing of specific items of information. The diffuse nature of cholinergic projections is more consistent with a regulatory role, as are the effects of anticholinergic compounds upon attentional processes (see above) and the evidence of attentional dysfunction in patients with DAT (to be reviewed in Chapter 10) is also of interest in this respect. It is important to remember that the separately-labelled cognitive processes are not in fact discrete and that the learning and memory deficits, traditionally considered to be the hallmarks of dementia, can at some levels be construed as evidence of insufficiency in, or less than optimal allocation of, available attentional resources. This point will be returned to in Part IV.

Clinical Studies Using Non-cholinergic Drugs

The foregoing review has been concerned with studies of drugs affecting the cholinergic system but it must be pointed out that there have been many other pharmacological approaches to the treatment of cognitive impairment and dementia in the elderly. These have included so-called cerebral vasodilators such as papaverine, the drug hydergine which is thought to have both vasodilator and metabolic-enhancing properties, 'nootropic' drugs of which the prototype is piracetam, peptides suh as ACTH analogues and vasopressin, stimulants including methylphenidate and dextroamphetamine, as well as precursors of other neurotransmitters, for example L-DOPA. These treatments have been reviewed by others (Bagne *et al.*, 1986; Funkenstein *et al.*, 1981; McDonald, 1982; Nicholson, 1990; Reisberg *et al.*, 1980, 1981; Whitford, 1986) and therefore will not be considered in any detail here. Such treatments have led to rather mixed and generally not very encouraging results. This is perhaps not surprising given that many of these approaches have been totally arbitrary while others, such as the use of vasodilators, have been based upon erroneous assumptions concerning the neurobiology of ageing and the pathological processes giving rise to dementia in the majority of cases, namely AD.

One of the major points in favour of studies using cholinomimetics in patients with AD is that they represent a rational pharmacological approach to a known biochemical deficiency. The same could of course be said for attempts to increase other neurotransmitters known to be deficient in this condition, particularly in the case of younger patients, but to date not so much attention has been directed towards other transmitters for a variety of reasons. These include the historical primacy of the discovery of marked cholinergic deficiency, the widely accepted belief that deficits in other neurotransmitter systems may be of secondary importance to the cholinergic changes (see Chapter 4) and the established role of cholinergic deficiency in memory dysfunction, together with the emphasis accorded to mnemonic deficits as core features of DAT, and of many other dementia syndromes (see Chapters 6 and 8). However, the time seems appropriate for a broadening of perspective. Not only is there now a substantial amount of data documenting changes in other neurotransmitter systems in DAT and various dementia-associated conditions, but there is also a growing body of knowledge concerning the role of certain of these transmitters in behavioural functions known to be affected by a number of dementia-producing conditions (see Chapter 6). For example, there is evidence implicating brain monoamine systems (specifically noradrenalin and serotonin) in the regulation of mood (see Gray, 1985; Meltzer, 1987; Willner, 1989) and the catecholamines (noradrenalin and dopamine) in attentional processes (Clark *et al.*, 1986a,b; Robbins and Everitt, 1987). Noradrenalin, dopamine and serotinin are each involved in various aspects of the regulation of food intake (Leibowitz, 1987). Serotonin, noradrenalin and dopamine (as well as ACh) are also involved in control of aggressive behaviour (see Meltzer, 1987). Of course it is important not to lose sight of the fact that the different neurotransmitter systems of the brain are intimately connected so that changes in the level of activity of one will lead to secondary changes in other systems. Ultimately the clinical features manifested will be the net result of these interactions.

Methodological Issues Raised by Pharmacological Studies

Several points emerge on consideration of the results of the studies reviewed in the preceding pages of this chapter which have profound relevance for ongoing attempts to develop optimal methods of assessment for use in clinical trials.

First, it is clear that treatment with cholinomimetics, in particular physostigmine, can produce significant improvements in cognitive functioning which, as emphasized by the results of Gustafson *et al.* (1987), Muramoto *et al.* (1979, 1984) and Sahakian *et al.* (1987), are not necessarily restricted to memory. However, with the possible exception of THA (Summers *et al.*, 1986), the changes produced are small and a number of workers (e.g. Christie *et al.*, 1981; Davis and Mohs, 1982; Sullivan *et al.*, 1982) rightly point out that, even with the improved level of functioning consequent upon treatment, patients remain quite impaired relative to non-demented control subjects. An important issue that must be considered with respect to physostigmine is the marked individual variation in response to a given dose. This emphasizes the need for individual titration of dosage level to achieve the optimum effect on cognitive functioning (see Stern *et al.*, 1987 for a dissenting view). Since the therapeutic window for physostigmine seems to be quite narrow, with a fine balance between potentiation *vs* impairment, it is possible that at least some of the failures to find significant improvements following treatment with physostigmine may have been due to a failure to optimize the dose. A similar situation may pertain to other anticholinesterases or to direct agonists (Penn *et al.*, 1988) and indeed to drugs which affect non-cholinergic transmitter systems.

Another important pharmacological limitation is that compounds such as physostigmine and arecoline have a short duration of action so that, although useful as research tools, they have limited therapeutic potential. However, if consistent effects of these compounds were to be demonstrated this might encourage the development of alternative preparations of cholinomimetic drugs which would be both potent and long-acting. In order to prove therapeutically viable, however, such compounds would also have to minimize the adverse side-effects of current drugs such as physostigmine and arecoline. These are non-selective agents and, because of the widespread cholinergic innervation of vital organs, can have profound and serious side-effects, including bradycardia, nausea and possibly depression. Such undesirable effects would clearly negate any beneficial effects upon cognition.

However, it must be acknowledged that even in the unlikely event of complete pharmacological restoration of cholinergic functioning, cognitive deficits might still be found. The biochemical evidence points to ACh as the major neurotransmitter system affected in AD but it is by no means the only system involved (see Chapter 4). Ultimately therefore, it may be that replacement therapy will depend upon finding the proper balance between stimulation and inhibition of the various neurotransmitter systems. In this context it is of interest that older patients have a more specific biochemical deficit, restricted essentially to the cholinergic system. Hence, as Rossor *et al.* (1984) suggested, simple cholinergic replacement therapy might be more likely to succeed in elderly patients. In younger patients with AD the more complex pattern of neurotransmitter and neuropeptide abnormalities might be expected to militate against the possible success of such a circumscribed approach.

To date the selection of tests for use in pharmacological studies appears to have been fairly arbitrary. Very few procedures have been employed in more than one study and this lack of replication must itself testify to the absence of an empirical or theoretical rationale underlying test selection. Their only common ground, it seems, is the assumption that they are measures of learning and memory. Moreover, the complex nature of memory (see Chapter 8) has all too often been neglected. The foregoing review points to a few exceptions to this 'tunnel vision' which seeks to concern itself only with memory (construed in rather global terms) and it is of note that these studies have produced some interesting results.

The challenge for neuropsychology is to lead the way in the development of measures which will be sensitive to small changes in relevant aspects of cognition and behaviour and sufficiently flexible to cope with the requirements of clinical trial design. Patients with DAT often differ substantially in their cognitive abilities so that it is difficult to develop a single set of memory or other cognitive tests which will be appropriate for evaluating the effects of cholinomimetic drugs in all patients. It is important to be able to adjust the difficulty of a test so that most patients can make a reasonable attempt and have scope for both improvement and deterioration. In addition, it is essential that alternative forms of equivalent difficulty be available and moreover, that the time required for test completion be limited, not only because of the difficulties patients with dementia have in sustaining effort for long periods of time, but also because of the temporal constraints imposed by drug pharmacokinetics. In 1977 the Medical Research Council, in a report on the senile and presenile dementias (MRC, 1977), called upon psychologists to direct their expertise to the task of satisfying these requirements and this call was reiterated by Lishman (1978). In order to meet these challenges it seems essential to develop a greater understanding of the psychological nature of the deficits heralded by AD and other dementia-producing conditions and to establish whether there are subtypes, identifiable stages and/or core areas of disability, either within or across aetiological conditions. It is also important to realize that in order to arrive at optimal assessment procedures for demonstrating the effects of cholinomimetics, or indeed other drugs, in such conditions a sufficient understanding is required of certain pharmacological factors including dose-response relationships, the duration of drug action and how these are influenced by route of administration. Such factors have implications for the timing of test administration in relation to drug treatment. However, as emphasized by Brinkman and Gershon (1983), the relationship between psychology and pharmacology is reciprocal so that understanding of pharmacological factors depends in turn on the availability of sensitive dependent measures of cognition. Thus, although many of the issues considered in this chapter, and particularly in this last section, may seem to be essentially pharmacological in nature, they must be of concern to neuropsychologists attempting to take up the challenge advanced by the Medical Research Council.

Another issue that emerges on consideration of the clinical drug studies is the need for diagnostic specificity and sensitivity so that patient selection will be appropriate. With respect to specificity, drug enhancement of cholinergic function may only be of therapeutic benefit to those patients in whom the cholinergic system is significantly compromised, including patients with AD, and may not enhance cognition in other impaired groups. If the benefits to be obtained from the currently available compounds are small then diagnostic homogeneity, both within and across groups of patients classified as having DAT, becomes a criterion of critical importance. Of course this consideration will also be relevant to the quest for adequate evaluation of any therapeutic intervention, including non-pharmacological approaches. It is also relevant for studies which seek to increase understanding of the nature of the cognitive deficits in DAT and it must be said that a major defect in much of the existing psychological literature on dementia is the lack of adequately detailed subject descriptions. Another issue with respect to appropriate patient selection concerns severity of cognitive dysfunction. There is evidence suggesting that improvements following drug treatment are more likely in less severely impaired patients (Christie *et al.*, 1979; Etienne *et al.*, 1978a; Signoret *et al.*, 1978; Sullivan *et al.*, 1982). In the early stages of the disease neuropathological and biochemical abnormalities will be less severe and thus it is more likely that there will be a residual neural substrate capable of responding to drug treatment. Moreover, because of their less severe cognitive impairment, such patients will be able better to understand what is required of them, quite apart from their ability to perform the index task. However, by definition, the deficits shown by patients in the early stages of the disease will be much less severe so that there is a need to devise measures which will be sufficiently sensitive to detect even relatively mild decrements and to monitor the effects of therapeutic interventions upon these. This again directs attention towards our need to delineate and understand the psychological nature of the disability heralded by this disease. Similar considerations will apply to other dementia-producing conditions.

Finally, it is indisputable that the ultimate criterion of success or failure of any approach to treatment, including pharmacological, in AD or in other dementias must be behavioural. Therefore, effective research on the treatment of demented patients is dependent upon the existence of precise behavioural methods of assessing the effects of proposed new forms of treatment. Here too, tools must be made available which are sufficiently sensitive to detect small but significant improvements in a patient's condition if potentially useful forms of treatment are not to be abandoned prematurely.

PART III

Having established in Part II that there are substantial differences between the various dementia-producing conditions in terms of neuropathological and neurochemical changes, and hence the importance of selecting appropriate patients as target subjects for attempts at rational pharmacological intervention, we now turn attention to the necessary prerequisites for achievement of this goal. In Chapter 6 we consider what is known (and perhaps more importantly what is not known) about the clinical manifestations of the different disease processes giving rise to dementia, before going on in Chapter 7 to consider issues relating to the early detection of dementia and to differential diagnosis between some of the many causes of this devastating clinical syndrome. We hope we have established in the foregoing chapters that the outcomes of such endeavours have very real practical implications and, in view of the scientific developments of recent years, can no longer be dismissed as merely irrelevant (even if intellectually satisfying) academic exercises. Chapter 7 will not provide a systematic overview of all the available neuropsychological data pertinent to attempts to increase diagnostic efficiency. This would constitute a volume in its own right. Rather we seek to highlight conceptual and methodological issues that arise in relation to attempts to pursue this endeavour. Our aim is to guide readers in consulting the literature which is available, to provide an appropriate critical and evaluative stance and thereby aid the planning of future research directed towards diagnostic issues.

PART III

Clinical Features of Alzheimer's Disease and Other Dementia-Producing Conditions

As in previous chapters the major emphasis will be on AD as this is the most prevalent cause of dementia and as such has been the focus of most research endeavour.

Alzheimer's Disease

An adequate knowledge of the clinical features of DAT would seem to be a prerequisite for differential diagnosis of this disorder within a patient's lifetime, given that biopsy to confirm Alzheimer-type neuropathology can rarely be justified on ethical grounds, not to mention the fact that, owing to sampling errors, this procedure might underestimate the severity of pathological changes.

Alzheimer's original description in 1907 (see Wilkins and Brody, 1969) was of a 51-year-old woman who had delusions of persecution and jealousy in addition to marked memory impairment and disorientation for time and place. Indeed, jealousy towards her husband was the first noticeable sign of the disease. This patient became perplexed and confused with phases of delirium. There was marked impairment of comprehension and speech with evidence of perseveration and paraphasia. The dementia was progressive and death occurred after 4 years.

In the decades since Alzheimer's original report of the case history and post-mortem examination of this patient there have been many studies of the clinical features shown by biopsy - or autopsy - proven cases of AD. One might expect that a condition with such a history of scientific investigation would have evolved to a point of general agreement and some degree of certainty concerning its clinical phenomeno-logy (the assumption being of course that it does indeed constitute a single nosological entity). This, however, is only partly true. The review which follows will be restricted for the most part to those studies where diagnosis was confirmed, either by biopsy or at autopsy, so that it can be concluded with reasonable confidence that the clinical features described do indeed represent those found in patients with AD. Of couse a potential bias might stem from this approach in that most of the pathologically-verified cases have been presenile.

There is a general consensus of opinion that memory disturbance is an early feature (Brun and Gustafson, 1976; Coblentz *et al.*, 1973; Constantinidis, 1978; Goodman, 1953; Hughes, 1970; Pearce and Miller, 1973; Sim *et al.*, 1966; Sjogren, 1952; Sulkava *et al.*, 1983) and this conclusion is echoed by many investigators who have looked at clinically diagnosed patients (Pearce and Miller, 1973; Rosenstock, 1970; Roth, 1980b; Roth and Myers, 1975; Ziegler, 1954). The memory disturbance initially manifests itself in relation to recent events while, in the early stages, recall of more remote occurrences may be well preserved. With further deterioration, however, memory for recent experiences becomes a void and for the past it is restricted to a few muddled recollections. Disorientation is noted by many (Coblentz *et al.*, 1973; Constantinidis *et al.*, 1978; Sim, 1965; Sim and Sussman, 1962; Sjogren, 1952) as another relatively early symptom but while some emphasize disorientation in space as a more significant early feature (Sim and Sussman, 1962; Sjogren, 1952) others place as much emphasis on temporal as on spatial disorientation (e.g. Constantinidis *et al.*, 1978). Disorientation for place and/or time is also noted in reports of clinically-diagnosed cases (Rosenstock, 1970; Roth and Myers, 1975). Spatial disorientation may manifest itself initially as an inability to cope in new environments but with further deterioration this impairment extends to even familiar surroundings such as the home, so that the patient may be lost and disorientated in what was previously a very familiar environment. With respect to temporal disorientation ignorance of the date becomes compounded by lack of awareness of the time of day.

Although Alzheimer's is a disease which ultimately leads to dementia, it is important to point out that early in the course of its progression patients do not manifest the global impairment of intellectual functioning required for the label 'dementia' to be appended. This is emphasized by Sim and Sussman (1962: 493) who state that, ' . . . although the patients were poorly orientated and demonstrated gross memory loss, they did not appear demented and were able to organize themselves and their environment to a remarkable degree, particularly in social intercourse'. However, patients gradually succumb to more generalized intellectual deterioration. Judgement and reasoning are impaired, abstract thought processes are increasingly compromised and patients lose the ability to either generate or grasp new ideas or to discern the significant from the trivial. While simple routine activities may still be carried out with reasonable proficiency the patient will prove unable to pursue a complex task to successful completion and novelty or change will present major difficulties. Indeed, it is well recognized that family awareness that something is amiss, and subsequent medical consultation, are often provoked by the individual's failure to cope adaptively with some change in circumstances. Eventually the condition progresses to a stage where there is loss of all intellectual faculties with extreme incoherence and irrationality.

Constantinidis and the Geneva group of investigators (Constantinidis, 1978; Constantinidis *et al.*, 1978; Todorov *et al.*, 1975) have emphasized the importance of aphasia, apraxia and agnosia in the clinical phenomenology of AD and indeed they, and others, have related the occurrence of these instrumental disorders to the presence of neocortical neurofibrillary tangles (see Chapter 3). These continental workers for a time made a distinction between Alzheimer's presenile dementia, Alzheimerized senile dementia and simple senile dementia (where memory and orientation problems predominate in the absence of aphasia, apraxia or agnosia), but more recently Constantinidis (1978), in line with most British and American workers, has agreed that a single disease process is operating in these three 'variants'. He has presented data suggesting that, among senile subjects, it is those who live longer after the onset of amnesia who more frequently develop sufficient quantities of neurofibrillary tangles and therefore symptoms of instrumental disorders. He considered that this finding was in agreement with the concept of evolutional continuity between simple senile dementia and Alzheimerized senile dementia.

A number of other investigators looking at pathologically-verified cases of AD (Brun and Gustafson, 1976; Coblentz *et al.*, 1973; Feldman *et al.*, 1963; Goodman, 1953; Jacob, 1970; Sim and Sussman, 1962; Sjogren, 1952; Stengel, 1943) have acknowledged that these instrumental disorders of aphasia, apraxia and agnosia are important clinical features, and similar conclusions can be drawn from various reports of clinically-diagnosed patients (e.g. Pearce and Miller, 1973; Rosenstock, 1970). Such 'focal' symptomatology has generally been considered to be of intermediate or late onset, rarely occurring before marked memory impairment has developed. Recently, however, Crystal *et al.* (1982) have published a case report of a 57-year-old woman with biopsy-proven AD who, on clinical presentation, showed a right parietal lobe syndrome with astereognosis and pseudoathetosis. She showed marked constructional apraxia at a time when there was still only mild impairment of recent memory and mild nominal dysphasia. This is an interesting example of a case of AD in whom focal neurological symptoms and signs preceded impairment of memory and it constitutes an important reminder that, within the context of global impairment of intellectual function, cognitive abilities may be differentially affected depending upon which areas of the brain are most severely involved. Moreover, Goodman (1953) reports that, although in the majority of his cases speech defects appeared after memory failure had been noticed, a few patients showed initial disturbance of language functions and in some 20 per cent of cases there was simultaneous involvement of speech and memory. Pogacar and Williams (1984) report the interesting case of a 56-year-old man who developed a fluent aphasia which progressed for almost 1 year before other symptoms of more generalized cerebral dysfunction emerged. Alzheimer's disease was confirmed on neuropathological examination following the patient's death 6 years later.

Generally the first linguistic change noted by clinicians assessing and/or caring for patients with AD has been a progressive simplification of the richness of language. The vocabulary becomes impoverished, phrases and tenses simplified, and the process of analogy and metaphor diminished, but the more classical signs of an anterior or posterior dysphasia, such as naming and word finding difficulties and syllabic transpositions, may also be seen, although generally, it has been thought, somewhat later in the course of the disease.

Emotional and personality changes are often noted in descriptions of patients with dementia, a substantial majority of whom presumably have DAT, even when this is not specified (Miller, 1977a; Neumann and Cohn, 1953; Pearce and Miller, 1973; Roth and Myers, 1975). With respect to personality, this may become a caricature of its premorbid features, with for example a very meticulous individual becoming frankly obsessional, but the reverse may also occur so that there is gross change from premorbid characteristics. Relative preservation of personality was considered by Mayer-Gross *et al.* (1969) to be a more characteristic feature of vascular dementia and thus it was included by Hachinski *et al.* (1975) in their ischaemic rating scale, devised to assist clinicians in differentiating between multi-infarct dementia and primary degenerative dementia. However, Rosen *et al.* (1980) carried out a pathological study to verify the utility of the ischaemic score and their results, although based on a small sample, cast doubt upon the diagnostic significance of relative preservation of personality. Changes in personality were noted in all of their dementia patients, irrespective of cerebral pathology. Most reports of the clinical features in pathologically verified cases make no specific mention of personality. Sim *et al.* (1966), however, are a notable exception and they emphasize that, in their series of patients with AD, personality and social behaviour were remarkably well preserved for quite a long time. Indeed, they note that some patients with gross intellectual deterioration were able to perform at an adequate social level.

Emotional changes are more often referred to in reports of pathologically-verified cases. These may include agitation or irritability and also a gloomy pessimistic attitude, apathy and retardation with perhaps carelessness in dress or personal hygiene. In some cases of AD emotional features are evident at quite an early stage (Parr, 1955; Sim and Sussman, 1962; Stengel, 1943) so that the disease may present as a depressive illness, rendering diagnosis more difficult (see Chapter 7). Such affective symptoms may be an intrinsic part of the disease process, precipitated by specific neurochemical changes, but they may also, to some extent at least, represent an understandable response on the part of patients to awareness of their progressively restricted ability to perform everyday tasks. As the disease progresses, however, affected individuals will become increasingly unaware of their predicament. As in the case of many other symptoms, there is considerable discrepancy between different studies regarding the relative frequency of occurrence of various emotional features. Coblentz *et al.* (1973) note that moderate agitation was present in five of their ten confirmed cases, and Sim and Sussman (1962) report its occurrence in eight of 22 proven cases. These latter workers point out that agitation cannot with certainty be considered an affective feature but this in no way diminishes the importance of affective symptomatology since 12 of their 22 proven cases were described as being unequivocally severely depressed early in the course of their illness. Stengel (1943: 13) considers that depressed anxious mood is a conspicious feature of AD and indeed states that in two of his nine cases, ' . . . depression and anxiety appeared first before loss of memory was obvious' . He also states that increased motor activity was a consistent feature in his patients, although not always very pronounced, and this was not characteristic of any particular stage of the disease. Sjogren (1952), in contrast, emphasizes that aspontaneity and reduced initiation were dominant features in his patients, and indeed these were noted as present early in the course of the disease in 15 of 18 cases. Although acknowledging that this contradicts the views of many previous investigators, Sjogren (1952: 80) states quite clearly that, 'Even if the Alzheimer patients show periods of increase in motor activity, especially in connection with depressions, hallucinations and paranoid reactions, these periods of motor unrest at intervals are not the essential feature in the picture of the disease'.

There is some discrepancy in the literature not only with respect to the prevalence of psychotic features but also the stage in the temporal progression of the disease at which they emerge. Sjogren (1952) reports that these were a relatively common feature and, at a comparatively early stage, hallucinations occurred in four and paranoid reactions in five of his 18 confirmed cases of AD. Similarly, Goodman (1953) reports that hallucinations, mostly visual, occurred frequently during the course of the disease in the majority of patients, and indeed in one case heralded the onset of the disease. Paranoid delusions were common fairly early in the course of the illness. In contrast, Sim and Sussman (1962: 493) report that psychotic features, observed at some time in seven of their 22 cases, ' . . . were absent in the early stages and were only seen as a very late manifestation' and Sim (1979), on the basis of further case studies, has reiterated this view. Coblentz et al. (1973) found psychotic behaviour in two of their ten patients but they give no indication as to when in the course of the disease these features were observed.

Extrapyramidal features, such as increased muscle tone or disturbance of posture and gait, which are undoubtedly characteristic of the later stages of the disease, can also be present to some extent relatively early in a number of patients (e.g. Pearce and Miller, 1973; Sjogren, 1952). Myoclonus, a recognized feature of Creutzfeldt–Jakob disease, has received relatively little attention in the literature on AD. However, it has been noted in some pathologically-verified cases and seems to occur at markedly different times after onset of the condition (Brun and Gustafson, 1976; Faden and Townsend, 1976; Feldman et al., 1963; Gimenez-Roldan et al., 1971; Jacob, 1970; Terry et al., 1964). Seizures may occur in some patients with AD, generally as a feature of the advanced stages (Brun and Gustafson, 1976; Coblentz et al., 1973; Feldman et al., 1963; Sim, 1979; Sim et al., 1966; Sjogren, 1952), although Hughes (1970) would assign them a more significant place in the symptomatology of the disease.

The occurrence of other neurological features, such as primitive reflexes and abnormalities of gaze, have also been noted (e.g. Heston *et al.*, 1966; Hughes, 1970; Neumann and Cohn, 1953; Paulson and Gottlieb, 1968; Sjogren, 1952). Unfortunately, the most detailed report in this respect, that by Paulson and Gottlieb (1968), lacks histological verification for some of the clinical diagnoses. However, the occurrence of these phenomena provides an important reminder that AD has other features besides those in the domain of mental function.

Coblentz *et al.* (1973) note that incontinence was present in five of their 10 pathologically-verified cases when hospitalized, which was on average 4.3 years after estimated onset. Sim and Sussman (1962) report finding incontinence in only one of 22 patients, and then only some 6 years after disease onset, while Sjogren (1952), in contrast, reports enuresis to be a common early feature.

Ultimately, if progress of the disease is not interrupted by death, the patient will decline into a state of mutism and unresponsiveness. By this stage most are likely to be totally bedridden and incontinent, showing marked signs of physical deterioration. Death often results from pneumonia or some other intercurrent infection. This applies not only to Alzheimer's disease, but to the degenerative dementias in general.

Although there is a wealth of clinical descriptive material, by no means all the reports are of pathologically-verified cases of AD and the above review has been confined essentially, although not exclusively, to biopsy- or autopsy-proven cases. Even in these verified cases, where the picture is not confounded by clinical diagnostic errors, it must be apparent, that, despite fairly broad agreement that memory disturbance is an early presenting symptom and a prominent one (and likewise orientation difficulties), there is considerable disagreement about the occurrence of other symptoms. This lack of consensus concerns not only whether the various clinical features occur late or early in the course of the disease, but also the proportion of patients who manifest them and, moreover, whether there are identifiable stages or subtypes. Questions that inevitably occur to the neuropsychologist concern the nature of the memory disturbance and the instruments and criteria (both qualitative and quantitative) used in screening for the presence of this or other symptoms. Such issues will be returned to in Part IV.

Most patients with AD present long after the disease begins (e.g. Coblentz *et al.*, 1973; Roth and Myers, 1975; Sim and Sussman, 1962; Sulkava, 1982) and since the onset is insidious it is difficult to plot the early course of events, having to rely upon the retrospective accounts of relatives who may be preoccupied with what they see as causative or precipitating factors. Indeed, it is important to note that although the onset is insidious, the patient often first comes to medical attention as a result of some acute disturbance. Sim and Sussman (1962) emphasized the need for early referral so that investigations could be commenced before the patient was rendered incapable of supplying information about disease onset and the early course of events. Early referral seems essential if we are to be able to refine our knowledge of the disorder and hopefully resolve apparent discrepancies in the literature. Furthermore, if methods for slowing or arresting progress of the disease were indeed to be developed it would be crucial to ensure that diagnosis was made before cognitive impairment became so global and severe as to militate against the possible efficacy of any intervention. However, early referral will only come about when relatives and carers abandon ageist models which assume inevitable cognitive decline and therefore are able to recognize that deterioration is abnormal before it becomes severe. The need for such attitudinal change applies likewise to GPs and other community workers who must also come to perceive early diagnosis and differential diagnosis as meaningful pursuits with important practical implications for case management. They will of course need to have available to them sensitive screening instruments and clear operational criteria to assist in decision making, requirements which may be satisfied, at least in part, by neuropsychological research.

Systematic studies of large numbers of patients while still in the early stages of the disease, with subsequent pathological verification of the diagnosis, should also allow us to determine whether there is an orderly pattern of decline, a necessary prerequisite for staging the disease. An adequate clinical description of each of the 'stages' (assuming that they exist), and widespread acceptance of the criteria, would facilitate clinical diagnosis and research progress, enabling the selection of homogenous groups for comparative studies. Patients continue to present at various intervals after estimated disease onset (see Hart, 1985) and it seems more than likely that this will continue to be so, although the availability of effective treatment might radically alter the picture. Different groups of investigators have in the past put forward ideas on criteria for stages (e.g. Berg, 1984; Constantinidis, 1978; Grunthal, 1926 summarized by Newton, 1948 and Sim and Sussman, 1962; Hughes *et al.*, 1982; Sjogren, 1952) but these have been quite discrepant. For example, while some have directed attention to aphasic symptoms, others have made no mention of these. The major commonality uniting these various investigators has been an underlying assumption of global and orderly progression, but the problem of staging is further complicated by the possibility that there may be distinct subgroups among patients afflicted by AD.

The presence or absence of language disturbance has been one issue of fundamental importance in the debate as to whether subtypes of DAT can be identified and, if so, how subtypes defined in terms of clinical symptomatology relate to those identified on the basis of differences in the extent and nature of neuropathological changes such as the density and/or distribution of neurofibrillary tangles (see Constantinidis, 1978; Tomlinson, 1982). Seltzer and Sherwin's (1983) comparison of the clinical features of patients in whom the onset of symptoms of DAT was first noted before the age of 65 years with those of patients who were over 65 years when the first symptoms were recorded suggested that 'early-onset' patients might be more likely to show abnormalities of spontaneous speech, verbal comprehension, object naming and writing. These younger patients were also more likely to be left-handed, though Chui *et al.* (1985) were unable to replicate the finding of a disproportionate representation of sinistrals among early-onset cases. Seltzer and Sherwin hypothesized that the left hemisphere was particularly vulnerable in patients who developed DAT at an early age and speculated that this vulnerability might be genetically determined. Studies by Folstein *et al.* (Breitner and Folstein, 1984; Folstein and Breitner, 1981) produced somewhat more direct evidence for possible genetic differences among patients with DAT in that the prevalence of dementia was higher amongst the first degree relatives of those patients in whom evidence of aphasia or agraphia (symptoms which were closely associated) was detected on administration of the Mini-Mental State Examination or MMSE (Folstein *et al.*, 1975). They estimated that the cumulative incidence of dementia was 50 per cent for first degree relatives by 90 years of age and considered their data to be consistent with an autosomal dominant pattern of inheritance. However, Heyman *et al.* (1983) did not find a higher cumulative incidence of DAT in the families of patients showing language disorders than amongst the relatives of those without aphasic symptoms. These workers also reported that the frequency and severity of linguistic disturbances in patients with DAT was closely related to the duration of illness and in this respect it is of interest that the agraphic group in Breitner and Folstein's (1984) study had been resident in the nursing homes from which subjects were recruited for longer than those who did not show agraphia. This illustrates well our fundamental caveat, namely that any pursuit of evidence in support of subtypes must also take account of the issue of severity and what 'stage' patients are at in the progression of the degenerative process. Like Heyman *et al.* (1983), Chui *et al.* (1985) found no association between a familial history of dementia and aphasia. However, even when duration of illness was equated, their data supported an association between early onset and more prevalent and prominent language disorder. This accords with the findings of Seltzer and Sherwin (1983).

Clearly there are many discrepancies between the results obtained by these various workers, all of whom (except Seltzer and Sherwin) employed the MMSE. An outstanding question concerns the extent to which this lack of consistency is simply further testimony to the variability of patients with DAT, or reflects limitations inherent in the assessment instrument employed. While the MMSE makes some attempt at achieving objectivity and standardization, much is left to the discretion of the administrator and this in itself may have contributed to the differing results obtained in these studies.

Martin *et al.* (Martin, 1987; Martin *et al.*, 1986) tentatively identified three subgroups of patients with DAT which could be characterized at a clinical level by qualitatively different profiles of cognitive impairment. Each of these subgroups corresponded to a distinct pattern of cerebral hypometabolism as revealed by positron emission tomography (see Chapter 7). The complexities inherent in the establishment of adequate criteria for delineating subtypes were reviewed by Jorm (1985) and to date research investigations have not met the criteria necessary to establish qualitatively different subtypes (on the basis of either clinical or neuropathological criteria). In the absence of histological confirmation the possibility of diagnostic error remains, but if subtypes do exist their presence will have profound implications (which might differ from those entailed by a severity or stage model) for attempts at early detection, determination of inclusion criteria for therapeutic trials and the selection of outcome measures.

Another unresolved issue concerns the relation of the patient's previous intellectual ability and educational level to disability at time of presentation, and indeed also to patients' capacity to compensate for their deficits, so that adequate performance can be maintained during the initial phases of the disease. It seems quite conceivable that more competent individuals might have more reserve capacity over and above that required for effective functioning. This might be especially so with respect to their particular areas of expertise, whether 'intellectual' or 'practical', which could, because of extensive practice, be carried out relatively automatically. Thus, for example, an accountant might retain arithmetic ability for longer than most patients. Of coure, it is also possible that a small decline in capability or efficiency might be more readily detected in those individuals who are engaged in more demanding occupations or activities. Thus such individuals might be more apt to come to medical attention and so be diagnosed earlier and more readily. This seems on the whole more likely to be true of presenile cases of AD than of older patients who will, for the most part, be in retirement. Stereotyped views of ageing as a process of inevitable intellectual decline might also serve to delay initial medical presentation and further referral of older patients.

There is no doubt that AD brings with it a prognosis of decreased life expectancy and indeed Katzman (1976) has labelled it a 'malignant' disorder. He has estimated that the senile form of the disease may rank as the fourth or fifth most common cause of death in the USA, although it is not even listed as a cause of death in the vital statistics tables of that country. A somewhat similar situation pertains to the UK (N.E.J. Wells, 1979).

The poor prognosis of this disease has long been recognized. Roth (1955) found that almost 60 per cent of senile dementia patients admitted to a psychiatric hospital were dead within 6 months, a higher mortality rate than for patients of a similar age with functional psychiatric disorders, and indeed a higher short-term mortality rate than was found in patients with vascular dementia. Numerous other workers have also provided evidence of increased mortality in victims of this disease (e.g. Kay, 1962; Nielsen *et al.*, 1977; Shah *et al.*, 1969; Whitehead and Hunt, 1982). Although there is general agreement on this point, mean estimates of disease duration tend to vary from study to study and there is undoubtedly considerable individual variation. In the studies referred to above, where the clinical diagnosis was confirmed by pathological examination, the duration of the disease ranged from 2.5 to 20 years, although the majority of cases did fall within a narrower band of 5–10 years approximately.

Another issue which arises in this respect is whether AD runs a shorter course in younger or in older victims, and here there appears to be a lack of consensus. Nielsen *et al.* (1977), for example, found that the course of the disease was longer in younger patients and Constantinidis (1978) would seem to support this view. He states that although the instrumental disorders of aphasia, apraxia and agnosia indicate a more severe clinical picture, and are typically more rapid in onset in presenile cases (see Constantinidis *et al.*, 1978), patients with these instrumental disorders paradoxically survive for longer after disease onset. This appears to be somewhat at odds with the report of McDonald (1969) on patients with senile dementia. In his study the presence of parieto-temporal dysfunction, again more marked in patients with a rather earlier age of onset, was associated with shorter survival. However, perhaps more important than the absolute duration of the disease is its effect upon the life expectancy of younger and older patients respectively. When this is considered it is clear that AD is more malignant in younger patients, even if it lasts somewhat longer in absolute terms (Wang, 1978).

The foregoing review has been concerned with Alzheimer's disease, the major cause of dementia, but a number of the issues raised will also be relevant to certain of the other dementia-producing conditions, the clinical features of which will be outlined below.

Pick's Disease

It has generally been considered that the early stages of Pick's disease are dominated by personality changes and emotional alterations including apathy, irritability, depression, jocularity and euphoria (Cummings and Benson, 1983). The condition is also marked by poor judgment and lack of insight. Social behaviour deteriorates and there may be evidence of disinhibition, including sexual indiscretion. Stereotyped behaviours and rigid rituals may also be observed.

A striking early feature of this condition is the appearance of at least some aspects of the Kluver–Bucy syndrome, which was first described in monkeys following lesions of the temporal lobes, amygdala and hippocampus (Kluver and Bucy, 1939). Symptoms exhibited by patients with Pick's disease have included affective disturbance, gluttony, hyperorality, agnosia and excessive exploratory responses to novel stimuli, and these in various combinations (Cummings and Duchen, 1981).

Although in the early stages of Pick's disease cognitive impairment is generally less marked than personality change and emotional disturbance, impairment of language can be an early feature and indeed may be the first symptom (Holland *et al.*, 1985; Wechsler, 1977; Wechsler *et al.*, 1982). Clinical reports highlight empty speech, circumlocution, word finding and confrontation naming difficulties as typical manifestations of the evolving language impairment. The case study reported by Holland *et al.* (1985) is of particular interest. Based on the writings of a victim who recorded his experience of the process of degeneration (over most of its 12.5-year course until his death at the age of 79 years), and the oral testimony of his family, it documents considerable preservation of other aspects of cognition, such as memory and arithmetic skills, in the face of profound deterioration of language. Such dissociation appears to be a general feature of Pick's disease (see Cummings and Benson, 1983).

Creutzfeldt–Jakob Disease and Kuru

Creutzfeldt–Jakob disease is a relatively uncommon disorder the onset of which is usually in the sixth or seventh decade of life, although younger and older cases have been recorded (Brown *et al.*, 1979a,b). In general the condition progresses rapidly, more than half of the patients being dead within 9 months and the great majority within 2 years.

There is considerable diversity in the clinical features presented by different patients and a number of clinical variants have been documented. Nevertheless, it seems that certain threads of commonality can be identified. There appears to be some concensus of opinion regarding the occurrence of a prodromal phase marked by feelings of physical discomfort, mild apprehension, affective disturbance, concentration difficulties, fatigue, weight loss and altered sleeping habits. Occasionally there may be mild elation of mood, perhaps with inappropriate laughter and excessive loquacity (Brown *et al.*, 1979b; Cummings and Benson, 1983; May, 1968; Will and Matthews, 1984). During this phase, which appears in about one-third of all cases (Brown *et al.*, 1979b; Will and Matthews, 1984), a functional psychiatric disorder is the most likely diagnosis, but after a period of weeks or months the prodromal neurasthenic symptoms are eclipsed by frank neurological disturbance. Typically, a dementia syndrome develops encompassing severe intellectual deterioration with features of aphasia (almost inevitably present), agnosia and apraxia, as well as impairment of memory plus hallucinations and delusions.

Questions remain concerning the pattern in which these cognitive deficits develop, and likewise the order or pattern of occurrence of the inevitable neurological abnormalities that accompany them. These include pyramidal and extrapyramidal signs, myoclonus, cerebellar disturbances, rigidity and tremor, choreoathetosis, somatosensory and visual disturbances and cranial nerve palsies (Brown *et al.*, 1979b; Cummings and Benson, 1983; May, 1968; Will and Matthews, 1984). Such neurological signs and symptoms may be the initial presenting features in at least a proportion of patients (Aronyk *et al.*, 1984; Brown *et al.*, 1979b).

In the terminal stages, patients with Creutzfeld–Jakob discase lapse into a mute, akinetic stuporous state with myoclonus, seizures, autonomic disturbances and decerebrate rigidity (Kirchenbaum, 1968). A period of deepening coma may last for several weeks before death ensues.

Ataxia of gait is generally the earliest symptom of Kuru. This is followed by more generalized ataxia, a characteristic shiver-like tremor (which gives rise to the name of this condition) and dysarthria. Dementia is generally a late feature of Kuru and is rarely severe, although behavioural disturbances and psychomotor slowing are common (see Cummings and Benson, 1983).

Progressive Supranuclear Palsy

Ocular, motor and neuropsychological dysfunction are characteristic of this condition (Steele *et al.*, 1964). Loss of voluntary eye movement is a notable feature. The most common early symptom is impairment of downward gaze, but as the condition progresses paresis of upward gaze develops and eventually volitional horizontal gaze is also lost (Cummings and Benson, 1983). These ocular abnormalities are accompanied by pseudobulbar palsy (manifested by mask-like facies, increased jaw and facial jerks, exaggerated palatal and pharyngeal reflexes, dysphagia and drooling). Axial rigidity of the trunk and neck results in the adoption of a hypererect posture (c.f. the stooped posture of patients with Parkinson's disease) with extension of the neck. During the course of the disease patients with progressive supranuclear palsy develop a profound bradykinesia which superficially resembles that seen in Parkinson's disease. They typically exhibit a variety of speech disorders (see Lebrun *et al.*, 1986) but the consensus of opinion is that language *per se* is for the most part spared. However, although aphasia is not noted on clinical examination it remains to be determined whether more subtle disturbances of language processing would be detected if patients were to undergo formal neuropsychological evaluation.

Personality changes and mild dementia were noted by Steele *et al.* (1964) and their observations have been confirmed and elaborated by subsequent investigators. Albert *et al.* (1974) considered the condition to be characterized by forgetfulness, slowing of thought processes, impaired ability to manipulate acquired information and alterations of personality including apathy and depression. The absence of clinical features considered typical of cortical pathology, such as agnosia and apraxia, led them to introduce the controversial term 'subcortical dementia' to describe the pattern of decline shown by patients with progressive supranuclear palsy. Quite apart from questions concerning the validity of the cortical/subcortical distinction, there remains controversy surrounding the frequency, type and severity of cognitive dysfunction in patients with progressive supranuclear palsy. Most studies have relied solely upon clinical observations, with all their inherent problems and pitfalls, and formal neuro-psychological investigations are clearly necessary. These have begun, but it seems from the first reports in the literature (Fisk *et al.*, 1982; Kimura *et al.*, 1981) that controversy concerning the presence and/or the extent of intellectual deterioration will not be readily resolved.

Parkinson's Disease

In 1817 James Parkinson concluded the opening paragraph of 'An essay on the Shaking Palsy' with the phrase 'the senses and intellect being uninjured', but contradictory evidence has emerged over the years. There is considerable controversy concerning the prevalence of cognitive deficits in patients with Parkinson's disease, and also their cause.

Estimates of the prevalence of dementia in patients affected by this disease have varied between 15 and 90 per cent (Celesia and Wanamaker, 1972; Hakim and Mathieson, 1979; Lieberman *et al.*, 1979; Martin *et al.*, 1973; Marttila and Rinne, 1976; Pirozzolo *et al.*, 1982; Pollock and Hornabrook, 1966; Sroka *et al.*, 1981; Sweet *et al.*, 1976). Different criteria for patient selection and for the designation of dementia, as well as different drug regimens, have undoubtedly contributed to the variance between estimates. These and other issues have been critically reviewed by Brown and Marsden (1984) who maintain that many of the published prevalence estimates are over inflated and that the 'true' prevalence of dementia in patients with Parkinson's disease is of the order of 20 per cent, although further research is required to establish this unequivocally.

Summarizing the contents of a large number of clinical reports, Cummings and Benson (1983) conclude that the principal features of the dementia in patients with Parkinson's disease include failure to initiate activities spontaneously, inability to develop a successful approach to problem solving, impaired and slowed memory, deficits in visuospatial perception, impaired concept formation, poor performance on word fluency tests, difficulties in shifting set and overall a reduced rate of information processing. The dementia is usually of mild to moderate severity. It has been considered that 'cortical' features such as aphasia and agnosia are unusual and, when manifest in a minority of patients, reflect the presence of significant Alzheimer-type neuropathological changes in the cortex (see Chapter 3). Such patients may raise important diagnostic questions (see Chapter 7). A higher proportion of patients with Parkinson's disease than with other chronic medical disorders show evidence of depression, the severity of which does not bear a strong relationship to the extent of physical disability, but does relate to cognitive dysfunction (Celesia and Wanamaker, 1972; Mayeux and Stern, 1983). Hence it has been considered that the depression manifested by such patients is not simply a reaction to the physical disability they experience, but rather is an intrinsic part of the disease process, although an alternative viewpoint has been expressed (e.g. Warburton, 1967).

Abnormalities of speech and writing compound the difficulties created by cognitive deficits. The voice acquires a monotonous quality and decreases in volume. Dysarthria, together with changes in the rate of speech (which may increase or decrease), makes for further difficulties. Micrographia is the initial feature in about 5 per cent of cases and is severe at some stage in the course of the illness in some 10–15 per cent of affected individuals. The morphology of the letters may remain intact apart from the reduction in size but patients' rigidity and tremor may further reduce legibility.

Movement disorder is, of course, the hallmark of Parkinson's disease. It is characterized by akinesia (i.e. difficulty in initiating movement), bradykinesia (i.e. motor slowing), rigidity of limb and trunk muscles as well as tremor. All of these symptoms contribute to loss of voluntary movement. In addition, patients with Parkinson's disease typically show abnormalities of eye movements and autonomic disturbances such as postural hypotension and oesophageal spasm.

Huntington's Disease

Huntington's disease is a progressive neurodegenerative condition that is inherited in an autosomal dominant manner. The duration of the condition from symptom onset (usually in the fourth or fifth decade of life) to death is of the order of 15 years, but may be as long as 30 years (Martin and Gusella, 1986).

In his original description, published in 1872, Huntington noted that, 'as the disease progresses the mind becomes more or less impaired, in many amounting to insanity, while in others mind and body gradually fail until death relieves them of their sufferings'. Personality changes, including irritability, untidyness and apathy are often the first indication of disease onset and in the majority of cases these precede the choreiform movements (Cummings and Benson, 1983). Mood disorders resembling unipolar or bipolar affective illness and psychotic features, particularly persecutory delusions are common. Rates of suicide and attempted suicide are very high.

These psychiatric features may be accompanied by increasing impairment of cognitive functioning. Memory disturbance is prominent, but patients also show impairment of concentration and judgment and have difficulty with tasks which require organization and planning ability, functions typically mediated by the frontal lobes which are known to be affected in this condition (see Chapter 3). The situation with respect to language is somewhat controversial. Choreiform movements of the lips and tongue can severely disrupt articulatory agility and abnormal movements of the diaphragm disturb the volume, rate and phrase length of patients' speech. In addition to dysarthria patients manifest word finding difficulties and typically fail on language tests that require organization, sequencing and linguistic elaboration. Such findings would seem to be at odds with the view of Cummings and Benson (1983) that Huntington's disease is one of the subcortical dementias since these are not typically associated with language impairment. However, Cummings and Benson (1983) maintain that the language tasks on which patients with Huntington's disease score poorly are those that require more than linguistic ability *per se*. These tasks also make demands upon memory and other cognitive operations. Clearly formal neuropsychological investigation will be necessary in order to determine the validity of this argument in relation to Huntington's disease, or indeed to the cortical/subcortical distinction in general.

Movement disorders are of course characteristic of Huntington's disease. In the early stages the victim may simply appear to be nervous, fidgety or clumsy but, as full-blown chorea develops, the abnormal movements become more frequent and exaggerated. Increasingly these impair, and eventually they eliminate, normal activity by interfering with the ability to stand, walk, write or perform any act that requires manual dexterity. Patients also experience difficulty swallowing.

Although chorea is the typical motor disturbance associated with Huntington's disease, a proportion of patients show extreme rigidity and thus may appear more similar to individuals suffering from Parkinson's disease. However, this rare presentation is more likely to be seen in juvenile onset cases (before the age of 20 years) than in older patients.

Multi-Infarct Dementia

In contrast to AD, multi-infarct dementia is more common in men than in women, reflecting the fact that cardiovascular disorders are more prevalent in males. The onset of dementia is abrupt and usually associated with a cerebrovascular accident. The progression of multi-infarct dementia is said to follow a step-like course with episodic exacerbations followed by plateaux or even some degree of remission, although the extent of any improvement diminishes as the condition progresses.

Initially, neuropsychological deficits are patchy, as might be expected, given the irregular but restricted distribution of pathology in the early stages of this condition. However, as the volume of infarcted tissue increases the functional consequences become more generalized and more apparent. Emotional lability and depression are often cited as key features of this condition. Nocturnal confusion is also considered to be an important symptom. There are inconsistencies in the literature regarding the preservation of personality. Slater and Roth (1969: 593), who provided what has come to be regarded as the classic description of the clinical features of vascular dementia, stated at one point that, 'Memory and intellectual impairment may be preceded by a caricature of one or more conspicuous character traits, a growing suspiciousness, pathological jealousy . . . ' but, in the same text, they also asserted that, 'the basic personality may be well preserved . . . '.

Psychological changes may be accompanied by a wide variety of somatic complaints, including headache, giddiness, tinnitus, general malaise and palpitations. Focal neurological symptoms and signs are generally present. Cerebrovascular accident is usually the cause of death.

Alcoholic Dementia

Neuropsychological investigations suggest that up to 50 per cent of chronic alcoholics show intellectual impairment (see Cummings and Benson, 1983). Such alcoholic dementia is more apparent in elderly individuals than in the young and occurs earlier and at lower levels of consumption in women than in men.

Mood change, in particular euphoria and lability, are frequently found, as are visual and auditory hallucinations and delusions (Cutting, 1978). Forgetfulness, psychomotor retardation, perseveration, poor attention and disorientation are also typical features of a dementia that is clinically mild and is either non-progressive or only slowly progressive. Formal neuropsychological testing produces variable results, but the majority of studies show poor abstracting abilities, memory deficits and impairment of verbal fluency (see Cummings and Benson, 1983).

Concluding Remarks

It will be apparent from the foregoing review that a wealth of descriptive data has accumulated over the years as clinicians have documented the presenting features of patients thought to be affected by various dementia-producing conditions. Of particular interest are reports of patients in whom the markers of a specific pathological process have subsequently been identified by biopsy or autopsy examination or even (although this is less ideal) by prolonged follow-up with documentation of the developmental course of the clinical symptomatology, together with the results of concomitant laboratory investigations. Clearly, the degree of interest aroused over the years, and the extent to which clinicians have raised and attempted to address penetrating questions, has been variable and often idiosyncratic. Hence the quality as well as quantity of the reporting has varied within and across conditions.

Although it would be churlish to deny the importance of extensive clinical experience with demented patients it is important to be aware of the limitations of un-controlled observations. Individual clinicians differ in the tools they employ and in their criteria for concluding that particular features are present or absent. Such criteria will also be influenced by their prior expectations regarding which features should or should not coexist or be present in particular conditions. Alas, a style of reporting in scientific journals that allows for premature reification of concepts which remain in effect merely hypotheses open to evaluation must be condemned as dangerous. It is our belief that lists of clinical features purported to distinguish between cortical and sub-cortical dementias (see Cummings, 1986) are being flaunted with a confidence that the scientific data do not yet merit. The utility and/or validity of the distinction between so-called cortical and subcortical dementias is at present uncertain. Although it would be presumptious to dismiss it outright, a number of objections must be borne in mind.

As outlined in Chapter 3, the distinction is undermined by neuropathological evidence of subcortical damage in patients with DAT and conversely of cortical damage in at least some conditions hitherto considered to be subcortical, such as Huntington's disease and Parkinson's disease. In terms of clinical features the presence or absence of language impairment has assumed an important position in the ongoing debate concerning the nosology and nosography of dementia (Hart, 1988a). Albert (1981), himself an early advocate of the cortical/subcortical distinction, rightly pointed out that some language impairment may occur in any type of dementia, although he maintained, as many others have subsequently done, that the linguistic deficits found in these two types of dementia are distinct. However, claims regarding qualitative differences seem premature as the question of whether there are qualitative, or indeed quantitative, differences between patients with dementias of differing aetiologies can only be established by systematic investigations using patient groups matched in terms of overall severity of cognitive impairment. Experimental investigations have begun (Bayles *et al.*, 1982; Bayles and Tomoeda, 1983) but the necessary matching of groups is a task which continues to pose very considerable methodological problems (see Mayeux *et al.*, 1983). Furthermore, not all patients with DAT (the quintessential example of a cortical dementia) show pronounced disturbance of language on clinical examination, even when some deficiency may be highlighted by more systematic and penetrating evaluation. This is especially true of older patients with DAT in whom pathological change tends to be restricted to the cortex, while linguistic deficits are more characteristic of younger patients in whom pathological damage also affects subcortical structures.

The heuristic value of clinical observations is irrefutable, but we would argue that these must be supported by systematic controlled investigations employing objective neuropsychological assessment and experimental procedures of the type that will be considered in the chapters of Part IV.

Chapter 7

Diagnosis and Differential Diagnosis

The diagnosis of dementia remains an imprecise art and much scientific endeavour is being directed towards the necessary attainment of a universally agreed definition embodying explicit operational criteria. However, important though it is, the task of diagnosing dementia reliably and accurately must never be seen as an end in itself. Rather, clinicians and researchers must proceed further and seek to identify the aetiological factors giving rise to the presenting clinical syndrome. This is often a difficult and lengthy process. Clinical differentiation between dementia syndromes of different aetiologies can often be difficult and a number of studies have pointed to diagnostic error in a not insignificant proportion of cases (Bradshaw et al., 1983; Homer et al., 1988; Kendell, 1974; Marsden and Harrison, 1972; Nott and Fleminger, 1975; Ron et al., 1979). Detailed investigations have been found to indicate a potentially reversible cause of the dementia syndrome in some 8–30 per cent of cases (Bradshaw et al., 1983; Freemon, 1976; Marsden and Harrison, 1972; Smith and Kiloh, 1981). Although specific treatment of the underlying cause may not completely reverse the cognitive deficit in all cases, it should arrest the dementing process and alleviate the associated symptoms in many patients. Findings such as these have prompted a number of writers to caution against the therapeutic nihilism which still tends to be evoked when patients with a dementia syndrome are encountered, especially elderly patients (Cummings et al., 1980; Steel and Feldman, 1979; Stoudemire and Thompson, 1981).

Quite apart from the possibility of uncovering treatable conditions, early referral and investigation is also relevant to the scientific endeavour of increasing knowledge about the natural history of the different, currently untreatable, degenerative diseases of the brain. Although at present this may seem a somewhat academic exercise, it is an important prerequisite for the development of therapeutic strategies applicable to hitherto irremediable dementia-producing conditions and indeed, even if this is not possible, it might enable clinicians to provide patients' families and supporters with accurate prognostic information, thereby allowing for better planning and provision of resources. Some of the problems surrounding diagnosis of dementia *per se* were discussed in Chapter 2. We shall consider below some of the differential diagnostic problems posed by various groups of conditions giving rise to dementia and also draw attention to some important conceptual and methodological issues that have arisen in relation to neuropsychological endeavours towards the resolution of diagnostic and differential diagnostic problems.

Functional Psychiatric Disorders

In addition to the numerous neurological and medical conditions that may present as dementia there are a number of psychiatric conditions which can give rise to this clinical syndrome. In such cases the term 'pseudodementia' has conventionally been applied (Janowsky, 1982; Kiloh, 1961; Post, 1975; C. E. Wells, 1979), although probably inappropriately (Caine, 1981; Mahendra, 1984; see also Chapter 2).

The reports of Liston (1977, 1978) are of particular interest. Liston carried out systematic retrospective analyses of the medical records of 50 cases in whom the discharge diagnosis was presenile dementia. Pathological examination to confirm the clinical diagnosis was lacking in all but one case of Creutzfeldt–Jakob disease. It was found that the interval between symptom onset and first contact with a physician was shorter for patients with a history of psychiatric treatment and for those who showed a spectrum of depressive symptomatology prior to final diagnosis than for patients without such histories. However, the delay between physician contact and final diagnosis was greater for these presumptive psychiatric cases. Liston (1977) used the term 'occult' to refer to cases in which an 'organic' dementing process was initially masked by a clinical presentation that could easily be mistaken for major affective disorder. Carlson (1976) provides a detailed case history of one such patient.

Such failure to recognize a primary dementia, usually early in its course, is not the only type of diagnostic error which can occur in differentiating between so-called 'organic' and 'functional' conditions. A much more frequent error is the diagnostic conclusion that the dementia is irreversible when the disorder is primarily 'functional'. There are a number of functional psychiatric conditions, including schizophrenia, hysteria, mania and paranoia, as well as depression, which may present a clinical picture of dementia but depression is undoubtedly the most common cause of such so-called pseudodementia (see Lishman, 1987: 561–75). The reported frequency of failure to recognize depression as the underlying cause of a dementia syndrome ranges from 2 per cent to 15 per cent (Duckworth and Ross, 1975; Freemon, 1976; Garcia *et al.*, 1981; Kendell, 1974; Marsden and Harrison, 1972; Nott and Fleminger, 1975; Ron *et al.*, 1979; Smith and Kiloh, 1981).

Depressive pseudodementia, more appropriately referred to as the dementia syndrome of depression (Caine, 1981), frequently gives rise to diagnostic problems in elderly patients. It has been estimated that, according to relatively strict criteria, some 4–10 per cent of the elderly suffer from moderate to severe clinical depression (Blazer and Williams, 1980; Gurland, 1976; Weissman and Myers, 1978) and a considerably higher proportion show less severe or more transient disturbances of mood (Wasylenki, 1980). In terms of referrals to psychiatric services, depression constitutes perhaps the largest single problem in the elderly (Pfeiffer and Busse, 1973; Pitt, 1982). Indeed Williamson (1978) has pointed out that it is only after the age of 75 years that dementia is found to have a higher incidence. The problem of so-called pseudodementia assumes particular importance in the elderly because in many older patients the presentation of depression may be somewhat atypical with cognitive symptoms, such as impairment of memory and concentration, faulty orientation and defective knowledge of current events, being particularly prominent, while affective disturbance is comparatively less apparent. In the presence of general psychomotor retardation, social withdrawal, carelessness and general self-neglect it is not difficult to appreciate that a diagnosis of depression might not seem obvious. Indeed, in some cases the patient may neither manifest nor complain of any affective disturbance (e.g. Case 1, McAllister and Price, 1982). Failure to recognize the primary role of depression in producing a clinical syndrome of dementia is not only a more frequent but also a much more serious diagnostic error than that of failing to detect occult dementia given the therapeutic nihilism that a diagnosis of dementia may evoke, together with the fact that depression is an eminently treatable condition (as indeed are many of the other 'functional' psychiatric conditions that may give rise to a clinical syndrome of dementia).

The diagnostic problem is further complicated by the fact that affective symptoms, or indeed a depressive illness, may coexist with a non-reversible dementia (Demuth and Rand, 1980; McAllister and Price, 1982; Reifler *et al.*, 1982; Shraberg, 1978). The frequency of this association is unclear but Reifler *et al.*'s (1982) study of a geriatric population indicated that depression was superimposed on dementia in some 19 per cent of cases. Marsden and Harrison (1972), reporting on presenile patients seen in a neurological setting, stated that some 25 per cent of patients with dementia were depressed. The case histories reported by a number of the above authors show clearly that a coexisting depression serves to exacerbate the cognitive and behavioural impairments of a primary dementia. All of these authors, like Post (1975), emphasize that vigorous treatment might lead to considerable clinical improvement. The danger is that the remediable depressive component may be obscured by the degree of 'organic' dementia. Dramatic responses to ECT have been reported in a number of such cases (Demuth and Rand, 1980; McAllister and Price, 1982). Indeed, patients have also been found to respond favourably to tricyclic antidepressants although, in view of the anticholinergic properties of this class of drugs, as well as the now well-documented deficit in cholinergic function in AD and certain other dementia-producing conditions, it might be more desirable to employ as a first choice some of the newer antidepressant drugs which do not have such marked anticholinergic effects.

Considering why functional psychiatric disorders are mistakenly diagnosed as primary dementias, various workers have suggested that such errors may occur because too much weight is attached to changes in cognition alone (e.g. Lishman, 1987; Post, 1975; Roth, 1978; C. E. Wells, 1978, 1979). Although cognitive impairment is the hallmark of the dementias, it not unique to them. It is also a frequent feature of many functional psychiatric disorders. C. E. Wells (1979) listed a number of features which he considered should aid clinicians in arriving at correct diagnoses. The importance of historical data in diagnostic decision making is borne out by the four patients described by McAllister and Price (1982), in all of whom it was the previous history of psychiatric illness, considered in the context of a current illness which had an abrupt onset and generally short duration (as well as a rapid progression of cognitive and behavioural deterioration in two cases) which suggested the possibility that an affective disorder was making a significant contribution to their clinical dysfunction. McAllister and Price (1982) pointed out that, while consideration of historical data proved useful in determining an appropriate course of therapeutic intervention, many of the other features suggested by C. E. Wells (1979) as indicative of pseudodementia, for example evidence of pervasive affective change, frequent 'don't know' responses, relatively well-preserved attention and concentration, or variability of performance across tasks of similar difficulty, were not in evidence in their patients.

Neither the CT scan (Jacoby and Levy, 1980) nor the EEG (see Wang, 1981; Wells, 1980) have proved particularly helpful in resolving this diagnostic dilemma, especially in elderly subjects because there is a large degree of overlap between normal and various abnormal groups (see below). It has been suggested that the dexamethasone suppression test (see Carroll *et al.*, 1981) might potentially help in identifying depression (Grunhaus *et al.*, 1983; McAllister *et al.*, 1982; Rudorfer and Clayton, 1981). However, other reports are less optimistic (see Hollander *et al.*, 1986).

The utility of psychological testing has also been questioned. Even authors who have upheld the usefulness of such evaluation (e.g. Janowsky, 1982; Roth, 1980b; C. E. Wells, 1979) have been at pains to draw attention to its limitations with respect to this diagnostic problem. The general consensus of opinion seems to have been that, at best, the results of tests carried out by psychologists would be in close agreement with the findings of a thorough clinical evaluation. Similar evidence prompted Post (1975: 109) to conclude, 'This agreement makes testing by a psychologist as a routine investigation quite unnecessary in clinically clear-cut cases'. However, he went beyond this fairly obvious conclusion and stated boldly that, 'Where . . . the clinical assessment suggests doubtful cognitive impairment, psychologic testing usually produces equally doubtful results'. One of the patients described by McAllister and Price (1982), who proved to be a 'pure' case of 'depressive pseudodementia' and responded to treatment, demonstrated such profound cognitive impairment as to preclude formal neuropsychological testing. Even if a patient is somewhat less retarded, the test results obtained are likely to be consistent with an organic diagnosis if the depressive illness is sufficiently severe to produce a dementia syndrome and so cause a clinical problem. Certainly, where depression and dementia coexist it is hardly surprising that psychological test results should be consistent with an organic diagnosis. This might result in failure to exploit a therapeutic opportunity, but only if undue weight is attached to changes in cognition alone or if the clinical presentation is particularly convoluted. In such situations it is particularly important that practitioners remember the adage of C. E. Wells (1979: 897) that, ' . . . it is the totality of the clinical picture that is important' in making a diagnosis. In a similar vein Roth (1980b: 214) warned that, ' . . . no psychological measure should be allowed to override a judgement derived from careful history-taking and thorough clinical evaluation', while rightly acknowledging that psychological testing provides a valuable adjunct in the clinical assessment of patients suspected of dementia.

Much of the dissatisfaction over the years amongst referring medical practitioners, and likewise amongst the clinical psychologists to whom they referred for diagnostic assistance, has derived from the misconceptions under which they laboured. One fundamental misconception concerned the nature of dementia. More specifically, both parties failed to differentiate further within this broad category of conditions. Furthermore, in their use of the general term organicity, they betrayed an implicit, even if not explicit, assumption that dementia was in essence equivalent to other forms of brain damage and that the cognitive and behavioural deficits of patients so afflicted differed only in quantitative terms. Not surprisingly, therefore, many of the tests employed by clinical psychologists for the purpose of differentiating between these so-called organic and functional conditions, and even some of those which were developed for this purpose, were gross and non-specific and lacked sound theoretical underpinnings, quite apart from any methodological shortcomings in their construction. Hence their lack of striking success in answering what was in any case an inappropriate question should cause no surprise.

Another fundamental misconception concerned the nature of depression, or indeed other functional psychiatric conditions. When used in this context the term functional was essentially synonymous with non-brain-damaged. It was not used, as might be considered appropriate today, to refer to an altered and dysfunctional pattern of neuronal activity which might be present in the absence of damage to the structure of the brain. The serendipitous discovery of pharmacological agents which were effective in ameliorating the symptoms of certain such conditions (specifically some depressive disorders and schizophrenia), and subsequent developments in understanding of the neurochemical disturbances mediating their clinical manifestations, have cast such conditions in a new light such that they now undoubtedly fall within the proper scope of investigators wishing to pursue understanding of brain-behaviour relationships. Experimental neuropsychologists, largely those working with animal subjects (e.g. Gray, 1977, 1985; Iversen, 1977; Stein *et al.*, 1977), have been quick to appreciate the potential of such developments for enhancing knowledge of the neural substrates of behaviour. It is in our view regrettable that many clinical neuropsychologists have been rather slow to recognize that such conditions rightly fall within the realm of those meriting application of their neuropsychological endeavours. This is as true of primary affective disorders as it is of those which are secondary to neurological lesions, although to date very few neuropsychologists have shown due interest in either class of condition. The latter deserve to be regarded as more than merely the cause of error variance which confounds attempts to measure cognitive impairment or impedes efforts at rehabilitation since they provide a window on the neuroanatomical basis of emotion. The growing availability of brain-imaging procedures now affords tremendous potential to advance understanding of the neurochemical substrates of the emotional, as well as the behavioural and cognitive, abnormalities heralded by depression and it is our belief that there is scope here for clinical neuropsychologists, as well as for human experimental and cognitive neuropsychologists.

In recent years a considerable amount of cognitive neuropsychological research has investigated the performance of depressed patients on cognitive tasks and there is a substantial body of evidence indicating impairment of memory, although controversy continues concerning the cognitive mechanisms mediating the impairment of performance on experimental tasks as well as the contribution of ECT or pharmacological agents to the deficits detected (Leight and Ellis, 1981; McAllister, 1981; Moore *et al.*, 1988; Weingartner, 1986; Williams and Broadbent, 1986). A complementary line of research has been conducted by cognitive psychologists who in the past decade have devoted increasing attention to exploration of the relationship between affect and memory by analysing the changes in performance on cognitive tasks produced by experimental manipulation of mood states (Blaney, 1986; Bower, 1981, 1983; Singer and Salovey, 1988; Teasdale, 1983). In view of the relatively recent but by now well-established evidence of memory dysfunction in depressed patients we can appreciate that herein lay yet another significant misconception confounding the early attempts by clinical psychologists to distinguish accurately between patients suffering from depression and other dementia-producing conditions. Many of the tests they employed for this purpose were founded on the basic premise that dementia was characterized by impairment of memory, as well as other aspects of cognition, while such functions were essentially spared by depression. It remains to be determined whether and how the memory impairment heralded by depression differs qualitatively from that which occurs in the course of normal ageing or as a symptom of another dementia-producing condition. Indeed, it is unknown whether the memory dysfunction consequent upon depression changes in fundamental nature, or only in extent, when the condition is of sufficient severity to produce a dementia syndrome.

Although the majority of depressed patients may show some cognitive impairment not all will manifest a dementia syndrome. Nevertheless, it is likely that those who posed diagnostic problems and so were most frequently referred to clinical psychologists for psychometric assessment were patients who showed a significant degree of cognitive dysfunction or perhaps manifested a dementia syndrome of depression. Hence what was viewed as a diagnostic question (i.e. detection of dementia) would, in the light of currently greater knowledge about depression and the definition of dementia as a clinical syndrome, be more correctly construed as a differential diagnostic problem (i.e. seeking to determine the aetiological basis of the syndrome). This is an interesting semantic issue but it also remains true that in construing it as a question of how to identify dementia clinical psychologists raised and attempted to address, however effectively or ineffectively, important conceptual and methodological issues. We shall return to these later in this chapter.

Before proceeding to consider another group of conditions giving rise to dementia it seems appropriate to digress briefly from the topics of diagnosis and differential diagnosis which are the major thrust of this chapter and return to the issue considered in Chapter 1, namely the nature of neuropsychology as a scientific discipline and the breadth of its scope. We wish to make explicit our view regarding the role of neuropsychology in relation to psychiatric conditions hitherto considered to be functional and we shall use depression to illustrate our case. Although certain depressive disorders are the consequence of a biological change, or certainly have a prominent biological component, others seem more directly attributable to adverse life events or at least an inappropriate attributional or cognitive processing style in relation to these. In some cases the most appropriate method of therapeutic intervention appears to be a direct biologically-targeted one while in others psychological intervention, for example applying cognitive-behavioural techniques, would appear to be more appropriate and efficacious. In many cases, of course, it is likely that the best outcome might be achieved by a judicious combination of these approaches. However, we wish to emphasize that the clinical manifestations of any depressive condition must ultimately be mediated by activity in a neuronal substrate. Similarly, any therapeutic intervention, whether biological or psychological must, in the final analysis, exert its remedial effects by altering the pattern of such activity.

Other Degenerative Dementias

The attempt to differentiate between functional psychiatric and organic states has enjoyed a long history of clinical and scientific endeavour. However, it now seems that with increasing knowledge and therefore growing prospects of treatment, particularly for DAT, an equally important challenge is reliable ante-mortem differentiation between aetiologically and pathologically distinct degenerative conditions. This is a necessary prerequisite for the selection of relatively homogeneous groups for clinical trials and for futher explorations of the nature of the cognitive deficit(s) in different conditions (Seltzer and Sherwin, 1978). In the event that a therapeutic agent or procedure does prove to be effective in combating the ravages of a particular degenerative disease process it will be important to have available accurate diagnostic information so that, in the case of an individual patient, an informed decision can be made about whether to prescribe such treatment. No therapeutic intervention is likely to be totally free of risk in fallible human hands and inappropriate application may prove detrimental.

Alzheimer's disease is the major cause of dementia and, although diagnosis thereof ultimately rests upon neuropathology, its identification remains a clinical problem. In the absence of cerebral biopsy, which cannot be justified as a routine procedure and in the absence of an ante-mortem biological marker (see Hollander *et al.*, 1986), diagnosis must of necessity be by exclusion, as far as is possible, of other neurological, psychiatric, metabolic or systemic conditions which might give rise to dementia. The extent to which this process of exclusion has been pursued systematically and exhaustively has varied considerably among clinicians and researchers alike. Not surprisingly, therefore, the concordance between clinical and pathological diagnoses has been variable (Merskey *et al.*, 1985; Sulkava *et al.*, 1983; Tierney *et al.*, 1988) and even at its best leaves an error rate in excess of 10 per cent. As in the case of dementia *per se*, one major factor limiting progress in this field has been the lack of consensus regarding criteria for establishing this diagnosis. In recognition of the need for greater uniformity the National Institute of Neurological and Communicative Disorders and Stroke together with the Alzheimer's Disease and Related Disorders Association of the United States convened a group of experts to refine the clinical diagnostic criteria for AD. The outcome of their deliberations was a set of guidelines for the diagnosis of PROBABLE, POSSIBLE and DEFINITE AD, as set out in Table 7.1. Although recognizing the continuing debate about which neuropsychological tests are best for measuring the specific cognitive functions they referred to, this working party made some suggestions about which measures might be usefully employed (see McKhann *et al.*, 1984). It is clear from recent research reports that the criteria they set out are being employed with increasing frequency and thus it would appear that progress is indeed being made towards the goal of standardizing clinical diagnostic criteria. However, the clinicopathologic concordance study of Tierney *et al.* (1988) reminds us that the supposedly gold standard of pathological diagnosis is not as immutable as is often assumed. Another thrust towards operationalization and standardization of pathological criteria for diagnosis of AD seems appropriate, given that the proposals made by Khachaturian (1985) have failed to achieve this goal.

In what follows; our purpose is not to consider the ultimate diagnosis of the rarer degenerative conditions selected for consideration as they, like AD, are often complex and variable in their presentation. Rather, our concern is to emphasize the differential diagnostic difficulties which may arise out of their symptomatology and also to highlight examples of clinical features which might prove useful in excluding such conditions for the purpose of arriving at a diagnosis of probable AD.

Table 7.1 NINCDS-ADRDA Criteria for the Clinical Diagnosis of Alzheimer's disease

I.	The criteria for the clinical diagnosis of PROBABLE Alzheimer's disease include:

    – dementia established by clinical examination and documented by the Mini-Mental State Examination, Blessed Dementia Scale, or some similar examination, and confirmed by neuropsychological tests;

    – deficits in two or more areas of cognition;

    – progressive worsening of memory and other cognitive functions;

    – no disturbance of consciousness;

    – onset between 40 and 90 years of age, most often after age 65 years; and

    – absence of systemic disorders or other brain diseases that in and of themselves could account for the progressive decline in memory and cognition.

II.   The diagnosis of PROBABLE Alzheimer's disease is supported by:

    – progressive deterioration of specific cognitive functions such as language (aphasia), motor skills (apraxia) and perception (agnosia);

    – impaired activities of daily living and altered patterns of behaviour;

    – family history of similar disorders, particularly if confirmed neuropathologically; and

    – laboratory results of:

        normal lumber puncture as evaluated by standard techniques,

        normal pattern or non-specific changes in EEG, such as increased slow-wave activity, and

        evidence of cerebral atrophy on CT scan with progression documented by serial observation.

III.   Other clinical features consistent with the diagnosis of PROBABLE Alzheimer's disease after exclusion of causes of dementia other than Alzheimer's disease, include:

    – plateaux in the course of progression of the illness;

    – associated symptoms of depression, insomnia, incontinence, delusions, illusions, hallucinations, catastrophic verbal, emotional or physical outbursts, sexual disorders and weight loss;

    – other neurological abnormalities in some patients, especially with more advanced disease and including motor signs such as increased muscle tone, myoclonus or gait disorder;

    – seizures in advanced disease; and

    – CT scan normal for age.

IV.   Features that make the diagnosis of PROBABLE Alzheimer's disease uncertain or unlikely include:

    – sudden, apoplectic onset;

    – focal neurological findings such as hemiparesis, sensory loss, visual field deficits, and incoordination early in the course of the illness; and

    – seizures or gait disturbances at the onset or very early in the course of the illness;

V.   Clinical diagnosis of POSSIBLE Alzheimer's disease:

    – may be made on the basis of the dementia syndrome, in the absence of other neurological, psychiatric, or systemic disorders sufficient to cause

dementia, and in the presence of variations in the onset, in the presentation, or in the clinical course;
- may be made in the presence of a second systemic or brain disorder sufficient to produce dementia, which is not considered to be *the* cause of the dementia; and
- should be used in research studies when a single, gradually progressive severe cognitive deficit is identified in the absence of other identifiable cause.

VI.   Criteria for diagnosis of DEFINITE Alzheimer's disease are:
- the clinical criteria for probable Alzheimer's disease and
- histopathological evidence obtained from a biopsy or autopsy.

VII.   Classification of Alzheimer's disease for research purposes should specify features that may differentiate subtypes of the disorder, such as:
- familial occurrence;
- onset before 65 years of age;
- presence of trisomy-21; and
- coexistence of other relevant conditions such as Parkinson's disease.

Creutzfeldt–Jakob disease can generally be differentiated from AD by its rapidly progressive clinical course and the host of neurological signs, including myoclonic jerking, which accompany the progressive dementia. Of course, given the rapid progression of Creutzfeldt–Jakob disease, with over 90 per cent of patients dying within 2 years (May, 1968), the late occurrence of myoclonus in AD is not likely to cause much diagnostic confusion. However, although it is not a common early feature of AD, myoclonus may appear quite early in some cases (Faden and Townsend, 1976; Jacob, 1970; Terry *et al.*, 1964). Abnormalities of the EEG, even if only appearing late in the course of the disease, have been reported in more than 90 per cent of Creutzfeldt–Jakob patients (May, 1968) and may therefore be of diagnostic utility. A characteristic (although not pathognomonic) feature is the appearance of periodic high amplitude slow spikes and spike-wave complexes superimposed on a slow, low voltage background activity. These may be accompanied by myoclonic jerking. This EEG pattern has not, on the whole, been found in cases of AD with myoclonus (Faden and Townsend, 1976; Gimenez-Roldan *et al.*, 1971; Mayeux *et al.*, 1980), although possible exceptions might be found in the reports of Jacob (1970) and Watson (1979). However, Watson's interpretation of the EEG evidence in his patient as that characteristic of Creutzfeldt–Jakob disease has been questioned (Gloor, 1980). Although the occurrence of prodromal psychiatric disturbances early in the course of Creutzfeldt–Jakob disease would initially tend to thwart diagnosis of this condition *per se*, such features would nevertheless favour, if not ensure, exclusion of patients so affected from a diagnosis of AD.

At any rate, the differentiation between AD and Creutzfeldt–Jakob disease is unlikely to prove a major diagnostic problem since the latter is a rare condition. This is also true of Huntington's disease which accounts for only a small percentage of all cases of dementia (Freemon, 1976; Marsden and Harrison, 1972; Smith and Kiloh, 1981). Although choreiform movements are characteristic of Huntington's disease and are typically an early sign of the disorder, it is not unknown for the associated dementia to be coincident with, or indeed to predate, the movement disorder (Bolt, 1970; Brackenridge, 1971; Corsellis, 1976; Curran, 1930; Dewhurst *et al.*, 1969; Lishman, 1987) and so become a cause of diagnostic confusion. The fact that some cases of AD may present with abnormal movements can be another source of confusion. Knowledge of the family history might prove helpful in reaching an accurate diagnosis since Huntington's disease is an inherited condition transmitted in a simple autosomal dominant fashion. Of course, it must be pointed out that a similar dominant pattern of inheritance for AD has also been reported in some families (Cook *et al.*, 1979; Kilpatrick *et al.*, 1983). As already noted, Huntington's is not a very frequently-occurring disease, especially in the elderly, although the onset may occasionally be delayed until old age. Moreover, it has been reported that in cases where the onset of choreiform movements is in the sixth or seventh decade the progression of the disease is very slow, without development of the dementia that is associated with chorea under the age of 50 years (Bird, 1978).

As noted in Chapter 6 a sizeable (although variously estimated) proportion of patients with Parkinson's disease manifest a dementia syndrome. Given the occurrence of movement disorders in certain patients with AD, a question may arise concerning whether a patient has DAT with extrapyramidal signs or parkinsonism with dementia (see Drachman and Stahl, 1975). It remains to be determined whether the dementia that occurs in a proportion of parkinsonian patients is an intrinsic feature of this condition or alternatively represents the simultaneous occurrence by chance of two independent age-related conditions. Even if we assume the former, and there is indeed therefore a differential diagnostic problem, it remains true that, in practice, by the time dementia develops in association with Parkinson's disease, the diagnosis is clear in most patients.

Pick's disease is a rather rare cause of dementia, typically presenile although it does also occur in old age (Binns and Robertson, 1962). Pick's disease and AD resemble each other very closely in their clinical manifestations although they are pathologically distinct, Pick's disease being characterized by circumscribed lobar atrophy, particularly in the frontal and temporal lobes, as opposed to the generalized atrophy of AD. The histological features of the two diseases are also different (see Lishman, 1987). Although some authorities consider that careful scrutiny of the clinical symptomatology, especially that of the initial stage, should uncover enough differences to enable a tentative differentiation, criteria for separating these two diseases on clinical grounds are not universally accepted (see Brun and Gustafson, 1976; Lishman, 1987; Robertson, 1978; Robertson *et al.*, 1958; Sim and Sussman, 1962; Sjogren, 1952; Stengel, 1943). There seems to be fairly general agreement that in Pick's disease changes of character and disposition are often noted from the outset, perhaps even before any changes in memory are apparent, whereas in AD memory disturbance is very frequently the presenting feature while personality and social skills are maintained for quite a long time. Spatial disorientation, generally quite an early and prominent sign in AD, is a late feature of Pick's disease. Dyspraxia and agnosia, typical parietal lobe symptoms, are considered to be much less common in Pick's disease than in AD and disturbances of gait, as well as other extrapyramidal features, are also said to be more characteristic of AD. Early incontinence has been regarded as indicative of Pick's disease, and would be consistent with marked frontal lobe pathology, but Sjogren (1952) has cited this as an early feature in his series of patients with AD. Stengel (1943) emphasized facile hilarity, lack of spontaneity and increasing apathy as characteristic of Pick's disease as opposed to the depressed anxious mood and overactivity of patients with AD, but Sjogren (1952), on the basis of a larger series of patients, emphasized inactivity and lack of spontaneity as prominent features of AD. Thus, while these various workers hold that the two diseases can be differentiated on clinical grounds, they are by no means agreed on the criteria for such a distinction and in practice it remains difficult to exclude Pick's disease in the absence of pathological evidence. Recently, however, Gustafson and Nilsson (1982) have published rating scales for AD (specifically excluding SDAT) and Pick's disease respectively which they claim will allow for differential diagnosis but any judgment regarding their utility must await subsequent pathological verification in a much larger series of patients. This might prove slow and difficult given that Pick's disease is a comparatively rare entity, although estimates of incidence are quite variable (Josephy, 1953; Malamud, 1972; Sjogren, 1952; Terry, 1976).

There are of course other diseases which cause primary neuronal degeneration and hence dementia. However these, together with those referred to above, account for only a small part of the growing problem of dementia.

Multi-Infarct Dementia

In terms of prevalence the major clinical problem is the differentiation between DAT and multi-infarct dementia. The latter term was introduced by Hachinski *et al.* (1974) who considered it a more accurate representation than the term 'cerebral arteriosclerosis' of the pathological processes giving rise to most cases of dementia of vascular origin. In an attempt to address the problem of differentiating between DAT and multi-infarct dementia, Hachinski *et al.* (1975) devised a rating scale giving rise to an ischaemic score. This was based upon clinical features acknowledged to be characteristic of vascular dementia (Mayer-Gross *et al.*, 1969), having been shown in clinicopathological studies to correlate well with ischaemic changes in the brain (Corsellis, 1962). According to the procedure of Hachinski *et al.* (1975) an ischaemic score is derived by assigning points as shown in Table 7.2.

Table 7.2 Ischaemic Rating Scales

Feature	Point Value	
	Hachinski *et al.*, 1975	Rosen *et al.*, 1980
Abrupt onset	2	2
Stepwise deterioration	1	1
Fluctuating course	2	–
Nocturnal confusion	1	–
Relative preservation of personality	1	–
Depression	1	–
Somatic complaints	1	1
Emotional incontinence	1	1
History or presence of hypertension	1	1
History of strokes	2	2
Evidence of associated atherosclerosis	1	–
Focal neurological symptoms	2	2
Focal neurological signs	2	2

Applying this scoring procedure to a group of 24 patients, Hachinski *et al.* (1975) found a bimodal distribution with two distinct groups, those scoring seven and above and those scoring four or below. Patients with high scores were labelled as having multi-infarct dementia and those with low scores primary degenerative dementia. Mean cerebral blood flow was found to differ between the two groups, being decreased in the multi-infarct dementia group but normal in the AD group and, since the degree of intellectual and behavioural impairment was judged to be comparable in both groups, the authors concluded that the difference in cerebral blood flow could not be attributed to group differences in the overall severity of dementia. It is unfortunate that autopsy results were not available to further validate the ante-mortem diagnoses as various workers have reported that regional blood flow is also reduced in AD and DAT (Gustafson, 1979; Gustafson and Risberg, 1979; Tachibana *et al.*, 1984). This is hardly surprising since the metabolic activitiy of the brain is reduced in DAT (Benson, 1982; Wang, 1981) and cerebral blood flow is, as a rule, directly under the control of brain metabolic need. However, Gustafson (1979) suggested that patterns of regional blood flow may assist in the differential diagnosis between AD, Pick's disease, multi-infarct dementia and depressive pseudodementia and independent verification of such claims in pathologically-confirmed cases, studied early in the course of deterioration, is therefore of some importance.

Rosen *et al.* (1980) attempted a pathological verification of the ischaemic score by looking at the clinical differentiation of patients with a known histological diagnosis of DAT, multi-infarct dementia or mixed pathology. They found the ischaemic score to be quite successful in differentiating SDAT from vascular dementia in patients with known histological diagnoses but suggested that a somewhat modified scoring system might increase the accuracy of clinical differentiation (see Table 7.2). However, the number of patients employed in this study was small and since clinical presentation of the dementias is known to be very variable, the generality of these findings remains unproven. Liston and La Rue (1983a,b) reviewed critically the evidence concerning clinical differentiation of primary degenerative dementias from multi-infarct dementia and concluded (1983a:1464) that, '... the margin of error associated with the ante-mortem diagnosis of mult-infarct dementia is unacceptably high'. Their position was supported by Brust (1983) who emphasized that vascular dementia is still overdiagnosed, not only clinically but also pathologically. Although a low ischaemic score tends to rule out vascular dementia, since it is unlikely that functionally significant ischaemic lesions will be neurologically silent, the converse does not necessarily hold. A high ischaemic score can never indicate that the dementia is of vascular origin since there is at present no clear way of determining to what extent, if any, the ischaemic lesions are causing or contributing to the dementia syndrome (see Chapter 3 for the threshold concept).

These criticisms of the ischaemic score present a problem mainly for investigators whose aim is to select cases of multi-infarct dementia. However, this does not present a major problem if the purpose is to arrive at a diagnosis of DAT (or another primary degenerative dementia) by exclusion, using a high ischaemic score as one of the exclusion criteria. The only danger is that it may cause one to needlessly reject a number of suitable patients and thereby potentially diminish the representativeness of the sample. However, it might be argued that in the early stages of research a cautious strategy would be indicated. Ultimately, of course, undue reliance upon the ischaemic score might serve to deprive some patients of a therapeutic intervention which might be appropriate and/or prove beneficial.

Gustafson and Nilsson (1982) suggested that the differentiation between vascular and primary degenerative dementias might be approached from the opposite direction, taking as a starting point the clinical criteria for primary degenerative dementia. While their initial data suggested that this approach might be worthy of further investigation any conclusions regarding its utility with respect to this differential diagnostic problem would be premature at this time.

Electrophysiology

Reference has already been made at various points to electrophysiological techniques. It seems appropriate, therefore, to provide a brief overview of the nature of these procedures, which hold significant potential for advancing knowledge about brain-behaviour relationships, and to present a summary appraisal of their diagnostic utility.

The use of electroencephalography (EEG) in the evaluation of patients with dementia dates back to the earliest days of its application to human subjects (Goodin,

1985), but there remains much uncertainty regarding its diagnostic utility. This may, in part, depend upon the patient's age. A slowing of the frequency and diminution in quantity of alpha activity, together with the appearance of theta and delta activity, is almost invariably noted in presenile patients with DAT (Gordon and Sim, 1967). However, it becomes more difficult to categorize these alterations as abnormal in elderly patients when they must be interpreted in the context of a general age-related trend towards similar changes. In presenile patients the EEG is more likely to be normal in Pick's disease than in AD (see Gordon and Sim, 1967) and presumably the same would be true of elderly patients. The characteristic appearance of spiking may aid recognition of Creutzfeldt–Jakob disease, although this feature may only be present in some 30 per cent of patients in the early stages of the disease (Torres and Hutton, 1986). A very low amplitude EEG might suggest Huntington's disease, but this does not appear to correlate with the severity of dementia, age at onset or severity of illness (Scott *et al.*, 1972) and only a minority of patients with Huntington's disease demonstrate this abnormality (Torres and Hutton, 1986). In many cases of multi-infarct dementia the EEG is normal; in others diffuse slowing can be seen but in some cases focal abnormalities may be detected in regions of extensive infarction (Lishman, 1987; Loeb, 1980). However, focal abnormalities can also be found in some 18 per cent of patients with DAT (Erkinjuntti *et al.*, 1988). Various workers have advocated comparison of recordings made at different points in time (e.g. Torres and Hutton, 1986). It has become almost axiomatic that EEG abnormalities will increase progressively throughout the course of DAT but this view has been challenged by Rae-Grant *et al.* (1987). A large proportion of patients with DAT in their longitudinal study showed stable EEGs. However, group data can be misleading and, in view of the difficulties surrounding clinical diagnosis, the crucial question is whether there can be a dissociation in individual patients between the results of EEG and cognitive assessments carried out serially. Unfortunately Rae-Grant *et al.* (1987) did not present their data in a manner that allows this question to be answered.

While the EEG can be surprisingly normal in many dementia-producing conditions, especially in the early stages of illness, most treatable causes of dementia such as mass lesions, toxicity and altered metabolic processes are associated with early and prominent EEG abnormalities. These alterations may antedate detectable cognitive impairment (Harner, 1975; Torres and Hutton, 1986). Diffuse infectious, toxic or metabolic encephalopathies can be excluded with a high degree of confidence if a normal EEG is obtained and herein lies the greatest diagnostic contribution of encephalography.

In summary, while EEG investigations can provide clues to the aetiology of a dementia syndrome the results they yield can rarely stand alone and must be interpreted in the context of other clinical information, including history and presenting symptomatology.

More recently techniques for studying evoked potentials have been applied to the investigation of patients with dementia. These involve computer averaging of the EEG to indicate electrical activity in response to repetitive stimuli. These can be conveniently classified into two broad categories, depending on the length of time after stimulus occurrence that the activity is sampled. The stimulus-related potentials occurring within approximately 250 msec represent the obligatory responses of the nervous system and are determined largely by the physical properties of the eliciting stimulus including its sensory modality. These stimulus-related potentials include the brainstem auditory evoked potential (BAEP) which is affected by pitch and loudness; the somatosensory evoked potential (SEP) which is sensitive to intensity and duration of the evoking stimulus; and the visual evoked potential (VEP) which depends upon characteristics such as brightness, contrast and visual angle and is referred to as flash VEP or pattern VEP depending upon the stimulus used. These stimulus-related potentials are relatively insensitive to cognitive factors such as attention or the manner in which the sensory information conveyed is to be used by the subject (e.g. Huisman *et al.*, 1987).

We shall consider stimulus-related potentials as indexes of the functional integrity of sensory systems in Chapter 11. As for their diagnostic utility, Goodin (1985) asserted that the changes reported in patients with dementia were too small and/or too inconsistent to be useful but the results of a recent series of investigations challenge this view (Bajalan *et al.*, 1986; Harding *et al.*, 1985; Wright *et al.*, 1984, 1986, 1987). In patients with DAT these workers found VEPs to be normal following pattern stimuli, but abnormal to flash stimuli with marked slowing of P2, the major positive component of the response. Serial recordings from a patient with DAT indicated that the abnormality of the response to flash stimuli, and hence the discrepancy between the flash and pattern VEPs, increased with severity of the condition (Orwin *et al.*, 1986). This pattern of relative impairment is at odds with that characteristic of a number of other neurological conditions (e.g. multiple sclerosis) in which the pattern VEP is typically abnormal while the flash VEP is normal. Young normal subjects treated with scopolamine showed the same differential pattern of responding as patients with DAT so implicating brain cholinergic systems in the abnormal responses of such patients (Bajalan *et al.*, 1986). It has recently been reported that individuals with multi-infarct dementia show the same phenomenon as those with DAT (Wright and Furlong, 1988). This may limit the differential diagnostic utility of such data. Of course, clinical diagnostic errors may have undermined its specificity and further investigations are warranted.

The second category of evoked responses are those which have been referred to as event-related potentials. These occur at longer latencies (250 msec and beyond) than stimulus-related potentials. They are relatively insensitive to the physical parameters of the eliciting stimulus and are not specific to one sensory modality. Rather they are highly dependent upon the psychological variables to which stimulus-related potentials are immune. Procedures designed to measure event-related potentials demand cognitive effort on the part of subjects who must make discriminative responses, in contrast to their relatively passive role during the measurement of stimulus-related potentials.

The measurement of event-related potentials, particularly P3 (also referred to as P300) has aroused much interest. This is a positive wave that develops about 300–400 msec after the occurrence of an infrequent and unexpected stimulus to which the subject has to respond. In Chapter 10 some of this work will be discussed in relation to attentional dysfunction, but it has also been suggested that the presence of abnormal P3 waves may be of diagnostic value. Squires *et al.* (1980) investigated a wide variety of patient groups and reported that P3 responses were abnormally delayed in some 74 per cent of their patients with dementia, irrespective of its aetiology. In contrast, only 3.5 per cent of their non-demented patients with neurological and psychiatric conditions, including depression, showed such delayed responses. Thus, although sensitive to dementia *per se*, the P3 response appears to lack differential diagnostic potential. Another event-related potential is the contingent negative variation or slow negative component of the electrical waveform that develops in the preparatory interval between a warning stimulus and an imperative stimulus to which some response is required. It has been reported that this is abnormal in patients with DAT (O'Connor, 1981; Tecce, 1983) but, since measurement of this potential requires a high level of patient cooperation, the limits of its differential diagnostic, or indeed prognostic, potential have not been explored.

Neuroimaging

A number of neuroimaging procedures have been developed and applied to patients with dementia-producing conditions. These include X-ray computed tomography (CT), positron emission tomography (PET), single photon emission computed tomography (SPECT) and nuclear magnetic resonance imaging (MRI). In what follows we shall consider briefly how such techniques may contribute to the resolution of diagnostic problems.

CT generates an image of brain structure in terms of the attenuation of X-rays. This procedure can provide evidence of cerebral atrophy, ventricular dilation or indicate the presence of space-occupying lesions. It is in the detection of the latter that CT has proved most useful. The considerable overlap between groups of elderly subjects (normal, depressed and demented), in terms of the degree of atrophy and ventricular dilation found (Jacoby and Levy, 1980), precludes a diagnosis of DAT based on these features alone. Even if areas of infarction are detected a question will remain concerning whether the infarction is causing, contributing to or is irrelevant to the dementia syndrome. Although focal accentuation in frontal and temporal areas might raise the question of Pick's disease, as in the case reported by Wechsler (1977), quite circumscribed cerebral atrophy has been reported in certain histopathologically-verified cases of AD (Tariska, 1970), consistent with the fact that focal symptomatology has sometimes been noted (see Chapter 6). In some cases of hydrocephalus, ventricular dilation may be accompanied by sulcal widening which, when seen on the CT scan, cannot be differentiated from primary cerebral atrophy (Editorial British Medical Journal, 1980).

The advantages of CT scanning, like other neuroimaging procedures, are limited by a number of as yet unresolved methodological problems, some of which will be referred to in subsequent paragraphs. One important factor confounding early CT studies was the essentially subjective nature of the measurements made and the use of overly simplistic rating scales, with the consequent problem of inadequate inter-rater reliability (see Hollander *et al.*, 1986). Various attempts have been made to circumvent this subjective element and thereby increase the diagnostic utility of CT scans, first, by operationalizing the rating systems applied to scan images, but perhaps more importantly by applying quantitative methods at a more fundamental level of data analysis, specifically to the digital CT density data that a scanner yields, rather than applying quantitative analysis only to the familiar CT scan images that are reconstructed from such data. However, comparisons of the CT density values from patients with DAT and control subjects have continued to yield variable results, with some workers finding lower attenuation densities in patients with DAT (e.g. Albert *et al.*, 1986; Bondareff *et al.*, 1981; Naeser *et al.*, 1982), although others have found no significant differences (e.g. Wilson *et al.*, 1982a; Gado *et al.*, 1983) or even increased densities (George *et al.*, 1981). A number of technical factors may have contributed to the variability of these results, including the type of scanner employed and its history of use (see Hollander *et al.*, 1986). It is of interest that one team failed to replicate their own results obtained some 5 years previously despite using the same procedure and the same equipment (see Colgan *et al.*, 1986). It must, therefore, be concluded that in the present state of the art, examination of attenuation densities and removal of the subjective element is not sufficient to mitigate the problems surrounding computed tomography. Achieving consistency regarding head placement (either across subjects or for the same person on different occasions in a longitudinal study) remains a problem for CT scanning, as well as for other neuroimaging procedures. Although studies which have involved serial CT scans (Brinkman *et al.*, 1986: Naguib and Levy, 1982) have found the rate of ventricular enlargement to be greater in groups of patients with DAT, there has been considerable within-group variance. This may reflect individual differences in the rate of neuronal degeneration but inconsistent positioning of subjects may also be a contributing factor.

PET allows for imaging and quantification of the local tissue concentration of injected radioactive tracers, so reflecting the physiological activity and functional status of the brain (Heiss *et al.*, 1986). The technique has been employed most frequently to investigate regional metabolism of glucose and blood flow (both of which are closely linked to neuronal activity). Many studies of patients with DAT have demonstrated an overall reduction in cerebral metabolism, with a further focal accentuation in the temporoparietal region. Later in the course of the degenerative process there may be additional focal attenuation of metabolic activity in the frontal cortex. There is evidence that the distribution of metabolic decline is in keeping with the pattern and magnitude of pathology found at autopsy (see Hollander *et al.*, 1986; Riege and Metter, 1988 for recent reviews). However, not all patients show the same pattern of focal accentuation. Martin *et al.* (1986) found a correspondence between those brain areas in which metabolic activity was particularly diminished and the cognitive deficits shown by patients. They interpreted their data as support for the notion that there are subtypes of DAT. It has been reported that PET can assist in making differential diagnoses among dementia-producing conditions as diverse as AD, multi-infarct dementia, Pick's disease, Parkinson's disease and Huntington's disease, as well as alcoholic dementia and depression (see Hollander *et al.*, 1986; Riege and Metter, 1988). However, it is of interest that one of the major proponents and users of PET has more recently asserted boldly that PET has a limited future as a diagnostic technique in dementia (Benson, 1988), although he continues to advocate its application in addressing novel research questions. Certainly the cost and limited availability of PET scanners precludes their widespread use for diagnostic purposes.

The more recent application of an alternative and cheaper method of neuroimaging which can also yield information about brain metabolism, namely SPECT, represents an important advance. There are now a number of reports that this can be usefully employed to distinguish between patients with various conditions including DAT, multi-infarct dementia and progressive supranuclear palsy (Jagust *et al.*, 1987; Neary *et al.*, 1987; see also Hollander *et al.*, 1986; Riege and Metter, 1988). Application of SPECT to patients with DAT has indicated temporoparietal accentuation of a more general cerebral hypometabolism, a result which corresponds to those obtained from such patients using PET (see above). Nevertheless, the more costly PET procedure continues to offer a number of technical advantages over SPECT (see Di Chiro, 1987) and it therefore appears that this will continue to be the functional imaging procedure of choice at specialized research centres seeking to unravel the mysteries of brain-behaviour relationships, even if not widely available for diagnostic purposes.

MRI provides both anatomical and biochemical information. There are different dependent measures of magnetic resonance from which images can be constructed. From the preliminary data available it would appear that these may serve different purposes. While images constructed from the T2 parameter seem to be particularly useful in distinguishing between DAT and normal ageing (Erkinjuntti *et al.*, 1984; Harrell *et al.*, 1987), analysis of T1 data may prove helpful in differentiating between DAT and multi-infarct dementia and/or Korsakoff's syndrome (Christie *et al.*, 1988). Having made a direct comparison of the relative merits of CT and MRI in patients with dementias of various aetiologies, Johnson *et al.* (1987) concluded that MRI was the method of choice for investigating changes in brain morphology as it proved more sensitive in detecting small areas of tissue damage. Hence it is superior to CT in the identification of small infarcts.

Although these neuroimaging techniques have provided new and exciting avenues through which to explore brain-behaviour relationships, it is important not to be overawed by their technical sophistication. A number of the limitations inherent in such procedures have already been referred to above. Furthermore, all are subject to motion artefact and require a not insignificant degree of cooperation from subjects. Comparative investigations which have employed neuroimaging technology, in common with those which have utilized other investigative procedures, have fallen foul of the problems associated with selection of suitable patient groups and of appropriate control subjects (see Hollander *et al.*, 1986). It must be apparent that many methodolgiocal criticisms can be directed at neuroimaging procedures and, depending upon the level of analysis, these may apply to one or more of the techniques: some are common to all. Indeed, a number of these criticisms are equally applicable to other approaches to neuropsychological investigation, such as those that use electrophysiological or cognitive measures as their independent variables. Hence it goes without saying that one approach cannot be used as a gold standard against which to assess another and when data derived from cognitive assessment instruments purporting to provide diagnostic information have been judged in relation to the data yielded by neuroimaging techniques for the purposes of validation it has been very much a case of assessing the imperfect against the imperfect. Although this unsatisfactory state of affairs does not necessarily preclude the achievement of progress towards increased diagnostic and/or differential diagnostic accuracy it is important to be aware of the inherent tautology.

The potential of techniques that yield information about the metabolic and physiological activity of the brain has not yet been fully exploited. Most studies to date have investigated only resting brain metabolism which may not be predictive of the metabolic response to demands imposed by performance of a task, whether experimental or in the course of everyday living. It is probable that any diminution in metabolic activity would be less apparent in the resting state. However, there is already some evidence that asymmetries in regional hemispheric glucose metabolism in this passive state correspond to the relative severity of naming *vs* visuoconstructive difficulties detected in patients with DAT (Martin *et al.*, 1986). *In vivo* measurement of the level of cerebral activity that accompanies engagement in different types of cognitive activity must afford a tremendous opportunity to enhance understanding of the neural substrates of cognitive processes, and thereby increase diagnostic sensitivity, but this potential has scarcely been probed. Further advances are heralded by the development of analogues which will allow for *in vivo* detection of changes in specific neurotransmitter systems and the effects of drugs upon different receptor types and subtypes (Wagner, 1986).

Cognitive Assessment

We have already referred to some of the conceptual difficulties which have militated against the diagnostic and differential diagnostic utility of psychometric assessments carried out by clinical psychologists over the years. These issues have largely gone unrecognized by the referring medical practitioners, and likewise by the clinical psychologists who attempted to assist in resolution of their diagnostic dilemmas. However, there has been much greater awareness (and staunch criticism) of some of the practical difficulties associated with administration of formally structured and standardized assessment procedures to elderly patients. Examples have included the time required for testing, the complexity of the stimulus materials and the degree of effort and cooperation required from subjects to perform on tasks that often lacked face validity. Readers wishing for an overview of the wide range of psychometric tests that have been employed for diagnostic purposes should consult E. Miller (1977a, 1980) Recognition of the practical difficulties inherent in the application of such tests has led to the development of shortened versions of existing tests or test batteries, such as the WAIS or Wechsler Adult Intelligence Scale (Wechsler, 1955). Many of these have been applied in the quest for diagnostic indicators, although they were not designed for this purpose. In addition, new assessment procedures specifically designed to address diagnostic questions have been introduced, and in some cases subsequently revised (see Kendrick and Moyes, 1979 on the replacement of the arduous Synonym Learning Test with the Object Learning Test in the second edition of a test battery developed for the purpose of distinguishing between depression and dementia in elderly subjects).

In more recent years an important parallel line of developement has been pursued by medical practitioners (as well as some psychologists) who, while becoming increasingly aware of the importance of cognitive impairment in elderly patients, have also recognized the frequent failure by physicians and other health-care personnel to detect such impairment (see DePaulo and Folstein, 1978; Knights and Folstein, 1977; Williamson *et al.*, 1964). It has been acknowledged that the unstructured and unscientific nature of bedside mental status examinations might be one significant factor contributing to this lack of sensitivity. There have been various attempts to incorporate some of the positive elements of the psychometric tradition into mental status examinations so as to arrive at standardized methods of data collection and interpretation and provide quantifiable results. Among the more popular instruments of this type are the Information-Memory-Concentration Test (Blessed *et al.*, 1968), the Mini-Mental State Examination (Folstein *et al.*, 1975), Kahn *et al.*'s (1960) Mental

Status Questionnaire, the Mattis (1976) Dementia Rating Scale, the Cognitive Assessment Scale from the Clifton Assessment Procedures for the Elderly (Pattie and Gilleard, 1979), the Cognitive Capacity Screening Examination (Jacobs *et al.*, 1977) and Pfeiffer's (1975) Short Portable Mental Status Questionnaire. References to such mental status questionnaires and dementia rating scales are abundant throughout the literature on dementia, but details of many of these, plus others, are brought together in Israel *et al.* (1984a,b).

With the upsurge of interest in the dementias that has been seen in the past decade, clinical neuropsychologists have begun to turn their attention to diagnostic issues as well as to the other assessment needs posed by this group of conditions. In pursuing other goals of assessment in patients with dementia (e.g. quantifying levels of impairment and devising measures of change) they have already drawn upon existing knowledge about brain-behaviour relationships and used this, together with their understanding of the models and concepts of cognitive psychology, in order to isolate and measure the component elements and stages of information processing affected by particular dementia-producing conditions (e.g. Corkin *et al.*, 1986). To date they have not on the whole sought to apply a thorough information processing approach to diagnostic problems. Rather, attempts to contribute to the resolution of diagnostic questions have been largely confined to efforts to enhance the information yielded by existing psychometric procedures (e.g. Fuld, 1982, 1984; Perez *et al.*, 1975, 1976) or to administration of a somewhat motley collection of neuropsychological tests, either alone or in combination. Multivariate statistical procedures such as discriminant function analysis are frequently applied to identify which test or group of tests allow for maximal separation of groups (e.g. Eslinger *et al.*, 1985; Storandt *et al.*, 1984).

The net result is that at the present time there is a plethora of instruments available for the purpose of assessing the cognitive status of elderly individuals and thereby making some contribution to the process of screening for dementia. The content and sophistication of these instruments is extremely variable. For example, they range from those which tap a single dimension of cognition to those which are multifactorial, and from what are very brief examinations to those which are more intensive and therefore more protracted. They vary also in degree of standardization and in the extent to which their psychometric properties have been formally established. Although some were intended to address only one of the assessment needs presented by the elderly (e.g. identification of cognitive dysfunction), others were developed with more than one assessment need in view (e.g. detection of poverty or abnormality in level of cognitive performance, rating the severity of cognitive dysfunction and/or measuring change). It is readily apparent from the literature that measures have sometimes been applied rather indiscriminately and applied for, or purported to fulfil, purposes for which they were not designed, without any attempt to engage in the processes of data collection and analysis necessary to validate the procedures in relation to pursuit of the respective goals.

The ideal screening instrument would be one that detected any abnormality in cognitive functioning with high sensitivity (i.e. a high hit rate) but also high specificity (i.e. a low false-positive rate). It would be one that required only a relatively short time for administration and could be administered, scored and the data it yielded interpreted without extensive prior training. These processes could be executed with reliability by different individuals and on more than one occasion if necessary. It would be acceptable to the target population and be insensitive to subject variables such as age, educational and sociocultural factors, or at least embody some adjustment procedure in relation to these. Such an ideal is probably unobtainable and any screeening test procedure will almost inevitably represent the outcome of a series of compromises. No single instrument has yet been designed which is generally considered to be adequately sensitive to mild degrees of impairment or sufficiently discriminating in relation to the broad range of dysfunction encountered in screening across diverse community and institutional settings and in people from different cultural, socioeconomic and educational backgrounds.

There are a number of unresolved and often unrecognized theoretical and conceptual difficulties surrounding efforts to date (over and above those which have already been considered above relating to the definition of dementia and the cognitive deficits which may accompany so-called functional disorders), together with often striking methodological inadequacies, in the construction and validation of screening instruments. In the remaining pages of this chapter we shall seek to highlight some of these difficulties. We shall not attempt to catalogue the tests or procedures already in use for diagnostic purposes but will refer to certain of these for illustrative purposes. Some of the different elements or stages of decision making that may be involved in the process of diagnosis will be used as a framework in pursuing this task. The first of these concerns determination of whether an individual's level of cognitive function is abnormally low and if so a second question arises, namely whether there has been a clinically significant degree of change from the premorbid level of function. Having established that an individual's level of function is below that to be expected from a member of the same cohort, and that there has been deterioration (and provided an acute confusional state or delirium has been excluded), a third question arises concerning whether the impairment pervades sufficient aspects of cognitive, emotional and behavioural functioning to constitute a dementia syndrome (or is such as to render highly probable progression towards this). If dementia is present or apparently looming efforts must then be directed towards differentiation amongst possible causes.

The first question forces us to confront the inadequacy of our theoretical understanding of the normal ageing process (see Kausler, 1982) and the related question of what level of performance should be considered 'normal' for a person of a given age. Interpretation of performance on any cognitive test requires that normative data be available. Unfortunately, many potentially useful measures are lacking in this respect (e.g. many mental status examinations). Even when norms have been established for older subjects the sampling procedures employed have often been less rigorous than in the case of younger age groups. For example, the original standardization sample for the WAIS did not include any subjects over 64 years of age and the same criticism applies to many other tests (e.g. the Wechsler Memory Scale and the Benton Visual Retention Test). Even when normative data have been collected from subjects covering a broader age range the results have often been reported in terms of a broad band elderly category (e.g. the Inglis Paired Associate Learning Test). When data were eventually collected documenting the performance of older subjects on the WAIS the strict selection criteria pertaining to the original sample were not applied. Wechsler's (1981) revision of the WAIS (WAIS-R) represents an improvement on the original scale in that the standardization sample includes individuals aged up to 74 years. However, in view of the rapidly increasing number of 'old' elderly (i.e. over 80 years of age), normative data with an upper age limit of 74 years are less than adequate. Leaving aside the issue of age-appropriate norms there are a number of other questions that remain outstanding concerning the diagnostic contribution of WAIS data (see below).

Although not the only reason for revising a test or test battery, an important spur can and has been recognition that the relevance of normative data can be eroded over time. This process of erosion derives from generational differences in knowledge and performance consequent upon changes in socioeconomic factors such as nutrition, health care and educational experiences (both formal and informal). The magnitude of these cohort effects is well illustrated in the research literature on ageing by the often striking discrepancies between the results of cross-sectional and longitudinal investigations, with age differences typically being more marked in the former (see Kausler, 1982). Cross-sectional studies of the sort employed by Wechsler (1958, 1981) confound age and cohort differences and tend to overestimate the decline in cognitive functioning that occurs as a result of normal ageing.

Criticism in terms of educational and/or sociocultural bias has long been levelled against intensive psychometric assessment procedures such as the WAIS which measure abstract knowledge and reasoning and employ stimulus materials that may be inappropriate given the age and culture of many subjects. However, it has become apparent that similar criticisms are equally pertinent to the more cursory assessments of cognitive performance embodied in more limited tests and indeed in mental status examinations commonly used for screening purposes, both in terms of the selection of test items and the failure to adjust scores according to the level of education (see Anthony *et al.*, 1982; Kittner *et al.*, 1986; Nelson *et al.*, 1986; Ritchie, 1988). Consequently, individuals from deprived backgrounds, those with limited educational attainments and immigrants who do not share the same cultural background tend to underperform. This reminds us of the sensitive issue raised in Chapter 2, namely that those having limited intellectual ability and/or little education are particularly likely to be considered cases of dementia. It emphasizes the importance of establishing that there has been decline and that any deficiency in performance relative to one's peers represents an acquired impairment.

Patients differ considerably in terms of intellectual and behavioural competence at the time of initial contact with would-be assessors so that absolute performance level is of little utility in and of itself. Patient groups consistently perform at a lower level than normal control groups on measures of general intellectual ability but, since increased variability is characteristic of the elderly in general and of patients in the throes of degenerative processes in particular, overlap between groups is to be expected. The net outcome is that despite reliable group differences on a given measure, performance on that measure may not enable useful decision making with respect to individuals. It is important to remember that a measured Intelligence Quotient (IQ) which is normal or even above average does not rule out dementia or a degenerative process any more than low intellectual ability establishes the presence of dementia without evidence of change. This is well illustrated by the first author's data documenting the performance of patients with probable AD and normal control subjects on a wide range of psychometric and experimental measures, including the WAIS: the most widely used measure of general intelligence (see, Hart 1985). However, any attempt to determine whether there has been decline raises a number of difficulties since decline can only be assessed in relation to some antecedent measure and test data from the period preceding presentation are rarely available. Various attempts have been made to devise indirect methods of assessing premorbid level of general intellectual functioning. There has been a long-standing tradition of inferring premordid ability from biographical data concerning educational and occupational attainments. More recently, some effort has been directed towards increasing the reliability of this approach by building regression equations to estimate premorbid IQ from demographic variables known to be related to IQ test performance (Crawford *et al.*, 1989; Wilson *et al.*, 1978). However, IQ levels may differ considerably between subjects falling within a given educational or occupational group and this is particularly true of those in lower occupational strata.

Alternative attempts to devise indirect methods of assessing intellectual decline have been based upon the fundamental premise that some aspects of cognitive functioning are more prone to deterioration than others, whether as a consequence of ageing, disease or injury. A further assumption has been that by comparing performance on measures that are subject to decline and on those that are more resistant, one can arrive at an estimate of the degree of change that has taken place. One popular approach has been to look for differential performance on the subtests of the WAIS. Various indexes have been produced using different combinations of subtest scores, but none has proved particularly successful (see Lezak, 1983). Other clinicians have preferred to look simply at the relationship between Verbal IQ (VIQ) and Performance IQ (PIQ) since a number of studies of patients with dementia have found PIQ to be lower than VIQ (see Miller, 1977a). Attempts have even been made to provide normative data so that the abnormality of a given VIQ-PIQ discrepancy can be assessed. It has been assumed that the verbal subtests of the WAIS, and in particular the Vocabulary subtest (like other measures of vocabulary), can be used to estimate premorbid level of ability but there are problems inherent in this approach. Although vocabulary scores are generally highly correlated with IQ the relationship is not sufficiently strong to prevent appreciable error if IQ is estimated solely on the basis of vocabulary test performance (Yates, 1956). Furthermore, although it is more resistant to decline than some aspects of cognition, vocabulary does not always remain unaffected by cerebral pathology (Hart, 1985). There is also empirical evidence undermining the reliability of VIQ-PIQ discrepancies in favour of VIQ in patients with dementia (Alexander, 1973a; Hart *et al.*, 1986a).

More recently it has been suggested that reading ability might be used to estimate premorbid intelligence (Nelson and McKenna, 1975; Nelson and O'Connell, 1978). Although not without its limitations, the National Adult Reading Test (NART) seems to be particularly useful in this respect (Crawford *et al.*, 1988; Hart *et al.*, 1986a). This test is currently being restandardized in relation to the WAIS-R and attempts are also being made to allow higher premorbid IQ levels to be predicted (Crawford and Nelson, in preparation). This would render the procedure of measuring predicted-obtained IQ discrepancies more sensitive to deterioration in subjects of higher intellectual ability. It is unfortunate, but not surprising in view of the obvious complexity of the task, that no attempt has yet been made to derive objective measures indicative of 'premorbid' competence in specific aspects of cognition such as memory, language or visuoconstructive skills, although tests of such abilities are often employed for diagnostic purposes.

Although progress has been made the search for indirect methods of determining whether intellectual ability has declined from a higher premorbid level has not yet produced wholly satisfactory results. Of course, after the time of initial assessment further decline becomes measureable by direct means and the same will apply to all aspects of cognition. This involves comparison of data obtained on two occasions. However, although apparently a simple exercise, the process of retesting is fraught with technical difficulties. If it is to provide data which are valid, a measure that is used on more than one occasion must have high test-retest reliability or exist in alternate forms, the psychometric equivalence of which has been formally established. Unless a test has high test-retest reliability any inference regarding an alteration in clinical status will only be possible if there has been a large change in score. In seeking to establish adequate test-retest reliability data an investigator must confront a number of significant methodological problems. If normal subjects are to be employed one must ensure that a ceiling effect does not give rise to a spuriously high test-retest reliability coefficient which could be potentially misleading. If patient groups are to be employed the progressive nature of many dementia-producing conditions requires that due consideration be given to the possibility that a genuine change in clinical status may occur over the test-retest interval (which must therefore be short). The more short-term and transitory day-to-day fluctuations that may occur in some patients with dementia constitute another potentially confounding factor that may affect the similarity of (or the discrepancy between) test scores obtained on two or more occasions.

Test-retest reliability data are lacking for many psychometric tests which have a long history of use in relation to diagnostic questions. Even when such data have been established they are often potentially inappropriate since elderly subjects were not employed (e.g. Matarazzo *et al.*'s 1973 test-retest reliability data for the WAIS), although it has not yet been determined that age is an irrelevant factor with respect to the reliability of performance on retesting. Test-retest reliability data have more frequently been collected for the less intensive bedside screening instruments, perhaps because data collection is less time consuming. Of course, if the test is being administered and/or scored by different assessors on the different occasions, it is also necessary to have information regarding inter-rater reliability and most investigators seem to have taken little account of this. The work of Folstein *et al.* (1975) represents a welcome exception.

Given that there is evidence of decline one must determine whether this is sufficiently pervasive to satisfy criteria for a diagnosis of dementia (see Chapter 2). The selection of test items is, therefore, a process of crucial significance and one that presents a number of practical problems. Would-be test constructors must strive to satisfy a number of divergent goals, for example, sampling different aspects of cognition while doing so sufficiently comprehensively to allow for reliable detection of what may be subtle and elusive changes, at least in the early stages, and all this while limiting the time required for administration. Some have attached high priority to limiting the time required for test administration but the result has been screening instruments that probe a restricted range of cognitive domains and/or do so very superficially. Typically items are selected for inclusion in mental status examinations in a somewhat arbitrary manner and without regard to any theory or model of normal cognition or of the mechanisms or course of cognitive decline. Furthermore, results are usually compressed into a single score so that even the rudimentary information that might be available about specific deficits is forfeited and cognition comes to be represented as a unitary function. Alas, the same lack of theoretical direction also limits the potential of some instruments that have sought to examine a single aspect of cognition more intensively. All too often the net result has simply been more items but little increase in the diversity of information yielded. Of course impairment of one aspect of cognition does not warrant a diagnosis of dementia. Nevertheless, information derived from tests that aim to tap specific cognitive functions may enhance the process of diagnostic decision making when combined with data from other sources, including that from tests of different facets of cognition.

Of course the demonstration of acquired impairment across a broad spectrum of cognitive functions does not *ipso facto* justify a diagnosis of dementia. Hence a patient should not be considered demented solely on the basis of a poor score on a mental status test or even on a battery of neuropsychological tests. As already noted a more global approach which takes account of cognitive and non-cognitive aspects of the clinical picture is required. Historical details of the onset and clinical course of deterioration are particularly important for the distinction between delirium and dementia (Lipowski, 1982) and such information is also crucial in the process of differentiating between different dementia-producing conditions. The recent introduction of the CAMDEX (Cambridge Mental Disorders of the Elderly Examination) represents a welcome attempt to standardize the collection, integration and evaluation of the different types of data pertinent to such diagnostic decision-making (see Roth *et al.*, 1986). Administration of the CAMDEX is certainly time consuming, but then the goal of achieving a rapid diagnosis of dementia, while conforming to high standards of accuracy, is probably unrealistic. Likewise, the quest for a measure which permits rapid yet accurate differentiation between the various conditions that may give rise to this clinical syndrome seems foolhardy.

The utility of any diagnostic or differential diagnostic test will be determined by its validity, that is the concordance between what it measures and what it purports to measure and the purity or specificity with which it achieves this. The validity of any measure must be determined with reference to the particular use for which it is intended. A measure which meets one assessment need admirably (e.g. quantifying severity) may not be useful for a different purpose (e.g. diagnosis). Furthermore, validity is not a unitary concept (see Anastasi, 1976) and therefore cannot be reported on in general terms. It is for this reason that various types of validity have been referred to in the literature.

Content validity concerns the nature of the items selected to make up a test or measure and whether they allow for adequate sampling from the cognitive/behavioural domains of interest. However, as already noted, the selection of test items for inclusion in cognitive screening tests has often been arbitrary and the same criticism also applies to a number of more intensive psychometric assessment procedures.

A closely related concept is that of construct validity. This refers to the extent to which a test measures a theoretical construct such as memory or language (or some subcomponent of these more global constructs). In practice, however, test items often tap many aspects of cognition in addition to that intended, whether because of methodological inadequacies or lack of adequate conceptual sophistication. Thus, for example, performance on an instrument such as the Benton Visual Retention Test requires not only memory for abstract shapes but also visuospatial processing and visuoconstructive skills. Poor performance on a test of this type need not reflect a deficit in memory *per se*. Memory is but one aspect of a complex information processing sequence which commences with perceptual analysis of the test stimuli and ends with execution of the graphomotor responses on which the interpretation of performance is based.

Face validity is often referred to in the literature and is an important notion, although it is not validity in the technical sense. It concerns what a test appears to measure rather than what it actually measures and is fundamentally an issue of rapport and public relations. Subjects may underperform (for what are in essence motivational reasons) on a test with low face validity which they perceive to be irrelevant. However, if they are provided with a convincing rationale and/or if tests employ stimulus materials that are age-appropriate then subjects are more likely to cooperate. Face validity will be particularly important in community studies using volunteer populations for the purposes of early detection and epidemiological research.

In developing instruments that screen for dementia the demonstration of external validity is of particular importance. This concerns the extent to which performance on the test instrument corresponds to data yielded by other relevant indexes employed at the same or at some later time (concurrent and predictive validity respectively). The search for suitable external validators presents problems which have yet to be resolved. Diagnostic instruments have often been validated against the judgments of experienced clinicians but these are often inaccurate. Alternatively, the pattern of diagnostic classification produced by the test under construction has been compared with that derived from existing tests, but the outcome is ultimately determined by the diagnostic accuracy of the latter. Others have used physical and/or physiological measures obtained from neuroimaging procedures or measures of brain electrical activity as validating criteria. However, while these may have a validation role in relation to differential diagnostic decisions, they cannot be used as external validators for a diagnosis of dementia which, as a clinical syndrome of cognitive/behavioural impairment, is defined without reference to structural or physiological parameters. Alas, all of the external validators that have been used to date are beset by their own errors of measurement and interpretation with the net result that their diagnostic accuracy is also limited. Attempts to validate new instruments against subjective clinical diagnoses or existing tests may be further confounded by the high degree of tautology that is often inherent in such endeavours.

Spuriously high levels of agreement with an external validator can arise through direct and indirect contamination. The former will arise if the test under construction, or items from it, were administered in the process of diagnostic decision making whereby a subject's criterion status (i.e. patient *vs* control) was determined before proceeding to analyse the correspondence between the test results and this diagnosis. The widespread habit of developing new tests by selecting items from established instruments predisposes to this methodological pitfall. In principle, therefore, it should be possible to avoid direct contamination, but indirect contamination is more subtle and is much more difficult to eliminate. For example, memory impairment is a common feature of dementia and its assessment would be included in any diagnostic examination. If a test instrument being evaluated embodies some assessment of memory, albeit using different items from those employed in arriving at the clinical diagnosis, there may be *a priori* correlation between the test under examination and the criterion against which it is being validated. Consequently a spuriously high impression of validity might result. It is not easy to determine the practical significance of indirect contamination or to conclude unequivocally that it is undesirable.

Many of the problems surrounding external validation of test instruments purporting to enhance diagnostic decision making relate to the selection of subject groups. The patients employed in validation studies are usually individuals in whom the dementing process is well established so that there is little uncertainty surrounding their diagnostic status. Of course, however accurately a test may discriminate between such patients and controls there is no guarantee that it will help resolve the diagnostic questions posed by problematic cases in whom symptoms and signs are more equivocal. Typically, the items included in cognitive tests are those which tap aspects of cognition at a level which is almost certain to be impaired in the later stages of evolution of the clinical syndrome and likewise cut-off points are set so as to maximize separation of control subjects from the unequivocally impaired individuals making up the patient group. It is likely that neither the items selected nor the cut-off scores identified will be appropriate when assessing an individual in whom the clinical symptomatology is more equivocal. Problematic cases of the sort likely to be encountered in day-to-day practice should be included in the validation process, with appropriate follow-up to confirm the provisional diagnosis, but this has seldom been done. Kendrick's inclusion of a 'pseudodementia' group in his early attempts to distinguish between depression and irreversible dementia represents a notable exception (Kendrick, 1972) but he did not include a similar group in his more recent work to revise the battery (Kendrick *et al.*, 1979). The selection of suitable control subjects is also potentially problematic. Their generally healthy status often renders them unrepresentative of that majority of elderly individuals who, although they do not suffer from dementia, may be affected by other neurological, medical or psychiatric conditions.

Little attention has been directed towards estimation of the incremental validity of putative diagnostic instruments, that is the diagnostic utility of the information they yield relative to that available from other sources and therefore the extent to which they enhance the accuracy of decision making. The introduction of a new diagnostic technique can only be justified if it is more accurate than existing methods of diagnosis or if its diagnostic accuracy is approximately equal to that of other methods but it has advantages in terms of patient comfort, time required for administration and/or cost efficiency. One relevant consideration with respect to incremental validity must be the base rate with which a condition occurs in the population being sampled. If this is sufficiently high for a particular condition it may be difficult to demonstrate the detection rate which could be achieved by consideration of the base rate alone. It is unfortunate that base rates have seldom been considered in developing assessment instruments, a noteable exception being the work of Kendrick *et al.* In their efforts to distinguish between depression and other causes of dementia they carried out a Bayesian analysis which incorporated base rate data (e.g. Gibson and Kendrick, 1979). Issues pertaining to incremental validity are illustrated by Branconnier's (1982) discussion of the utility of so-called intrusion errors as a diagnostic marker for DAT. The question of where to set the cut-off point poses a number of problems. Typically cut-off scores are selected so as to maximize the overall correct classification, but these will almost inevitably be imperfect and in setting cut-offs investigators must therefore take account of the consequences for an individual of being falsely assigned to a particular diagnostic category (Type I error) or conversely the consequences of not being so designated when this would be appropriate (Type II error).

Many of the points raised in the foregoing discussion are of crucial significance, not only in relation to development of measures to enhance diagnosis of dementia *per se*, but also *vis a vis* instruments which might be directed at differential diagnosis. To date there have been few attempts to devise cognitive assessment instruments which contribute to the process of differential diagnosis. This neglect has been appropriate given the lack of fundamental knowledge about the cognitive changes brought about by different conditions since differential diagnostic instruments should be based upon such information. However, some investigators have sought to exploit the data yielded by existing psychometric instruments (e.g. the WAIS and the Wechsler Memory Scale) for differential diagnostic purposes. It is not surprising that they have failed to achieve dramatic success (e.g. Aminoff *et al.*, 1975; Gandolfo *et al.*, 1986; Mazzucchi *et al.*, 1987; Perez *et al.*, 1975, 1976, 1978; Whitehead, 1973a). Quantitative differences have emerged but investigators have generally been unable to detect qualitative differences in group performance across the subtests making up these test batteries. Although discriminant function analysis has sometimes allowed for significant separation of patient groups such results are unlikely to be relevant to decision making about individuals. Moreover, such positive findings cannot necessarily be replicated by the same investigators (e.g. Perez *et al.*, 1978) let alone by others working in different centres and therefore with different patient samples. This emphasizes the need for cross-validation studies before making premature claims.

Miller (1977a :109) warned that,' . . . the search for the right Wechsler subtest combination still goes on, rather like the medieval alchemists' search for the philosopher's stone, and with as little likelihood of ultimate success'. The search does indeed go on. For example, Fuld (1982, 1984) presented a profile of WAIS performance which she claimed to be characteristic of cholinergic dysfunction, whether drug-induced or disease-induced, and evidence supporting her position has since been reported by others (Brinkman and Braun, 1984; Satz *et al.*, 1987; Tuokko and Crockett, 1987). However, while Fuld's formula appears to have high specificity, its sensitivity is too low for it to be of much practical use in the diagnosis of DAT (Filley *et al.*, 1987; Hart, 1985).

We believe that the contribution of cognitive assessment to diagnostic and differential diagnostic decision making will only be advanced by the development of tests specifically designed for such purposes. These must be based on knowledge of the nature of the cognitive changes consequent upon different dementia-producing conditions. Investigations directed towards acquiring this understanding will be the subject of Part IV. However, before proceeding further it is worth emphasizing that any skilled and experienced clinical psychologist or clinical neuropsychologist would not rely solely upon the quantitative results of psychometric tests but would combine these with the case history and the clinical impression gained from detailed behavioural observations during interview and test administration in order to arrive at a formulation relevant to the referral questions. The same would, of course, apply to medical practitioners applying mental status examinations.

PART IV

In the next five chapters we shall consider studies that have sought to elucidate the nature of the cognitive and behavioural deficits manifested by patients with dementia-producing conditions. Many of these have employed an experimental or information processing approach as opposed to the largely psychometric orientation of studies considered in Chapter 7. Until comparatively recently experimental research of this type was almost exclusively restricted to the investigation of memory (Chapter 8), but there has been a welcome growth of interest in other apsects of cognition, notably language (Chapter 9), but also attention (Chapter 10), perception (Chapter 11) and praxis (Chapter 12). To date, it has been investigations of memory dysfunction in patients with dementia that have drawn most heavily upon models and theories from cognitive psychology, but there are signs that research into other cognitive domains, in particular language, is developing towards greater theoretical sophistication. However, some areas of research remain relatively atheoretical from the point of view of cognitive models, partly because such models have not been developed. Research into the dementias is, therefore, setting the pace for enquiry into aspects of cognition (such as the processing of olfactory information) that have hitherto been largely neglected by cognitive psychologists (see Chapter 11).

As indicated in Chapter 1, the relationship between cognitive psychology and cognitive neuropsychology is bi-directional. It will become apparent in the chapters to follow (especially Chapter 8) that the study of patients with dementia-producing conditions can yield data with important implications for the models proposed to account for normal cognitive operations.

At the end of Chapter 7 it was indicated that greater understanding of the nature of the cognitive deficits heralded by different dementia-associated conditions should allow for development of more sensitive diagnostic and differential diagnostic instruments. However, developments in understanding or conceptualization of cognitive dysfunction are themselves dependent upon increased diagnostic sophistication. Readers must therefore appreciate that a high level of diagnostic accuracy will be necessary in order to demonstrate subtle differences between aetiologically distinct dementia syndromes. Hence, progress on one front will require parallel advances on the other and issues of diagnosis (and staging) are crucial to the interpretation of data to be reported in the following chapters.

Chapter 8

Memory

Memory impairment is one of the most prominent clinical features of dementia and it is this aspect of cognitive dysfunction more than any other that has been the focus of experimental investigation. Over the years cognitive psychologists have made numerous attempts to fractionate the processes involved in learning and memory for descriptive and heuristic purposes, the net result being a bewildering array of partially overlapping categories and subcategories. Tulving (1987) rightly drew attention to the important question that remains outstanding, namely whether there is any correspondence between these postulated constructs and the neurobiological substrates to which they must ultimately relate.

Research on individuals with memory impairments has already made important contributions to this debate by demonstrating double dissociations between different types of memory impairment following selective damage to specific brain structures (see Chapter 1; Markowitsch and Pritzel, 1985; Weiskrantz, 1987). More recently, evidence has begun to accumulate regarding the selective involvement of particular neurotransmitter systems in certain types of memory function or processing activity. Thus, for example, blockade of the cholinergic system by scopolamine affects some aspects of memory but leaves others intact (Kopelman and Corn, 1988; Nissen *et al.*, 1987). We believe that investigation of patients with dementia will provide further information concerning the nature of memory processes themselves, their interactions with other aspects of cognition and their anatomical and neurochemical substrates.

In order to organize the large body of data already available it seems appropriate to employ as a basic framework the long-standing and all-embracing tripartite distinction between sensory, short-term (or primary) and long-term (or secondary) memory (see Baddeley, 1986). Traditionally it was the structural properties of these hypothetical divisions or stores that were emphasized but over the years the focus of research has shifted away from the stores *per se* to the processes which determine what is stored, how it is stored and the manner in which it is accessed and retrieved in order to be used, either as an end in itself or as an input to some other cognitive operation. This has been exemplified by developments such as the concept of working memory proposed by Baddeley *et al.* in relation to short-term memory (see Baddeley, 1987). In the case of long-term memory this emphasis on processing operations is illustrated by a greater concern with encoding mechanisms at input and retrieval strategies at output, exemplified by the notion of levels of processing (Craik and Lockhart, 1972) and the encoding specificity principle (Tulving and Thompson, 1973). Furthermore, there have been numerous attempts at fractionation within long-term memory with distinctions being proposed between, for example, episodic and semantic memory, declarative *vs* procedural memory and implicit as opposed to explicit memory (see Tulving, 1987). These will be returned to later in this chapter, but before proceeding it is important to emphasize that such developments are essentially elaborations of the traditional three-store model rather than attempts to replace it. Even the levels of processing approach of Craik and Lockhart does not represent the radical alternative it was originally claimed to be since it is primarily concerned with how encoding operations affect the entry of material into long-term memory and the efficiency with which it is retained and retrieved.

In reviewing data pertaining to the memory impairments of patients with dementia we shall once again be concerned for the most part with those afflicted by DAT which, as the most common type of dementia, has been the focus of most research endeavour. We shall include some data obtained from patients whose diagnosis has been the alcoholic Korsakoff syndrome although there is often doubt concerning the cognitive status of such individuals. As previously noted, they may lie anywhere along a continuum from relatively pure amnesia to more generalized cognitive impairment which would warrant the label dementia. Various research groups appear to be sampling from different points along this continuum and consequently, even when comparable experimental paradigms are employed, a critical factor in determining the outcome of one investigation relative to another will be the criteria for selecting subjects. It seems likely that differences in these criteria, such as selection on the basis of functional impairment as opposed to diagnostic category, could account for some of the apparent discrepancies in the literature on amnesia. Similar uncertainties often surround the exact cognitive status of patients with Huntington's and Parkinson's diseases.

Sensory Memory

In research on dementia little attention has been devoted to the modality-specific sensory input buffers that constitute the initial stage of the three-store model. Studies to date have addressed only the visual sensory store (iconic memory). Miller (1977b) used a tachistoscope to present patients with DAT with an array of letters for brief but varying lengths of time, followed immediately by onset of a patterned mask to disrupt any figural after-effects. It emerged that patients required a longer duration of stimulus exposure before they could begin to report any of the letters reliably. Furthermore, at all exposure durations they reported fewer letters than control subjects. Schlotterer *et al.* (1984) confirmed Miller's finding that patients with DAT required a longer duration of exposure in order to identify a stimulus, but demonstrated that this was only true when the mask was patterned and was therefore assumed to exert its effects centrally. When the mask was a homogeneous flash, which only disrupts processing monoptically and therefore peripherally (see Turvey, 1973), patients performed as well as age-matched controls. Although these workers based their conclusion of intact peripheral *vs* impaired central processing on the work of Turvey (1973), their methodology (which involved presentation of stimuli to both eyes simultaneously) was not sufficiently rigorous to allow them to demonstrate conclusively that the masking effect produced by the pattern was indeed central in origin. Nevertheless, Schlotterer *et al.* (1984) went on to suggest that the pattern of results they obtained was consistent with the known distribution of histopathology in AD. They noted that the absence of neurofibrillary tangles (even if not neuritic plaques) in the geniculostriate pathway up to and including area 17, the primary visual cortex, would provide support for their interpretation (see Chapter 11 for a fuller discussion of the supposed integrity or otherwise of the visual system in such patients). The increased susceptibility of patients with DAT to a patterned mask might be consistent with evidence that the secondary or association cortices which mediate higher-order perceptual functions are differentially affected by AD (see Chapter 11).

The results of these studies are in keeping with the notion that DAT may entail impairment at quite an early stage in the processing of incoming information. Few comparable investigations have been carried out using patients with other dementia-associated conditions. However, Butters and Cermak (1980) reported impairment of iconic memory in alcoholic Korsakoff patients. To date echoic memory (the sensory store for auditory information) has been neglected, despite the substantial body of data accrued by cognitive psychologists outlining the properties of the system. Although it is widely assumed that comparable sensory memory systems exist for the other modalities of touch, taste and smell, these have not been investigated experimentally, even in normal subjects.

In their reports all researchers have commented upon the practical difficulties inherent in attempts to investigate the iconic memory of patients with dementia. Such difficulties notwithstanding, there is a need for further research to determine the nature of the deficits that have been documented. A number of factors, or combinations thereof, might account for the deficient performance of patients. These include poor attentional control, perhaps in terms of preparatory processing or selective focusing (see Chapter 10), and more rapid decay of information from iconic memory. The possibility of methodolgical artefact must also be considered. A deficit at a higher level of perceptual/linguistic/mnemonic processing (whereby, for example, a name is attached to the visual stimulus identified as a letter so that it can then be reported as such) could result in a distorted representation of the processing that had taken place at this early stage. It is perhaps worth noting that dysfunction in a sensory memory system is most likely to be identified clinically as a perceptual deficit. As will become apparent in Chapter 11, there is increasing awareness of the importance of sensory and perceptual abilities and deficits in patients with dementia-associated conditions.

Short-term (Primary) Memory

Psychologists use the term short-term memory in a more restricted sense than do members of other disciplines for many of whom it can refer to retention of information over periods of minutes, hours, days or even weeks. In the psychological literature, and in the research to be reported in this section, the term short-term (or primary) memory denotes storage (and manipulation) of small amounts of information for relatively short periods of time (up to about 30 seconds).

Several lines of evidence point to impairments of short-term memory in patients with dementia. These include poor performance on dichotic listening and free recall tasks, decreased memory span for various types of material and more rapid forgetting. After presenting some relevant data we shall report on attempts to go beyond mere documentation of impairment and elucidate the nature of the short-term memory deficits reported.

Amongst the first reports of experimental investigations into the short-term memory of patients with probable dementia were those of Inglis *et al.* (see Inglis, 1958, 1970) who used a dichotic listening paradigm. When separate lists of up to three digits each were presented simultaneously (one to each ear) before subjects engaged in immediate recall patients performed as well as control subjects with respect to the list reported first, although differences did emerge for longer lists. However, they performed very poorly in recalling items from the list reported second, irrespective of its length. In accordance with the models in vogue amongst cognitive psychologists of the time (Broadbent, 1958), these workers considered that recall of the second list represented output from a short-term memory store, and therefore interpreted their findings as evidence that patients' short-term memory was impaired. However, other interpretations are possible. For example, Craik (1977) suggested that the differential recall of information presented on the two channels in a dichotic listening task might reflect differences in the attentional resources directed towards each and/or the perceptual processing carried out.

Reductions in the digit span of patients with dementia have been reported by some workers (Kaszniak *et al.*, 1979; Kopelman, 1985; Larner, 1977; Morris, 1987b; Nebes *et al.*, 1984), but not by others (Caird and Hannah, 1964; Crook *et al.*, 1980; Weingartner *et al.*, 1981; Whitehead, 1973a). It seems likely that differences in aetiology and/or diagnostic criteria might be one factor contributing to such discrepancies in the literature. Another factor is likely to be differences in the severity of dementia in the subjects studied and longitudinal studies have demonstrated that this is indeed an important determinant of the results obtained. Hart (1985) found forward digit span to be unimpaired in patients with mild-to-moderate DAT, although backward span was reduced, but as the degenerative process continued forward span too came to be reduced. Similar longitudinal data have been reported by Botwinick *et al.* (1986). It is hardly surprising that backward span or recall of digits in reverse order should prove a more sensitive measure of short-term memory impairment. Performance on this task requires that subjects not only hold but also manipulate information so that backward span places a heavier load upon short-term working memory (see below). Digit span is also impaired in patients with Huntington's disease (Cantone *et al.*, 1978; Orsini *et al.*, 1987) and indeed in children at-risk for this condition (Catona *et al.*, 1985). It is unimpaired, or only mildly decreased, in patients with Korsakoff's syndrome (Kopelman, 1985) and likewise in those with progressive supranuclear palsy or Parkinson's disease (Huber *et al.*, 1986; Orsini *et al.*, 1987; Pirozzolo *et al.*, 1982), even when the parkinsonian patients have identified dementia (Huber *et al.*, 1986). In patients with DAT the span for recall of letters and of words is also reduced (Corkin, 1982; Miller, 1973; Morris, 1984). Block span is likewise reduced in patients with DAT (Cantone *et al.*, 1978; Corkin, 1982) and comparative investigations have indicated that patients with Huntington's disease, progressive supranuclear palsy and Parkinson's disease demonstrate smaller reductions on this measure of non-verbal memory capacity than do those with DAT (Cantone *et al.*, 1978; Orsini *et al.*, 1987). Indeed Morris *et al.* (1988a) failed to find a reduction in block span in their parkinsonian patients but procedural differences may account for this discrepancy. These workers (unlike other investigators) employed a computerized version of the test.

Turning to free recall, Miller (1971) investigated serial position effects in the free recall of patients with DAT and reported reductions in both the primacy and recency effects, i.e. the tendency for subjects to show differential recall of items at the beginning and end of a list. Following Glanzer and Cunitz (1966) the recency effect has traditionally been construed as a measure of short-term memory and Miller (1971), therefore, concluded that this was deficient in patients with DAT. However, Baddeley and Hitch (1977) have raised questions concerning the theoretical interpretation of recency effects in free recall as the output from a short-term memory store. Furthermore, in relation to patients with dementia, results pertaining to the recency effect have been inconsistent. Gibson (1981) failed to replicate Miller's finding of a reduced recency effect and Harris and Dowson (1982) only found it to be reduced in more severely impaired subjects. However, both of these studies confirmed Miller's finding of a reduction in the primacy effect or long-term memory component of the serial position curve. Certain investigators have chosen to analyse free recall performance according to the method of Tulving and Colotla (1970). A word retrieved with only six or fewer stimulus presentations or recall productions intervening between presentation and recall of that particular item was assumed to be retrieved from primary memory. All other words recalled were considered to represent output from secondary memory. Both Martin *et al.* (1985) and Wilson *et al.* (1983) reported moderate impairment of primary or short-term memory, as well as deficits in long-term or secondary memory. Moreover, Wilson *et al.* (1983) reported that, although independent in control subjects, performance on the short-term and long-term memory components were significantly correlated in their patient group. They, therefore, suggested that the secondary memory deficit of patients with DAT might be due in part to impairment of primary memory.

The questions of diagnostic homogeneity and severity of impairment already raised in relation to memory span also apply to reports concerning the short-term component(s) of free recall performance. There is little mention in the literature of the performance of patients in whom other dementia-associated conditions have been explicitly diagnosed. However, Della Sala *et al.* (1987a) reported that patients with Parkinson's disease show a normal recency effect. This has also been documented for patients with the alcoholic Korsakoff syndrome (Baddeley and Warrington, 1970; Cermak *et al.*, 1976), although Cermak *et al.*'s (1976) data suggest that the effect may operate over a smaller number of items, possibly implying more rapid loss of information. This brings us to the next point of consideration in relation to the short-term memory of patients with dementia.

Thus far the data presented have been concerned with estimating the capacity of short-term memory but another important parameter is the rate at which information is lost. Attempts to measure the rate at which information is lost from short-term memory have employed the Brown–Peterson distractor paradigm or various tasks hitherto used to investigate memory in non-human primates.

The Brown–Peterson distractor paradigm requires subjects to retain information for variable periods of time while simultaneously performing a distractor task to prevent rehearsal. When assessed using this procedure the performance of patients with DAT is significantly impaired (Corkin, 1982; Kopelman, 1985; Morris, 1986). Patients with Parkinson's disease (Tweedy *et al.*, 1982) and with Huntington's disease (Butters *et al.*, 1986) also perform poorly, as do those with the alcoholic Korsakoff syndrome (Butters *et al.*, 1986). However, Kopelman (1985) reported that Korsakoff patients were less severely impaired than those with DAT. It is important to be aware of Baddeley's (1986) cautionary note concerning the interpretation of results obtained using the Brown–Peterson paradigm and to recognize that poor performance does not necessarily reflect a faster rate of decay of information held in short-term memory.

Patients with DAT show delay-dependent deficits when assessed using the delayed matching-to-sample and delayed non-matching-to-sample tasks originally devised to investigate memory in non-human primates. These two paradigms require that subjects retain a representation of presented stimuli so that they can subsequently discriminate between items which have been shown previously and those that are novel when they are confronted with an array of stimuli after brief but varying time intervals. Patients with DAT also show time-dependent deficits on delayed response procedures in which presentation of stimuli and the opportunity to respond is separated by a retention interval (Flicker *et al.*, 1984; Freedman and Oscar-Berman, 1986; Irle *et al.*, 1987; Sahakian *et al.*, 1988). Patients with Parkinson's disease also show impairment on such tasks (Freedman and Oscar-Berman 1986; Sahakian *et al.*, 1988), but on delayed matching-to-sample (i.e. selecting from an array the stimulus which was presented a short time before) the performance deficit of parkinsonian patients is independent of the duration of the delay interval. Thus they perform poorly even when there is no delay, so that the task is reduced to one of simultaneous matching without a memory component. This would imply some perceptual and/or attentional impairment (Sahakian *et al.*, 1988). Alcoholic Korsakoff patients also show deficits when assessed using delayed response procedures adapted from primate research (e.g. Kessler *et al.*, 1986).

The literature reviewed above documents deficits in the performance of patients with some dementia-associated conditions on a number of tasks and points to reduction in the capacity of and/or rapid loss of information from short-term memory. We now turn attention to research which has been directed towards establishing what factors affect performance on the respective tasks and ultimately determining the nature of those deficits.

The contribution of proactive interference to the poor performance of patients on the Brown–Peterson procedure has been examined. In a comparative study Butters *et al.* (1979) found differences in the types of error made by patients with Huntington's disease and the alcoholic Korsakoff syndrome respectively, although their overall level of performance was comparable. Amnesic Korsakoff patients made many prior-list intrusion errors (i.e. their erroneous responses were often stimuli which had been employed on previous trials) and their error rate increased under conditions designed to increase proactive interference, namely massed presentation of stimuli. Performance improved following a procedural manipulation designed to reduce the build-up of proactive interference, namely repeatedly alternating the nature of the stimulus material between consonant and word trigrams. In contrast, the errors made by patients with Huntington's disease were typically non-list intrusions and these did not vary in response to procedural changes that affected the performance of alcoholic Korsakoff patients. However, in a more recent study, Beatty and Butters (1986) have demonstrated that patients with Huntington's disease do show release from proactive interference on the Brown–Peterson paradigm under certain circumstances, specifically when the stimuli are word triads and there is a shift in the semantic category of the words from trial to trial. It has been reported that, relative to control subjects, individuals with Parkinson's disease show less release from proactive interference on this paradigm (Tweedy *et al.*, 1982). The role of proactive interference in the poor performance of patients with DAT on this task has yet to be examined.

Of course proactive interference is but one of the factors that might account for forgetting of material held in short-term memory as indexed by performance on the Brown–Peterson paradigm. Over the years cognitive psychologists have directed attention to other possible mechanisms including simple trace decay, displacement and interference between material to be remembered and that presented in relation to the distractor task. On considering the results of studies in which the nature of the distractor tasks differed, Morris (1986) suggested that forgetting on the Brown–Peterson paradigm could be interpreted in terms of the working memory model. This model (see Baddeley, 1987) comprises a number of subsystems including a passive auditory-verbal or phonological input store and an articulatory rehearsal mechanism, together with an equivalent system for visuospatial information, referred to as the visuospatial scratchpad. These various subsystems are all coordinated by another, namely the central executive. This central processor determines the allocation or distribution of the limited processing resources or attentional capacity available to an individual. Although there is considerable consensus of opinion regarding the active role of short-term memory as a system which utilizes processing resources cognitive psychologists are not necessarily agreed as to whether it is a unitary system or one that comprises multiple subsystems, as Baddeley *et al.* suggest. They may also disagree about whether it, or the subsystem concerned with allocation of resources, should be construed primarily as a memory or as an attentional system. All of course recognize the interplay between different cognitive operations, however they are labelled.

Using the working memory model as a theoretical framework for research on patients with DAT, Morris (1986) hypothesized that a reduction in the resources available to the central executive could account for their poor performance when assessed using the Brown–Peterson paradigm. In effect, when subjects engaged in the performance of a distractor task there would be insufficient residual capacity to allow for effective maintainance rehearsal of stimuli that were to be recalled subsequently. Morris (1986) varied the complexity (and hence the processing demands) of distractor tasks and demonstrated that this affected the short-term retention of patients with DAT, although none of the secondary tasks employed affected the recall of control subjects. Similarly, results obtained by Baddeley *et al.* (1986) from patients with DAT under a variety of dual processing conditions pointed to a deficiency in the central executive.

Morris (1984) examined the functioning of other components of the working memory model in patients with DAT, namely the passive phonological store and the articulatory loop. He investigated the effects of phonological similarity on recall accuracy using lists of acoustically similar and dissimilar letters. Although their overall level of functioning was substantially lower than that of age-matched control subjects, patients with DAT demonstrated an equally marked reduction in immediate recall when phonological similarity was increased. This suggested that the passive phonological store was functioning normally. Such results are at odds with the earlier report of Miller (1972) that patients with DAT were less sensitive than normal control subjects to the phonological properties of words. However, Miller's results were confounded by a floor effect and Morris (1984) avoided this by employing a span procedure as opposed to Miller's use of longer lists of constant length.

Morris (1984) also examined the articulatory loop in patients with DAT by measuring memory span for long and short words. The so-called word-length effect (i.e. longer memory span for short words) was as strong in the patients as in control subjects and concurrent articulation suppressed the effect of word length to a similar extent in both groups. It was therefore concluded that the articulatory loop system was relatively intact in patients with DAT. Additional supportive evidence was obtained in subsequent studies demonstrating that patients with DAT could rehearse at a normal rate and that concurrent articulation reduced memory span to a comparable extent in patients and control subjects (Morris, 1987b,c).

Application of the working memory model to the short-term memory deficits of patients with DAT represents an interesting example of the heuristic value of models of cognitive function derived from experimental investigations of normal subjects when used to analyse the deficits of patients suffering from memory impairment. The suggestion that the deficit in short-term memory shown by patients with DAT can be attributed to the central executive component of the working memory system is particularly thought-provoking. A reduction in processing capacity, and/or in the efficiency with which the central executive distributes this across the other subsystems and the functional operations they sustain, can of course be construed as an attentional deficit. This is consistent with other evidence to be reviewed in Chapter 10 and with growing recognition of the importance of attentional processes in memory, as exemplified by the distinction between automatic and effortful processing (Hasher and Zacks, 1979) which will be taken up below. As yet few attempts have been made to examine the memory deficits of other patient groups within the framework of the working memory model but Della Sala *et al.* (1987a) invoked the model retrospectively in relation to research on patients with Parkinson's disease and suggested that the central executive was defective. However, Morris *et al.*'s (1988a) data suggest that the visuospatial scratchpad may be spared in patients with Parkinson's disease, at least in those considered to be without dementia. Litvan *et al.* (1988) demonstrated that the articulatory loop was deficient in memory-impaired individuals with multiple sclerosis. This study is of some interest because, although the patients they investigated did not have dementia, multiple sclerosis is another condition that can give rise to a dementia syndrome.

In summary, patients with dementia-associated conditions show impairments on a variety of tasks designed to look at different aspects of short-term memory. The extent of these deficits is generally related to the overall severity of the clinical condition. There remains a need for further research into the underlying nature of these deficits, as well as for explorations of hitherto neglected aspects of short-term memory. The visuospatial scratchpad component of the working memory model merits further attention as the evidence of reduced block span and impaired performance on delayed matching-to-sample tasks cited above would give grounds for suspicion that this too might be impaired, at least in some patients. There is also a need for further comparative studies of patients whose dementia syndromes arise out of different aetiologies.

Long-term (Secondary) Memory

The abundant clinical descriptions of memory impairment in patients with dementia, as documented in Chapter 6, generally refer to what would be considered secondary or long-term memory in the terminology of cognitive psychology. This memory system is concerned with recall of information that has been stored for any period in excess of approximately 30 seconds (in the absence of continuous rehearsal) and hence it encompasses material from both the very recent and the remote past.

Examinations of the efficiency of retrieval of list items as a function of their serial position at presentation and recall have revealed not only poor recall from short-term memory but also deficient retrieval of information supposedly held in secondary or long-term memory. Such evidence of impairment of long-term memory has been documented in relation to patients with the alcoholic Korsakoff syndrome (see Butters and Cermak, 1980) and with Parkinson's disease (Della Sala *et al.*, 1987a), as well as those with DAT (Gibson, 1981; Harris and Dowson, 1982; Martin *et al.*, 1985; Miller, 1971; Wilson *et al.*, 1983). Of course, while documenting the impairment(s) heralded by different dementia-producing conditions is an important first step, the real challenge must lie in proceeding to devise experimental procedures that will yield explanatory information.

In their efforts to account for the deficient performance of patients with dementia many researchers have sought to attribute deficits to one or more of the stages involved in acquiring, storing and later retrieving information. However, while conceptually distinct, these three stages are not in fact independent. Evidence has been marshalled to show that the durability of storage is related to the encoding processes carried out at the time of acquisition (Craik and Lockhart, 1972) and that optimal retrieval occurs when the recall strategy adopted is consistent with that employed during acquisition (Tulving and Thompson, 1973). Furthermore, since acquisition and retention cannot be measured directly they must be inferred from the efficiency with which information is retrieved. Squire (1980) presented an interesting appraisal of the debate concerning the implications of different deficits in performance on memory tests for the integrity of operations at particular stages of information processing. He rightly emphasized (Squire, 1980: 370) that 'much of the argument is semantic' and that the choice of terms used (e.g. acquisition, encoding, storage, consolidation, retrieval) 'seems to turn as much on personal preference as on empirical evidence'. These difficulties notwithstanding the text that follows shall be organized in terms of headings that denote different stages of information processing and we shall attempt to avoid repetition although the same data are often relevant to more than one stage and therefore could be presented in different places.

Acquisition

Cognitive psychologists have now amassed a large body of evidence concerning the many procedural variables that affect the ease with which lists of items can be learned. These include rate of presentation, the relationship between items comprising a list, whether the items are pictures or words and in the case of words properties such as their frequency of occurrence, imagery ratings and the concreteness of their lexical referents (see Morris, 1978). A number of investigations have been carried out to assess the sensitivity of patients with dementia to these variables, with abnormal encoding being inferred when this is altered.

Having demonstrated a significantly reduced primacy effect in the recall protocols of patients with DAT, Miller (1971) proposed that the inferred long-term memory deficit was due to inefficient transfer of information from short-term memory. His hypothesis was consistent with the then current belief that information entering long-term memory must necessarily have passed through short-term memory. However, when Miller (1971) slowed the rate at which items were presented to allow for more effective transfer of material from short-term into long-term memory recall performance was not enhanced. In a subsequent investigation Miller (1973) demonstrated that supraspan learning was impaired in patients with DAT and again interpreted this as evidence of an acquisition deficit.

Young adults recall pictures better than words and concrete words are recalled more readily than abstract words for which it is more difficult to evoke visual images. Rissenberg and Glanzer (1986) reported that the superior recall of pictures over words declined in the course of normal ageing and was further diminished by DAT. In a subsequent study these workers (Rissenberg and Glanzer, 1987) found that the discrepancy between superior recall of concrete words and less efficient retrieval of abstract words also became less marked in the course of normal ageing, but the performance of patients with DAT was contrary to expectation. They showed a differential recall effect comparable to that exhibited by young normal subjects. However, Rissenberg and Glanzer (1987) considered their surprising results to be an artefact of the word finding difficulties of patients with DAT (in whom retrieval of abstract words is particularly impaired), rather than an alteration in encoding processes *per se*.

Although recognition memory is the subject of a later section it is worth noting here that the first author's data from patients with mild-to-moderate DAT assessed on a continuous recognition paradigm would also be consistent with the notion that such patients are not particularly sensitive to the imagery values of words. Neither hit nor false-positive rates were affected by manipulations of this variable (Hart *et al.*, 1985). Conflicting results have emerged from investigations of the effects of word imagery ratings upon the recall performance of patients with Huntington's disease. While Weingartner *et al.* (1979) failed to detect a significant effect of word imagery, Beatty and Butters (1986) demonstrated that their sample of patients with Huntington's disease showed better recall of high as opposed to low imagery words. Clearly, further research is necessary to determine the extent to which patients with these and other degenerative conditions can exploit the potential for enriched encoding afforded by high imagery words and incorporate the visual as well as the verbal properties of stimulus material to be learned.

In their efforts to understand the nature of the memory deficits exhibited by patients with dementia a number of researchers have drawn upon the levels of processing framework of Craik and Lockhart (1972). At the heart of this framework lies the notion that formation of memory traces is essentially a by-product of the various encoding operations and analyses carried out upon incoming information for the primary purposes of perception and comprehension. Different ways of analysing information have been viewed as lying on a continuum from 'shallow' to 'deep', with shallow levels of analysis being essentially structural (i.e. concerned with sensory and physical aspects of stimuli) whereas deeper levels involve more abstract, semantic and associative processing. Craik and Lockhart suggested that deeper semantic processing led to stronger and more durable memory traces but it is now recognized that 'depth' is not the sole determinant of memory performance, with a major role being assigned to the concept of 'elaboration'. While depth refers to the qualitative type of analysis, elaboration refers to the extensiveness or richness of processing carried out at any given depth. Materials processed in a deep and elaborate manner are more likely to give rise to distinctive, and therefore more discriminable, encodings, resulting in better recall and recognition. However, such processing requires greater effort or attention (Eysenck and Eysenck, 1979; Griffith, 1976) in the sense of amount of processing resources necessary for performance of the task (Kahneman, 1973). The original levels of processing ideas dealt exclusively with encoding at input but, in the light of subsequent research findings (Fisher and Craik, 1977; Kolers, 1973; Tulving and Thomson, 1973), they were extended to encompass retrieval. The encoding specificity principle (Tulving and Thomson, 1973), according to which retrieval operations must be compatible with the initial encoding operations for efficient recall to occur, has come to assume an important place in subsequent thinking.

The levels of processing approach with its emphasis on control processes is an attractive framework within which to approach the question of memory impairment in patients with dementia. In view of the neuropathological and neurochemical changes that accompany dementia-associated conditions it is reasonable to suppose that the processing resources of afflicted patients would be reduced relative to those of their healthy peers. However, the question remains as to whether there is optimal allocation of the resources that remain available. If this is not the case a suitable orientation procedure might serve to focus available resources leading to deeper and more elaborative processing, and hence better retention, with obvious practical implications for attempts at rehabilitation and management.

There are in the literature reports of a number of studies of patients with DAT, Huntington's disease and the Korsakoff syndrome which have implications for encoding deficit hypotheses concerning their memory dysfunction. Data from patients with Huntington's disease will not be considered further in this section as these have, almost without exception, been construed as evidence of a retrieval deficit and will therefore be dealt with below. As for patients with the Korsakoff syndrome (diagnostic questions concerning whether dementia is present notwithstanding) the consensus of opinion is that such patients tend not to engage spontaneously in deeper levels of processing, but are able to do so when presented with tasks designed to elicit this. Such procedures do not inevitably result in improved performance during memory testing, although there has been some alleviation of memory impairment in certain circumstances (e.g. Biber *et al.*, 1981). Readers wishing to learn more about studies of Korsakoff patients which have sought to determine whether their memory disorder could be attributed to inadequate processing of information should consult reviews by Cermak (1979, 1982) and Hirst (1982).

Miller's (1975) study of patients with DAT is relevant to the question of whether the encoding operations carried out by such patients are deficient, although this study was designed to test a retrieval deficit rather than an encoding deficit hypothesis (drawing upon the work of Warrington and Weiskrantz, 1970) and was interpreted as confirmation of the former. It was found that recall cues (in the form of the first three letters of each list item) were of no benefit to control subjects but improved the performance of patients with DAT so as to render between-group differences statistically non-significant. Other studies in which letter cues were employed have yielded similar results (Davis and Mumford, 1984; Hart, 1985; Morris *et al.*, 1983). Interpreted in terms of the encoding specificity principle, these data suggest that patients with DAT spontaneously employ only a superficial encoding strategy at the time of acquisition. This notion would be consistent with Weingartner *et al.*'s (1981) finding that such patients differed from control subjects in that they did not recall categorized word lists any better than lists of unrelated items. Retrieval will be the subject of a later section of this chapter but it is worth noting here that the findings just reported imply a mismatch between the retrieval strategy adopted spontaneously by patients with DAT and the cognitive strategy they employed at the time of acquisition.

Even if it is indeed the case that patients with DAT do not spontaneously engage in deep and elaborative processing, questions remain concerning whether they can be induced to do so and, if so, whether this will result in improved recall performance. A

147

number of investigators (Corkin, 1982; Diesfeldt, 1984; Hart, 1985; Martin *et al.*, 1985; Wilson *et al.*, 1982b) have required patients to engage in orienting tasks designed to elicit processing at particular depths, but in only one of these studies (Martin *et al.*, 1985) did a deep processing manipulation independently produce beneficial effects on free recall. This fairly consistent finding of no enhancement of recall following orientating procedures designed to promote deep processing cannot be attributed to an inability to carry out deep semantic processing. The first author found that patients with mild-to-moderate DAT had no difficulty in deciding whether stimulus items belonged to specific semantic categories. Indeed, they sometimes spontaneously elaborated their responses by providing additional information which was relevant and appropriate, even if unnecessary (Hart, 1985). In one of the few studies that has investigated memory in patients with depression (as opposed to normal subjects who have undergone a mood induction procedure), Weingartner (1986) found that carrying out an 'effortful' orientating procedure that placed heavy demands upon attentional resources actually impaired the subsequent free recall performance of depressed patients. Taken together, these results lend further support to the view that although an important prerequisite in most circumstances, deep semantic processing at the time of acquisition is not necessarily sufficient to ensure good recall performance (see Baddeley, 1978; Craik, 1979; Tulving, 1979). The question remains as to why the semantic orienting procedures employed in the studies reviewed above (Corkin, 1982; Diesfeldt, 1984; Hart 1985; Martin *et al.*, 1985) failed to enhance free recall. One explanation might be that patients did not spontaneously initiate a retrieval strategy that was consistent with their initial encoding of the material. If so it might be possible to enhance recall performance selectively by providing retrieval cues compatible with those prevailing at the time of encoding. This issue will be considered below in the section on retrieval, but before turning to this third stage of information processing we shall overview the small amount of data relevant to the second stage, namely storage.

Storage

The extent to which information stored in long-term memory is lost with the passage of time has been investigated by comparing recall at different intervals after initial learning. There have been a number of investigations of this type examining the performance of patients with various clinical conditions and the results have given rise to a distinction between 'temporal' and 'diencephalic' amnesic syndromes (see Markowitsch and Pritzel, 1985; Squire, 1987). It has been asserted that the former, which are produced by damage to the temporal lobe itself and/or to proximal structures such as the hippocampus and amygdala, or by ECT (which is presumed to disrupt the normal processing activities of these structures), are characterized by abnormally rapid forgetting (Huppert and Piercy, 1978, 1979; Squire 1981). In contrast, individuals, such as those with Korsakoff's syndrome or with Huntington's disease, in whom pathology affects predominantly diencephalic structures (see Chapter 3), show normal rates of forgetting (Corkin *et al.*, 1984; Huppert and Piercy, 1978; Kopelman, 1985; Martone *et al.*, 1986).

Studies of patients with DAT, in whom there is typically damage to both temporal and diencephalic structures, have yielded contradictory results. While Hart (1985) and Moss *et al.* (1986) reported abnormally rapid forgetting of prose passages and word lists, other investigators who employed similar verbal materials and/or pictorial stimuli have failed to do so (Becker *et al.*, 1987; Corkin *et al.*, 1984; Kopelman, 1985; Martone *et al.*, 1986). However, Hart (R. P.) *et al.*'s (1988) results are consistent with both outcomes in that their patients with DAT showed accelerated forgetting during the first 10 minutes of retention, but normal rates of loss thereafter. In certain of the investigations referred to above (Corkin *et al.*, 1984; Kopelman, 1985; Martone *et al.*, 1986) it would not have been possible to detect an accelerated rate of forgetting in the initial stages of retention as measurement only commenced 10 minutes after acquisition. In these studies the investigators manipulated the duration of stimulus exposure differentially during training so as to equate levels of performance 10 minutes after stimulus presentation. There is clearly a need for further research to determine more precisely the circumstances under which patients with DAT show abnormally rapid forgetting and to specify in detail the conditions that promote a normal degree of stability in the pattern of retention. Such studies must take account of the fact that comparisons of rate of decline will, for the most part, only be justified when they are made between subjects who have been matched in terms of the amount of information initially acquired or in terms of the information held at some point in the course of forgetting, although the second alternative would be methodologically less sound. Some of the issues relevant to problems posed by comparative research of this type are considered by Woods and Piercy (1974).

Retrieval

Although availability in store is a necessary prerequiste for subsequent retrieval of information it is not a sufficient one. The contents of memory must also be accessible. In the following paragraphs we shall review the results of studies examining the efficiency with which patients with dementia-producing conditions can recover from memory items that are indeed held in store. In so doing we shall concentrate upon four major topics: (1) the phenomenon of intrusion errors, (2) the effects of providing retrieval cues, (3) performance on recognition tasks, and (4) retrieval of information that has been held in store for long periods of time and has, therefore, been referred to as remote memory.

Intrusion errors. Much of the current interest in intrusion errors, which may be considered instances of inappropriate retrieval, can be traced to the report of Fuld *et al.* (1982) that patients with DAT made such errors (defined as the inappropriate recurrence of a response, or type of response, from a preceding test item, test or procedure) during the course of neuropsychological assessment. These workers distinguished between intrusion errors and the more general phenomenon of response perseveration known to occur in patients with many kinds of brain damage, including dementia-producing conditions (Freeman and Gathercole, 1966). As noted in Chapter 7, Fuld *et al.* (1982) proposed that such errors were of diagnostic significance, but this view has been disputed by subsequent workers (Branconnier, 1982; Shindler *et al.*, 1984). Fuld *et al.* (1982) also reported evidence suggesting that intrusion errors were related to cholinergic dysfunction. The results of an earlier study by Smith and Swash (1979) of a single patient with biopsy-proven AD provide tentative support for Fuld *et al.*'s hypothesis concerning cholinergic mediation of this phenomenon in that some 80 per cent of the errors made by this man when learning successive word lists were items that had been included in previous lists. When treated with the anticholinesterase drug physostigmine he made fewer intrusion errors, but there was no increase in the number of words recalled correctly. However, Thal *et al.* (1983) subsequently reported improvement in total recall and retrieval from long-term memory as well as a decrease in the number of intrusion errors, following administration of physostigmine to enhance cholingeric function.

There remain a number of unresolved issues concerning the phenomenon of so-called intrusion errors in the responses of patients with DAT, or indeed other types of dementia. Questions that remain to be addressed include the proportion of patients who make such errors and, for a given individual, their absolute and relative frequency of occurrence, as well as the circumstances under which they occur. Miller's (1978) investigation of patients with DAT, which was designed to test the more general disinhibition hypothesis of retrieval dysfunction, is relevant to certain of these issues. This study involved single presentations of 20 consecutive lists, each followed immediately by free recall. Patients with DAT not only made fewer correct responses but fewer responses overall than control subjects. They also made fewer intrusion errors in absolute terms but such errors constituted a higher proportion of their total responses than was true of control subjects. Unfortunately, Miller (1978) did not specify whether he considered only prior-list errors or whether his intrusion category included extra-list errors. The latter have also been referred to as random errors and have been documented as a prominent feature of the response protocols of patients with dementia (e.g. Whitehead, 1973b). The distinction between prior list and extra-list commission errors is important since only prior-list intrusion errors indicate adequate registration and maintenance of information that is subsequently retrieved inappropriately.

In a study designed to elicit information about the conditions under which prior-

and extra-list intrusions occurred, Hart (1985) found that although patients with DAT made more intrusion errors (prior- and extra-list combined) than controls, the difference was not statistically significant. However, intrusion errors constituted a significantly greater proportion of their total responses, a result that probably amounts to a replication of Miller's (1978) finding. Both groups made more prior-list intrusion errors under a test condition that was designed to increase the probabilty of proactive interference (presenting successive lists one after another, as opposed to separating them by 10–15 minutes occupied by other activities) but there was little evidence that patients with DAT exhibited a marked propensity towards errors of this subtype. Similar conclusions can be drawn from the study of Wilson *et al.* (1983) and from another study in which the first author used pictorial stimuli (Hart *et al.*, 1986b). However, it is important to note the data of Butters *et al.* (1987). In a comparative study involving patients with DAT, Huntington's disease and the alcoholic Korsakoff syndrome they assessed recall of short prose passages. They concluded that the occurrence of large numbers of prior-story and extra-story intrusions may be an important characteristic of patients with DAT and, to a lesser extent, those with an alcoholic Korsakoff syndrome. In contrast, patients with Huntington's disease made few such errors.

It has been suggested that the frequency of intrusion errors should be employed as a dependent variable in therapeutic trials involving patients with DAT (Brinkman and Gershon, 1983). However, in the present state of ignorance and confusion concerning their nature and the circumstances that promote their occurrence, caution must be exercised in interpreting any findings relating to such errors. This is especially so since high levels of intrusion errors may only be characteristic of a small minority of patients with DAT (Hart, 1985).

Cueing. We have already noted in our discussion of encoding processes that patients with DAT consistently retrieve information more efficiently when provided with letter cues (Davis and Mumford, 1984; Hart, 1985; Miller, 1975; Morris *et al.*, 1983). Investigations of semantic cueing operations have produced more equivocal results. Although Davis and Mumford (1984) found first letter cueing to be effective in enhancing the recall of patients with DAT, they found no improvement following semantic retrieval cues. Other investigators have reported beneficial effects in certain circumstances. In Diesfeldt's (1984) study semantic cues enhanced the recall of patients with DAT, but only if they had undergone a semantic orientation procedure during acquisition. This result is consistent with the encoding specificity principle of Tulving and Thompson (1973) and with the evidence already presented that patients with DAT do not spontaneously engage in deep semantic processing. Hart (1985) also found that recall performance improved when semantic retrieval cues were provided, but this effect was independent of the orientation conditions that had been imposed at acquisition in order to manipulate the depth to which list items were processed. Hart's

(1985) study therefore provided little support for the encoding specificity principle. The same is true of Martin *et al.*'s (1985) investigation which revealed a generalized facilitatory effect of semantic cueing. Butters and Cermak (1980) did produce evidence of encoding specificity. Their alcoholic Korsakoff patients demonstrated enhanced retrieval when their attention was directed to semantic properties of stimuli at the time of presentation and semantic cues were provided at recall, but only if the retrieval cues concerned the same semantic dimension(s) as were highlighted during acquisition.

In summary, there is evidence that when provided with retrieval cues, at least in certain circumstances, patients with some dementia-associated conditions can gain access to information that is stored in memory although they are unable to retrieve this on demand. In view of the obvious practical implications of any procedure that enhances retrieval, there is an urgent need to determine what are the optimal conditions for learning and what cueing procedures to implement at the time of retrieval. Another important question to be addressed concerns the extent to which optimal encoding and retrieval conditions respectively depend upon the aetiology of the degenerative process and/or what stage a given individual has reached in the progression of their disease process.

Recognition. Recognition tasks can be considered a special class of cued recall in which the retrieval cue is the stimulus itself. It has been widely assumed that recognition tests provide the most sensitive indication of the availability of items in memory as they render an active search strategy unnecessary and so make fewer processing demands upon the subject. However, while not wishing to deny the sensitivity of recognition tests to the availability of information in store, it is important to be aware that subjects are sometimes able to recall stimulus items that they fail to recognize (see Tulving and Thomson, 1973). Nevertheless, recognition procedures have proved very popular and a considerable body of information has accumulated concerning the performance of patients with different dementia-associated conditions.

Whitehead (1973b) found that patients with dementia had lower hit rates and made more false-positive errors than a group of elderly depressed patients. The aetiology of the dementia in these patients was unspecified but their admission as psychiatric inpatients had been related to the emergence of psychotic or depressive symptoms rather than diminished mental function *per se*. In a second study Whitehead (1975) found that the performance of such patients was somewhat better when a forced-choice (as opposed to a yes-no) procedure was employed, although this superiority was only significant for a subgroup of better learners. Contrary to expectation, the forced-choice procedure increased the number of correct identifications but had little effect upon the rate of false-positive responses. It was therefore suggested that the forced-choice test format encouraged emission of correct but low confidence responses. Such findings emphasize the importance of readiness to respond as a critical determinant of overall performance on recognition tests. Miller's

(1975) data from patients in the early stages of DAT, also point to the superiority of a forced-choice recognition format. Within-subject comparisons revealed that patients performed best on this condition, although from the point of view of between-group comparisons it was only when provided with partial information (in the form of the initial letters of each item) that the difference in performance between patient and control subjects was eliminated.

In an attempt to control for guessing many workers have applied measures derived from signal detection theory in their analyses of recognition memory data (see Banks, 1970), although not without criticism (Lockhart and Murdock, 1970). By taking account of the proportion of correct and false-positive responses this approach purports to yield independent measures of signal discriminability (memory strength) and decision strategy. Whether or not one considers signal detection theory a suitable model of memory processes, the sensitivity indexes derived from this theory have considerable descriptive utility and represent sophisticated corrections for guessing (Banks, 1970). When such measures have been applied to data from patients with dementia (Ferris *et al.*, 1980; Larner, 1977; Miller and Lewis, 1977; Wilson *et al.*, 1982b) the results have been inconsistent regarding changes in stimulus sensitivity and response bias. Such inconsistencies give rise to a number of questions and Hart *et al.* (1985) explored the hypothesis that different results emerged because investigators employed different stimulus materials. In this study the first author employed a continuous recognition procedure to investigate recognition of verbal and non-verbal stimuli (faces, drawings of everyday objects, abstract but verbally encodable geometric shapes and complex abstract material that was not readily amenable to verbal encoding). Although patients with DAT showed a fairly generalized impairment of performance, the extent and nature of their deficit depended upon the type of stimulus material presented. The data for each type of material were, by and large, consistent with previously published results. It emerged that patients with DAT adopted their most lax response criterion when confronted with photographs of faces and this finding is of interest since relatives reported that these patients often recognized family members and friends whom they were unable to name. They also reported instances when patients apparently 'recognized' people who were in fact strangers. However, it is significant that Hart *et al.*'s (1985) signal detection analysis did not provide any evidence of a generalized disinhibition of responding in patients with DAT. Indeed, for some types of stimulus material they adopted more conservative response criteria than normal elderly control subjects. The results of this study also demonstrate the sensitivity of indexes derived from signal detection theory. Although the hit rates of the patients with DAT and the normal elderly control subjects did not differ significantly for verbal stimuli or for the most familiar types of non-verbal stimuli (drawings of everyday objects and photographs of faces), signal detection analyses clearly indicated that patients were less able to discriminate between novel and repeated items.

Butters *et al.* have carried out comparative investigations of recognition memory in patients with Huntington's disease and the alcoholic Korsakoff syndrome. More recently they have also included patients with DAT in their studies. Their results suggest qualitative differences in the performance of patients with these aetiologically distinct conditions. For example, patients with Huntington's disease and the Korsakoff syndrome show equally poor recall of words, but only those with Huntington's disease perform better when tested on recognition paradigms. Changes from a recall to a recognition test format do not produce comparable facilitory effects upon retrieval in alcoholic Korsakoff patients (Butters *et al.*, 1987; Martone *et al.*, 1986; Moss *et al.*, 1986). Such evidence has exerted a significant influence upon Butters *et al.*'s theorizing concerning the nature of the mnemonic deficits heralded by Huntington's disease (see Butters *et al.*, 1986). These workers hypothesized that the fundamental deficiency leading to poor performance by patients with this degenerative condition on various memory tasks is failure to initiate efficient search strategies to recall information that is indeed held in store. Free recall data provide further support for the notion that there is a primary retrieval deficit in patients with Huntington's disease. Caine *et al.* (1977) and Fisher *et al.* (1983) used a selective reminding procedure whereby, following each free recall trial, subjects were only reminded of items they had failed to retrieve and were then required to retrieve all items during the subsequent free recall trial. Patients with Huntington's disease showed inconsistent patterns of retrieval, while control subjects, once they had recalled a word from long-term memory, continued to do so consistently on consecutive trials.

Data to be reported below concerning the remote memory of patients with Huntington's disease are consistent with the hypothesis that their memory impairment derives primarily from a retrieval deficit. However, there remains a need for more rigorous testing to determine the generality of this apparent retrieval deficit, especially since there is some evidence to suggest that it may only apply to verbal material (Moss *et al.*, 1986). Further comparative investigations are required. These should involve patients with other dementia-associated conditions and should include a number of test paradigms, ideally with several dependent measures of performance on each of these. Patients whose dementia is associated with Parkinson's disease would seem to be prime candidates for inclusion in comparative studies, especially in view of the reports by Flower's *et al.* (1984) and by Lees and Smith (1983) that recognition memory is unimpaired in such patients.

Remote memory. The preceding review has been concerned with retrieval of information that has only recently entered long-term memory, but it is often necessary to access information acquired months, years or even decades before. It is the fate of such so-called remote memories in patients with dementia that will be considered in the following paragraphs.

Clinical descriptions of patients with dementia tend to emphasize a disproportionate loss of recent memories and relative sparing of remote memories. This is in accord with conventional wisdom, as expressed by members of the lay public, concerning the nature of dementia or in more common parlance, senility. Such views conform to the law of regression proposed by Ribot (1882), according to which the probability of forgetting an event is inversely related to the time that has elapsed since its registration in memory. In recent years attempts have been made to subject such long held notions to rigorous scientific scrutiny. Various objective methods have been developed to allow for more systematic assessment of remote memory (see Erber, 1981). These include tests of public information pertaining to different periods in the life histories of individuals assessed (e.g. questionnaires relating to public events or television shows screened at designated times in the past, together with assessments of the subjects' ability to identify pictorial material depicting famous events or individuals) as well as tests of access to more personal or autobiographical information (e.g. assessment procedures that require subjects to provide the names of classmates and to identify individuals portrayed in school/family photographs). There are many methodological difficulties inherent in all of these approaches such as lack of control over the conditions of original learning and the problems of generating test items of equivalent difficulty for successive periods of time. Tests of autobiographical memory confront the additional difficulty of determining the veracity of responses concerning personal information (Kopelman *et al.*, 1989). Despite these problems, a number of investigators have now made noteable attempts at systematic exploration of remote memory in patients with dementia-producing conditions.

Impaired recall and recognition of information relating to major public events and to famous individuals from the past have been documented for patients with DAT (Beatty *et al.*, 1988; Flicker *et al.*, 1987; Sagar *et al.*, 1988; Wilson *et al.*, 1981), Huntington's disease (Albert *et al.*, 1981a,b; Beatty *et al.*, 1988), and dementia associated with Parkinson's disease (Huber *et al.*, 1986; Sagar *et al.*, 1988). In all of these patient groups the magnitude of deficits tends to be related to overall severity of dementia. However, Sagar *et al.* (1988) did note that the difficulty experienced by patients with Parkinson's disease in dating events and in judging the period of prominence of famous individuals whose faces were presented was independent of the presence of dementia. They speculated that there might be a relationship between this temporal ordering difficulty and the disproportionate deficits in recency discrimination that these patients display (Sagar *et al.*, 1985). Deficits in remote memory have also been documented for alcoholic Korsakoff patients (e.g. Albert *et al.*, 1981a; Cohen and Squire, 1981; Kopelman, 1989) but are less severe than those typically found in patients with DAT (Kopelman, 1989). The preliminary data from other comparative investigations suggest that the remote memory deficits heralded by DAT are also more severe than those associated with Huntington's disease (Beatty *et al.*, 1988) or Parkinson's disease (Sagar *et al.*, 1988). However, the results of comparative studies must be interpreted with caution in view of the difficulties inherent in matching patient groups for overall severity of dementia.

A number of investigators have reported that the remote memory deficits of patients with DAT show a temporal gradient with relative preservation of memories pertaining to the more distant past (Beatty *et al.*, 1988; Kopelman, 1989; Sagar *et al.*, 1988; Wilson *et al.*, 1981) although the gradient is not as steep as that shown by alcoholic Korsakoff patients (Kopelman, 1989). On the other hand patients with Huntington's disease exhibit a rather flat temporal gradient with recall of information acquired in the distant past being just as impaired as retrieval of knowledge about more recent events (Albert *et al.*, 1981a,b; Betty *et al.*, 1988). Studies of cognitively impaired patients with Parkinson's disease have yielded contradictory results. While Huber *et al.*, (1986) did not find a temporal gradient Sagar *et al.*, (1988) did so, but the deficit in recalling information from remote memory extended over a shorter time span than was true of patients with DAT.

The presence or absence of a temporal gradient has important implications for the nature of remote memory deficits. The flat retrograde amnesia exhibited by patients with Huntington's disease when assessed on tests of remote memory provides further support for the hypothesis of Butters *et al.* (referred to above) that this disease entails a generalized inability to initiate systematic retrieval strategies in order to gain access to stored information. As for patients with other conditions (specifically DAT, Parkinson's disease and the alcoholic Korsakoff syndrome), a retrieval deficit may make some contribution to their poor performance on tests of remote memory, but this would not account for the temporal gradient. Hence a deficit at some other stage of information processing must be sought to explain their pattern(s) of performance. Shimamura and Squire (1986) suggested that the temporal gradient manifest by Korsakoff patients reflects a progressively developing anterograde amnesia, induced by excessive consumption of alcohol over a prolonged period prior to development of overt Wernicke–Korsakoff symptoms. Although not denying the importance of a retrieval deficit this explanation shifts the emphasis away from retrieval to the earlier stages of initial encoding and storage. However, acquisition deficits could scarcely account for the gradient manifest by patients with DAT since their remote memory deficits extend back over many decades and include years when they operated without any evidence of cognitive impairment, and which almost certainly predated the onset of decline.

Investigations of remote memory in patients with dementia have proved a fruitful line of research. The differential pattern of deficits shown by various patient groups may be an important pointer towards the neural mechanisms that underly retention of information over extensive periods of time and allow access to such remote memories. For example, it might be significant that those conditions in which temporal gradients are most marked, namely DAT and the alcoholic Korsakoff syndrome, involve damage to the nucleus basalis of Meynert, the origin of cholinergic projections to the cortex (see Chapter 3). Further investigation of patients with Parkinson's disease could yeild important information since this condition is also associated with cell loss from the nucleus basalis. However, data concerning the presence of a temporal retrieval gradient are equivocal for such patients.

Semantic Memory

Most research on long-term memory reviewed in the foregoing pages concerns what has been designated episodic memory. This term was introduced by Tulving (1972) to denote an autobiographical record of events or episodes, personally experienced by an individual, and encoded in relation to a particular temporal and spatial context. The majority of investigative procedures traditionally employed in experimental or clinical assessment situations have tapped episodic memory. However, some measures of remote memory do not tap this type of information, drawing rather upon what Tulving (1972) termed semantic memory. This he defined as a system of organized knowledge concerning words and concepts and the rules which govern manipulation and utilization of these. Information in semantic memory is stored in a relatively context-free manner and lacks the autobiographical referents which characterize that held in episodic memory. The term semantic memory as used by Tulving has broad connotations and encompasses not only linguistic or lexical information. It is concerned with the entire domain of non-personal factual knowledge (Chang, 1986). Nevertheless, most investigations that have systematically sought to examine semantic memory in patients with dementia have been concerned with linguistic information (or more specifically with lexical access, the integrity of associational networks and the preservation of syntax). Hence we shall defer detailed consideration of these until the chapter on language and communication. For the present purposes it is sufficient to note that, although the data are not entirely consistent, the contents of semantic memory seem to be relatively well preserved, at least until the later stages of dementia. However, the facility with which this information can be accessed is variable and depends critically upon the processing demands of the retrieval task. Studies of so-called priming phenomena have given rise to a body of data that is relevant to questions concerning the integrity of associational networks. However, such studies will be considered in detail in the next section of this chapter as they also bear upon the issue of implicit (as opposed to explicit) memory. Suffice it to say here that the results to date point towards relative preservation, though there are some contradictory findings regarding patients with DAT.

As yet there has been little systematic investigation of the integrity of non-lexical factual information or the efficiency with which patients with dementia can access and use such information, if it does indeed remain in store. Mental status examinations typically tap information of this type (e.g. with questions relating to heads of state/government, historical information or recitation of familiar sequences such as the letters of the alphabet etc.) and the poor performance of patients with moderate or severe dementia in response to questions of this type indicates that non-lexical factual information is lost or at least becomes difficult to access. The Information Subtest of the WAIS also taps factual information, but although the WAIS itself (or selected subtests from it) is widely employed by researchers, data for individual subtests are seldom published. The first author found that patients with mild-to-moderate DAT were significantly impaired on this subtest (Hart, 1985) and similar results were reported by Pillon *et al.* (1986). Pirozzolo *et al.*'s (1982) patients with Parkinson's disease performed poorly although Pillon *et al.* (1986) failed to detect significant impairment in their parkinsonian subjects or in patients with progressive supranuclear palsy. Butters *et al.* (1978) found that when Huntington's disease was well advanced patients performed poorly on the Information Subtest, although recently diagnosed individuals did not. However, Fisher *et al.* (1983) could not distinguish between groups of moderately and severely disabled patients with this disease. Bieliauskas and Fox (1987) carried out a longitudinal investigation of a single patient with Creutzfeldt–Jakob disease and found rapid decline in performance on this subtest, but it was commensurate with deterioration of other aspects of cognition. The small group of patients with vascular dementia studied by Hart (1985) obtained Information Subtest scores that were comparable to those of normal elderly control subjects, although the same patients were significantly impaired on tests of episodic memory and on other measures of cognitive processing. In a comparative study Perez *et al.* (1975) reported that patients with multi-infarct dementia performed significantly better than those with DAT on this WAIS subtest but these workers failed to replicate their findings in a subsequent study (Perez *et al.*, 1976), thereby highlighting the need for validation studies. Finally, Butters and Cermak (1980) reported that patients with the alcoholic Korsakoff syndrome were not impaired on the Information Subtest, but they provided insufficient data concerning the overall cognitive status of their sample to allow one to determine whether they had dementia.

In summary, the available data suggest that patients afflicted by various dementia-producing conditions may differ in terms of whether and at what stage non-personal factual information is lost or becomes difficult to access. There is clearly a need for more systematic investigation, comparing performance across different patient groups and drawing different samples from those afflicted by any specific condition. It will also be important to determine relative levels of functioning on different measures of semantic memory and to assess these in relation to other aspects of cognition.

Procedural Memory/Implicit Memory

Drawing on work carried out in the field of artificial intelligence, Squire *et al.* (see Squire, 1986) proposed a different system for fractionating long-term memory. They distinguished between declarative and procedural subsystems. Declarative memory (knowing what) is explicit and accessible to conscious awareness. Its contents can be 'declared', that is brought to mind verbally as a proposition or non-verbally as an image. Both episodic and semantic memory can be construed as subordinate categories of declarative memory (see Tulving, 1987). In contrast, procedural memory (knowing how) is implicit and can only be accessed via performance, that is by engaging in the skills or operations in which the knowledge is embedded.

There is much evidence that patients with specific amnesic syndromes show marked deficits in explicit memory while their implicit memory is much less impaired (see Shimamura, 1986). Some investigtions have now been carried out to determine whether patients with dementia-producing conditions show a similar dissociation. Moscovitch (1982) found that patients with DAT showed a repetition priming effect when assessed on a lexical decision task. Subjects were required to decide whether strings of letters formed words and their decision latency was reduced on re-exposure of a previously presented word. However, explicit memory was deficient in that patients subsequently showed poor recognition of words that had been used as stimuli during the lexical decision phase of the investigation. Ober and Shenaut (1988) reported similar facilitative effects of repetition priming in patients with DAT. Nebes *et al.* (1984, 1986) found that although such patients took significantly longer than control subjects to name visually presented words, they nevertheless showed semantic priming in that identification latencies were reduced when stimuli were preceded by semantically related words or congruent sentences. Furthermore, Nebes *et al.*'s (1986) patients were even more sensitive than control subjects to the semantic context, whether congruent or incongruent, provided by the priming sentences. Such findings imply that semantic fields are intact (see also Chapter 9) but other workers have been unable to demonstrate semantic priming in patients with DAT (Ober and Shenaut, 1988; Shimamura *et al.*, 1987; Salmon *et al.*, 1988). Preliminary data suggest that patients with Huntington's disease and with Parkinson's disease show semantic priming effects (Hines and Volpe, 1985; Salmon *et al.*, 1988).

Shimamura *et al.* (1987) and Salmon *et al.* (1988) compared the performance of patients with DAT, Huntington's disease and the alcoholic Korsakoff syndrome using another dependent measure of priming efficacy. Following exposure to various procedures designed to activate particular information in semantic memory subjects were assessed on a letter stem completion task in which they were presented with letters and required to add others to make a word. Although the patients with DAT produced more words that were semantically related to the priming stimulus than would have been expected on the basis of guessing, they demonstrated a less marked semantic priming effect than patients with the other aetiological conditions. Patients with Huntington's disease were also impaired relative to their control subjects. However, all patient groups were equally impaired on conventional recall and recognition tasks.

Another body of data bearing upon the integrity of implicit memory in patients with dementia derives from investigations of their motor skills learning. There are many reports of preserved skills learning in amnesic patients, including those with the alcoholic Korsakoff syndrome (see Squire, 1986), and some investigators have reported that patients with DAT demonstrate learning in terms of their performance on a rotary pursuit task (Eslinger and Damasio, 1986; Heindel *et al.*, 1988). Hart (1985) also found evidence of skills learning in patients with DAT: when re-assessed on simple, choice and cross-modal reaction time tasks, as well as on a computerized version of the continuous performance test (see Chapter 10), their reaction time and/or its variability was significantly reduced although initial exposure had taken place some weeks before. Knopman and Nissen (1987) demonstrated that patients with DAT were able to exploit the sequential redundancy in a stimulus sequence on a choice reaction time task and so reduce their reaction time over successive blocks of trials. The final block of trials did not include the redundant sequence and reaction time increased once more, thereby indicating that the previous reduction in response latency reflected implicit learning of the stimulus sequence, rather than the beneficial effects of practice *per se*.

Studies that have compared the skills learning ability of patients with different clinical conditions have yielded interesting results. Martone *et al.* (1984) found that alcoholic Korsakoff patients showed good skills learning when required to read mirror-transformed sentences but their subsequent recognition of the words employed in the test was poor. Patients with Huntington's disease showed the opposite pattern of relative performance. They were less proficient than Korsakoff patients in acquiring the skill of mirror reading, but later demonstrated better recognition memory for the stimuli presented during the procedural learning phase of the experiment. These are interesting results and merit validation studies to determine the reliability of the double dissociation revealed by this preliminary investigation. Moscovitch *et al.* (1986) also used transformed script and demonstrated relative preservation of implicit memory in a miscellaneous group of amnesic patients, many of whom had DAT or other dementia syndromes. Like control subjects, the patient group read material to which they had been exposed previously more quickly than novel items, but they differed from control subjects in that they were unable to identify this material as being familiar in a declarative test condition.

Investigations demonstrating dissociation of performance on tasks measuring different aspects of memory in certain patient groups (with, for example, explicit memory being impaired while implicit memory remains essentially intact) are of considerable theoretical importance. They provide support for the distinction between these subtypes of long-term memory and imply that different neural substrates may be involved. The demonstration that some patients with dementia are capable of learning quite specific information throws down a challenge to clinical neuropsychologists to devise strategies whereby these capabilities may be utilized to full effect in order to enhance or maintain functional capacity and thereby quality of life.

Concluding Remarks

The data reported in this chapter suggest that different patterns of memory deficit may be associated with aetiologically distinct dementia syndromes. Detailed longitudinal investigations have yet to be carried out but there are good grounds for supposing that different patterns of deficit will only be manifest by patients in the earlier stages of their respective dementing processes. This emphasizes that, in order to avoid unnecessary error variance, future researchers must seek to employ diagnostically homogeneous patient groups. It also draws attention to the importance of providing adequate descriptive data concerning subjects selected for study in order to allow for some estimate of the overall severity of their clinical condition (in terms of the range of cognitive domains affected as well as the degree of impairment) and, in the case of certain clinical conditions, a decision about whether a diagnosis of dementia is warranted at the time of investigation. However, attempts to establish consistent and accurate diagnostic criteria pose significant methodological difficulties. Likewise, efforts towards quantifying severity of the overall aggregate of cognitive and behavioural impairment, or establishing definable stages in a particular degenerative process, have proved challenging, with only modest success being achieved so far (see Chapters 6 and 7). In comparative studies the problem of quantifying overall severity of impairment becomes particularly complicated. Nevertheless, overcoming this methodological hurdle remains a necessary prerequisite for matching subject groups so that differences in performance due to aetiology are not confounded by differences in overall severity.

In describing their patient samples it is not only important that investigators report detailed information concerning cognitive and behavioural competence or disability, but also that they document any medication consumed in relation to the dementia syndrome or any other condition, whether or not this is related. Such treatments could affect quantitative and/or qualitative aspects of performance on dependent measures applied for the purpose of the study or on indexes used for descriptive purposes. For example, patients with Parkinson's disease are frequently treated with anticholinergic drugs to control their movement disorder but, as already documented (Chapter 5), such compounds can themselves impair cognition. Similar considerations would also apply to many antidepressant drugs which are not infrequently prescribed for patients with probable dementia.

Putative differences in the pattern of memory deficits shown by patients with aetiologically distinct dementia syndromes have important implications regarding what aspects of memory should be the target of therapeutic interventions. They also bear upon the selection of appropriate outcome measures to assess therapeutic efficacy.

Baddeley (1982b: 306) noted that models are ' . . . tools, useful fictions that summarize what one already knows in ways that make it easier to ask sensible further questions' and these functions are amply demonstrated by research on memory impairment in patients with dementia. The models evolved by cognitive psychologists to account for mnemonic processing have proved invaluable in making sense of the large body of data now available, quite apart from their heuristic contribution in prompting application of novel investigative procedures. The demonstration of different patterns of deficit between patient groups in which there are distinctive structural and neuro-chemical pathologies has been particularly important. Such data have given further credence to the validity of current models and classificatory systems. By providing important neuropsychological pointers they allow for generation of hypotheses concerning the neural mechanisms that might mediate different aspects of memory. The importance of comparative investigations is also apparent and further studies are required. These should include patients whose dementia syndromes arise out of different aetiologies and should incorporate measures of more than one of the purported memory subsystems, together with assessments of other aspects of cognition.

Readers will have noted the prominence of attention-related concepts in current work on memory, for example the central executive in the working memory model of short-term memory (Baddeley, 1987) and the frequency with which the concepts of effortful and automatic processing (Hasher and Zacks, 1979) have been invoked. Indeed, in the gerontological literature some workers have attempted to account for age-related changes in memory solely in terms of attentional phenomena (Craik and Byrd, 1982; Craik and Simon, 1980; Kinsbourne 1980; Rabinowitz *et al.*, 1982; Wingfield, 1980). Interested readers wishing to pursue the role of attention in memory processes should consult sources such as Baddeley (1987), Cowan (1988), Griffith (1976), Hasher and Zacks (1979), Schneider and Shiffrin (1977), Shiffrin and Schneider (1977). Of course, no aspect of cognition stands or functions in isolation and the interdependence of different cognitive processes will be emphasized many times in forthcoming chapters. In relation to the topic of this chapter it must be noted that the relationship between memory and attention is bi-directional. Norman and Bobrow's (1975) distinction between resource-driven (top-down) and data-driven (bottom-up) cognitive processes alluded to the role of memory in attentional operations and this was rendered more explicit by Rabbitt's (1979) choice of the label 'memory-driven' in preference to 'resource-driven' to refer to top-down processes.

Intact attention (at some level of analysis) is indeed an essential prerequisite for the efficient execution of all information processing operations, but it is unfortunate that it is all too often invoked as a global construct and as an explanation by default. As will be emphasised in Chapter 10, attention is not a unitary concept and it is therefore necessary to specify more precisely the sense in which the term is used. Alas, even investigators who do employ the term attention in a more restricted sense (specifically to refer to the amount of processing resources available and/or allocation thereof) all too often resort *post hoc* to designation of information processing activities as either automatic or effortful. If we are to avoid tautology there is an urgent need for independent criteria whereby such terms can be defined without resort to their effects upon performance.

In summary, considerable progress has undoubtedly been made in recent years towards understanding the nature of memory dysfunction in patients with dementia-associated conditions. However, many questions remain to be addressed as we seek to consolidate this knowledge and confront the new challenges that greater knowledge inevitably brings in its wake.

Chapter 9

Language and Communication

Over the years there have been numerous reports in the literature of language dysfunction or 'aphasia' in patients with dementia (e.g. Bayles *et al.*, 1982; Constantinidis *et al.*, 1978; Critchley, 1964; Ernst *et al.*, 1970; Miller, 1977a; Obler, 1983; Sjogren, 1952; Stengel, 1964a,b). Indeed, disturbance in this realm of cognition was noted by Alzheimer (1907) when he described the case history and post-morten examination of his original patient (see Wilkins and Brody, 1969). Although generally considered to be a feature that emerges late in the progression of AD there is evidence to suggest that patients afflicted by this disease and indeed by other primary degenerative dementia-producing conditions, including Pick's disease, may present with relatively specific impairment of language (Goodman, 1953; Holland *et al.*, 1985; Kirshner *et al.*, 1984; Morris *et al.*, 1984; Neary *et al.*, 1986; Pogacar and Williams, 1984; Wechsler *et al.*, 1982). Given the extensive literature on vascular pathology in relation to aphasia, it goes without saying that disturbances of language may be noteable in patients with multi-infarct dementia. Quite apart from those patients in whom language deficits are striking, and therefore readily apparent on clinical examination, the results of neuropsychological screening investigations suggest that some impairment of language may be common even in the relatively early stages of a degenerative process (Code and Lodge, 1987; Hart, 1985). This has important implications for the long-standing practice of using verbal tests, in particular measures of vocabulary, to estimate premorbid level of function (see Chapter 7).

Language is a fundamental tool of human communication and accordingly is crucial for the evaluation of most cognitive abilities. Thus an important issue must be the extent to which linguistic impairment might contribute to the intellectual decline and memory dysfunction that have been considered the hallmarks of dementia. For example, poor performance on a learning and memory test employing pictures of objects as stimuli may simply reflect confrontation naming difficulties. Similarly, any impairment of a subject's ability to comprehend test instructions, whether conveyed orally or in writing, may compromise that person's performance on almost any cognitive task. The converse is also true so that impairments of language and communication might be secondary to deficiencies in other cognitive processes.

   The issue of whether the language disturbances of patients with dementia can be considered instrumental disorders comparable to those found in patients with circumscribed cerebral lesions is one that has drawn comment from many writers over the years. Some have maintained that the term 'aphasia' (or 'dysphasia') should only be used when the language disturbance is thought to be associated with a localized cerebral lesion (e.g. Critchley, 1964; Weinstein and Kahn, 1952). However, Stengel (1964a) rightly pointed out that this position embodies a confusion of psychological with anatomical concepts and it is important to recognize that the definition of aphasia, like that of dementia, remains open to controversy (see Au *et al.*, 1988). Applying the techniques, terminology and theories of aphasia to the study of patients with dementia may prove fruitful (Au *et al.*, 1988). However, use of global terms such as aphasia in relation to the language disturbances of patients with dementia does not in itself have any implications regarding the extent to which these are considered similar to linguistic deficits consequent upon more focal cerebral lesions. Likewise, it does not have any connotations with respect to aetiology, onset of language dysfunction or the degree of linguistic impairment relative to general cognitive dysfunction. Approaching the issue from an alternative perspective, there has also been debate concerning whether other intellectual processes are indeed spared in patients with aphasic disturbances that result from more circumscribed lesions (Hamsher, 1981; Zangwill, 1964).

   The last decade has seen a tremendous burgeoning of interest in the language of patients with dementia, in particular DAT. As already noted in Chapter 6 this has become a pivotal issue in relation to a number of nosological and nosographic issues such as the controversial classification of dementia syndromes into cortical and subcortical types and the identification of subtypes of DAT. Furthermore, a number of workers (e.g. Bayles and Boone, 1982; Skelton-Robinson and Jones, 1984; Weeks, 1988) have asserted that tests of language function may have potential as sensitive diagnostic tools and as indexes of severity in patients with dementia. Kaszniak *et al.* (1978) have further suggested that, in the absence of relevant focal lesions, the presence of expressive language deficits in patients with dementia may be predictive of a poor prognosis for survival. With respect to diagnostic claims, we have already emphasized in Chapter 7 that evidence of impairment in a single domain of cognition is insufficient to warrant a diagnosis of dementia. It is also important to be aware that slowly progressive aphasia need not necessarily develop into generalized cognitive dysfunction of sufficient severity to justify assignment of this diagnosis (Chawluk *et al.*, 1986; Heath *et al.*, 1983; Kirshner *et al.*, 1987; Mesulam, 1982, 1987). It has been suggested that in patients showing such slowly progressive aphasia there may be focal pathological changes in the left perisylvian cortex (see Figure 9.1).

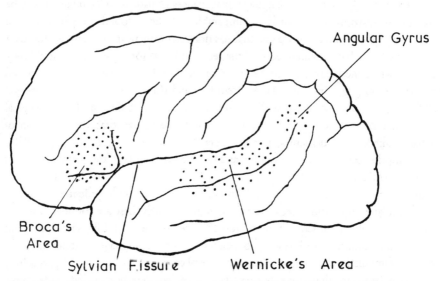

Figure 9.1 Left hemisphere of the brain showing the Sylvian Fissure and the approximate location of Broca's and Wernicke's areas and of the angular gyrus.

Empirical Investigations into the Language of Patients with Dementia

There are in the literature a number of rich descriptions of the language behaviour of patients with dementia (e.g. Critchley, 1964; Obler, 1983; Stengel, 1964a) and the heuristic value of such reports is irrefutable. However, it is our contention that they must be supported by systematic single-case investigations incorporating within-person controls and ultimately between-group comparisons before generalized conclusions can be drawn. Group data pertaining to different dementia-producing conditions will be particularly important if common core features are to be distinguished from the often striking, but nevertheless uncommon, features which may capture the attention of clinicians and receive undue emphasis.

Of course, evidence suggesting impairment of language consequent upon a dementia syndrome can only be evaluated in the context of knowledge about the performance of normal elderly individuals. Although one encounters in the literature sweeping statements about changes in language heralded by the normal ageing process (e.g. Stengel, 1964a) there has been a paucity of controlled studies into the effects of ageing *per se* on verbal communication (Brookshire and Manthie, 1980). In the past decade steps have been taken to remedy this deficit as researchers have come to appreciate the necessity of objective investigation (see Ulatowska *et al.*, 1985 and Chapter 5 in Bayles and Kaszniak, 1987). It must also be emphasized that clinicians' impressions are likely to be suspect since, by definition, they encounter elderly invidi-duals whose mental state is such as to cause concern or who suffer from physical or psychiatric conditions likely to predispose them to cognitive dysfunction. Hence the need for controlled investigations.

Receptive Language

Comparatively little attention has been directed to the receptive language of patients with dementia. However, it has been demonstrated that the ability of patients with DAT to respond to the auditory commands of the Token Test (De Renzi and Faglioni, 1978) decreases as these require them to decode progressively more information or when correct execution involves several steps (Emery and Emery, 1983; Hart, 1985). Of course intact comprehension of oral instructions will not in itself guarantee adequate performance on the Token Test. This test also places demands upon other non-linguistic cognitive processes. Failure to execute commands might, therefore, reflect inadequate short-term memory, perceptual disability and/or deficient motor programming (Lesser, 1976). The performance of patients with DAT on the Token Test has indeed been found to show a significant correlation with scores on the Wechsler Memory Scale and the WAIS (Hart, 1985) but correlation need not imply causation and the relationship between memory or intellectual impairment and receptive language deficits remains to be clarified. However, the first author has found that patients with this condition sometimes fail items in the final part of the test which, although linguistically more complex, are of shorter verbal span and require less complex motor programming, than commands in the penultimate section which they can execute without error. Moreover, patients sometimes repeat commands aloud correctly but remain unable to execute them. Thus it seems unlikely that the poor per-formance of patients with DAT on the Token Test can be attributed entirely to non-linguistic factors.

The commands of the Token Test are low in verbal redundancy and situational or contextual cues cannot be exploited to assist comprehension. Although these features undoubtedly contribute to the demonstrated sensitivity of the test to impairments of receptive language (see Boller and Dennis, 1979), deficiencies in performance on this test may be disproportionate to patients' difficulties in comprehending language in real-life situations. Indeed, the extent to which some linguistically impaired patients with DAT remain attuned to the non-verbal and paralinguistic cues that orchestrate social interaction is often striking (Hart, 1985), an observation which might be exploited to advantage in management programmes and will be returned to later in this chapter.

Although not immune to the ravages of DAT, ability to read words aloud remains relatively intact until the degenerative process is well advanced (Hart *et al.*,

167

1986a). Indeed, this can be used to estimate the premorbid intellectual level of individuals afflicted by this and other dementia-producing conditions (Crawford *et al.*, 1988; Hart *et al.*, 1986a; Nelson, 1982; Nelson and O'Connell, 1978). The relative stability of performance on word reading tests, and in particular the preservation of patients' ability to read words of irregular orthography (Nelson and O'Connell, 1978; Hart *et al.*, 1986a), clearly implies that the lexicon itself remains comparatively intact in the face of progressive degeneration. This issue will be considered further when reviewing data on expressive language and evidence for reduced efficiency of lexical access, together with data pertaining to the structure and organizational integrity of semantic memory.

Of course oral reading *per se* cannot be taken as an index of reading comprehension. Patients sometimes make errors when required to match words to pictures, although they can read the same words aloud without error (Hart, 1985). Preliminary data obtained by the first author from patients in the early stages of DAT indicated that they were less accurate in executing commands if these were written than if the same commands were delivered orally. This suggested inability to exploit the continuing presence of the written material, although other cognitively impaired patients (who did not meet strict inclusion criteria for DAT) were able to do so (Hart, 1985). Other workers too have reported similar difficulties in reading for meaning in patients with DAT although the precise nature of the difficulties that they, or victims of other dementia-producing conditions, might experience remains to be determined (Cummings *et al.*, 1986; Stevens, 1985). Possible contributory factors might include disruption of sensory input consequent upon abnormal eye movements, perceptual abnormalities and/or loss of concentration.

In conclusion, the limited data available suggest that auditory comprehension fares better than reading comprehension in patients with DAT, and that reading for meaning is more impaired than reading aloud. Indeed Benson *et al.* (1982) have suggested that the tendency towards differential impairment of reading aloud and reading for meaning in patients with DAT may be one feature of relevance for clinicians attempting to distinguish between this and the angular gyrus syndrome, in which both reading aloud and reading comprehension are usually seriously compromised. Of course both areas of reading ability will be severely impaired in patients with advanced dementia. There have been few objective studies of the language of patients with other dementia-producing conditions and this is particularly true of those with Creutzfeldt–Jakob disease. Therefore, Bieliauskas and Fox's (1987) single case study of a patient with this disease is of particular interest. It is relevant to the topic of receptive language just discussed in that their data pointed to impairment of reading comprehension at a time when comprehension of words presented in the auditory modality (as measured by the Peabody Picture Vocabulary Test) remained essentially intact.

Expressive Language

Naming

Impairment of naming ability is undoubtedly one of the most commonly reported language deficits in patients with dementia and it is one of the few aspects of linguistic function in such patients which has been subjected to systematic experimental investigation. There have been many reports that confrontation naming is impaired in patients with dementia (Appell *et al.*, 1982; Bayles, 1982; Bayles and Boone, 1982; Bayles and Tomoeda, 1983; Flicker *et al.*, 1987; Huff *et al.*, 1986; Kirshner *et al.*, 1984; Lawson and Barker, 1968; Martin and Fedio, 1983; Rochford, 1971; Schwartz *et al.*, 1979; Shuttleworth and Huber, 1988; Skelton-Robinson and Jones, 1984; Warrington, 1975). However, many of the early reports provided few details of diagnostic criteria and employed what were probably heterogeneous samples. A number of studies have documented impairment of confrontation naming ability in patients with so-called subcortical dementias (Globus *et al.*, 1985; Matison *et al.*, 1982; Smith *et al.*, 1988) although there have been some exceptions (Maher *et al.*, 1985; Pillon *et al.*, 1986; Pirozzolo *et al.*, 1982). However, when comparative studies have been carried out, the results have suggested that the nominal deficits of patients with subcortical dementias, such as Parkinson's disease and Huntington's disease, are indeed less severe than those characteristic of patients with dementias purported to be cortical in nature, such as DAT (Bayles and Tomoeda, 1983; Cummings *et al.*, 1988). However, the conclusions to be drawn from such studies must remain tentative given the unresolved methodological problems of matching patient groups in terms of overall severity of cognitive impairment. The nature of the nominal disorder shown by patients with dementia remains controversial and is the subject of much research, especially in patients with DAT.

Word frequency has an important effect upon naming difficulty, with patients showing greater impairment when required to produce less frequent words (Barker and Lawson, 1968; Kirshner *et al.*, 1984; Lawson and Barker, 1968; Shuttleworth and Huber, 1988; Skelton-Robinson and Jones, 1984). Thus word frequency should be taken into account when selecting stimuli to assess confrontation naming ability. Word frequency is also a critical determinant of naming latency in normal individuals (Lawson and Barker, 1968; Oldfield and Wingfield, 1965), with less common names taking longer to produce. This relationship is exacerbated in dementia and Lawson and Barker (1968) suggested that reaction time might provide a more sensitive measure of dysfunction than response accuracy.

In addition to linguistic factors, such as frequency, which affect the word search stage of naming (Oldfield and Wingfield, 1965), certain non-linguistic factors have been implicated in the naming disorder of patients with dementia. Barker and Lawson (1968) found that the naming performance of their heterogeneous group of demented patients was facilitated when the uses of the stimulus objects were demonstrated or when patients were allowed to handle them (see also Appell *et al.*, 1982). This facilitative effect of additional cues applied to the naming of both common and uncommon objects. Barker and Lawson (1968) therefore concluded that, quite apart from any linguistic factors that might impair naming, demented patients were less efficient in identifying the objects. Rochford (1971) likewise concluded that impairment of visual recognition was an important factor in the naming impairment of demented patients. When presented with line drawings of objects their most common error was to supply the name of an object which looked similar to the stimulus depicted. In contrast, the most common errors made by patients with dysphasia resulting from localized cerebral lesions were failure to verbalize and provision of descriptive phrases. Moreover, demented but not dysphasic patients showed a dramatic improvement in accuracy when required to name parts of the body. These constitute very familiar and therefore easily recognized stimuli, although their names vary considerably in terms of word frequency. On the basis of clinical observations Stengel (1964a,b) expressed a similar view that the nominal dysphasia that occurs in dementia differs from that found in aphasia due to focal lesions. He noted that, when called upon to name objects, demented patients would often 'boldly and sometimes recklessly improvise and produce words on the spur of the moment' (Stengel, 1964a: 289), while a response more typical of patients with amnesic or nominal dysphasia consequent upon focal lesions was to say 'I know what it is, but I can't find the word' or to correctly describe the use of the object instead of naming it.

Kirshner *et al.* (1984) also reported data suggesting that perceptual difficulty was an important determinant of naming performance. Patients with DAT were most efficient when presented with real objects, but their accuracy declined progressively when the stimuli were respectively photographs of objects, line drawings of these and masked drawings (i.e. line drawings superimposed on a background of intersecting lines). Likewise Shuttleworth and Huber's (1988) patients with DAT made fewer errors when naming real objects as opposed to line drawings of objects. These findings lend support to Barker and Lawson's (1968: 1355) cautionary note that 'methods of assessment using pictures may be biased towards eliciting difficulties of identification rather than of word finding', clearly an important practical consideration.

However, the contention that perceptual difficulty is a major contributor to the nominal deficit of patients with dementia has been challenged. Bayles (1982) recorded the naming responses of patients with 'severe senile dementia' and reported finding no evidence to substantiate previous suggestions of perceptual failure. Similar conclusions were drawn from the results of a comparative study (one of the few to date) carried out by Bayles and Tomoeda (1983) in which they investigated the confrontation naming impairment of patients with dementias of different aetiologies (DAT, Huntington's disease, Parkinson's disease and multi-infarct dementia) as well as different degrees of severity. The misnaming responses of all patients (irrespective of the aetiology of their dementia) were most likely to be semantically associated with the target stimulus. Many errors were visually as well as semantically related to the target item, but Bayles and Tomoeda (1983) argued that such instances need not indicate misperception; rather they might suggest some interplay between perceptual and linguistic-cognitive mechanisms. Quite correctly, they also drew attention to the lack of clarity concerning what was meant when demented patients were described by earlier workers as being perceptually impaired. This could mean that the visual signal was degraded, so that the name of an object matching the impaired image was selected. Alternatively, the incoming visual signal might have remained intact but patients were unable to match this with its lexical referent (either because the referent no longer existed or the features of the stimulus were no longer meaningful), in which case it would be more appropriate to describe the deficit as linguistic-cognitive since it would reflect a change in the structure and/or organizational integrity of the semantic memory system or the mechanism and/or efficiency by which information held therein could be accessed. Data bearing upon the question of whether and to what extent visual perceptual systems are compromised by DAT or other dementia-producing conditions will be considered in Chapter 11.

Schwartz *et al*.'s (1979) longitudinal study of a single case provides further support for a linguistic-cognitive interpretation. When first assessed this 62-year-old patient showed profound anomia but although she could name only one of the 70 pictures of objects presented, she demonstrated recognition of these through gestural responses. However, when required to match the pictures to words, she made many errors, more than 80 per cent of which were due to selection of semantically related items rather than unrelated items or those which were phonologically (and orthographically) related. Martin and Fedio (1983) classified the errors made by patients with DAT on the Boston Naming Test and found that perceptual errors were only a small percentage of the total. Most errors were classified as language-related and there were also more instances of failure to respond than of perceptual errors (c.f. Rochford, 1971; Bayles and Tomoeda, 1983). The first author has found that the performance of patients with DAT is also deficient when they are provided with a description of a stimulus or an outline of its function and required to produce the appropriate name (Hart, 1985). Such findings point to a linguistic-cognitive deficit.

It must be apparent that there is considerable controversy surrounding the role of perceptual and linguistic factors in the naming impairment of patients with dementia. Most experimental investigations have focused on patients with DAT, but the under-lying nature of the nominal deficit might differ according to aetiology as well as the localization of focal concentrations of neuropathology. Thus it is possible, indeed probable, that even in a homogeneous group of patients, all of whom have DAT, there will be individual differences in the extent to which different cognitive factors contribute to the manifest impairment of naming because of variations in the topography of neural damage. Moreover, DAT, like many other dementia-producing conditions, is a progressive degenerative disorder so that the pattern of deficits, and the relative importance of the different contributory factors, may change over time.

Word Fluency

Irrespective of its role in the deficient nominal ability apparent on confrontation naming tests, visual perceptual impairment can make little contribution to the demonstrated poor performance of patients with DAT on word fluency tests. These allow subjects only a limited time to access items from the lexicon according to specified rules (Appell *et al.*, 1982; Diesfeldt, 1985; Hart, S. *et al.*, 1988; Martin and Fedio, 1983; Miller, 1984b; Miller and Hague, 1975; Ober *et al.*, 1986; Rosen, 1980; Weingartner *et al.*, 1981). With the exception of Murdoch *et al.*'s (1987) investigation, comparative studies have found performance to be more deficient under these test conditions than when confrontation naming is assessed (Appell *et al.*, 1982; Benson, 1979; Corkin *et al.*, 1984; Huff *et al.*, 1986). Such data lend tentative support to the notion advanced by Isaacs and Kennie (1973) that a measure of word fluency might make a useful contribution to the process of screening for dementia (see Hart, S. *et al.*, 1988).

Word fluency is also impaired in patients with Huntington's disease (Butters *et al.*, 1986; Smith *et al.*, 1988), Parkinson's disease (Globus *et al.*, 1985; Matison *et al.*, 1982; Pillon *et al.*, 1986) and progressive supranuclear palsy (Maher *et al.*, 1985; Pillon *et al.*, 1986). Indeed, when the performance of patients with DAT, Parkinson's disease and progressive supranuclear palsy was compared in the same study (Pillon *et al.*, 1986) it was those with progressive supranuclear palsy who showed the most severe impairment.

Word fluency tests exist in many forms. Subjects may, for example, be required to access words from the lexicon according to membership of a semantic category or by first letter. The existing literature on the cognitive deficits of patients with DAT would allow for opposing predictions concerning their relative performance on semantically and orthographically constrained word fluency tests (see Hart, S. *et al.*, 1988). Indeed studies which have addressed this question have produced inconsistent results. Weingartner *et al.* (1981) reported that most of their mildly impaired patients with progressive idiopathic dementia (presumed DAT) showed greater facility in producing words beginning with designated first letters than in supplying members of semantic categories while the majority of control subjects showed the reverse pattern of relative productivity. Moreover, word fluency was impaired by a scopolamine challenge to the already compromised cholinergic system of patients with DAT and this drug-induced impairment was most marked when retrieval was semantically constrained (Sunderland *et al.*, 1985). However, other workers who studied patients with mild-to-moderate DAT have reported the converse pattern of results with retrieval from semantic categories being superior to that according to first letter (Hart, S. *et al.*, 1988; Ober *et al.*, 1986; Rosen *et al.*, 1980). Hart, S. *et al.* (1988) noted that the particular letters and categories chosen had a significant effect upon the level of performance on either type of fluency task. This finding may partially account for the apparently descrepant results of Weingartner *et al.* (1981).

Contradictory results have also been reported regarding the relative performance of patients with Parkinson's disease on semantically and orthographically constrained word fluency tasks (Globus *et al.*, 1985; Matison *et al.*, 1982) and similar methodological considerations might go some way towards accounting for these discrepancies. Of course it is possible that subject selection variables might be important. A particularly moot question concerns whether dementia is present in the parkinsonian patient groups (and if so its severity). Subject selection variables may also be important in relation to the performance of patients with a history of excessive alcohol consumption. Mattis *et al.* (1981) reported deficits in retrieval of category exemplars in alcoholic Korsakoff patients, although other workers had previously failed to do so. However, as noted in earlier chapters of this book, and most recently in Chapter 8, the classification of patients whose cognitive impairment is alcohol-induced is problematic. Their status in terms of the Korsakoff amnesic syndrome *vis a vis* alcoholic dementia (in which cognitive impairment is more generalized) is often unclear or unspecified.

Advocates of the cortical/subcortical distinction, and of the notion that language is spared in the latter, have attempted to account for the impaired word fluency of patients with subcortical dementias in terms of the cognitive processes, other than language, which are tapped by word list generation tasks (see Chapter 6). One of these other factors might be speed of processing as this is held to be particularly vulnerable in patients with subcortical dementia. The data of Cummings *et al.* (1988) are of interest in that patients having Parkinson's disease with overt dementia generated more category exemplars than patients with DAT, despite more marked slowing of their verbal output. Questions have also been raised concerning whether the word fluency deficit of patients with DAT represents an impairment of language *per se*. Miller (1984b) suggested that the deficit shown by patients with mild to moderate DAT in retrieving words according to first letter could be predicted on the basis of their general level of verbal intelligence, but Hart, S. *et al.*'s (1988) data point to a more specific impairment.

Data from word fluency tests have also been used to address the question of whether there are changes in the structure and organization of the lexicon in patients with DAT, over and above the demonstrated decline in retrieval efficiency. Miller and Hague (1975) found that patients with DAT not only produced fewer words than control subjects on a fluency task but that their responses demonstrated a differential paucity of low frequency words. While this finding might suggest a selective loss of low frequency words from the lexicon in patients with DAT, the results obtained by

Miller and Hague (1975) in a follow-up study did not concur with this (see below). Moreover, Ober *et al.* (1986) failed to replicate Miller and Hague's original observation. However, they allowed less time for response generation and this may have been insufficient for differences to emerge.

Martin and Fedio (1983) investigated the organizational structure of semantic memory by requiring subjects to generate the names of items that could be found in a supermarket. Normal control subjects proceeded in a systematic fashion from one superordinate category to another (e.g. vegetables, dairy products, household items, etc.). Their patients, whose dementia was mild to moderate, generated both fewer categories and fewer examplars per category than control subjects. These findings have been replicated by Ober *et al.* (1986), who also demonstrated that the changes were more marked in severely demented patients. Such results strongly suggest that, in addition to deterioration in the efficiency of lexical access, there may be some loss of information from the lexicon itself in patients with dementia.

It is worth noting that the data of Warrington (1975) and Schwartz *et al.* (1979), which will be returned to later in this chapter, are consistent with the notion that the organizational structure of semantic memory is altered in the course of a dementing process.

Generation and Selection of Word Associates

Gewirth *et al.* (1984), who studied the word associations of patients with dementia, reported a decrease in paradigmatic responses (i.e. responses which were semantically related to the stimulus and of the same grammatical class). This decrease was exacerbated by increasing severity of dementia but there were no significant differences between aetiologically distinct subgroups of dementia patients. Dementia did not reduce the incidence of syntagmatic responses (i.e. words of a different grammatical class from the stimulus word and words that could occur sequentially within the same sentence as the stimulus). Gewirth *et al.* (1984) concluded that their data pointed to loss of, or at least impairment of access to, semantic markers and loosening of associational networks. However, they asserted that knowledge of syntax remained comparatively intact, a point which will be returned to below. Essentially similar conclusions were drawn by Santo Pietro and Goldfarb (1985) from their word association study. Grober *et al.*'s (1985) finding that patients with DAT were impaired in ranking the salience of each of three attributes relative to an index noun would also suggest an alteration in the organization of semantic memory in such patients.

However, other data suggest that the organization of semantic memory remains comparatively intact in patients with dementia. Diesfeldt (1985) reported that while patients with DAT were poor at spontaneously generating category exemplars on a word fluency task their ability to select the member of a designated category from amongst four alternatives was unimpaired. Moreover, Hart (1985) found that patients with mild-to-moderate DAT, and likewise those whose dementia was probably of vascular origin, had little difficulty when required to make judgements about the category membership of stimulus words. Furthermore, despite difficulty in ranking the salience of attributes, the patients studied by Grober *et al.* (1985) were able to discriminate between words which were and were not related to a stimulus item. Similarly, Nebes and Brady (1988) found that patients with DAT were highly accurate in deciding whether words were related to target stimuli. Such findings suggest that the contents of semantic memory remain intact, even when the organizational integrity of the semantic network has been compromised by the advance of dementia.

Narrative Discourse

Several methods have been employed to elicit connected sequences of expositive speech. The first is to engage the subject in open-ended conversation or in free narrative. This approach was employed by Miller and Hague (1975). On the basis of a sample of some 2000 words they concluded that the free speech of patients with DAT did not point to a selective loss of rare words. This result was at odds with their previous finding of a paucity of low frequency words on a fluency test. Kempler *et al.* (1987) analysed samples of spontaneous conversational speech from patients with DAT and found that these contained a normal range and frequency of syntactic constructions but poor lexical use. Such data provide empirical support for the often quoted assertion that syntax is selectively preserved in such patients. Likewise, Ripich and Terrell (1988) elicited expositive speech by engaging subjects in topic-directed interviews. In analysing their data they focused on the patterns of discourse, as reflected in subjects' use of propositions and cohesion devices and in listeners' judgements of the coherence of their utterances. Relative to control subjects patients with DAT used significantly more words and these occurred in shorter conversational turns. Moreover, independent judges rated their speech as more incoherent, principally because of missing referents, and Ripich and Terrell concluded that this failure by patients with DAT to make explicit for listeners the information necessary for comprehension reflected an inability on their part to take account of another person's perspective. Data collected using different methodology point towards similar conclusions (see below).

Although an open-ended conversational approach is appropriate for some purposes, it is less than adequate for addressing other research questions because there is no precise standard of reference against which to compare a subject's verbal behaviour. Alternatively, subjects may be asked to describe the uses of objects. Patients with DAT are often unable to provide more extensive verbal information about objects which they can name (Hart, 1985). It has been suggested that the problem lies in conceptualizing the action associated with use of an object rather than in description *per se* as would be the case with patients whose expressive difficulties were part of a more specific dysphasia (Stevens, 1985). Requiring the subject to describe a picture should also elicit connected sequences of words and here too there is a standard of reference. Picture description tasks are included in a number of the well-known batteries for examination of aphasia such as the Boston Diagnostic Aphasia Examination (BDAE) of Goodglass and Kaplan (1976), the Western Aphasia Battery (Kertesz, 1980) and Whurr's (1974) Aphasia Screening Test (AST). Obler and Albert (1981) present some interesting examples of the responses of patients with DAT to the Cookie Theft Picture from the BDAE. An analysis of the responses made by patients with DAT to this picture allowed Nicholas *et al.* (1985) to present quantitative data in support of the long-standing clinical contention that empty speech is typical of such patients. Hier *et al.* (1985) also employed this picture and made a detailed linguistic analysis of the responses of patients with DAT and of those whose dementia was stroke-related. They concluded that increasing severity of dementia had differential effects upon language depending upon the aetiology of the condition. The speech of patients with mild DAT was similar to that of patients with anomic or semantic aphasia, but in the later stages of the degenerative process it was more typical of Wernicke or transcortical sensory aphasia, becoming progressively more verbose and less concise while at the same time conveying less information. Conversely, the utterances of patients with vascular dementia became increasingly similar to those of Broca-type aphasics as the severity of their dementia increased. Their speech was more laconic than that of patients with DAT but aposiopesis, logorrhoea and palilalia were more characteristic of the latter. Perseverations featured in the utterances of patients having dementia, irrespective of its aetiology. Hier *et al.* (1985) suggested that the aposiopesis shown by patients with DAT might represent a non-linguistic deficit, namely failure to perceive the necessity of completing utterances. A similar notion was advanced by Hart (1985) to account for some of the errors made by patients with DAT on the Reporter's Test (see below). Hier *et al.*'s (1985) report that the pattern of impairment depends upon the aetiology of the dementia is important. It emphasizes the need for some degree of aetiological homogeneity if meaningful conclusions are to be drawn from group studies of the changes in language heralded by different conditions giving rise to dementia.

When describing pictures subjects retain considerable freedom in the choice of what to say. Furthermore, non-linguistic factors such as how the picture is perceived can be important determinants of their verbal responses. For example, Hart (1985) found that when patients with mild to moderate DAT were required to describe the picture from Whurr's AST their responses were not only linguistically deficient relative to those of controls but also showed lower levels of abstraction. Many patients failed to perceive the picture as an integrated whole. Stevens (1985) likewise reported that her mixed group of elderly patients with dementia showed evidence of failure to achieve perceptual integration or abstraction in describing the same picture.

An alternative approach to the problem of eliciting connected sequences of organized speech, yet limiting the range of acceptable responses, is exemplified by the Reporter's Test devised by De Renzi and Ferrari (1978). These workers conceived of the possibility of using the commands and stimuli from the Token Test to elicit expositive speech in a controlled manner. In the Reporter's Test the patient is required to describe actions carried out by the examiner with respect to the token stimuli, providing sufficient information to allow for exact reproduction of the examiner's action(s) by an imaginary third person confronted with the same stimulus array but unable to observe the examiner. Hart (1985) found that patients with DAT were impaired relative to normal control subjects irrespective of whether a pass-fail or a more lenient weighted scoring procedure (allowing credit for each relevant word reported, with the exception of verbs) was applied.

One of the claimed strengths of the Reporter's Test, namely the limited number of words it involves, could also be regarded as a source of weakness. The test does not tap the wealth of the vocabulary that may be available to an individual. Nevertheless, patients' responses can contain a rich variety of linguistic errors, as indicated by a qualitative analysis carried out by the first author (Hart, 1985). This revealed the not-infrequent occurrence of semantic paraphasias, a finding which concurs with the report of Stengel (1964b). However, it is at odds with claims made by Benson (1975) and Critchley (1964) that errors of this type were not a feature of the language of patients with dementia. Nicholas *et al.* (1985) also found that patients with DAT produced many semantic paraphasias and could not be distinguished from those with Wernicke's aphasia in terms of this linguistic feature. They did, however, utter fewer literal and verbal paraphasias than patients with a classical Wernicke-type aphasia and also produced fewer neologisms.

Several aspects of Hart's (1985) data on the Reporter's Test attest to the futility of considering language in isolation from other aspects of cognition. Non-linguistic cognitive errors were very apparent in the responses made to items in the final and most complex part of the test. For example, patients often made responses which, although verbally elaborate, showed rather egocentric utilization of a restricted context-dependent code. These responses contained insufficient information to allow for the examiner's action(s) to be reproduced solely on the basis of the descriptions rendered. Such findings are consistent with a view often expressed in the literature that the pragmatic or complex extra-linguistic aspects of language are severely compromised in patients with dementia. Moreover, the performance of patients and controls alike on all parts of the Reporter's Test correlated significantly with WAIS Full Scale IQ and with performance on the Wechsler Memory Scale, though the direction of causality, if any, remains to be determined. The Reporter's Test is certainly very sensitive to impairment in patients with DAT and Hart's (1985) data support McKhann *et al.*'s (1984) suggestion that it should be used routinely in the neuropsychological assessment of patients in whom a dementing process is suspected.

Repetition

In attempting to conceptualize the language deficits of patients with different types of dementia a number of authors (e.g. Appell *et al.*, 1982; Cummings *et al.*, 1985; Hier *et al.*, 1985) have invoked some of the categories of the Wernicke–Lichtheim taxonomy of the aphasias (see Marshall, 1986). In particular, attempts have been made to subsume the language of patients with DAT within the categories of anomic, transcortical sensory or Wernicke's aphasia.

The question of whether, and at what stage in the degenerative process, repetition becomes impaired is a central issue in such taxonomic endeavours. Although repetition remains relatively intact in the early stages of DAT, it can be impaired under certain circumstances. Rosen (1983) found that while mildly impaired patients could repeat sentences composed of high-frequency words accurately, repetition of sentences comprising low-frequency words was impaired relative to that of normal elderly control subjects and to their own performance on sentences of high-frequency words. Patients with dementia also show impairment in repetition of semantically anomalous sentences (Kopelman, 1986; Weeks, 1988). Furthermore, there has long been a debate in the literature concerning whether forward digit span is reduced in demented patients, with some workers (e.g. Caird and Hannah, 1964; Hart, 1985; Weingartner *et al.*, 1981; Whitehead, 1973a) failing to find significant impairment, while others (e.g. Larner, 1977; Kaszniak *et al.*, 1979; Kopelman, 1985; Nebes *et al.*, 1984) have done so. One factor contributing to the inconsistency of the results may be lack of aetiological homogeneity across patient samples, while another (see Corkin, 1982) may be variation in the severity of dementia. However, even patients whose repetition remains for the most part intact may still perform poorly when asked to recite over-learned sequences such as the alphabet (Hart, 1985), and in this respect they differ from patients with classical transcortical sensory aphasia (Cummings *et al.*, 1985). Such errors in the production of automatic sequences might arise because of deficient self-monitoring of verbal output.

Data on repetition have also been important with respect to the issue of whether there is a dissociation of language functions in the course of dementing processes, with knowledge of phonology and syntax remaining largely intact, while the semantic aspects of language are more vulnerable. Whitaker's (1976) single-case study of a 59-year-old woman with dementia (but not AD or Pick's disease according to autopsy data) is often quoted in relation to this debate. This patient was unresponsive to commands and her language was effectively restricted to echolalia and reading aloud. Nevertheless, she spontaneously corrected deliberate errors of syntax and phonology when she echoed the examiner's sentences, although she did not at any time correct semantic errors. This contrasts with Kopelman's (1986) observation that patients with DAT sometimes attempted to 'normalize' semantically anomalous sentences. Irigaray's (1973) data (see Obler, 1981) suggested that the pragmatic and semantic aspects of language were more vulnerable in patients with DAT than competence with respect to phonological and morphosyntactic features. Although this differential pattern of impairment has received much attention in the literature, it is important that clinicians do not lose sight of the aetiological and nosographic heterogeneity of dementia syndromes and recognize that the empirical research to date has yielded some apparently inconsistent results. Holland *et al.*'s (1985) report charting the progression of deterioration in a patient with Pick's disease is of note in this respect. This individual's syntactic ability showed marked deterioration before semantic competence was severely impaired.

Reading Aloud

It has already been noted that ability to read single words aloud remains remarkably intact in patients with dementia. However, there is a paucity of data concerning their ability to read sentences or prose passages. Cummings *et al.* (1986) found that patients with DAT could read written commands aloud without difficulty, but Stevens (1985) reported that her patients were impaired on the sentence reading subtest of Whurr's AST. These were a mixed group, some of whom had DAT while others probably had vascular dementia. However, using the same test materials as Stevens, Hart (1985) found patients with DAT to be impaired. Moreover, Hart's (1985) data suggested that ability to read sentences aloud might be more impaired than word-reading ability, quite apart from the issue of comprehension. A disruption of visual scanning mechanisms may contribute to this. Scanning difficulties can also disrupt performance on single word reading tests, but on these it is possible to redirect a patient's attention to the appropriate location without confounding the dependent measure of reading efficiency (Hart *et al.*, 1986a).

Writing

While agraphia is recognized as a symptom of DAT there is a lack of concensus regarding the frequency of this symptom or the proportion of patients in whom it is apparent before the final stages of vegetative mutism. As already noted, some workers (e.g. Breitner and Folstein, 1984; Seltzer and Sherwin, 1983) have suggested that the presence or absence of this symptom may be a criterion of some significance in the debate about whether subtypes of DAT exist. However, the assessments of agraphia carried out by such workers have been somewhat superficial. Before drawing conclusions about the presence or absence of dysgraphia it is necessary to assess writing performance under a variety of circumstances, including copying, writing to dictation and the more creative process of 'spontaneous' writing. Patients are often asked to write their name and address but may fail to do so for different reasons. Those who are unable to remember their address may nevertheless be able to write it perfectly, once reminded, while others who can provide this personal information orally, upon request, may be quite unable to execute the required graphic response (see Hart, 1985). Needless to say, patients whose dementia is associated with movement disorders, such as those with Parkinson's disease and Huntington's disease, manifest impairments of writing (see Chapter 6).

The figures which follow depict examples of writing collected by the first author from patients with DAT. Figure 9.2 illustrates the responses of a 71-year-old man when required to write five words to dictation (book, dart, gate, string and

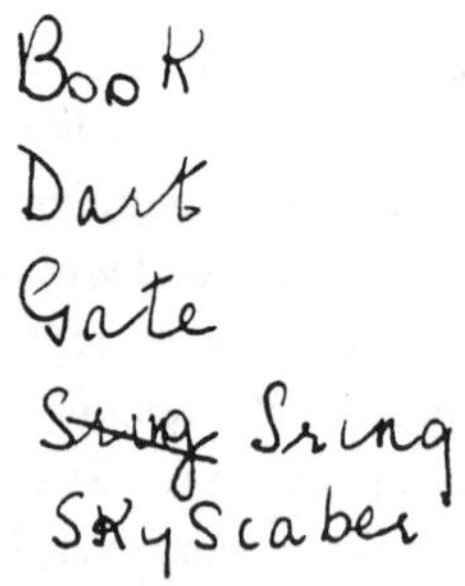

Figure 9.2   Writing to dictation.

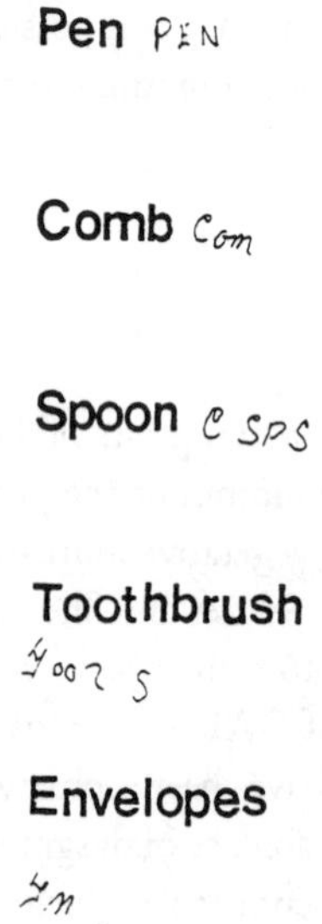

Figure 9.3   Copying words.

skyscraper), following Whurr (1974). It demonstrates letter omission errors as well as substitution of a letter which is phonologically and visually similar to the target (b for p). These errors were particularly significant in view of this individual's educational and occupational background and his still average level of general intellectual functioning at the time of testing when he achieved a Full Scale IQ score of 106 (± 5.1 S.E.M.) on the WAIS. This was, however, lower than the premorbid estimate derived from performance on the NART (Full Scale IQ = 119 ± 7.6 S.E. est) and represented a decline from the Full Scale IQ measure of 122 (± 5.1 S.E.M.) obtained on the WAIS 1 year before. Figure 9.3 depicts attempts at copying made by a 74-year-old man with a 2-year history of cognitive decline and marked frontal signs. It shows omission of letters and evidence of preservation across stimuli. Figure 9.4 illustrates deterioration of writing ability over a period of 18 months in a woman who presented at 66 years of age with a history of decline dating back some 2½–3 years according to her family (Patient E; Hart, 1985).

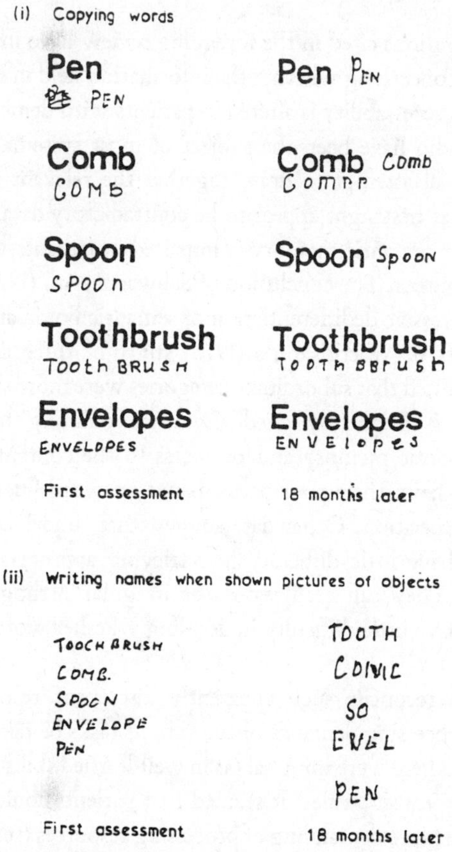

Figure 9.4   Deterioration in writing ability.

The stimulus materials employed in these writing tests were from Whurr's AST and have been reduced from the original size (as presented to patients) for the purposes of reproduction in this text. The illustrations of patients' responses have also been reduced proportionately.

Holland *et al.*'s (1985) single case study is of interest in that their patient with Pick's disease retained the capacity to express his thoughts and feelings in writing long after he had ceased to speak. Admittedly he did so in a somewhat distorted manner.

Behrendt (1984) draws attention to some of the negative implications of impairment of handwriting for individuals who, although in the throes of a dementing process, might nevertheless be able to sustain some degree of independence in society. In particular, he emphasizes the legal implications of inability to render one's signature as in former times.

Semantic Memory

Many of the investigations cited in the foregoing review have important implications for the controversy concerning whether the information held in semantic memory, its organization and/or accessability is altered in patients with dementia and in particular those with DAT, who have been the subject of most systematic investigations. In what follows we shall attempt to draw together the relevant information so as to reconcile what may at first sight appear to be contradictory data. Evidence consistent with the notion that semantic memory is impaired in patients with dementia comes from a number of sources. The conclusion of Schwartz *et al.* (1979) that their patient, WLP, showed progressive dedifferentiation of semantic boundaries is widely quoted. Likewise, the results of Warrington's (1975) study of three patients with cortical atrophy which suggested that subordinate categories were more vulnerable than superordinate categories is frequently cited. Evidence pointing to alterations in the organization of semantic memory and/or access to the contents thereof in patients having DAT comes from their poor performance on word fluency tasks and altered patterns of word association. Other data suggest that, under certain circumstances, such patients may have little difficulty in retrieving appropriate information from semantic memory. They can read words of irregular orthography, they observe syntactic rules and have little difficulty in deciding whether words belong to specified semantic categories.

Attempting to reconcile such apparently discrepant results, the first author proposed that the processing demands of the various tasks be taken into consideration (Hart, 1985). When these were minimal (as in well-learned skills such as reading aloud or compliance with syntactic rules) it seemed that patients could perform efficiently, but when tasks were more demanding of processing resources (requiring, for example, a self-directed search of information held in semantic memory as in word fluency tasks) their performance was poorer. Others have arrived at similar conclusions (e.g. Jorm, 1986). The results of word association studies are consistent with this notion in that patients with DAT make few errors in deciding whether stimuli are related, but are poor at generating associate responses or at ranking the salience of associates for a given target (Gewirth *et al.*, 1984; Grober *et al.*, 1985; Santo Pietro and Goldfarb, 1985). If the structure and organization of semantic memory does indeed remain intact in patients with DAT and the deficits detected arise because they do not have available the attentional capacity necessary to utilize the information, then one might expect that these patients would show evidence of semantic priming. This is widely considered to be an automatic process and thereby one that demands little processing capacity. Unfortunately, the available data are inconsistent (see Chapter 8) and further research is necessary to establish the exact circumstances under which semantic priming does and does not occur in patients with DAT. Comparative investigations must also be carried out to determine the relative integrity of priming operations in patients whose dementias arise out of different disease processes.

A distinction between the automatic *vs* effortful processing demands of different tasks not only allows one to reconcile much of the available data, but also serves to focus attention upon the extent to which different cognitive processes interact. For the moment it remains little more than a *posthoc* rationalization, but it should be possible to demonstrate by means of appropriate experimental methodology that the semantic processing operations which patients with DAT perform poorly are indeed more demanding of cognitive resources. Dual-task paradigms might be one likely candidate.

Non-verbal Communication

Although language is undoubtedly of crucial significance in human interactive processes we must not lose sight of the reality that communication entails more than language. The prosodic features of speech such as pitch, loudness, rate and the intonation, melody and variability of the speaker's voice are important elements in the communication of emotion and contribute to the contextual framework out of which meaning is extracted. These features are used in synergy with aspects of body language such as gesture, gaze, relative positioning and physical contact to produce the rich and complex medium of non-verbal communication.

The normal ageing process involves atrophy of the vocal chords and alterations in the larynx and associated speech musculature. These give rise to changes in the acoustic and articulatory properties of speech such as its intensity, pitch and rate, its nasal properties and the modulation, tremor or breathiness with which it is uttered. Such changes in motor speech performance are further compounded by a number of neurological conditions including some dementia-producing diseases.

Dysarthria, which results from weakness, paralysis or incoordination of the speech apparatus itself, typically occurs without the symbolic processes of language being compromised. It is a recognized clinical feature of a number of so-called sub-cortical dementias in which infracortical pathology affects brainstem nuclei that innervate the speech musculature. Different types of dysarthria have been identified (Darley *et al.*, 1975) and in Parkinson's disease and progressive supranuclear palsy it is typically of the hypokinetic type, while patients with Huntington's disease manifest hyperkinetic dysarthria. In stroke patients, also brainstem lesions may give rise to dysarthria and by implication therefore certain patients with multi-infarct dementia will manifest this motor speech impairment. Likewise, the reports of aprosodias or compromised affective communication following right hemisphere strokes (Ross, 1981) would lead to the expectation of impairment in this domain of non-verbal communication in at least some patients with vascular dementia. Frontal lobe disease can lead to alterations in prosody (see Sapir and Aronson, 1985). This may have implications for dementia-producing conditions in which neuropathology shows a propensity for the frontal lobes (as in Pick's disease and certain cases of AD) or by less direct means interferes with the functioning of this brain region (as, for example, in Huntington's disease).

The capacity of patients with Parkinson's disease to convey affective information is not only compromised by dysarthria, but also by the masking of facial expression which is another characteristic feature of this disease. In a controlled experimental investigation Scott *et al.* (1984) demonstrated that receptive as well as expressive abilities were impaired in patients with Parkinson's disease whose appreciation of both facial expressions and the prosodic elements of speech was deficient. It remains to be determined whether such difficulties are exacerbated in patients with Parkinson's disease plus dementia. Studies of heterogeneous groups of institutionalized patients with purported dementia led Kurucz and colleagues (Brosgole *et al.*, 1981; Kurucz and Feldmar, 1979; Kurucz *et al.*, 1979) to conclude that their ability to decode facial expressions depicted in pictorial representations was impaired, although these patients achieved greater accuracy in recognizing 'happy' faces than those which were 'sad' or 'angry'. In the studies carried out by Kurucz *et al.* subjects were exposed to very unrealistic situations. In real-life circumstances non-verbal communication is usually multi-modal and multi-factorial and people typically respond to non-verbal communication using non-verbal as well as verbal channels. Hoffman *et al.* (1985) attempted to circumvent some of the methodological pitfalls of the earlier work by having an actor convey emotional information and recording non-verbal as well as verbal responses. These workers concluded that non-verbal communicative abilities were not significantly compromised by dementia. Even patients with severe dementia remained responsive to the emotional undertones in their environment, although their responses were often delayed. In this study patients were responsive to negative as well as to positive affective communications. These findings have important implications for the behaviour of caregivers and are in agreement with views expressed in the nursing literature based largely (but not exclusively) on anecdotal observations (e.g. Bartol, 1979; Burnside, 1973; Langland and Panicucci, 1982). The importance of touch is often mentioned in this literature which is targeted primarily at those who deliver care directly.

Information about objects and actions can be conveyed through pantomime, but comprehension of information delivered via this medium is deficient in patients with DAT (Huff *et al.*, 1988; Kempler, 1988). Kempler (1988) found that these patients were also deficient in producing pantomime, but most of their errors were clearly related to the gestural target. Since patients could execute non-symbolic movements without difficulty he concluded that their problem was not simply one of inability to perform purposeful coordinated movements. Given that the same patients showed deficits in both comprehension and production of pantomime, together with parallel receptive and expressive impairments on lexical tasks, Kempler (1988) concluded that DAT heralded disruption of a general symbolic system underlying both gestural and lexical abilities.

Concluding Remarks

It must be apparent from the foregoing review that there are many discrepancies in the literature regarding the language and communication of patients with dementia. A number of interrelated factors have combined to produce this state of affairs. Most studies have focused on patients who have DAT, but there is considerable heterogeneity in terms of the symptoms displayed by individuals with this diagnosis and the rate and manner of disease progression. Lack of consistent diagnostic criteria for dementia and its different causes must also militate against homogeneity across patient samples. Most dementias arise out of progressive degenerative conditions and the nature and extent of language deficits can, therefore, be expected to change during their course. At the present time there is a lack of consensus regarding criteria for staging the progress of deterioration and there are no accepted instruments (psychometric or otherwise) to index levels of severity in anything but crude terms. Hence, it is necessary to provide detailed descriptions of the patient samples under investigation. There is an urgent need for detailed longitudinal investigations to chart the progression of communicative dysfunction within the same individuals and reduce the potentially confounding effects of between-subject variance, that inevitably complicates cross-sectional approaches.

It is clear from the recency of many of the papers referred to in this chapter that interest in the language of patients with dementia is growing and that there has been a welcome increase in awareness of the importance of aetiological considerations. There remain many unanswered questions. Detailed comparative studies employing groups of carefully selected patients with different types of dementia might generate data pertinent to the resolution of outstanding nosological and nosographic questions. The receptive language of patients with dementia has been rather neglected while non-verbal communicative abilities have been largely ignored. These require more systematic investigation. Furthermore the issue of whether, and to what extent, dissociation of language functions occurs routinely in dementia is one that requires attention. Although a number of investigators have suggested that the pragmatic and semantic aspects of language are more vulnerable than competence with respect to syntax and phonology (a contention which is fast approaching the status of dogma) such conclusions have not gone unchallenged (Obler, 1983). It remains possible that these linguistic modules may be differentially impaired depending upon the aetiology of the dementia. There is a need for carefully designed studies which use semantic and syntactic tasks of comparable difficulty.

A major thrust behind much of the current upsurge of interest in the dementias has been the quest for sensitive indexes for assessing pharmacological efficacy. Greater understanding of language may permit development of sensitive measures of change that might be of use in assessing the efficacy of any therapeutic intervention.

Given the interdependence of language and other cognitive functions, the search for an understanding of language dysfunction in demented patients must go hand in hand with explorations of other aspects of cognition (see Obler, 1983). Bayles and Boone (1982) rightly point out that the responses of demented patients may hold a wealth of theoretically rich information which might permit a better conceptualization of the relation of thought to language. In addition to these more abstract academic questions, increased understanding of the nature of the impairment(s) of language and communication heralded by different dementia-associated conditions may lay the foundations for therapeutic interventions. It must at least allow for more informed, and therefore more appropriate, approaches to the day-to-day management of afflicted patients. This is important since impaired communication is a major contributor to the burden experienced by carers (Gilleard, 1984) and must also be a cause of great frustration to patients.

Chapter 10

Attention

Attentional dysfunction has been noted in some clinical descriptions as an important feature of DAT (e.g. Brun and Gustafson, 1978; Eisdorfer, 1981; Eisdorfer and Cohen, 1980; Chapter 6) and as noted in earlier chapters, attentional concepts are becoming increasingly important in attempts to account for memory and language dysfunction in patients with dementia. It has also been asserted that impairments of learning and memory in the so-called subcortical dementias are associated with disturbances of arousal and attention. However, despite recognition of its importance, systematic investigation of this critical aspect of cognition has been conspicuously lacking (Miller, 1981a). A major difficulty confronting researchers has been the lack of a unified concept of attention. Moray (1969) listed six different meanings of the term then in use in the psychological literature and Meldman (1970) provided an even more extensive list. However, in a highly influential paper, Posner and Boies (1971) proposed that, underlying this diversity, three core concepts of attention could be identified. The first of these concerned maintenance of attention in the sense of sustaining alertness or arousal and the second related to the ability to select information from one source or kind rather than another. The third concept concerned limitations upon available processing capacity and therefore related to the notion of mental effort. Further evidence that attention is not a unitary concept can be found in the experimental psychopathology literature where it has been demonstrated that different procedures purporting to be measures of attention often display minimal intercorrelation (see Spring, 1980).

The attempts of researchers and theorists to fractionate attention have undoubtedly proved useful in organizing the available data and allowing new questions to be formulated. However, there is in practice a continuous dynamic interaction between these different attentional processes or constructs. This is exemplified by Kahneman's (1973) attempt to link the amount of processing capacity available to level of arousal. One consequence of the highly interactive nature of attentional processes is that performance on any task or measure of attention will generally represent the net result of contributions from each of the components, however many one chooses to construe. Thus, for example, ability to focus attention upon an appropriate target and resist interference from others will require more than selective operations and efficiency in regulating the direction of attention. It will, in addition, depend upon intensive aspects of attention such as arousal and the focusing power or degree of concentration that can be mustered for information processing. Readers who wish to learn more about the historical development of concepts of attention and the diversity inherent in current conceptualizations might wish to consult Parasuraman and Davies (1984).

Comparatively little is known about the neural mechanisms that underly attentional processes. However, it is widely accepted that they involve complex interactions between many cortical and subcortical areas and pathways of the brain (Mesulam, 1981, 1985; Pribram and McGuinness, 1975; Sheer, 1984). Equally complex is the role played by various neurotransmitters. Acetylcholine, dopamine and noradrenalin have all been implicated (Clark *et al.*, 1986a,b; Joseph *et al.*, 1979; Mason, 1980; Robbins and Everitt, 1987; Sheer, 1984; see also Chapter 5).

In reviewing the limited amount of experimental data available from patients with dementia it has proved expedient to simply divide attentional phenomena into two broad classes, namely selective and intensive. Other workers too have chosen to use this simple dichotomy (see Section 2 in Boller and Grafman, 1988).

Selective Aspects of Attention

To what extent can patients with dementia sample information adequately from all sources and exclude or ignore 'irrelevant' stimuli while being ready to shift the focus of attention under appropriate circumstances?

In a study of the visual perceptual ability of a group of patients with senile dementia, Williams (1956) showed that their slow and inaccurate performance was largely due to inability to select appropriate and ignore irrelevant cues in the perceptual field. She concluded (1956: 278) that, ' . . . what the demented patient lacks is not so much the ability to behave in a fitting manner as the ability to select from his environment the cues to tell him what is fitting. It is not so much that he is unable to receive information through his senses, but that he is unable to select or abstract from all the information available that which is relevant'.

At the heart of the Stroop effect lies an inability to focus attention upon a single input and exclude from processing (or at least inhibit responses to) other inputs defined in advance as being irrelevant. Indeed, Allport (1980: 130) has described the Stroop task as 'a microcosm of selective responding'. In the original Stroop paradigm interference was generated by requiring subjects to name the colour in which incongruous colour words were printed (i.e. red printed in blue, green printed in red etc.) while ignoring the printed words. However, an interference effect can also be demonstrated using other types of material (e.g. Cohen and Martin, 1975; Jensen and Rohwer, 1966

Morton, 1969; and reviews by Dyer, 1973) and Stroop-like paradigms are increasingly being used to tap the unconscious operations of the semantic memory system.

Hart (1985) employed a modified version of the Stroop colour-word task in an investigation of patients with DAT and a small group of patients whose dementia was probably of vascular origin. When required to name the print colour of incongruous colour words patients with DAT were impaired on measures of accuracy and speed of response. They were also impaired, albeit less severely, on a second interference condition in which they were required to name the colours in which non-colour words were printed. Since the magnitude of interference on Stroop tasks depends upon the strength of the semantic relationship between the competing responses (Klein, 1964; Warren, 1972) the finding of a more generalized interference phenomenon is consistent with the suggestion that there may be some disruption in the organization of semantic memory in patients with DAT (see Chapters 8 and 9). Patients with supposedly vascular dementia were also impaired relative to age-matched controls, but only in terms of response speed on the more difficult conflict condition of incongruous colour words. It is possible that the difference in performance between the two patient groups simply reflected the relative severity of their dementia since those with DAT scored significantly lower on a brief mental status examination (Blessed *et al.*, 1968). A particularly interesting outcome of this investigation was the finding that patients improved their performance on repeated presentation of the stimulus material. This suggests that they were learning to overcome the disruptive effects of interference so as to focus attention more selectively.

Brown and Marsden (1988) reported that patients with Parkinson's disease were impaired on the Stroop colour-word task under normal test conditions, but not when they were cued regarding the relevant response dimension before presentation of each stimulus word. They concluded that patients with this basal ganglia disorder have reduced attentional resources. When tested on the more effortful processing condition that required internal self-directed control their limited capacity was exceeded.

The difficulties that patients with DAT experience when attempting to exclude irrelevant information are also demonstrated by poor performance on Gottschaldt's Hidden Figures Test (Capitani *et al.*, 1988). This visual perceptual task requires subjects to disentangle a target (a meaningless geometric figure which is not amenable to verbal encoding) from a larger background of similar material in which it is embedded.

Electrophysiological procedures have often been used to study selective attention. Laurian *et al.* (1982) employed a fast habituation paradigm in which they presented subjects with short sequences of auditory stimuli separated by longer periods of silence. Young normal subjects showed a marked attenuation in the amplitude of their evoked responses to successive stimuli within sequences, but patients, described (1982: 288) as suffering from 'simple senile dementia' and 'senile dementia evolving towards an Alzheimer condition', did not demonstrate such attenuation. Indeed, patients' responses were enhanced. These results suggest failure to habituate on repeated presentation of a stimulus, but the significance of the findings are difficult to determine in the absence of an age-matched control group. This study should be repeated using more appropriate control subjects.

It has already been noted in Chapter 7 that a 'rare' tone which has been designated as a target stimulus for detection tends to evoke a large positive response, termed P3 (or P300) some 300 milliseconds after stimulus presentation. This component of the waveform is absent from electrophysiological responses to 'frequent' but irrelevant tones of a different frequency. The magnitude of the P3 response is generally insensitive to physical parameters of the signal, but it is affected by a variety of psychological factors (Johnson, 1984). Hence it has been referred to as a cognitive event-related potential. In patients with DAT the amplitude of the P3 potential is reduced and its latency is increased (e.g. Blackwood and Christie, 1986; Blackwood *et al.*, 1987; Pfefferbaum *et al.*, 1984; St. Clair *et al.*, 1985, 1988; Syndulko *et al.*, 1982). Longitudinal investigation of patients with DAT over the course of 1 year pointed to further increases in P3 latency which were very marked in some cases and were accompanied by severe cognitive decline (St. Clair *et al.*, 1988).

Brain cholinergic systems may be involved in the generation of P3 responses since the amplitude of this component of the waveform is reduced by treatment with scopolamine (Meador *et al.*, 1987). Blackwood and Christie (1986) found that although physostigmine enhanced learning and memory in a group of patients with DAT, P3 remained unchanged but Neshige *et al.* (1988) reported a reduction in P3 latency in patients with DAT following oral administration of physostigmine. Drug treatment also led to improved performance on the WAIS. However, while the muscarinic agonist RS86 also increased the amplitude of the P3 response, it had only modest effects upon cognitive status (Hollander *et al.*, 1987).

Changes in P3 are by no means unique to patients with DAT. They occur in the course of normal ageing (e.g. Goodin *et al.*, 1978, St. Clair *et al.*, 1985) and in other dementia-associated conditions including Parkinson's and Huntington's diseases (Goodin and Aminoff, 1987; Homberg *et al.*, 1986) and multi-infarct dementia (Neshige *et al.*, 1988). In Parkinson's disease these changes appear to be related to cognitive status rather than motoric impairment (Goodin and Aminoff, 1987; Hansch *et al.*, 1982; O'Donnell *et al.*, 1987). The same applies to Huntington's disease. Likewise, in multi-infarct dementia delays in P3 are related to severity of cognitive impairment (Homberg *et al.*, 1986; Neshige *et al.*, 1988). There have been reports of alterations in P3 in chronic alcoholics (Begleiter *et al.*, 1980; Pfefferbaum *et al.*, 1979), but these were not apparent in the recent study of Blackwood *et al.* (1987).

Selection for attention of particular stimuli or features of stimuli, and maintenance of this selection over time (a topic to be considered in the next section) are clearly necessary, but not in themselves sufficient, to support efficient cognitive processing. To function effectively an individual must steer a course between rigid fixation on the one hand and excessive distractibility on the other (see Geschwind, 1982) and demonstrate a certain degree of flexibility with respect to the focus, locus and maintenance of attention over time (Kinsbourne, 1980).

During the course of a general neuropsychological assessment of patients with DAT the first author noted many instances of inappropriate shifting of attention. Patients often seemed to be excessively distracted by irrelevant stimuli, especially in the auditory modality. Trivial sounds evoked marked orienting responses in some patients and these apparently failed to habituate. There were also occasions when patients noted trivial visual stimuli but it was less certain that their responses were inappropriate in the context in which they occurred. At other times patients failed to shift attention long after it was appropriate to do so. The phenomenon of so-called intrusion errors documented by Fuld and others (see Chapter 8) may represent another example of inappropriate shifting in the focus of attention. In contrast, perseverative responses, from which intrusion errors have been differentiated, may reflect a failure to shift the focus of attention when it would be appropriate to do so.

Hart (1985) employed a cross-modal reaction time task to investigate the ability of patients with DAT to shift the focus of attention under controlled experimental conditions. She compared reaction time to stimuli preceded by others in the same modality to response latency when they followed immediately after stimuli in a different modality. Two ipsimodal test conditions, visual and auditory, were also employed in order to control for the effects of stimulus change *per se*. These involved within-modality changes, in either colour of light or frequency of tone. Patients with DAT showed no effect of stimulus change in the visual modality, but some slowing in response to change within the auditory modality (consistent with the previously mentioned anecdotal evidence). However they demonstrated a very marked cross-modal retardation effect which was significantly greater than that demonstrated by normal control subjects. The enhanced modality shift effect observed in these patients was not simply an artefact of a generalized increase in response latency. Similar results were obtained when the retardation of reaction time following stimulus transition was expressed as a percentage of baseline response latency to non-transition stimuli in the same modality. Nevertheless, attempts to interpret the disproportionate slowing of patients with DAT on cross-modal transition trials as evidence of a deficit in ability to switch attention must be tempered by consideration of the methodological complexities inherent in any attempt to compare the size of a performance deficit across two or more tasks or conditions (Chapman and Chapman, 1973, 1978). Hence, it is possible that the performance differences apparent on the cross-modal and ipsimodal control conditions may simply reflect the psychometric characteristics of these particular tasks together with the generally lower competence of the patients with DAT.

In view of the already mentioned anecdotal evidence that patients with DAT over-reacted to auditory stimuli, it might have been predicted that these patients would not show cross-modal retardation on transitions from light to sound stimuli. Indeed, a comparative facilitation effect might have been expected, contrary to the bi-directional cross-modal retardation effect that was observed. Hart's (1985) study should be repeated while simultaneously measuring cortical evoked responses and other physiological elements of the orienting response. The relationship between the latency and magnitude of these neurophysiological components and reaction times to transition and non-transition stimuli could then be examined. In view of the inverted U-shaped relationship between arousal and performance, it is possible that a very marked orienting response, and increase in arousal when a new stimulus is presented, could render patients incapable of executing the required response efficiently. Rapid awareness need not *ipso facto* result in an immediate voluntary response. The possibility that there might be a discrepancy between physiological and behavioural responses merits further exploration. It would also be of interest to investigate cross-modal reaction times in patients with other dementia-associated conditions.

By means of sophisticated experimental methodology Posner *et al.* (Posner *et al.*, 1982; Rafal *et al.*, 1988) demonstrated empirically that normal subjects could orientate attention covertly without concomitant head or eye movements. They then sought confirmatory evidence of this dissociation between overt and covert orienting of attention from patients with progressive supranuclear palsy whose eye movements are restricted in the vertical plane. While maintaining fixation on the centre of a visual display subjects were required to press a response key when they detected a visual target. On each trial a preparatory cue preceded appearance of the target. This cue conveyed information regarding the probability of a stimulus appearing at each of four target locations (above, below, to right or left of the fixation point). Eye movements were monitored so that trials on which the eyes did not remain fixated could be excluded. Covert orientation of attention was inferred from facilitation of response speed when the stimulus appeared at the cued location. Patients with progressive supranuclear palsy were slower to shift attention in the vertical than in the horizontal plane, consistent with their known difficulties in executing vertical eye movements (see Chapter 6). This result suggests that the midbrain retinotectal pathways that are important for controlling eye movements also subserve covert orientation of attention. In patients with Parkinson's disease the facilitation produced by cues was equally marked in the horizontal and vertical planes. Since a normal control group was not included it is not possible to determine whether there was an overall diminution in the efficiency with which parkinsonian patients oriented attention. However, patients with Parkinson's disease find it difficult to redirect or reorientate attention in other situations. For example, they perform poorly on tasks which require them to shift conceptual sets (Cools *et al.*, 1984; Flowers and Robertson, 1985; Lees and Smith, 1983).

There is a growing consensus of opinion that attentional disturbance may be central to the phenomenon of unilateral neglect of extrapersonal space. This has been documented most frequently following injury to the right hemisphere of the brain. Attentional disturbance may also underlie related disorders involving neglect of personal space (Bisiach and Vallar, 1988). Under a variety of stimulus and performance conditions patients without elementary sensory or motor defects (and whose cerebral pathology is usually vascular in origin) manifest unilateral neglect in that they fail to report, respond to or orient towards stimuli presented on the side contralateral to the cerebral lesion. There remains much debate concerning the precise nature of the disruption(s) of attentional mechanisms that may be involved, but some selective components appear to be implicated (Rizzolatti and Gallese, 1988). Mesulam (1981, 1985) proposed that four cerebral components (posterior parietal, cingulate, frontal and reticular) formed an integrated neural network that mediated selective attention to events in external space. According to this theory mechanisms providing an internal sensory representation of the external environment reside in the parietal lobule while the cingulate cortex regulates those processes whereby motivational significance is attached to stimuli and events. Frontal mechanisms provide for coordination of motor sequences to enable scanning and exploration of the environment while the reticular system ensures an adequate overall level of arousal and vigilance. Mesulam proposed that different aspects of the clinical syndrome of neglect could be linked to damage occurring at different sites in the circuit. Mesulam's model serves to remind us that the efficiency of selective operations will be influenced by tonic or intensive components of attention and it is to these that we now turn.

Intensive Aspects of Attention

In this section we will report investigations of preparatory processes, overall processing capacity and ability to sustain attention over time in patients with dementia-associated conditions. Many studies concerned with the tonic or intensive aspects of attention have employed reaction time as an index of available processing resources. Although it is possible to have relatively specific or restricted deficits in selective attention, any disruption of the intensive component(s) will inevitably exert more widespread detrimental effects upon information processing.

Historically, some of the earliest attempts at measuring attention employed simple reaction time paradigms (Woodworth and Schlosberg, 1954; Zubin, 1975). Simple reaction time refers to the time required to make a response following occurrence of a single stimulus designated in advance as the target to be detected. As its name implies, it requires a relatively elementary level of information processing, but performance nevertheless depends upon a number of factors including neural conduction velocity, exteroceptor and effector operations and efficient central stimulus-response integration. The latter involves attentional components such as ability to develop and maintain an appropriate state of readiness to respond to the designated imperative stimulus.

Slowing of simple reaction time with age is probably one of the most replicated findings of behavioural gerontology. In their reviews Welford (1977) and Birren *et al.* (1980) concluded that the increase in simple reaction time was of the order of 20 per cent when subjects in their sixties were compared with those in their twenties and they cited experimental evidence pointing to a predominant central component in this slowing. Salthouse (1980) argued that slower functioning of the central nervous system was the principal mechanism giving rise to age differences in nearly all aspects of cognition. However, under certain conditions, elderly subjects do not show marked deficits in response speed relative to young subjects (Gottsdanker, 1982; Nebes, 1978) and this emphasizes the importance of procedural variables. Spirduso (1975) high-lighted the importance of subject selection criteria for the extent of slowing observed. Consideration of the difficulties surrounding early detection of dementia (see Chapter 7) prompts one to question whether and to what extent the subjects employed in much of this gerontological research have indeed exemplified the normal ageing process.

To date only a few investigations of patients with DAT have used simple reaction time paradigms. Miller (1974) examined the psychomotor performance of patients with presenile dementia and reported significant slowing relative to control subjects on the more complex aspect of the task but not on the component he considered equivalent to simple reaction time. However, a number of investigators have found simple reaction time to be significantly slower in their patients with DAT (Ferris *et al.*, 1976; Hart, 1985; Pirozzolo *et al.*, 1981). Hart (1985) varied the interval between execution of a response and occurrence of the next stimulus. She demonstrated that patients with DAT responded faster at all response-stimulus intervals when these were regular (i.e. constant within a block of trials), as opposed to when they were irregular and varied randomly from trial to trial. Patients were severely disadvantaged by short response-stimulus intervals occurring in the context of an irregular series. This suggested that patients with DAT were attempting to generate and utilize a model of the temporal sequence of events so that they were able to make at least gross predictions concerning the time of occurrence of the next signal. Hart (1985) hypothesized that impairment of short-term working memory might force the patients with DAT to base their models upon limited sampling. Since short response-stimulus intervals in an irregular series were likely to have been preceded by longer intervals, patients tended to be unprepared. On the other hand normal elderly subjects, whose models of the stimulus sequence were based upon more extensive sampling, were less likely to be so adversely affected. Electrophysiological evidence of impaired preparatory processes has been obtained from investigation of contingent negative variation (O'Connor, 1981; Tecce, 1983). Hart's (1985) data, from the study described above and from another experiment (in which she demonstrated that patients' simple reaction time showed the normal orderly relationship to stimulus intensity), revealed two other important aspects of the performance of patients with DAT. First, their responses were more variable than those of control subjects, and second, practice led to a decrease in response latency and/or variability.

Recently Bloxham *et al.* (1987) employed a simple reaction time paradigm to investigate preparatory processes in patients with Parkinson's disease. Their patients derived as much benefit as control subjects from provision of a warning signal at various intervals before onset of the imperative stimulus. These findings implied that preparatory processes were intact. However, Bloxham *et al.*'s patients were not considered to be cognitively impaired on the basis of a mental status examination. It, therefore, remains to be determined whether similar results would be obtained from parkinsonian patients who also showed evidence of cognitive decline.

Choice reaction time involves all of the underlying components of simple reaction time but it also requires additional central processing. This includes stimulus discrimination and differential response selection. Age differences in choice reaction time are well documented (see Welford, 1977, 1980a). Increases in the intercept and slope of the function relating response speed to the number of choice alternatives have been reported. The greater separation between young and old subject groups as the number of choice alternatives increases has been interpreted as support for the so-called complexity hypothesis, according to which age differences in speed of performance on any test paradigm are proportional to the difficulty of the task (Cerella *et al.*, 1980). However, age differences in choice reaction time are reduced dramatically, even if not eliminated, following prolonged practice (Rabbitt, 1980; Welford, 1977).

In view of the increased processing demands imposed by choice reaction time tasks it might be expected that these would be particularly sensitive to reductions in attentional capacity or the amount of processing resources available. Studies comparing the performance of patients with DAT on simple and choice reaction time tasks have provided support for the conclusion that choice reaction time is a more sensitive discriminator between patients and normal elderly control subjects (Ferris *et al.*, 1976; Miller, 1974; Pirozzolo *et al.*, 1981).

Miller's (1974) paradigm allowed him to derive a measure of movement time as well as decision time. He reported significant impairment on both components of the overall reaction time. The first author's data also highlight the importance of employing methodology that allows overall response times to be decomposed into decision and movement components (Hart, 1985). Like Miller (1974), she found that the movement time of patients with DAT was significantly longer than that of normal elderly control subjects. She also reported that it was more variable. This was also true of a small group of patients in whom vascular pathology was the likely cause of dementia. All groups showed an increase in decision time as the number of response alternatives was increased (from one to two to four) but there was no evidence that patients were differentially impaired on the more complex conditions of the task.

Unlike decision time, movement time was unaffected by the number of stimulus-response alternatives. Hart (1985) also demonstrated improved performance on a second occasion of testing when response speed was increased and its variability reduced. Such results are consistent with the notion that patients with DAT are capable of procedural learning (see Chapter 8).

A marked slowing of thought processes is purported to be one of the defining characteristics of so-called subcortical dementia (Cummings, 1986). In Parkinson's disease this presumed slowing has been termed bradyphrenia. It has been considered analogous to the difficulties that parkinsonian patients experience in carrying out movements (bradykinesia). Clearly, attempts to validate the concept of bradyphrenia experimentally are complicated by the inevitable presence of motor slowing in patients with Parkinson's disease. One widely adopted approach has been to examine response latency as a function of the processing demands of the task, while keeping response requirements as constant as possible across task conditions.

The results of a number of investigations have seriously challenged the existence of bradyphrenia. Evarts *et al.* (1981) found that patients with Parkinson's disease were not selectively impaired on choice as opposed to simple reaction time tasks. Bloxham *et al.* (1987) reported that, although their simple reaction time was slower than that of age-matched controls, the response speed of patients with Parkinson's disease was not differentially decreased when simultaneous performance on a tracking task was required. As already noted, one selection criterion for inclusion of patients with Parkinson's disease in Bloxham *et al.*'s study was absence of cognitive impairment, but Dubois *et al.* (1988), whose patients with Parkinson's disease were cognitively impaired, also failed to show a differential increase in response latency when the complexity of the task was increased. However, they found that patients with progressive supranuclear palsy, whose motoric impairment was similar to that of parkinsonian subjects, required significantly longer to undertake the additional processing required by a disjunctive reaction time, as opposed to a simple reaction time, task. Finally, Rafal *et al.* (1984) failed to replicate Wilson *et al.*'s (1980) finding that patients with Parkinson's disease displayed a disproportionate decrement in performance on a memory scanning task when the number of elements to be processed was increased. The rate of high speed memory scanning manifest by their patients was well within the normal range. Moreover, although treatment with L-DOPA/carbidopa enhanced speed of responding, it did not affect the slope of the function relating response latency to the number of items being processed. They therefore concluded that the effect of treatment was to reduce bradykinesia rather than increase speed of cognitive processing.

The investigations of patients with Parkinson's disease reviewed above provide little experimental evidence of slowing in the rate of information processing. They do not, therefore, provide support for the notion of reduced attentional capacity. However, reports of impairment on the Continuous Performance Test (Mayeux *et al.*,

1987; Stern *et al.*, 1984) suggest that these patients may have difficulty in sustaining attention or mental effort over time. It is to this aspect of attention that we now turn.

There have been many variants of the Continuous Performance Test since its development by Rosvold *et al.* (1956) as a diagnostic instrument for the detection of brain damage. All versions require subjects to sustain attention over time in order to detect targets from amongst distractors. Target stimuli can be simple (e.g. the letter X) or compounds of two or more stimuli (e.g. X, but only when preceded by the letter A). The Continuous Performance Test has proved sensitive in detecting deficits in various clinical groups and in monitoring the effects of drug treatments (see Hart, 1985). Indeed the performance of young normal volunteers on this test paradigm can be impaired by cholinergic blockade and enhanced by stimulation of brain cholinergic systems (e.g. Wesnes and Revell, 1984; Wesnes and Warburton, 1983a, b).

Alexander (1973b: 229) examined the performance of hospitalized patients with 'unequivocal senile dementia' relative to that of normal control subjects and patients with functional psychiatric disorders. Patients with dementia were not significantly impaired on the simple condition of the Continuous Performance Test in which they were required to respond to occurrence of the letter X. However, they were disproportionately impaired when selective short-term retention of information was required in order to respond appropriately (X if preceded by an A). Using patients with more rigorous diagnoses of DAT, Hart (1985) replicated this finding of more severe impairment on the memory-load condition. By measuring speed as well as accuracy of responding, and by analysing performance in terms of signal detection theory, she also demonstrated impairment on the simpler condition of the task. A small group of patients with vascular dementia did not differ significantly from normal elderly control subjects on any measure of response accuracy but, like patients with DAT, they were significantly slower and their response latency more variable than that of control subjects. Hence, reaction time and its variability were the most sensitive of the performance measures employed from the point of view of discriminating between patients with mild-to-moderate dementia and their non-impaired peers. Although these results are consistent with an inability to sustain attention for a prolonged period of time, or indeed to maintain it so as to respond efficiently in the short term, the exact nature of the dysfunction shown by patients with DAT remains to be determined. More specifically, the contribution of language and mnemonic deficits requires investigation since observations made during the course of this study led Hart (1985) to question whether less than perfect memory for the instructional set and/or inability to translate this into action might be contributory factors. Control subjects could readily reinstate appropriate responding after a momentary lapse of concentration resulted in an omission error but patients were frequently unable to do so. Failure to remember the instructions might be construed as a deficit in working memory (Welford, 1980b) and other evidence for impairment of this short-term memory system has already been reviewed in Chapter 8.

There is little information available concerning the extent to which patients with other dementia-associated conditions can sustain attention. The findings by Mayeux *et al.* (1987) and Stern *et al.* (1984) of impaired performance by patients with Parkinson's disease on the Continuous Performance Test have already been cited. There is a clear need for efforts to expand the comparative data base.

Concluding Remarks

Systematic investigation of attentional deficits in patients with dementia is still in its infancy but important results are already emerging. Clinical observations of attentional disorder in patients with DAT have received strong support from experimental studies. These patients have difficulty in selecting information from one source or kind rather than another, are poor at sustaining attention and have diminished processing resources. In contrast, investigations of patients with Parkinson's disease have challenged the widely-held belief that cognitive slowing is a prominent aspect of this condition. The finding of cognitive slowing in patients with progressive supranuclear palsy, whose levels of motor impairment were comparable to those of patients with Parkinson's disease, is important. This points to a dissociation between bradyphrenia (and by implication cognitive processing resources) and bradykinesia. It also emphasizes the utility of comparative investigations whereby differential patterns of performance may ultimately be linked to established differences in pathology and provide valuable clues to underlying neural mechanisms.

Jorm (1986) argued that, because of their diminished processing resources, patients with dementia would be particularly impaired on tasks that required effortful or controlled (as opposed to automatic) processing and that such tasks could prove useful as screening procedures. However, Weingartner (1986) rightly pointed out that a similar pattern of differential impairment may be found in other patient groups including those with depression and schizophrenia and in normal elderly individuals. Of course the extent to which various groups show differential impairment on effortful as opposed to automatic tasks may differ, and likewise the magnitude of their impairment. Hence Jorm's suggestion regarding screening potential cannot be dismissed. The distinction between automatic and effortful processing has proved extremely popular and it certainly allows for ready description of a large body of data. Its heuristic contribution is indisputable but the lack of well-defined operational criteria for what constitutes automatic and effortful processing affords potential for misuse. We must beware lest description and explanation become so enmeshed as to constitute a tautology. It is clearly necessary to arrive at some independent metric whereby tasks can be rated in terms of the automatic-effortful processing dimension and electrophysiological measures might go some way towards meeting this need. Sheer (1984) has suggested that level of electrical activity in the 40 Hz frequency band may be a marker of active cognitive processing and it would be of interest to determine whether performance on tasks purported to be effortful or automatic is associated with different amounts of activity in this frequency range. Sheer's data emphasize that attempts to relate electrophysiological activity to performance measures could provide a powerful paradigm for neuropsychological research.

In conclusion, investigations of attentional dysfunction in patients with dementia-associated conditions are beginning to yield important results. These promise to facilitate understanding of the nature of cognitive change in those afflicted by dementia-producing conditions. They are also providing information regarding the neural mechanisms that underly attentional processes.

Chapter 11

Sensation and Perception

The terms used in the title of this chapter are controversial and there is a large body of literature concerned with the question of how to define and distinguish between them. Essentially, sensation is the elementary process whereby stimuli become encoded within the nervous system. Perception is a higher order process concerned with extracting information from the neural impulses relayed by peripheral sense organs so that it can be organized and interpreted in the context of the subject's prior experiences and the knowledge base that constitutes semantic memory. Although sensation and perception have sometimes been considered dichotomous concepts it is difficult to determine where sensation ends and perception begins. However, it is important to emphasize that perception is not a passive one-way process driven by incoming sensory impulses. Rather it is an active exploratory venture whereby a subject seeks to make sense of an impinging array guided by existing semantic schemata or knowledge structures which give rise to expectations.

A related and equally controversial concept is that of agnosia to which reference has already been made at a number of points in preceding chapters of this book. This has been highlighted as a symptom which may be more characteristic of certain dementia-producing conditions than of others. Specifically, it has been considered a feature of cortical as opposed to subcortical dementias, and within the broad category of so-called cortical dementias it has been suggested that some conditions may show a particular propensity for dysfunction in this domain of perceptual processing. However, authors have not agreed as to which conditions herald differential vulnerability. Clearly an agnosia might occur at any point in the development of multi-infarct dementia, depending upon the location and extent of infarction. Although some have reported that agnosias occur early in the course of Pick's disease (Cummings and Duchen, 1981), others have not considered them to be a particularly prominent feature of this condition (Lishman, 1987). Although it has been documented as an early feature in certain patients with DAT (Crystal et al., 1982) agnosia is more typically considered to be a feature of the middle or later stages of this degenerative process. For anyone familiar with the concept of agnosia, as defined in the classical literature, this must give rise to certain questions. Traditionally, agnosia has been considered a disorder of recognition that cannot be explained in terms of sensory dysfunction, language deficits, attentional disturbances or generalized intellectual deterioration. However, in the later stages of a dementing illness, a specific disorder of recognition in the absence of elementary sensory dysfunction or significant impairment of other higher-order cognitive processes, not to mention one that was modality specific (one hallmark of agnosic disorders as conventionally construed), would be conceptually anomalous.

Quite apart from any difficulties that arise in relation to dementia, the concept of agnosia has been surrounded by controversy and is central to a number of on-going debates in the neuropsychological literature (Bauer and Rubens, 1985; Hecaen and Albert, 1978). It is not a unitary concept and some of the attempts at subclassification provide a focus for consideration of semantic issues which have received attention in the literature on dementia.

One question concerns whether a distinction can or should be made between perception and recognition. Lissauer's distinction between apperceptive and associative forms of visual agnosia remains an influential framework, although this stage model has been the subject of considerable debate over the years and has not met with universal acceptance (see Hecaen and Albert, 1978). Patients with so-called apperceptive agnosia are typically unable to draw misidentified items accurately or to match them to sample, but the striking feature of associative visual agnosia is that patients can copy and/or match-to-sample items that they fail to identify visually. Vignolo's (1969) division of auditory sound agnosia (i.e. inability to recognize non-speech sounds) into a perceptual-discriminative form (marked by predominantly acoustic errors on picture-sound matching tasks and associated with right hemisphere lesions) and an associative-semantic type (marked by predominantly semantic errors in matching pictures to sounds and associated with left hemisphere lesions) resembles Lissauer's apperceptive-associative dichotomy. The recognition failures of patients with the associative type of agnosia cannot be attributed to an inability to extract information from the impinging array of sensory stimulation or to an inability to integrate or organize the features extracted. Their deficit appears to satisfy the narrow definition of 'a normal percept that has somehow been stripped of its meaning' (Teuber, 1968: 293) but, whatever the merits of attempting to fractionate complex visual processes (and this we uphold) and however strongly the empirical data validate this decomposition, there is nevertheless a strong case for arguing that perceptual activity embodies the process whereby meaning is attached to the features extracted from sensory information. Data pertinent to the associative function whereby recognition is achieved will be included in this chapter. In more recent years, another classification system has been proposed in which a distinction is made between agnosias which are for object classes or superordinate categories as opposed to those which are for specific items or individual exemplars of the superordinate category. Patients with so-called prosopagnosia are typically unable to recognize the faces of certain individuals (specifically relatives and friends, and even their own faces in a mirror), but they remain aware of the general nature of the stimulus insofar as they recognize that it constitutes a face. On the other hand, a patient with a visual-object agnosia may be unable to recognize the identity not only of a specific object (e.g. apple) but also of the general semantic class to which it belongs (namely fruit). This proposed classification of agnosic disorders is particularly pertinent in relation to dementia. Readers will recall that this notion of hierarchical structuring in the semantic memory system, with the possibility of distinguishable types of defect reflecting impairment at different levels in the hierarchy, has already been referred to in Chapter 9.

Having highlighted certain controversial issues bearing upon the conceptualization of agnosia field, we now turn attention to the empirical data pertaining to the integrity or otherwise of sensory and perceptual systems in patients with dementia. For reasons of space we must assume that readers possess a certain knowledge of the anatomy and physiology of the sensory systems, but those who require further details of these systems should consult sources such as Fitzgerald (1985) and Kendall and Schwartz (1985). References such as Lindsay and Norman (1972) and Birren and Schaie (1985) may prove useful in relation to the visual and auditory systems.

Taste and Smell

The chemosensory modalities of taste and smell are closely related and hence will be considered together. Schiffman (1983a,b) documents the functional significance of these sensory modalities and highlights the diversity of diseases, nutritional and endocrine disorders, as well as drug treatments, to which they are vulnerable. A number of studies have examined the effects of ageing on olfactory and gustatory detection thresholds and most of the data have pointed to higher thresholds in older subjects (Grzegorczyk *et al.*, 1979; Kimbrell and Furchtgott, 1963; Murphy, 1979, 1983; Schiffman *et al.*, 1976, 1979). However, the finding of decreased chemosensory acuity has not been unanimous (Engen, 1977) and future studies must address key methodological questions relating to the experimental paradigms employed and more importantly to the cognitive status of the elderly subjects under study. Specifically, rigorous cognitive assessment will be necessary to determine whether the participants in such investigations exemplify the normal ageing process. Careful documentation of cognitive status is required for all comparative purposes.

In recent years the results of a number of converging lines of investigation into AD have pointed to pathological changes in the neuroanatomical and neurochemical substrates of the olfactory system and have served to focus attention upon the functional integrity of different components of this important sensory window on the world. Brain structures such as the uncus and the hippocampus, the medial group of amygdaloid nuclei and the temporal lobe, which form part of (or are linked to) the olfactory system (Eslinger *et al.*, 1982) are particularly vulnerable to the degenerative processes of AD. More recent data have implicated the anterior olfactory nuclei which are involved at a rather earlier stage in the processing of olfactory information (Esiri and Wilcock, 1984) and there may be pathological changes in the sensory epithelium of the nose in patients with AD (Talamo *et al.*, 1989). It is, therefore, not surprising that reports are emerging of olfactory deficits in patients with DAT (see below). Furthermore, there have been reports that a number of other neurological conditions (e.g. Korsakoff's syndrome) and dementia-related diseases (e.g. Pick's disease, Parkinson's disease and Huntington's disease) are also associated with olfactory dysfunction. In certain of these (specifically Korsakoff's syndrome and Pick's disease) there is evidence of damage to some of the anatomical structures involved in olfaction, although in other conditions data pertaining to the integrity or otherwise of such brain regions are somewhat more circumstantial. Of course it is important to consider not only anatomical structures, but also the neurochemical substrates which mediate the processing of information acquired via the olfactory modality. The report of Simpson *et al.* (1984) is of particular interest in this respect as these workers found choline acetyltransferase (ChAT) activity to be significantly reduced in the olfactory tubercle of patients with DAT as well as in those with Huntington's disease. Such findings augment long-established evidence of markedly reduced ChAT activity in other areas of the rhinencephalon, particularly the amygdala (Davies, 1979; Yates *et al.*, 1980b).

Turning to the empirical literature documenting olfactory deficits in DAT and other dementia-associated conditions, it rapidly becomes apparent that researchers have employed a wide variety of test paradigms. These impose very different cognitive demands and require that different processing abilities be intact. Olfactory deficits could result from disruption of neural activity at a number of points in the system concerned with the processing of information acquired through the nose. In the review which follows we shall consider first evidence pertaining to lower level olfactory functions and then proceed through data bearing upon higher order processes.

The most basic form of deficit is an elevation of olfactory thresholds, i.e. an increase in the concentration at which a stimulus must be presented in order to be detected. A number of studies have provided evidence of impaired ability to detect olfactory stimuli in patients with DAT (e.g. Doty *et al.*, 1987; Knupfer and Spiegel, 1986; Rezek, 1987), although other investigators have failed to find increased detection thresholds (Koss *et al.*, 1988; Peabody and Tinklenberg, 1985). Procedural differences may have contributed to the emergence of discrepant results. Indeed, Rezek (1987) demonstrated empirically that the sensitivity of patients with DAT relative to control subjects differed across stimuli so that whether or not detection deficits are found is likely to depend upon the stimuli employed in a given investigation. Deficits in the detection of olfactory stimuli have also been reported in patients with Parkinson's disease (Ansari and Johnson, 1975; Quinn *et al.*, 1987; Ward *et al.*, 1983), as well as in those with multi-infarct dementia (Knupfer and Spiegel, 1986). In parkinsonian patients this detection deficit may be more pronounced in those in whom the disease progresses rapidly (Ansari and Johnson, 1975). There has been some speculation about whether dementia is more likely to occur in this subset of parkinsonian patients (Serby, 1987). The presence or absence of olfactory detection deficits in patients with Parkinson's disease seems to be independent of concomitant treatment with L-DOPA or anticholinergic drugs. Moberg *et al.* (1987) found that the capacity of their patients with Huntington's disease to detect olfactory stimuli was intact, despite deficits in some higher order olfactory functions.

In a number of experimental investigations subjects have been required to judge whether a given odour is one that has already been presented in the test situation. The serial presentation of stimuli in such test paradigms requires that subjects form a transient representation of the stimulus odour but they are not required to generate or choose verbal labels appropriate to the stimuli. Individuals suffering from DAT (Kesslak *et al.*, 1988; Knupfer and Spiegel, 1986; Moberg *et al.*, 1987), multi-infarct dementia (Knupfer and Spiegel, 1986) and Huntington's disease (Moberg *et al.*, 1987) have all been found to perform poorly when assessed using such procedures. However, little is known about the nature of these deficits. While they might arise out of deficient ability to evaluate the qualitative properties of stimuli, they could also reflect a deficit in short-term working memory which might be specific for this sensory modality or more generalized. Moberg *et al.* (1987) are exceptional among investigators to date in that they made some attempt to address such issues. They found that although patients in the early stages of Huntington's disease showed a specific deficit, restricted to olfactory stimuli, those in the early stages of DAT were also impaired in recognition of visual and verbal material. Given the obvious difficulties in matching patient groups in terms of severity and tasks in terms of their discriminative power (see Chapman and Chapman, 1973, 1978) such results can only be considered preliminary, but they clearly suggest that further comparative studies should be carried out.

It has been reported that performance in matching olfactory stimuli to supplied verbal labels is deficient in patients with DAT (Knupfer and Spiegel, 1986; Peabody and Tinklenberg, 1985; Rezek, 1987; Serby, 1987), multi-infarct dementia (Knupfer and Spiegel, 1986) and Parkinson's disease (Serby, 1987), but not in those with alcoholic dementia (Serby, 1987) although Mair *et al.* (1986) found that alcoholic Korsakoff patients performed poorly on an odour-word matching task. Once again we should remind readers of the possible uncertainty surrounding the diagnostic labels assigned to patients with a history of chronic and excessive consumption of alcohol. Performance on such tasks requires that the sensory features extracted be matched to information in semantic memory. However, as already noted in Chapter 9, at least some patients with dementia become inefficient in gaining access to and/or retrieving information from semantic memory and there is evidence to suggest that data may even be lost from this memory system. Serby's (1987) report is of particular interest in this respect. He found that while patients with DAT and Parkinson's disease were impaired in matching verbal labels to olfactory stimuli, their performance was not deficient on an analogous task requiring them to match verbal labels to tactile stimuli. Such results raise the possibility of a modality-specific deficit, although they may simply reflect differences in the discriminative power of the two tasks.

In view of the evidence reported above, as well as in preceding chapters of this book, it is hardly surprising that patients with DAT perform poorly when required to name olfactory stimuli (Doty *et al.*, 1987; Kesslak *et al.*, 1988; Knupfer and Spiegel, 1986; Peabody and Tinklenberg, 1985; Warner *et al.*, 1986), a test paradigm referred to in the literature as 'smell identification'. The perceptual-cognitive functions required for performance on this task are also compromised by multi-infarct dementia, but less severely than by DAT (Knupfer and Spiegel, 1986). However, Parkinson's disease is exceptional in causing impairment comparable to, or perhaps even greater than, that resulting from DAT (Kesslak *et al.*, 1988). Performance on identification or naming tasks requires retrieval of information from semantic memory, but parkinsonian patients do not typically show confrontation naming deficits when presented with visual stimuli. Therefore it is unlikely that language impairment contributes significantly to their odour identification deficit. Nominal deficits might contribute to the impairment of smell identification in patients with DAT and multi-infarct dementia, but Doty *et al.*'s (1987) results, which raise the possibility of a modality-specific deficit in some patients with DAT, must not be forgotten. The patients with DAT whom they assessed were not significantly impaired on a picture identification task but smell identification was deficient. Results such as these once again raise the question of whether the odour and picture identification tasks were of comparable discriminative power. Furthermore, the odour detection ability of Doty *et al.*'s (1987) patients with DAT was impaired and this may confound the interpretation of data bearing upon smell identification *per se*.

Little attention has been paid to gustation in patients with dementia-producing conditions. Koss *et al.* (1988) and Morris *et al.* (1989) are exceptional in having investigated this sensory modality. Koss *et al.* (1988) reported that taste detection thresholds were unchanged in patients with DAT but they did not attempt to assess higher order gustatory processes such as taste recognition and identification. Morris *et al.* (1989) documented a number of important changes in the eating habits of patients with dementia (DAT, multi-infarct dementia and 'mixed' dementia). These included both increased and decreased food intake and alterations in item selection. The most common change in selection involved increased consumption of sweet foods, but some subjects showed a desire for more spicy foods than they had previously been accumstomed to eating. A substantial number of subjects exhibited inappropriate oral behaviour, attempting to eat inedible objects or consuming foods that were inappropriate, either in quantity or because they were uncooked. Morris *et al.*

speculated that altered taste perception might be one factor contributing to the changes observed in the eating habits of patients in their sample.

From the foregoing review it is clear that interest in the olfactory deficits of patients with dementia has grown rapidly during the past decade and several important conclusions can be drawn from the data collected to date. First, olfactory deficits are common in individuals suffering from a number of dementia-associated conditions. As they are also to be found in individuals afflicted by other types of neural damage, including head injury, focal excision, brain tumours and epilepsy (e.g. Abraham and Mathai, 1983; Eichenbaum *et al.*, 1983; Eslinger *et al.*, 1982; Jones-Gotman and Zatorre, 1988) they cannot in themselves be diagnostic indicators of dementia or any of the conditions that give rise to it. Second, olfactory deficits may occur relatively early in the course of certain dementia-producing conditions, suggesting that olfactory structures, and those associated with them, may be particularly vulnerable to pathological change. Indeed, Roberts (1986) suggested that Alzheimer's disease is caused by aluminosilicates entering sensory neurons in the olfactory epithelium and being transported transneuronally to several olfactory (and related) structures in the brain, thereby initiating changes that eventually result in the widespread neuronal damage characteristic of AD. However, as will be made clear in subsequent sections of this chapter, olfaction is by no means unique among the sensory systems in being compromised in AD. It has been asserted that the olfactory cortex is the only primary sensory cortex to be affected in AD, but this is only true if one restricts consideration to neurofibrillary tangles: neuritic plaques are more uniformly distributed throughout the cortex (Lewis *et al.*, 1987). Third, it is clear that olfactory defiicits are multi-dimensional in nature. Although some reflect fairly specific sensory/perceptual failures others point to a breakdown in the interaction between olfactory and other information processing systems. This emphasizes what is a basic tenet of neuropsychology, namely that it is not enough to simply document the presence of a deficit. One must go further and carry out detailed behavioural analyses to specify the nature of the deficit. Fourth, attempts to link olfactory deficits to disruptions of specific neurotransmitter systems have so far been unsuccessful. A large number of neurotransmitters are to be found in olfactory structures (Halasz and Shepherd, 1983) and many of these, such as acetylcholine, dopamine and noradrenaline, are disrupted in conditions associated with dementia (see Chapter 4). However the pharmaco-behavioural data accrued so far, mostly from incidental observations of the effects of drugs prescribed for management of movement disorder in patients with Parkinson's disease, have not proved convincing in implicating either of the target neurotransmitters, namely acetylcholine and dopamine, in the genesis of olfactory deficits.

In conclusion, it can be said that although knowledge has grown rapidly in recent years much remains to be learned about the presence, extent and nature of olfactory deficits in patients with dementias of different aetiologies, and knowledge about gustatory functions is pitifully lacking. Before proceeding to consider other sensory modalities it seems important to emphasize the practical implications of the evidence so far available. The sense of smell has an important role in monitoring the safety of the environment. Olfactory deficits might render an individual unable to detect the smell of leaking gas, smoke, dangerous fumes or food spoilage and, even if able to detect such warning stimuli, their significance might not be appreciated (and appropriate action taken) because of a deficit at the level of smell identification or recognition. It is important to recognize that victims are likely to be unaware of changes in their sense of smell and rather dramatic displays of deficit will often be necessary before family members or other carers are alerted to it. Hence the need for detailed investigation of all individuals in whom a dementia-associated condition is present or suspected. Since understanding of the relationship between threshold and suprathreshold olfactory functioning is less than adequate, it is important that clinicians do not rely on threshold measures as the sole index of olfactory functioning but rather apply such tests in conjunction with measures of recognition and identification. Furthermore, it is important to recognize that chemosensory disorders can reduce victims' enjoyment and quality of life. Diminished olfactory or gustatory ability may affect food choices and dietary habits and by implication might influence the nutritional status of afflicted individuals. The contribution of such deficits to the altered eating behaviour and hyperorality seen in at least some patients with dementia (Cummings and Duchen, 1981) is presently unknown, but would seem to merit investigation.

Somesthesia

The widespread distribution of its receptors throughout the body and the variety of stimuli to which it responds, together with the diverse range of sensations which it mediates all serve to render the somatosensory system unique among sensory modalities. It comprises three broad categories of receptor. Exteroceptive components respond to stimuli originating in the external environment while proprioceptive mechanisms are concerned with information pertaining to how body parts are positioned in relation to one another, as well as the orientation of the body in space, and interoceptive systems monitor aspects of the internal environment, such as blood pressure and biochemistry, most of which do not reach conscious awareness. Within the somatosensory system four major perceptual submodalities have conventionally been distinguished. These relate to: (1) sensation of touch and pressure; (2) pain sensation; (3) position sense, which includes awareness of static limb positions as well as of limb movement (kinaesthesia); and (4) thermal sensations relating to both warmth and cold.

To date there has been comparatively little research interest in the integrity (or otherwise) of somatosensory systems in patients with dementia-associated conditions. However, some data pertinent to this issue are available. In an investigation of tactile discrimination learning Freedman and Oscar-Berman (1987) found that patients with DAT could differentiate between stimuli using only tactile cues, although they showed poor learning. Patients with Parkinson's disease, including those with dementia (claimed to be of comparable severity to that of patients in the DAT group), were also unimpaired in discriminating between stimuli but, unlike patients with DAT, were able to associate shapes with reward, although they too were impaired in reversal learning.

Crystal *et al.* (1982) reported on a patient with biopsy-proven Alzheimer's disease in whom astereognosis (i.e. inability to identify objects by touch alone) was prominent at the time of initial clinical presentation in the absence of more global deterioration. However, Hart (1985) found little evidence of astereognosis in her sample of patients with DAT and Barker and Lawson (1968) reported that the naming performance of patients with dementia, many of whom probably had DAT, was facilitated by allowing them to handle the stimulus objects. Readers will recall that Serby (1987) reported on patients with DAT who could match verbal labels to tactile stimuli but whose matching performance was poor when the stimuli were olfactory. Hart (1985) also failed to find evidence of astereognosis in a small group of patients whose dementia was probably due to vascular pathology, although this has been documented for individuals with damage to the post-central gyrus consequent upon a vascular accident (Mauguiere *et al.*, 1983).

Huff *et al.* (1987) found that patients with DAT responded normally to pin and vibratory stimuli applied to single loci. However, it has been reported that they perform poorly on the Face-Hand Test, as do patients with many types of brain damage (Fink *et al.*, 1952; Frederiks, 1969; Hughes *et al.*, 1982; Irving *et al.*, 1970; Kahn *et al.*, 1960, 1975; N. E. Miller, 1980; Yesavage, 1979; Zarit *et al.*, 1978). The Face-Hand Test requires perception of two stimuli applied simultaneously to the cheek and the back of the hand in varying asymmetric combinations. The most common errors on this test involve misperception of the stimulus applied to the back of the hand, either extinction (when the stimulus is not reported) or displacement (whereby the stimulus applied to the hand is reported as being felt on the cheek). Hart (1985) found that most of the misperception errors made by her patients with DAT involved extinction, an error type that has been attributed to attentional dysfunction (Frederiks, 1969). However, there is considerable intersubject variability in performance on this test and even mildly demented patients may perform poorly (Berg *et al.*, 1988; Hart, 1985). Therefore, it is unlikely to be a good indicator of severity. It has been suggested that the Face-Hand Test may be particularly useful in the diagnosis of dementia as it produces worthwhile levels of discrimination between patients with so-called funtional disorders and those with dementia, but E. Miller (1980) has drawn attention to the lack of standardization data. Furthermore, the first author's data (Hart, 1985) indicated that performance on the test correlated poorly with other global indicators of the integrity of cerebral function such as Full Scale IQ and performance on the

the Information Memory and Concentration Test of Blessed *et al*. (1968).

Hart (1985) found that patients with DAT were impaired in making right-left discriminations with respect to their own body parts but they also made errors in discriminating between right and left on a diagram of a person facing towards them. This latter situation requires subjects to take account of the relativistic nature of right and left as they pertain to body parts and raises a question concerning the extent to which the problems patients experience in discriminating right from left in relation to their own bodies represents a disorder of body schema *per se* as opposed to a more general problem of visuospatial processing. To what extent is awareness of one's own body a crucial mediating factor in making judgments about the body parts of others? Body schema is not, of course, a unitary concept. Conclusions about its integrity can only be drawn if errors on tasks purported to measure body schema are viewed in the context of performance in other test situations that require similar judgments but not in relation to one's own body parts. Hart's (1985) finding that patients with DAT were particularly impaired when the instructions specified which hand they were to use in pointing to a named body part depicted on a diagram would suggest a deficit in body schema. Of course the possibility of an attentional deficit must also be entertained. Patients with Parkinson's disease are impaired on similar right-left discrimination tasks (F. P. Bowen *et al*., 1976), as indeed are many other patient groups (see Benton, 1959).

A number of investigators have documented a high incidence of abnormal somatosensory symptoms in patients with Parkinson's disease (e.g. Koller, 1984; Quinn *et al*., 1986; Sandyk, 1986; Snider *et al*., 1976). Such patients often describe positive sensory symptoms which include numbness, tingling, pain, coldness and burning. The origin of these sensations is not well understood but it has been suggested that they reflect basal ganglia dysfunction (Koller, 1984) and important mediating roles have been proposed for both dopaminergic (Quinn *et al*., 1986) and cholinergic systems (Sandyk, 1986), at least with respect to sensations of pain. Such sensations occur in the absence of detectable changes in sensory thresholds (Koller, 1984; Snider *et al*., 1976), as does the hyperalgesia which occurs in Pick's disease. Robertson (1978) reported that patients with Pick's disease tend to wince if mild pressure is applied to the trunk or limbs and may utter cries of pain and attempt to withdraw from deep pressure or venepuncture.

Dinnerstein *et al*. (1964) found that the processing of tactile information was slowed in patients with Parkinson's disease, but investigations of somatosensory evoked responses in patients with this condition have generally revealed no significant abnormalities (e.g. Chiappa, 1983; Jorg and Gerhard, 1987; Koller, 1984). A notable exception is the report by Rossi *et al*. (1985) of abnormal responses which could be ameliorated by treatment with L-dopa. It has been reported that somatosensory evoked responses are abnormal in a number of other dementia-associated conditions, including Creutzfeldt–Jakob disease, Huntington's disease and progressive supranuclear palsy, and they are also abnormal following cerebral infarction (see Chiappa, 1983; Mauguiere *et al.*, 1983). The findings with respect to progressive supranuclear palsy are particularly intriguing. Such patients display enhanced responses (Chiappa, 1983).

Vision

The incidence of visual dysfunction rises dramatically with age. Changes occur not only in the optics of the eye, but also in all neural components of the visual system, beginning at the level of the retina and continuing through the optic nerve to the lateral geniculate bodies and hence to the primary and association visual cortices (see Kline and Schieber, 1985). However, the effects of visual ageing are usually gradual and in many cases can be compensated for so that most older people do not experience severe and disabling visual impairment. Of course various pathologies of the visual system, which are not linked directly to the ageing process, do show an increased incidence among elderly people (e.g. cataract, glaucoma, macular degeneration and diabetic retinopathy). Furthermore, the incidence and prevalence of stroke increases with age and it is well established that such vascular episodes can give rise to a number of abnormalities in the processing of visual information. These include visual field defects (partial or complete hemianopias); disorders of visual attention (referred to as visual/visuospatial neglect or unilateral neglect) which have already been mentioned in Chapter 10; and visual agnosias (inability to recognize specific aspects of visual information despite intact sensory and attentional mechanisms). Although the first two of these deficit classes often occur together (and indeed all three may be coincident on more rare occasions), it is important to emphasize that each can occur independently (see Chapter 10).

Although a history of completed stroke may be surprisingly uncommon in individuals with vascular or mixed dementias, visual abnormalities such as those just mentioned may be prominent in some patients with multi-infarct dementia, particularly following occlusion of the posterior cerebral artery. Right-sided lesions involving the territory irrigated by this artery may give rise to visual hallucinations, palinopsia (i.e. visual perseveration with recurrence of the perceptual experience elicited by a stimulus when that stimulus is no longer present) and abnormalities in the perceptual processing of facial information. Bilateral posterior cerebral artery infarctions may produce cortical blindness, achromatopsia (i.e. dilution of object colours), visual object agnosia, or prosopagnosia depending upon the location and extent of the lesions. Ross (1980) drew attention to the phenomenon whereby patients may manifest a sensory-specific visual memory disorder despite minimal damage to the occipital lobe *per se* if the infarction of tissue supplied by the posterior cerebral artery causes a disconnection between the visual areas of the brain and the temporal lobes.

The extent to which visual or other sensory-specific memory disorders occur in the context of multi-infarct dementia has not been documented. Indeed, there has been surprisingly little formal and systematic investigation into the cognitive deficits that may occur in this, the second most common cause of dementia.

Visual defects as a consequence of vascular pathology have long been recognized. A number of recent reports indicate that non-specific complaints of visual impairment are also frequently made by individuals suffering from DAT and by their carers (Cogan, 1985; Olson, 1989; Sadun *et al.*, 1987; Steffes and Thralow, 1987). These have been expressed in terms of problems with reading (such as losing one's place on the page), glare, misreaching for objects on a table, clumsiness, walking into door frames, bumping into people, knocking things over and tripping. In addition, there are reports of visual hallucinations and of propopagnosia, with patients frequently mistaking their own image in a mirror for that of another person (a misperception which may fuel paranoid delusions about 'intruders'). Patients sometimes converse with their own reflection in a mirror and indeed may believe that individuals on a television screen are present in the room with them (Neary *et al.*, 1986). Recently there has been some discussion in the psychiatric literature about the occurrence of the Capgras syndrome (the delusion that familiar persons are being impersonated by identical doubles) in patients with dementia (Burns and Philpot, 1987; Kumar, 1987; Wrigley, 1987). Such reports are of particular interest, occurring as they do in the context of continuing controversy about the relative contribution of organic/neurological and functional/psychological factors to the occurrence of this syndrome, which some have attempted to link to prosopagnosia (see Dohn and Crews, 1986; Lewis, 1987). Consideration of the possible occurrence of the Capgras syndrome in patients with dementia has served to focus attention upon the uncertain nosological status of the syndrome.

Reference has already been made in Chapter 6 to the occurrence of visual hallucinations in other dementia-producing conditions. In Parkinson's disease these are generally considered to be side-effects of medication rather than an intrinsic feature of the condition. Visual hallucinations are a common feature of Creutzfeldt–Jakob disease. Other visual abnormalities also occur frequently in this condition including diplopia, blurring, distortion of the visual image, hemianopia and altered perception of colour (Brown *et al.*, 1979b, 1986; Will and Matthews, 1984). Unfortunately, the visual abnormalities which have been documented in clinical reports on patients with Creutzfeldt–Jakob disease have not yet been the subject of systematic neuro-psychological investigation.

Various experimental paradigms and different types of stimuli have been employed in order to investigate systematically the visual processing capability of patients with certain other dementia-associated conditions. There is a substantial body of data pertaining to patients with Parkinson's disease and this continues to grow as researchers seek to resolve the controversy concerning whether visuospatial impairment is a fundamental feature of the condition and not simply an artefact of the move-ment disorder. It is unfortunate that many investigators have employed inadequate research methodology and attempted to measure visuospatial processing ability via tasks that required motor skills (Brown and Marsden, 1986; Della Sala *et al.*, 1986). Therefore, the results to date are largely equivocal. However, even those who assert that visuospatial impairment is a specific deficit have failed to produce evidence suggestive of differential prevalence in those parkinsonian patients who show dementia (Boller *et al.*, 1984; Ransmayr *et al.*, 1987; Sahakian *et al.*, 1988; Villardita *et al.*, 1982).

Compared with normal control subjects, patients with DAT require longer exposure durations to identify tachistoscopically presented stimuli (Schlotterer *et al.*, 1984) and are more susceptible to the disruptive effects of patterned masks in backward masking paradigms. A number of reports suggest that they find it difficult to arrive at organized perceptual constructs if presented with stimuli that are incomplete or ambiguous. For example, ability to identify incomplete letters or to recognize objects from fragmented drawings is impaired (Corkin, 1982; Hart, 1985). Patients with DAT also perform poorly when required to locate differences between pairs of abstract mosaic patterns and patients with Huntington's disease show comparable deficits (Brouwers *et al.*, 1984). It will be recalled that the possible role of visual perceptual dysfunction in the confrontation naming difficulties of patients with DAT was considered at some length in Chapter 9, but it was concluded that the balance of evidence favoured an explanation in terms of a semantic/lexical deficit rather than visual perception. Hart (1985) noted that the erroneous responses made by patients with DAT on the Token Test of receptive language generally related to the shape of the token, although mistakes in relation to the colour of target stimuli were rare. Such findings suggest preservation of colour perception in patients with DAT and are consistent with other clinical observations (Cogan, 1985; Sadun *et al.*, 1987).

Patients with progressive supranuclear palsy performed normally when Maher *et al.* (1985) required them to identify fragmented letters and common objects photographed from unusual views. However, such patients did show impairment on tasks which required visual scanning (Fisk *et al.*, 1982; Kimura *et al.*, 1981). As well as difficulty in executing voluntary eye movements to command (see Chapter 6), individuals with progressive supranuclear palsy produced hypometric saccades when required to shift gaze horizontally towards a target stimulus on either side of a central fixation point when this target became illuminated (Fisk *et al.*, 1982). Furthermore, their attempts to maintain visual fixation were disrupted by square-wave jerks (i.e. rapid involuntary saccadic eye movements away from and back to the fixation point) which Fisk *et al.* (1982) suggested might make a significant contribution to the poor performance of patients with this condition on visual scanning tasks. Time is typically an important dependent measure of performance on such tasks and the repeated sampling required to arrive at an accurate assimilation of the visual stimulus can only be achieved at the cost of reduced scanning speed.

Abnormal eye movements have also been documented in patients with other dementia-producing conditions including DAT, Parkinson's disease and Huntington's disease. Several studies of patients with DAT have pointed to disruption of the normal pattern of smooth occular pursuit when required to track regularly-moving targets. Although a normal subject can visually track a slowly moving target with only occasional retinal slippage the smooth eye movements of patients with DAT fail to match movement of the target. Hence, large and frequent compensatory catch-up saccades become necessary (Fletcher and Sharpe, 1988; Hutton, 1985; Hutton *et al.*, 1984). There have been reports of another eye movement abnormality in patients with DAT, namely large amplitude saccadic intrusions in the form of square-wave jerks (Feldon and Langston, 1977; Fletcher and Sharpe, 1988; Jones *et al.*, 1983). These occur when patients attempt to fixate upon stationary stimuli or to track slowly moving targets. Such square-wave jerks can result in the subjective impression of objects continually jumping from side to side (Feldon and Langston, 1977). White *et al.* (1983a,b) have documented abnormalities in the eye movements of patients with Parkinson's disease. When this condition is severe patients may demonstrate reductions in the vestibulo-ocular reflex (which subserves vision during head movement by stabilizing the eyes relative to the environment) plus impairments of smooth ocular pursuit. Furthermore, their latency to initiate saccades is increased and these are typically slower and hypometric so that they fall short of the target. Saccadic intrusions in the form of square-wave jerks, of the type previously described in patients with DAT and progressive supranuclear palsy, can also occur. Lasker *et al.* (1988) reported that patients with Huntington's disease had difficulty in suppressing involuntary saccades and were, therefore, inefficient in maintaining steady fixation in the face of a distracting visual stimulus.

Hutton (1985) reported the results of various investigations into the eye movements of patients with DAT. His analyses indicated that the scanpaths of normal control subjects were highly predictable in response to questions designed to focus gaze upon 'relevant' aspects of an informative visual scene. However, the scanpaths of patients with DAT were poorly regulated and resembled those typical of patients with frontal lobe tumours. A preseverative pattern was evident in the eye movements of some patients with DAT. Hart (1985) noted that many of her patients with DAT were unable to apprehend a complex picture as whole although they could perceive individual parts one at a time. Scanpath abnormalities such as those reported by Hutton (1985) might go some way towards accounting for this pattern of performance suggestive of so-called simultanagnosia (Kinsbourne and Warrington, 1962).

Hutton (1985) also reported that fixation times were significantly longer in patients with DAT than in control subjects. These results are consistent with the report by Schlotterer *et al.* (1984) that patients with DAT require longer exposure times in order to identify visual stimuli and point to slower encoding of visual information. Like patients with progressive supranuclear palsy, those with DAT find it difficult to execute eye movements upon command. This deficit is particularly marked with respect to upward gaze (Hutton, 1985; Semple *et al.*, 1982). The practical consequences of this disability can be readily appreciated. For example notices and information in public places are often located above head height and will thus be less accessible to individuals with restricted upward gaze.

The evidence presented above clearly points to impairments of visual processing in patients with dementias of various aetiologies. However, the visual acuity of such individuals generally falls within the normal range, at least when assessed using conventional methodology. This typically involves presentation of small, high contrast stimuli, but the visual environment that subjects must negotiate in the course of everyday life is one that often requires them to detect coarse low-contrast targets (Bodis-Wollner and Onofrj, 1986). Hence, measures of visual contrast sensitivity would seem more appropriate and are likely to have greater predictive power and relevance in relation to the demands placed upon subjects outside the context of a laboratory or clinic. Such measurements involve manipulating the contrast of sinusoidal grids of various spatial frequencies (defined in terms of the number of cycles of light intensity change per degree of visual angle) in order to determine the threshold at which the pattern becomes discernible.

The results obtained to date from investigations of contrast sensitivity have been inconsistent. While Schlotterer *et al.* (1984) found normal visual contrast sensitivity in their patients with DAT, Nissen *et al.* (1985) reported elevated thresholds for all spatial frequencies assessed. They noted particularly poor sensitivity at low and intermediate spatial frequencies in one patient whose clinical symptomatology included severely impaired recognition of objects and faces. In view of these discrepant results further investigations into this aspect of vision in patients with DAT are required. A number of workers have measured the visual contrast sensitivity of patients with Parkinson's disease and, although there is general agreement that this is reduced, there is a lack of consensus regarding which frequencies are affected. While Skrandies and Gottlob (1986) reported loss of sensitivity across a broad range of spatial frequencies, Bodis-Wollner *et al.* (1987) found that decrements were selective for high frequencies and in the studies of Bulens *et al.* (1986, 1988) there was a 'notch' effect with maximum loss of sensitivity at intermediate frequencies. Evidence suggesting that the loss of visual contrast sensitivity in patients with Parkinson's disease may be orientation-specific (Bulens *et al.*, 1988; Regan and Maxner, 1987) is of particular interest. Orientation-selective neurons are only found in the visual cortex of primates and an orientation-specific deficit would, therefore, imply that the changes in visual contrast sensitivity noted in patients with Parkinson's disease reflect a cortical dysfunction.

Electrophysiological investigations have also highlighted abnormalities in the processing of visual information by patients having various dementia-producing conditions. As already noted in Chapter 7, Wright *et al.* reported that the visual evoked responses of patients with DAT were normal to repeated reversal of a patterned stimulus whereas the P2 component of their evoked responses to diffuse flashes of light was markedly delayed (e.g. Harding *et al.*, 1985; Wright *et al.*, 1984, 1986, 1987). These workers asserted that their results were consistent with the known distribution of cortical pathology in AD in which the primary visual cortex (believed to be the origin of the evoked responses to patterned stimuli) is largely spared of neurofibrillary tangles, even if not neuritic plaques. The delay in the evoked response to flash stimuli was thought to reflect damage to the association cortices. Wright and Furlong (1988) have subsequently reported that patients with multi-infarct dementia show a similar differential response to pattern reversal and diffuse stimuli. Electrophysiological investigations suggest that abnormalities in the processing of visual information are present in patients with Parkinson's disease even at the level of the retina (Gawel *et al.*, 1981; Gottlob *et al.*, 1987; Nightingale *et al.*, 1986). Although the retina is rich in dopamine it is not clear that the electroretinographic abnormalities which have been documented are related to this transmitter since they are unaffected by treatment with L-dopa (Gottlob *et al.*, 1987; Nightingale *et al.*, 1986). However, it has been speculated that impairments of visual processing at the level of the retina could make a significant contribution to the increased latency and/or reduced amplitude of the cortical evoked responses elicited by patterned stimuli (Gawel *et al.*, 1981; Gottlob *et al.*, 1987; Jorg and Gerhard, 1987; Marx *et al.*, 1986; Nightingale *et al.*, 1986). Preliminary data from patients with Huntington's disease suggest that the amplitude of the P100 component of the visual evoked response elicited by pattern reversal is reduced although latency is unchanged (see Chiappa, 1983).

The accumulating evidence of functional abnormalities in the processing of visual information is accompanied by a growing body of data demonstrating structural damage to visual pathways in victims of some dementia-producing conditions. Hinton *et al.* (1986) reported loss of retinal ganglion cells and widespread axonal degeneration in the optic nerves of patients with DAT, although Scholtz *et al.* (1981) found a slight reduction in the number of lateral geniculate cells in patients with this condition. Mean neuron diameter was also decreased, suggesting cell shrinkage, and there was loss of myelin from the visual cortex. Similar changes were found in brains from patients with multi-infarct dementia (Scholtz *et al.*, 1981). In AD neurofibrillary tangles are sparce in the primary visual cortex, but there is a 20-fold increase in the adjacent visual association cortex and a further doubling in the higher order visual association cortex located in the inferior temporal gyrus (Lewis *et al.*, 1987). The distribution of neuritic plaques is more even across these brain regions (Lewis *et al.*, 1987). The eye movement abnormalities characteristic of progressive supranuclear palsy have been attributed to extensive destruction of the superior colliculus (Steele *et al.*, 1964). However, the pathological changes underlying observed alterations of visual processing in patients with Huntington's and Parkinson's diseases await specific attention.

In summary, visual abnormalities are commonly associated with dementia-producing conditions and are clearly multifactorial in nature. In some conditions these impairments have already received systematic investigation and initial attempts have been made to relate the deficits to underlying structural changes and altered physiological activity. Other conditions await controlled investigation to supplement the clinical observations which have been documented. The relationship between dementia and the visual processing deficits shown by patients with Parkinson's disease calls for further clarification. It is clear that dementia is not a necessary condition for the presence of visual dysfunction in such patients, but the extent to which its presence might alter the nature and/or severity of any visual processing deficit remains to be determined. It goes without saying that any visual impairment will distort the information available to an individual and exacerbate the impact of deficits in other cognitive functions. It is therefore important that efforts be made to identify, elucidate the nature of and, where possible, compensate for such deficits. Already some attempts have been made at correcting for certain of these difficulties, by for example masking part of a page in order to ensure that only a few words are exposed at a time, thereby reducing the disruptive effects of losing one's place (Sadun *et al.*, 1987).

Hearing

It has long been known that ageing is accompanied by a decline in sensitivity to higher frequency tones (a condition referred as presbycusis). Although these threshold changes have been replicated consistently there is less concensus regarding their functional significance. It has been suggested that perception of some spoken words, especially those involving high frequency consonant sounds, may be distorted and could lead to an underestimation of the competence of older subjects in performing any task that requires oral comprehension (see Kausler, 1982). However, other workers have concluded that decibel decreases in sensitivity for higher frequency sounds in the range typical of most older people will have only negligible effects upon their perception of speech and do not in themselves account for the often reported age-related deficits in auditory processing (see Olsho *et al.*, 1985). This is not to deny the practical significance of presbycusis for older subjects whose perception of music (and hence potentially their quality of life) will almost inevitably be affected since higher frequency sounds must be amplified if they are to be heard.

The prevalence of hearing impairment in elderly people with dementia has been the subject of some controversy. Early studies by Kay *et al.* (1964) and by Hodkinson (1973), looking at community and hospitalized samples respectively, suggested that hearing impairment was disproportionately frequent among those with dementia. These early studies are open to criticism as they employed non-audiometric methods of low or unproven validity to identify hearing impairment. Recent investigators have adopted more rigorous test procedures but have produced conflicting results. Although the results of some studies have suggested no association between hearing loss and dementia *per se* (Gilhome-Herbst and Humphrey, 1980; Jones *et al.*, 1984), other data do point to a positive relationship (Thomas *et al.*, 1983; Uhlmann *et al.*, 1989). Such results, and the associated debate, occur in the context of a growing body of evidence suggesting a higher than hitherto recognized prevalence of significant hearing impairment amongst the elderly in general, together with an acknowledgment that it remains uncorrected in a high proportion of those for whom a hearing aid would prove beneficial. In the words of Gilhome-Herbst and Humphrey (1980: 905), 'deafness is the norm and not the exception, particularly in those aged over 80'.

In view of the conflicting results regarding the relationship of deafness to dementia, the outcome of Uhlmann *et al.*'s (1986) longitudinal study is of particular interest. Cross-sectional analysis of their initial evaluation data failed to support the hypothesis that hearing impairment is associated with greater cognitive dysfunction, in agreement with the results of Gilhome-Herbst and Humphrey (1980) and Jones *et al.* (1984). However, a different picture emerged from their longitudinal data. Specifically, decline in cognitive function over a 1-year period was significantly greater in patients with DAT whose hearing was impaired than in patients whose hearing was not considered deficient on the basis of formal evaluation. Uhlmann *et al.*'s (1986) finding of more rapid cognitive decline in hearing-impaired patients with DAT has been confirmed by Peters *et al.* (1988) who employed superior audiometric methodology. The extent to which hearing impairment has the same prognostic implications for patients whose dementias arise out of different aetiologies remains to be determined (see Peters *et al.*, 1988).

It will be recalled that an individual with confirmed Pick's disease who was studied longitudinally by Holland *et al.* (1985) was referred to previously in this text (Chapter 9) because of the detail with which he recorded his own experience of the process of degeneration. Recognizing the potential implications of the dissolution of some aspects of his linguistic abilities, this man carried with him at all times a card which he could present to strangers in order to account for himself. On this he had written, 'Hearing is good physically. Language sounds – not sense – noise' (1985: 37), thereby indicating that speech had become a meaningless noise. This was so at a time when he remained able to read, write and speak in a relatively normal manner. This patient's self-reports raise the question of whether he experienced an auditory agnosia, specifically pure word deafness. However, Holland *et al.* (1985) based their report of this patient largely upon anamnestic data and it is unfortunate that formal neuropsychological investigation was not conducted to determine the extent and nature of his recognition deficit or agnosia and specifically to investigate his recognition of non-speech sounds.

An obvious concern for the neuropsychologist must be the availability of evidence pointing to neuroanatomical, neurochemical and neurophysiological changes commensurate with the functional deficits being reported and the extent to which such changes are peripheral or central. In AD, neurofibrillary tangles are rare in the brain stem auditory nuclei (Ohm and Braak, 1989) and the primary auditory cortex, but they are common in the auditory association cortex (Lewis *et al.*, 1987). However, neuritic plaques are numerous in the primary auditory as well as in the association cortex (Lewis *et al.*, 1987). Plaques are also to be found in the relatively more peripheral brainstem auditory nuclei where it has been suggested that they may occur at a comparatively late stage in the progression of the disease (Ohm and Braak, 1989).

Neurophysiological measures of brainstem auditory evoked responses (BAERs) can throw light upon the functional integrity of the brainstem auditory pathway (see Chiappa, 1983). Grimes *et al.* (1987) reported that BAERs were normal in patients with DAT. They have also been found to be normal in patients with Huntington's disease (Bollen *et al.*, 1986). In a study of chronic alcoholic subjects Chan *et al.* (1985) found that BAERs were more likely to be abnormal in those who showed the Wernicke–Korsakoff syndrome. Most of Rossi *et al.*'s (1985) patients with Parkinson's disease demonstrated abnormal BAERs, but treatment with L-Dopa or carbidopa reduced the abnormality of these.

Many questions remain unanswered concerning the integrity of the neural substrates of auditory processing in different dementia-producing conditions. Likewise, there is uncertainty about the extent and nature of functional impairment in patients afflicted by such conditions. Nevertheless, the preceding literature review allows us to draw some tentative conclusions and direct attention to their practical implications. In summary, while it is unlikely that hearing impairment is itself a cause of dementia, it appears that deafness and dementia are often co-existent. This is not surprising since the prevalence of each increases with age. Since hearing impairment seems to be prevalent in at least some conditions that give rise to dementia, it may impose a significant additional disability. Subjects whose hearing is impaired may be able to compensate for reduced auditory sensitivity by allocating more processing (attentional) resources to the early stages of stimulus detection and analysis. However, Rabbitt (1988) rightly reminds us that the cost of doing so may become apparent in less than ideal comprehension of the information presented and impaired ability to judge its significance or to act upon it. Hence, even when they appear to have grasped a message (insofar as they can repeat it accurately) hearing impairment may, nevertheless, place elderly people at a disadvantage by limiting the additional capacity available to complete higher order cognitive operations.

Since the processing resources available to patients afflicted by dementia will be reduced it goes without saying that hearing impairment will impose a severe additional burden and exacerbate cognitive dysfunction. The crucial question that remains to be answered is whether correcting for hearing loss will serve to ameliorate cognitive impairment or slow the rate of decline. However, in the present state of knowledge we would argue that there is a responsibility upon all who work with elderly individuals afflicted by dementia, whether as researchers, therapists or carers, to ensure that corrective aids are made available when appropriate and that patients are encouraged and helped to use them to good effect. Furthermore, we would remind all such workers to beware that use of subjects' self-reports to detect hearing impairment has been documented to be insensitive and inaccurate, even in non-demented subjects (Corbin *et al.*, 1984).

Concluding Remarks

It is clear from the foregoing review that disorders of sensation and perception are common in patients with various dementia-associated conditions and are to be found in relation to all sensory modalities. Nevertheless, it remains possible that certain modalities may be differentially vulnerable, as Roberts (1986) has suggested with respect to the olfactory system in AD. To date no study has examined all sensory modalities in the same individuals and this must clearly be an important goal for future research. Furthermore, it is essential that all researchers be aware of the possible implications of sensory and perceptual disorders when they seek to investigate other aspects of cognition. From the point of view of therapeutic intervention studies there would seem to be grounds for including multimodal perceptual measures as dependent variables, but this has not yet been done. It is imperative that all demented individuals undergo thorough examination to determine whether sensory and/or perceptual deficits are present and when these are detected appropriate intervention must be initiated. Even if deficits cannot be ameliorated it is nevertheless important that carers be made aware of the presence of sensory and perceptual problems and of their implications so that they are better placed to comprehend the failures of those in their care to respond to environmental stimuli, and are alerted to potentially hazardous situations which might otherwise go unrecognized.

Chapter 12

Movement and Praxis

Disorders of motor control and movement are common in patients with dementia and indeed they are the hallmark of those dementia-associated conditions in which basal ganglia dysfunction is pathognomonic, specifically Parkinson's disease and Huntington's disease. In the past two decades there has been a tremendous burgeoning of scientific and clinical interest in the field of movement disorders, spurred on by the discovery of striatal dopamine deficiency in Parkinson's disease, and its dramatic response to treatment with the precursor L-Dopa. With the successful application of L-Dopa clinical medicine came to be perceived as increasingly relevant, not only to Parkinson's disease but also to other hitherto largely intractable conditions marked by movement disorder. A growing number of neuroscientists concentrated their efforts on the task of unravelling the mechanisms operating at different levels in the hierarchy of neural systems controlling movement, from the relatively simple reflex arcs in the spinal cord and brainstem to the increasingly complex voluntary command systems in the cerebral cortex. Specification of the structure and function of motor systems at different levels in this hierarchy has been, and will undoubtedly continue to be, a major neuroscientific theme exciting the minds of workers from various disciplines, including psychology. For neuropsychologists the most intriguing questions concern where voluntary command signals originate and the stages that mediate between motor planning and programming of the requisite movement(s) and their subsequent initiation and execution.

Patients with Parkinson's disease have been the major focus of research endeavour and many theories have been proposed regarding the impairment of movement shown by the victims of this, the most common of the basal ganglia disorders. These have included delayed proprioceptive feedback (Dinnerstein *et al.*, 1962), faulty transmission of motor commands between decision making and effector mechanisms (Angel *et al.*, 1970) and inability to carry out ballistic (i.e. preprogrammed or 'open-loop') movements which are executed without the aid of feedback (Flowers, 1975, 1976, 1978). There is evidence that patients with Parkinson's disease do not spontaneously engage in the process of generating predictions, as control subjects do, in order to guide the execution of purposeful movements (Flowers, 1978; Stern *et al.*, 1983, 1984).

Moreover, they find it difficult to carry out two actions simultaneously (Flowers, 1975).

In a seminal paper, Marsden (1982) proposed that the basal ganglia were responsible for the integration, sequencing and execution of series of motor programmes, thereby implicating these subcortical structures in rather more complex movement control processes than was hitherto believed. There is evidence that performance is impaired when patients with Parkinson's disease attempt to carry out sequential movements, not only because the individual movements are performed more slowly, but also because the interval between movements is prolonged. Ability to switch from one programme to another in a sequence may also be impaired so that patients cannot proceed from the first to the second movement (Benecke *et al.*, 1987). Other workers too have highlighted abnormalities occurring within motor programmes, emphasizing slowness in initiation and in subsequent execution as well as the difficulties that these patients have in maintaining the force of their muscle contractions over time (see Sheridan *et al.*, 1987). It is possible that many factors may be involved simultaneously (Sheridan *et al.*, 1987).

In terms of gross clinical features the movement disorders of Parkinson's disease and Huntington's disease represent opposing poles, the former being characterized by hypokinesia while the latter typically heralds hyperkinetic symptoms. Hence Hefter *et al.*'s (1987) finding that patients with Huntington's disease can show marked slowing of motor responses when required to execute rapid voluntary movements was of particular interest as it pointed to a similarity between these two conditions. However, on carrying out a detailed microanalysis, Hefter *et al.* established that, despite superficial resemblance, there remained subtle differences between the patterns of deficit occurring in Huntington's disease and Parkinson's disease.

We have touched very briefly upon attempts to explicate the movement disorders characteristic of some of the conditions that give rise to so-called subcortical dementia. It now seems appropriate to remind readers of frequent references in earlier chapters of this book to a higher-order movement disorder, namely apraxia. It has been purported that apraxia does not typically occur in subcortical dementias while being found in a number of the so-called cortical dementias. The term apraxia defines a distinctive category of movement disorder characterized by inability to carry out purposeful movements voluntarily despite normal primary motor skills (i.e. normal reflexes, muscle power, tone and coordination, and an absence of tremor, chorea or akinesia), unimpaired comprehension of what is required and absence of sensory deficits or general intellectual impairment. Operationally, therefore, apraxia is defined by exclusion but in practice the rigid criteria outlined above are seldom met. There may well be dysfunction in some of the areas listed, and this will undoubtedly be so in patients with dementia. However, deficits in other aspects of cognition must be insufficient to account for the degree or nature of the errors of praxis displayed by a patient.

While the term apraxia implies a complete absence of volitional movement it is frequently applied when the impairment is less severe and we shall do so in this chapter. However, some authors use the term dyspraxia when the degree of incapacity is less than total. These global terms imply a unitary disorder, but there is evidence that disorders of praxis differ in more than quantitative terms. Many classification schemes have been attempted. Some have sought to distinguish between different disorders of praxis on the basis of the underlying cognitive operations. Thus they have highlighted the spatial or temporal aspects of the disruption or have made a distinction between disorders that involve the conceptual programming of movements or movement sequences and those which affect the executive processes whereby movements are carried out. Others have focused upon behavioural analyses of the situations in which apraxic disorders become manifest, highlighting the significance of the eliciting stimuli (e.g. verbal command, gesture, pictorial representation or presentation of a real object) and the nature of the response. The latter can be symbolic or meaningless, proximal or distal. In addition, responses may be transitive (i.e. involve manipulation of an object) or intransitive and they can require a single movement or a sequence of actions. Clearly the apraxias constitute a highly complex group of disorders. Detailed consideration of the many unresolved conceptual and methodological issues is beyond the scope of this text, but can be found in Hecaen and Albert (1978), Heilman and Rothi (1985), Miller (1986) and Roy (1985).

In this chapter we shall discuss only the major forms of apraxia that have been considered in relation to dementia or are likely to be of significance in patients with this clinical syndrome, namely dressing, ideomotor, ideational, constructional and bucco-facial apraxia.

Dressing Apraxia

Dressing apraxia can occur in apparent isolation, although it is often part of a more generalized apraxic disorder or the syndrome of global impairment of cognitive and behavioural functioning that constitutes dementia. Indeed Miller (1986: 151) emphasizes that, 'Those studies that claim cases of a discrete dressing dyspraxia can generally be criticized for their limited assessment approach'. The phenomenon occurs more frequently following right hemisphere lesions. More than 20 per cent of patients with damage to the parietal and occipital areas of the non-speech dominant hemisphere show this type of disability, while only about 4 per cent of patients with damage to these areas in the left hemisphere find dressing particularly difficult (see Miller, 1986). Of course not all patients who have problems with dressing are apraxic. For example, patients who display a dressing problem in relation to one side of their body in association with a more generalized syndrome of neglect of one side of corporeal or extracorporeal space do not manifest dressing apraxia. The latter is a bilateral problem and goes far beyond the phenomenon of neglect.

Although semi-automatic, the process of dressing nevertheless requires that items be selected in an appropriate sequence and that they be orientated correctly so as to facilitate appropriate disposition in relation to the body. Patients with dressing apraxia are typically unable to select articles of clothing in an appropriate sequence and they also show impairment in subsequent manipulation of items. They may attempt to put on shoes before socks, jacket before shirt or try to put underwear over outer garments. Individual items of clothing are handled haphazardly, tried on inside out, upside down, back-to-front and may even be disposed in relation to the wrong body part.

Although impairment of dressing ability is noteworthy on empirical grounds, there is little justification from a conceptual point of view for isolating this as a distinctive type of apraxia. To do so implies a unique set of motor processes pertinent to dressing. Attempts have been made to link dressing apraxia to other forms of apraxia and it emerges that it is often associated with constructional apraxia, although the latter is more common (the ratio being approximately four to one). There have been no formal studies of dressing apraxia in patients with dementia but difficulties in dressing have often been noted in clinical reports.

Constructional Apraxia

Unlike the situation pertaining to dressing apraxia, there has been no controversy concerning the existence of constructional apraxia as an independent syndrome. This is essentially a disorder of formative activities. Drawing on the writings of earlier workers Benton (1969: 130) defined it succinctly as, 'a disturbance in formative activities such as assembling, building and drawing in which the spatial form of the product proves to be unsuccessful without there being an apraxia of single movements'. There has, however, been some debate concerning whether constructional apraxia is a unitary disorder. Benton's (1969) demonstration that there may be some dissociation of performance on different tests of constructional ability would suggest that there may be a need for subtyping within the broader category of constructional apraxia. For example, patients may show impairment on assembling tasks while graphic performance remains intact and *vice versa*. Clinicopathological studies support the notion that there are qualitatively different forms of constructional apraxia. When the lesion is located in the left hemisphere the disorder appears to represent a defect of execution or inability to establish the programme for the desired action. Following right hemisphere lesions, however, the apraxia is associated with disturbance of visuospatial processing.

Tests of constructional ability have long been included in formal clinical and neuropsychological assessments of patients with, or suspected of having, dementia.

Neuropsychology and the dementias

Measures of graphic ability (specifically tests of spontaneous drawing or ability to copy drawings) are increasingly being included in mental status examination protocols intended for initial screening purposes. A striking characteristic of the spontaneous drawings produced by the first author's patients with DAT was simplification (see Figure 12.1). This is a feature that is typically associated with left hemisphere lesions (see Walsh, 1978). The drawing represented in Figure 12.1 was quite large as produced

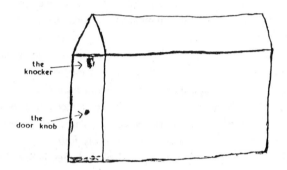

Figure 12.1   Drawing of a house as produced by a 66-year-old woman with DAT and a 2-year history of cognitive decline. Unhappy with her production, she was persistent in her efforts to improve it but merely went over the lines repeatedly. After a further 5 minutes had elapsed she had produced no significant change and was persuaded to proceed to another task. The parts labelled are as designated orally by the patient.

by the patient but a number of the spontaneous drawings rendered by patients with DAT were notably small and/or cramped relative to those produced by control subjects. Cramping was also apparent in the copies rendered by some patients. While free drawing of a cube proved a difficult task for subjects in all groups, control subjects could copy from a model without error but patients with DAT or vascular dementia

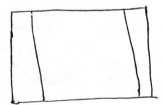

Figure 12.2   Copy of a cube rendered by a 60-year-old man with DAT in whom cognitive decline had been in progress for some 3–4 years.

often continued to fail on this task. Their reproductions sometimes lacked any semblance of perspective (Figure 12.2). Another frequent error was incorrect

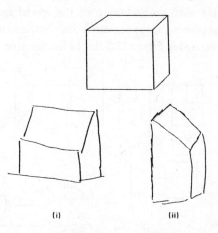

(i)   (ii)

Figure 12.3   Copies of a cube as rendered by (i) a 62-year-old man with vascular dementia of 1-year duration and (ii) a 73-year-old woman with in whom dementia had been present for at least 2 years and was thought to be of vascular or mixed aetiology.

orientation of the representation (Figure 12.3). In copying drawings patients with both types of dementia also displayed fragmentation (see Figure 12.4) and loss of spatial

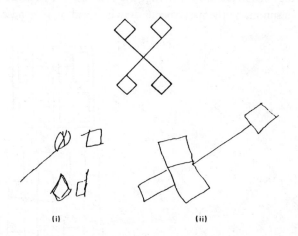

(i)   (ii)

Figure 12.4   Copies of a stimulus from the Wechsler Memory Scale made by two patients with DAT: (i) a 67-year-old women with dementia for 3 ½ years and (ii) a 72-year-old man with dementia of 2 ½ years duration. They show fragmentation and scattering of elements.

relations, with some tendency towards scattering of elements that should have been in closer proximity. It was not uncommon for patients to add further lines in order to bring together disparate elements (whether of the model or of their erroneous reproduction of it), so producing a representation that contained many more lines than the original. This is illustrated in Figure 12.5. In the literature on apraxia such features

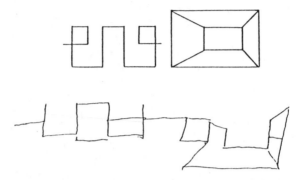

Figure 12.5   Copy of a compound stimulus from the Wechsler Memory Scale, as rendered by a 72-year-old man with DAT of some 2 ½ years duration, showing insertion of additional lines.

have typically been considered more characteristic of patients with damage to the right hemisphere. However when asked, if not spontaneously, many of the first author's patients recognized that their drawings were not accurate representations of the stimuli presented (an observation which suggests that visuospatial processing remained fairly intact). In summary, the spontaneous drawings and copies rendered by patients

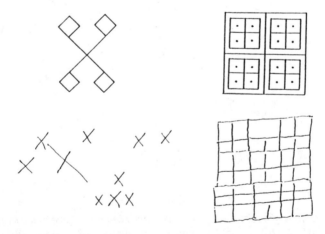

Figure 12.6   Examples of perseveration made by a 72-year-old man with a 2 ½-year history of DAT when copying stimuli from the Wechsler Memory Scale.

with dementia typically include features characteristic of patients with lesions restricted to the right and left hemispheres respectively. A similar conclusion was reached by Moore and Wyke (1984). In considering the drawings of patients with dementia it is difficult to attribute errors to a single cause. The contribution of a perseverative tendency must also be considered (see Figure 12.6).

Needless to say, patients with Parkinson's and Huntington's diseases are likely to show impairment on such drawing and copying tasks. However, it remains to be explored how far their difficulties are the product of their tremor and movement disorders. The extent to which higher-order cognitive deficits contribute remains to be determined.

When severe, constructional apraxia may manifest itself in an individual's reduced capacity to execute tasks required in the course of everyday living. For example, it may interfere with activities such as laying a table, setting up an ironing board or carrying out basic mechanical repairs. If mild, it may only become apparent in the course of formal neuropsychological examination and in this it is similar to the next type of apraxia to be considered, namely ideomotor apraxia.

Ideomotor Apraxia

The context in which a gesture or motor act is to be carried out and the stimulus presented are important determinants of whether ideomotor apraxia will become apparent. A naive observer is likely to perceive ideomotor apraxia as awkwardness or lack of cooperation on the part of the patient. An individual with this type of apraxia may perform a particular movement automatically in the normal course of events but will be unable to do so when asked to repeat it 'on demand' in an artificial situation or out of context. Ideomotor apraxia is predominantly (although not exclusively) a result of damage to the left hemisphere and is particularly frequent and severe following left parietal lesions. Performance may improve somewhat when the subject imitates gestures but it generally remains defective and will undoubtedly be less efficient than when real objects are provided for manipulation. Execution of designated movements in relation to real objects is the easiest category of gestural behaviour for patients with ideomotor apraxia who frequently substitute a body part for a missing object. For example, if asked to pretend to clean their teeth, patients with this type of apraxia may rub a finger against the teeth as if it were a toothbrush rather than responding as if they were holding a toothbrush. Intransitive movements prove particularly problematic for such patients. Imitation of meaningless gestures is generally significantly worse than imitation of meaningful gestures. Typically, patients with ideomotor apraxia will fail to execute even isolated single movements successfully. Hence it is seldom necessary to require that they perform sequential acts in order to demonstrate the presence of this praxic deficiency.

Della Sala *et al.* (1987b) investigated patients with mild DAT using De Renzi's assessment procedure (see De Renzi *et al.*, 1980). This involved imitation of both symbolic and meaningless transitive gestures and therefore constituted a demanding test procedure. Nevertheless, only one-third of the patients assessed showed ideomotor apraxia and on retesting 6 months later there was only a slight increase in the severity of their apraxia or in the number of patients demonstrating the phenomenon. One traditional approach to assessing for ideomotor apraxia is to require patients to pantomime the use of objects which they can see but not touch. Kempler (1988) applied this paradigm to patients with DAT. Subjects were presented with pictures of objects and required to mime their use. The pantomime performance of his patients was deficient but so too was their recognition of pantomime. His patients also performed poorly on measures of verbal recognition and production. Kempler therefore concluded that, even if the deficit in pantomime production could be ascribed to apraxia, there must have been a more profound deficit in symbolic processing to account for the intercorrelation between the scores obtained by his patients on all four measures employed. Foster *et al.* (1986) required patients with DAT to pantomime transitive gestures, to imitate similar gestures in accordance with a model and to manipulate real objects in response to verbal commands. They also assessed other aspects of cognition and measured regional glucose metabolism by PET scanning. Their results suggested that evidence of apraxia in response to oral commands and on imitation respectively reflected neuronal dysfunction in distinct cerebral regions. Imitation showed a significant correlation with performance on tests of visuospatial ability and with glucose metabolism in the right parietal lobe. However, inability to respond to spoken commands was correlated with performance on tests of verbal ability and with resting metabolism in the inferolateral regions of the left hemisphere. It would be particularly interesting to measure *in vivo* metabolism during performance on tests of praxis and to extend multidimensional investigations of this type to other patient groups.

As already noted apraxia has been considered one of the features that discriminate between so-called cortical and subcortical dementias, being found in the former but not in the latter. Furthermore, it has been maintained that the exclusion criteria used to define apraxia preclude its identification in patients with Parkinson's disease by virtue of their motor deficits. However, at least two studies have examined the performance of patients with Parkinson's disease on tests for ideomotor apraxia (Goldenberg *et al.*, 1986; Pirozzolo *et al.* 1982). Although neither found impairment in executing gestures to oral command, Goldenberg *et al.* (1986) produced evidence of impairment when patients imitated meaningless gestures. These workers examined the relationship between apraxia scores and motor disability and concluded that the deficits shown by their parkinsonian patients on tests of praxis were not simply a sequel of lower-order motor deficits such as akinesia or tremor. Unfortunately this study was methodologically flawed and it is therefore necessary that its results be substantiated.

Ideational Apraxia

Although ideomotor apraxia is essentially a disorder of motor execution, ideational apraxia represents a failure to conceptualize the plan of action required to achieve a desired goal. Therefore, the overall schema or cognitive representation of the intended act is lost. Although the individual elements or components of a sequential activity may be carried out correctly and fluently (as opposed to the clumsy and hesitant performance of patients with ideomotor apraxia), there is a breakdown in their ordering. Hence the logical succession of elements is disrupted. Patients with ideational apraxia perform much better on imitation tests than on those that require them to evoke the gesture spontaneously. In contrast to ideomotor apraxia, which is least apparent when real objects are manipulated, ideational apraxia manifests itself particularly in acts of voluntary motor behaviour that involve manipulation of real objects. Hence (once again in contrast to ideomotor apraxia) it will become apparent as a disorder in the course of everyday routine behaviour.

Despite many differencs between ideomotor and ideational apraxia, including those referred to above, there has long been controversy concerning whether they represent separate disorders or simply different degrees of severity of what is essentially the same problem. Although there is some evidence that they may occur independently (see De Renzi, 1985), in practice ideational apraxia commonly co-occurs with other types of apraxia (especially ideomotor) and with deficits in other aspects of cognition. This type of apraxia is almost inevitably accompanied by receptive language disturbance. Miller (1986: 22) rightly emphasized that, 'Many ideational dyspraxics have almost certainly been falsely classified as demented, or low performance on tests has been put down to poor comprehension'. It is important to recognize the possibility of misdiagnosing dementia in patients with ideational apraxia but it is also important to be aware of the suggestion that this type of apraxia is secondary to dementia (Miller, 1986).

Patients with dementia often use objects inappropriately. For example, they may use an object other than a comb or a hairbrush when attempting to put their hair in order. They also tend to fail in sequential manipulation of objects so that preparing a meal, for example, proves difficult. Schedules for assessing competence in activities of daily living (e.g. Kuriansky and Gurland, 1976; Lawton and Brody, 1969) may go some way towards quantification of such difficulties, although there is undoubtedly room for improvement.

Buccofacial (Oral) Apraxia

Patients with buccofacial apraxia resemble those with ideomotor apraxia in that specific testing is generally necessary for their deficit to become apparent. This type of oral-facial apraxia is characterized by difficulty in performing voluntary movements (not linked to speech) which involve the lower parts of the face such as the lips, tongue and cheeks. Patients with this form of apraxia may be unable to perform to verbal command actions such as sticking out the tongue, blowing a kiss, sucking on a straw or chewing (and meaningless movements are likewise impaired). However, in natural settings, they will demonstrate preserved ability to perform automatic and reflexive movements that involve the same muscle groups (as for example in eating, chewing, swallowing or blowing out a match).

It is important that the presence of buccofacial apraxia is recognized as it could bias the outcome of investigations into other functions e.g. receptive language. We have also chosen to make brief mention of it in this chapter because of its implications for management of patients with dementia. Specifically, when assisting a buccofacially apraxic patient to eat, it might be more appropriate to simply put a spoon to the person's lips without a verbal request that they open their mouth. The latter approach is interactive, and would therefore be more desirable in most circumstances. However, it could prove counterproductive in a patient with this type of apraxia by inducing voluntary control that might militate against accurate performance of the desired response.

Concluding Remarks

Some degree of apraxia is common in patients with DAT, and presumably in those with multi-infarct dementia in whom infarction is located in key brain regions, although there is a striking dearth of relevant information. Furthermore, systematic investigations are required to determine the frequency, nature and extent of praxic deficits in the rarer 'cortical' dementias. Apraxia may also occur in patients with dementia-associated conditions that involve basal ganglia dysfunction, although the presence of other types of movement disorder may obscure its presence or preclude identification.

Disorders of praxis may have profound effects upon patients' capacity to cope with their environment. Conditions such as ideomotor and buccofacial apraxia, in which there is inability to perform actions that are requested although the same actions can be performed spontaneously, may seem esoteric abstractions. However, they can have important implications for management of patients with dementia. Those who are observed to carry out motor acts spontaneously but fail to do so when requested by carers may be misperceived as awkward or uncooperative. Such negative attributions could have adverse effects upon the relationship between carers and patients. Attempts to verbally guide patients through a sequence of actions, such as those required for feeding, may prove counter-productive. By invoking voluntary control, verbal instruction could over-ride the automatic or reflexive responses that might allow for accurate execution of the desired movement. This serves to emphasize that any approach to therapeutic intervention must be founded upon awareness of the underlying nature of the neuropsychological deficits displayed by patients. Baseline and continuing assessment must be integral components of any management programme.

Part V

In the preceding chapters of this book we have documented some of the advances in knowledge about the dementias in general, and Alzheimer's disease in particular, that have been achieved over the past 15–20 years. In this final chapter we shall draw attention to some of the implications of the current state of neuropsychological understanding for treatment and management programmes. We shall also highlight elements of the knowledge base that may inspire optimism regarding future developments.

Chapter 13

Rehabilitation and Management: Present and Future

Cure must be the only acceptable goal for those who work with or, in whatever context, are confronted by the plight of individuals afflicted by dementia, a condition that strikes at the very humanity of its victims. However, treatment is always possible even if cure is not. Hence, there can be no justification for the all too prevalent therapeutic nihilism that thwarts attempts to provide high quality care and thereby foster a higher quality of life for patients and their families. By maximizing the victims' ability to utilize any functional assets or resources they retain, it should be possible to promote individuality and respect and ensure that they continue to be viewed as people of dignity and worth. Likewise, carers can be counselled and helped to construe their own role positively so that they can continue to perceive it as meaningful and worthwhile, providing that adequate practical, financial and social support are also made available. However blunted the perceptions of those afflicted by dementia, the individuality, dignity and worth of each victim must be preserved in order to ensure that the entire life of that person is not overshadowed. The destruction wrought by dementia must not be allowed to stand for surviving loved ones as the only monument to the life that was.

Even at this time when knowledge is less than adequate, neuropsychological understanding can make a significant contribution towards the achievement of high quality care. We have drawn attention to management issues at various points in previous chapters. It is our contention that further advances in neuropsychological understanding of the dementias can be achieved and that these will increase the efficacy of palliative care as well as facilitating progress towards the ultimate goal of arresting and reversing pathological change. However, as in many other scientific and medical fields, increases in knowledge herald new questions and dilemmas. The possibility of different forms of treatment raises many moral and ethical issues. These relate specifically to the desirability of treatments which are only partially effective. For example, any intervention which slows the rate of decline, and therefore prolongs the course of a degenerative process, might be open to the criticism that it simply draws out the suffering entailed and denies victims and their carers a timely end to their ordeal. Likewise, an intervention strategy that produces modest improvements in cognitive ability might, while failing to free patients from the dependency inflicted by dementia, run the risk of increasing their awareness of their plight, thereby exacerbating the suffering entailed. Hence therapeutic advances that are less then complete set the scene for profound philosophical debate which must inevitably go beyond the confines of medical and research establishments. We do not propose to dwell further on these issues here.

Quite apart from such ethical questions, there is a major psychosocial impediment to more rapid acquisition of knowledge about the neuropsychology of the dementias and to development and implementation of therapeutic interventions. Society is ridden with negative ageist attitudes. Old age is widely viewed as a period in which cognitive and behavioural decline is marked and inevitable. Elderly people themselves often subscribe to such views, as do many health-care professionals. Consequently, evidence of failing abilities in an elderly person is all too often accepted passively when the occurrence of similar deficits in a younger individual would undoubtedly trigger detailed investigation. Objective evidence is now available to challenge the view that dementia is an inevitable terminal stage of life in the absence of 'premature' death due to other causes. The epidemiological investigations which have done so much to heighten public awareness of the extent of the problem(s) posed by dementia have at the same time established unequivocally that only a minority of elderly people are afflicted by this condition: albeit an important minority with pressing needs that cannot be ignored. Even amongst the very old, in whom the prevalence of dementia is highest, victims are outnumbered by undemented peers.

Although it has been postulated that AD constitutes an acceleration of the normal ageing process there is considerable evidence to counter this view. Differences exist in terms of the extent of pathological change and its distribution throughout the brain, as well as in the pattern of neurotransmitter alterations. The qualitative and quantitative differences in cognition and behaviour documented in Part IV are also consistent with the view that DAT is an abnormal condition. In view of the implications of an accelerated ageing hypothesis for the lot of elderly people as a whole, it is particularly important that we do not lose sight of evidence which counters the notion that DAT is in any sense normal. It is important therefore that society at large (including professionals), the relatives, friends and acquaintances of afflicted individuals, and indeed the victims themselves, do not subscribe to an accelerated ageing hypothesis.

The nihilism that the concept or label of dementia evokes is unfortunate. It is particularly inappropriate since, in the present state of medical knowledge, it is already possible to reverse, or at least halt the progression of, some dementia syndromes. These were mentioned in Chapter 7 and will be returned to below. Even if we consider the majority of victims of dementia (namely those afflicted by AD or other conditions for which there is presently no cure), it is essential that detailed multi-faceted investigations of cognition and behaviour and of biological parameters be carried out in the early stages, and on longitudinal follow-up, in order to accrue the knowledge from which a cure is most likely to be derived.

The ideal of prompt and detailed neuropsychological investigation following reports of alterations in personality, cognition or behaviour would have immediate practical implications, quite apart from any facilitative effects upon progress towards the longer-term research goals referred to above and considered further below. Detailed neuropsychological examination should provide objective information regarding the nature and extent of an individual's deficits and highlight residual assets that could be utilized in devising strategies to meet the needs of that person. There are of course important unresolved questions concerning how neuropsychological test data relate to an examinee's competence in meeting the demands of everyday living (Sunderland *et al.*, 1983; Wilson, 1987b). These questions notwithstanding, neuropsychological test data can provide a useful basis for counselling victims who present in the early stages of a degenerative process, as well as their supporters and carers. Bewildered and distressed, these secondary victims often misinterpret aberrant behaviour as wantonness on the part of patients. It is important for all concerned that carers and supporters be provided with information that allows them to reconstrue the changes they are encountering as the consequences of neural damage. Holden (1988) provides illustrative examples of misinterpretations and discusses their implications at some length.

Ermini-Fuenfschilling *et al.* (1989) reported that relatives are generally inaccurate in their estimates of the cognitive capacities of the victims of dementia for whom they are providing support. This can have detrimental consequences for the relationship between carer and patient. Overestimation of a dependant's ability can give rise to inappropriately high expectations and failure to fulfil these may be construed as deliberate lack of cooperation. Conversely, underestimation can result in a pattern of caregiving that, however well-meaning, is patronizing and over-protective. A carer's failure to recognize or acknowledge residual capability can undermine the autonomy and self-esteem of the individual being supported and generate feelings of helplessness which become self-fulfilling by prematurely eroding functional competence. Ermini-Fuenfschilling *et al.* (1989) found that the adverse consequences of inaccurate appraisal of competence could be forestalled by early neuropsychological assessment followed by appropriate counselling of carers. However, their data indicated that, once established, potentially destructive patterns of interaction were difficult to modify.

Ultimately it is to be hoped that public awareness will grow to the extent that patients will present in the very earliest stages of cognitive decline, either spontaneously or in response to prompts from concerned relatives and friends. Ideally, they would be investigated before deficits became sufficiently global or severe to warrant a diagnosis of dementia. Patients identified early in the course of decline would retain greater neural and cognitive capacity and this should increase the probability that they would derive significant benefit from pharmacological agents. Likewise, their residual resources should still be adequate to allow them to derive maximal benefit from rehabilitation techniques designed to ameliorate the effects of specific cognitive deficits. In recent years growing numbers of clinical neuropsychologists have become enthusiastic about the development and application of cognitive rehabilitation programmes (see Brooks, 1984; Meier *et al.*, 1987; Miller, 1984a; Powell, 1981; Uzzell and Gross, 1986; Wilson, 1987b) designed 'to enable clients or patients and their families to live with, manage, bypass, reduce or come to terms with cognitive deficits precipitated by injury to the brain' (Wilson, 1988: 117). A significant characteristic of such programmes has been rigorous application of scientific methodology which has allowed for adequate evaluation of the efficacy of specific interventions. These more recent developments complement the long-standing efforts of other health-care professionals such as speech therapists, occupational therapists and physiotherapists.

Amelioration of the detrimental consequences of memory impairment has been the central focus in many cognitive rehabilitation programmes. The various approaches that have been adopted can be divided into three broad categories, namely: (1) teaching internal strategies (whether verbal or visual) that seek to promote maximally efficient use of residual resources; (2) use of techniques that supplement existing capabilities by means of external memory aids; and (3) manipulating the environment to reduce the memory load it imposes, thereby obviating the need for the cognitive function that has been compromised. Some illustrative examples are shown in Table 13.1. Of course, these approaches are not mutually exclusive and elements of all three can be included in the rehabilitation programme designed to meet a particular individual's needs.

Many of the internal strategies devised to promote effective encoding and retrieval appear to require significant mental effort and it might therefore be presumed that they would be inappropriate for patients with dementia. However, it will be recalled from Chapter 8 that experimental investigations have demonstrated beneficial effects of first letter cueing in patients with dementia. Some might be able to employ an alphabetical search strategy whereby they would in effect provide themselves with first letter cues in order to promote access to information that could not be retrieved spontaneously. Moreover, Hill *et al.* (1987) reported on a patient with primary degenerative dementia who successfully learned to use a visual imagery mnemonic to enhance retention of information. The improvement in performance that resulted was still apparent when the patient was reassessed 1 month later. Further research is required to determine the extent to which patients with dementia, or with conditions that eventually give rise to a dementia syndrome, can derive benefit from internal strategies and whether they can employ these spontaneously. However, the evidence to date from patients with other types of brain injury suggests that memory-impaired patients are unlikely to use strategies such as these without prompting (Wilson, 1987b).

Reports of systematic investigations into the utility of external memory aids are conspicuously absent from the growing literature on dementia. However,

Table 13.1 Cognitive rehabilitation strategies to circumvent memory impairment

---

Internal Strategies
    Use of visual imagery
    – peg-type mnemonics
    – fragmenting a person's name into imageable components
    – face-name association by exaggerating distinctive facial features and
      associating these with fragments of the person's name.
    – method of loci whereby information is 'deposited' at specific locations in
      images of familiar environments

    Enhanced verbal encoding and recall cueing
    – verbal associations between items to form a story
    – rhymes containing relevant information
    – alphabetical cueing
    – semantic processing

External Memory Aids
    Note books
    Tape recorders
    Diaries
    Calendars
    Timers/alarm clocks
    Personal computers/'intelligent' electronic note books
    Routinely placing items in specific locations
    Other people

Environmental Manipulation
    Signposts
    Colour coding of doors
    Labels and pictures indicating the contents of rooms, cupboards, drawers etc.

For further details of these and other procedures see Harris (1984), Moffat (1984) and Wilson (1987b).

unpublished data collected by the first author indicate that some patients with mild-to-moderate cognitive impairment can use external memory aids to good effect. For example, one 59-year-old patient with a history of transient ischaemic attacks and possibly one completed stroke had significant memory impairment but was able to remain in full-time employment because of systematic and very extensive note taking. Another patient presented at the age of 73 years with a 3-year history of cognitive decline and met strict diagnostic criteria for DAT. At this time he was able to supply his address either orally or in writing. When assessed 1 year later he was unable to remember his address but he knew that he carried with him a notebook in which it was written. When asked where he lived, he was able to produce the notebook from his pocket, locate the relevant information and respond appropriately. This was a very significant residual asset in a man who tended to wander and who had become lost on more than one occasion so that he required assistance from others in order to get home. As his DAT progressed he became unable to utilize this memory aid to good effect. These two case vignettes illustrate that early in the course of dementia-producing conditions patients may be able to derive as much benefit from memory aids as those with other types of brain injury. Needless to say, the benefits accrued are likely to be less enduring since most dementia-producing conditions are progressive.

Dementia is such that there will almost inevitably come a time when the only viable option for treatment and management will be to manipulate the physical and social environment so that the memory load imposed on victims is minimized. For example, key features of the environment can be labelled, signposts can be placed at strategic points to convey directional information and the route to a significant location, such as the toilet, can be marked on the floor (see Holden and Woods, 1988; Woods and Britton, 1985). In order to optimize their effectiveness, environmental manipulations should be based on knowledge of the deficits and residual assets of those for whom they are intended. Written labels will be of little assistance to patients who cannot read and/or comprehend them. Pictorial representations might then prove useful, but only for patients whose visual perceptual processing remains largely intact. Of course, the mere fact that signs and labels are available does not guarantee that patients who could usefully exploit these will in fact do so. Such a failure would be analogous to the lack of spontaneous use of internal memory aids already noted. Hanley's (1981) report casts doubt upon the efficacy of orientation aids when used alone, but indicates that they can be beneficial when provided in conjunction with an active environmental orientation programme and that they promote maintenance of any improvement derived from the latter.

This combined approach embodies many of the significant elements of Reality Orientation, probably the most widely applied and certainly the most extensively researched form of psychological treatment for elderly people with dementia (see Holden and Woods, 1988 for an excellent review of this and other psychological treatments for patients with dementia). The scientific literature on Reality Orientation is both large and confusing. Many of the seemingly contradictory results may stem from methodological differences in terms of subject selection, the control groups employed, the duration of therapeutic intervention and the measures used to evaluate outcome. Nevertheless, some general conclusions can be drawn regarding the efficacy of this treatment approach. While Reality Orientation interventions enhance verbal orientation, there is little evidence of improvement in other aspects of adaptive behaviour. Moreover, with the notable exception of the recent study of Baines *et al.* (1987), patients fail to maintain improvements after cessation of treatment. Perhaps surprisingly, there is no clear evidence that Reality Orientation is more effective when applied on a continuous 24-hour basis than if information orienting patients to person, time and place is only presented in short intensive sessions. However, it has been suggested by Hanley (1984) that this lack of differential efficacy may reflect carers' inability to sustain the principles of Reality Orientation continuously in all of their interactions with patients, even when they believe themselves to be doing so. The effectiveness of Reality Orientation applied in non-institutional settings remains to be determined empirically.

There is also controversy surrounding the mechanism(s) by which Reality Orientation might exert any beneficial effects. Stephens (1969) proposed that Reality Orientation could activate unused neural pathways and stimulate patients to develop new ways of compensating for organic brain damage. Holden and Woods (1988) have speculated on several neuropsychological mechanisms which might mediate improvement following stimulation according to Reality Orientation principles. However, they rightly point out that there is no empirical evidence that Reality Orientation alters the functional connectivity of neurons or leads to regeneration in pathologically damaged pathways. Indeed, some have asserted that the principal effects of Reality Orientation are mediated indirectly via the enhanced morale and enthusiasm of carers. This would be a significant achievement in its own right, but one which is devoid of neuropsychological relevance.

Many psychological approaches to the treatment and management of the diverse problems posed by dementia depend critically upon patients' communicative abilities but these are known to be compromised by a number of dementia-producing conditions (see Chapter 9). Likewise, the quality of the relationship between victims and their carers is vulnerable to communication deficits. Bayles and Kaszniak (1987) have outlined a number of behavioural management techniques for optimizing communication. These are based upon recognition of the information processing limitations that accompany most dementia-producing conditions at some stage in their progression. The mnemonic processing that communication entails can be reduced to a minimum by using short simple sentences where possible and employing 'right-branching' sentences in preference to 'left-branching' sentences (in which later clauses must be presented to allow comprehension of the kernel). Frequent use of pronouns also imposes an excessive memory load as the patient must remember their referents in order to comprehend. It is, therefore, better to repeat the referents. Indeed all communications should be highly redundant so that they provide repeated reminders of the salient points of the message. Patients with dementia often find it difficult to generate sequences of ideas. Consequently, it is generally more appropriate to employ 'closed' questions which entail a limited range of discrete response alternatives as opposed to 'open' questions that require extended and possibly complex replies. Since abstract concepts and relationships prove problematic, conversation should revolve around things that are directly observable and familiar, avoiding consideration of hypothetical situations and communications that require logical inference on the part of the patient. Likewise, similies and metaphors should be employed infrequently, if at all.

Attempts at communication can also be undermined by attentional dysfunction. It is important to reduce potential distractors. This can be done by reducing extraneous noise and by minimizing the number of individuals participating in a communicative interaction. Patients with dementia communicate best when in face-to-face interaction with one other person. Being part of a group imposes additional processing demands in that subjects must repeatedly shift and refocus attention and cope with the memory load involved in keeping track of who says what. Good eye contact should be established. This ensures that the patient is attending to the speaker and also allows the spoken word to be supplemented by non-verbal cues such as facial expression, hand gestures and posture. It will be recalled from Chapter 9 that non-verbal communication seems to be more resistant to the ravages of dementia-producing conditions than processing of information in the verbal domain. It may also be possible to supplement the spoken word with pictorial information or to allow patients to touch objects that are referred to since this facilitates access to information in semantic memory (Appell *et al.*, 1982; Barker and Lawson, 1968).

The therapeutic implications of knowledge about sensory and perceptual deficits have been considered in Chapter 11. Likewise identification of praxic deficits may be relevant to the development of management programmes, as indicated in Chapter 12.

In summary, providing that expectations are realistic, there is much that can be done by way of psychological treatments to ameliorate the diverse cognitive and behavioural impairments that constitute dementia. Of equal, if not greater, importance are programmes directed at carers to help them manage the behaviour of their dependants more effectively and introduce them to and/or encourage their use of cognitive strategies that will help them reduce the burden of caring (see Caranasos *et al.*, 1985; Clark and Rakowski, 1983; Eisdorfer and Cohen, 1981; Gendron *et al.*, 1986; Hepburn and Wasow, 1986; Kahan *et al.*, 1985). Treatment and management programmes must be tailored to the needs of each individual and draw upon their residual strengths. Detailed neuropsychological examination to determine the nature and extent of deficits in cognition, behaviour and emotion is not a sterile academic exercise. Rather it lays the foundations for all therapeutic interventions. It will be necessary to ensure regular monitoring of the efficacy of treatment programmes and make whatever adjustments are necessary as the dementia progresses over time. In short, and in keeping with the overall goal of maintaining the individuality of those afflicted, individual programme plans are required. At present pharmacological interventions have not proved notably effective in enhancing cognition, but it is to be hoped that the massive scientific effort currently being directed towards this end will eventually produce more clinically significant results. It is important to emphasize that pharmacological and psychological interventions are not mutually exclusive alternatives and it is likely that a combination of these approaches will be synergistic.

We turn now from consideration of palliative treatments and management strategies to the more ambitious goals of preventing pathological change and promoting neural regeneration. Achievement of these will almost certainly require understanding of the aetiologies of dementia-associated conditions and knowledge of the molecular mechanisms underlying pathological change. Of course, it must not be forgotten that it is already possible to halt the progression of a number of dementia syndromes and even to reverse some of these, partially if not completely.

To date most success has been achieved in combating dementia syndromes brought about by depression, drug toxicity and metabolic disorders (Clarfield, 1988). Evidence suggests that it may soon be possible to add further conditions to this list. By far the most important of these would be multi-infarct dementia since multiple infarction is the second most common cause of dementia in its own right and frequently co-exists with Alzheimer-type pathology to give rise to so-called mixed dementia (see Chapters 2 and 3). The predisposing factors for multi-infarct dementia are well known and it is, therefore, possible in principle to identify individuals at risk for this condition. Meyer *et al*. (1986) reported that the clinical course of multi-infarct dementia can be significantly altered by management of certain risk factors. In a longitudinal study these workers demonstrated that patients with multi-infarct dementia who were hypertensive improved their performance on a simple cognitive screening test (Jacobs *et al*., 1977) after their blood pressure had been stabilized in the high normal range (between 135 and 150 mmHg). However, if systolic blood pressure were reduced too dramatically, so that it fell significantly below the level of 135 mmHg, their neurological status and performance on the cognitive screening examination were likely to deteriorate. Among multi-infarct dementia patients who were normotensive, improved cognition was associated with cessation of smoking. More recently, Meyer *et al*. (1989) reported that treatment with daily doses of aspirin for more than 1 year led to significant increases in cerebral blood flow and enhanced the cognitive performance of patients with multi-infarct dementia. Patients treated with aspirin also became more independent in performing activities of daily living.

Management of risk factors and prophylactic treatment with aspirin are designed to prevent the occurrence of cerebral infarction but tentative evidence suggests that when infarction has occurred it may still be possible to minimize the extent of the tissue damage that results. There is now evidence of excessive release of excitatory amino acids (such as the neurotransmitter glutamate) following ischaemia and that this initiates a chain of events that lead to cell death (see Porsche–Wiebking, 1989). Research on animals has identified a number of compounds that are cytoprotective in that they reduce the amount of tissue damage that results from experimentally-induced ischaemia (Porsche-Wiebking, 1989). Consequently, there has been much speculation in the literature concerning the clinical utility of agents such as these in preventing the cerebral damage that occurs in humans following vascular accidents.

It has been suggested that a number of the primary degenerative conditions that give rise to dementia, such as AD and Huntington's disease, might also be caused by endogenous excitotoxins in the form of excessive amounts of excitatory amino acid transmitters or closely related substances (see Chapter 4). A number of studies have shown that when animals are treated with excitatory amino acid receptor antagonists there is a substantial reduction in the extent of cell damage that results from infusion of excitotoxins such as ibotenic and kianic acids (Wilmot, 1989). It has also been demonstrated that nerve growth factor protects cholinergic neurons from degeneration following various assaults (see Hefti *et al.*, 1989). Consequently, it has been suggested that this or some other trophic factor may prove useful in arresting neural degeneration. However, Butcher and Woolf (1989) have argued that neurotrophic factors may exacerbate the intensity and accelerate the pace of neuronal degeneration.

It has been proposed that a neurotoxin, which has not yet been identified, might contribute to the neuronal degeneration associated with Parkinson's disease. This suggestion was prompted by the results of a series of investigations that took place following the observation that a number of young heroin addicts in California developed severe parkinsonian symptoms (Langston *et al.*, 1983). It emerged that carelessness in the production of a synthetic heroin had resulted in distribution of material that was contaminated by MPTP (1-methyl-4-phenyl-1,2,3,6-tetrahydropyridine), a substance that was shown to be toxic to dopaminergic neurons in the substantia nigra which are lost in Parkinson's disease. Subsequent research demonstrated that it was not MPTP, but rather one of its metabolites, that proved toxic to this group of neurons. Production of the toxic metabolite was catalyzed by the enzyme monoamine oxidase B. When research from a number of laboratories confirmed that monoamine oxidase B inhibitors could block the devastating damage that occurred when MPTP was given to experimental animals (Chiba *et al.*, 1984; Langston *et al.*, 1984), Langston *et al.* hypothesized that an MPTP-like substance might be involved in the genesis of idiopathic Parkinson's disease. If this were indeed the case, inhibition of monoamine oxidase B might delay or prevent the degeneration of dopaminergic neurons in patients with this clinical condition. Positive results have emerged from at least two substantial clinical trials in which patients with Parkinson disease were treated with the monoamine oxidase inhibitor deprenyl, in that the rate of progression of their condition was slowed (Tetrud and Langston, 1989; The Parkinson's Study Group, 1989). However, findings to date have not proved totally unequivocal (Elizan *et al.*, 1989). Furthermore, it remains to be determined whether monoamine oxidase inhibitors ameliorate the cognitive deterioration that occurs in some patients with Parkinson's disease.

Although halting, or even slowing, the course of a degenerative process would constitute a significant achievement, researchers continue to strive towards the more ambitious goal of reversing pathological change. One approach has been the use of grafted neural tissue to replace that which has succumbed to pathological change. The first implantation study in human subjects involved two patients with severe

Parkinson's disease that was resistant to drug treatment (Backlund *et al.*, 1985). Dopamine-producing tissue which had been surgically removed from the adrenal medulla of these patients was implanted into the striatum, but produced only modestly beneficial results. When Madrazo *et al.* (1987) later claimed spectacular success using a similar, though cruder, technique their results gave rise to much controversy which remains unresolved. In subsequent clinical studies human fetal tissue was implanted and although encouraging results emerged from two studies (Hitchcock *et al.*, 1988; Madrazo *et al.*, 1988), the more thorough investigation of Lindvall *et al.* (1989) indicated only small (although sometimes statistically significant) improvements during the first 6 months after implantation. However, the same group (Lindvall *et al.*, 1990) have since reported that unilateral transplantation of fetal tissue was followed by marked and sustained symptomatic relief in a patient with severe Parkinson's disease that had been poorly controlled by drug treatment.

The grafting of neural tissue has become an important investigative paradigm within neuropsychology (see Dunnett, 1989). Much research effort is being directed towards improving transplantation methodology and determining the precise mechanisms by which transplanted tissue exerts its effects. The clinical utility of brain tissue implantation remains speculative (see Lindvall *et al.*, 1989). For example, the fate of any neural graft introduced into a patient's brain will depend upon the original cause of neural degeneration. In the event of an intrinsic deficit in the cells which have degenerated it would be unlikely that transplanted tissue would suffer the same fate. However, if degeneration resulted from infection or exposure to a toxin (endogenous or exogenous) the same fate might befall the grafted tissue. Furthermore, the use of human fetal tissue raises important ethical questions that must be considered by society at large. However, it may be possible to circumvent these ethical problems through genetic engineering. In a study involving rodents, Rosenberg *et al.* (1988) showed that the expected reduction in hippocampal ChAT activity that follows lesions of the fimbria-fornix pathway could be prevented by implantation of fibroblast cells that had been manipulated by genetic engineering to produce nerve growth factor. This raises the possibility of using patients as their own 'donors', at least where the aim is to provide a supply of trophic factors or other chemical substances.

Another significant determinant of whether neural transplants produce beneficial effects will be the precise role of the neurons that have degenerated. If these had been involved in complex circuits conveying information from one specific set of neurons to another restoration of function would require exact reconstruction of the previously existing connections. It is unrealistic to expect that such precise reconnections could be achieved. Hence transplantation would be unlikely to prove beneficial under these circumstances. However, the chances of success would be higher if the role of the degenerating system were modulatory. If this were so, the overall level of activity in a particular area of the brain might be the important parameter. Clearly, neural transplantation does not yet constitute a viable treatment option for dementia-producing conditions. Indeed, it is presently uncertain whether it will ever have any practical impact in this respect.

Concluding Remarks

The tremendous burgeoning of research that has taken place in the past 25 years has dramatically transformed our understanding of what was once an obscure and neglected group of conditions. Nevertheless, much remains to be learned. Readers of this book cannot have failed to notice the paucity of experimental data regarding the nature, extent and inter-correlation of cognitive changes in patients with multi-infarct dementia, despite the fact that multiple infarction is the second most common cause of dementia. We have consistently argued the merits of early referral and diagnosis. However, it must be conceded that we do not yet have available diagnostic tests of sufficient sensitivity to detect, in its earliest stages, cognitive decline that will progress to become dementia. There is a similar lack of sensitive differential diagnostic tests. The development of instruments to fulfil these needs will depend on research into the earliest stages of dementia-producing conditions. It will also require much greater undestanding of the nature and extent of any cognitive change that occurs in the course of normal ageing.

The unsuccessful attempts to produce clinically meaningful cognitive enhancement through manipulation of brain cholinergic systems has highlighted the need for more effective pharmacological agents. It has also drawn attention to the need for better methods of measuring change and assessing therapeutic efficacy. Development of sensitive and reliable measures of change which have predictive validity for performance in the real world will require a greater understanding of the psychological changes that are brought about by dementia-producing conditions.

Application of the powerful tools of molecular biology to investigation of dementia-associated conditions has already made a significant impact upon the level at which the pathological changes that take place in AD are understood. Amino acid sequences have been determined for amyloid, the major component of neuritic plaques, as well as for its precursor protein, and the gene that controls synthesis of this protein has been localized on chromosome 21. Progress has also been made towards identification and further analysis of the molecular components of paired helical filaments. This research can be expected to lead to a greater understanding of how pathological change comes about and how it affects cellular metabolism. It may also lead to the development of new therapeutic strategies aimed at halting or even reversing pathological change in surviving neurons. Glenner (1989), Muller–Hill and Beyreuther (1989), Selkoe (1989) and Tanzi et al. (1989) provide recent reviews of various aspects of this very rapidly advancing field. Molecular biologists have also been making strenuous efforts to locate the gene for familial AD (which affects a minority of cases). Initial findings suggested that this too was located on chromosome 21, close to the gene for amyloid, but more recent work suggests that the situation is more complicated and possibly involves more than one gene.

A major aim of this research has been to develop predictive DNA markers so as to identify individuals likely to be at risk for AD. For some time markers have been available that allow for identification of those individuals who are highly likely to develop Huntington's disease. Indeed, the increased predictive capacity afforded by this technology has already been applied clinically (Brock *et al.*, 1989), although a number of technical and ethical problems remain (Harper and Morris, 1989). Determination of the exact location and nature of gene mutations might offer new possibilities, such as genetic engineering to correct the deficits.

Just as neuropsychology has revolutionized our understanding of the dementias, so too recent investigations of the dementias have, in a very real sense, revolutionized neuropsychology. By focusing attention on the multiple, and often interdependent, facets of the problems posed by the dementias, the research of the past two decades has broken down some of the barriers that traditionally separated different neuroscientific disciplines. Practitioners from different specialties have come to appreciate more acutely than ever before the extent to which the outcomes of their own research endeavours must be viewed in the context of knowledge acquired by their colleagues in other disciplines. Such developments must bode well for neuropsychology as a whole and must ultimately prove beneficial for victims of the dementias and their families, friends and carers.

References

ABRAHAM, A. and MATHAI, K. V. (1983) 'The effect of right temporal lobe lesions on matching of smells,' *Neuropsychologia*, 21, pp. 277–81.

ADOLFSSON, R., GOTTFRIES, C. G., ROOS, B. E. and WINBLAD, B. (1979) 'Changes in the brain catecholamines in patients with dementia of Alzheimer type,' *British Journal of Psychiatry*, 135, pp. 216–23.

AGID, Y., AGID, J. F., RUBERG, M., PILLON, B., DUBOIS, B., DUYCKAERTS, C., HUAW, J. J., BARON, J. C. and SCATTON, B. (1986) 'Progressive supranuclear palsy: anatomo-clinical and biochemical considerations,' in Yahr, M. D. and Bergman, K. J. (Eds) *Advances in Neurology*, Vol. 45, New York, Raven Press, pp. 191–206.

ALBERT, M. L. (1978) 'Subcortical dementia,' in Katzman, R., Terry, R. D. and Bick, K. L. (Eds) *Alzheimer's Disease: Senile Dementia and Related Disorders, Aging*, Vol. 7, New York, Raven Press, pp. 121–30.

ALBERT, M. L. (1981) 'Changes in language with ageing,' *Seminars in Neurology*, 1, pp. 43–6.

ALBERT, M. L., FELDMAN, R. G. and WILLIS, A. L. (1974) 'The "subcortical dementia" of progressive supranuclear palsy,' *Journal of Neurology, Neurosurgery and Psychiatry*, 37, 121–30.

ALBERT, M. S., BUTTERS, N. and BRANDT, J. (1981a) 'Patterns of remote memory loss in amnesic and demented patients,' *Archives of Neurology*, 38, pp. 495–500.

ALBERT, M. S., BUTTERS, N. and BRANDT, J. (1981b) 'Development of remote memory loss in patients with Huntington's disease,' *Journal of Clinical Neuropsychology*, 3, pp. 1–12.

ALBERT, M. S., NAESER, M. A., DUFFY, F. H. and MCANULTY, G. (1986) 'CT and EEG validators for Alzheimer's disease,' in Poon, L. W. (Ed.) *Handbook of Clinical Memory Assessment of Older Adults*, Washington, American Psychological Association, pp. 383–92.

ALEXANDER, D. A. (1973a) 'Some tests of intelligence and learning for elderly psychiatric patients: a validation study,' *British Journal of Social and Clinical Psychology*, 12, pp. 188–93.

ALEXANDER, D. A. (1973b) 'Attention dysfunction in senile dementia,' *Psychological Reports*, 32, pp. 229–30.

ALLPORT, D. A. (1980) 'Attention and performance,' in Claxton, G, (ed.) *Cognitive Psychology: New Directions*. London, Routledge & Kegan Paul, pp. 112–53.

AMERICAN PSYCHIATRIC ASSOCIATION (1980) *Diagnostic and Statistical Manual of Mental Disorders*, 3rd ed., Washington, American Psychiatric Association.

AMERICAN PSYCHIATRIC ASSOCIATION (1987) *Diagnostic and Statistical Manual of Mental Disorders,*, 3rd ed, Revised, Washington, American Psychiatric Association.

AMINOFF, M. J., MARSHALL, J., SMITH, E. M. and WYKE, M. A. (1975), 'Pattern of intellectual impairment in Huntington's chorea,' *Psychological Medicine*, 5, pp. 169–72.

ANASTASI, A. (1976) *Psychological testing*, 4th ed., New York, Macmillan.

ANGEL, R. W., ALSTON, W. and HIGGINS, J. R. (1970) 'Control of movement in Parkinson's disease,' *Brain*, 93, pp. 1–14.

ANSARI, K. A. and JOHNSON, A. (1975) 'Olfactory function in patients with Parkinson's disease,' *Journal of Chronic Diseases*, 28, pp. 493–7.

ANTHONY, J. C., LeRESCHE, L., NIAZ, U., VON KORFF, M. R. and FOLSTEIN, M. F. (1982) 'Limits of the 'Mini-Mental State' as a screening test for dementia and delirium among hospital patients,' *Psychological Medicine*, 12, pp. 397–408.

APPEL, S. M. (1981) 'A unifying hypothesis for the cause of amyotrophic lateral sclerosis, parkinsonism and Alzheimer disease,' *Annals of Neurology*, 10, pp. 499–505.

APPELL, J., KERTESZ, A. and FISMAN, M. (1982) 'A study of language functioning in Alzheimer disease,' *Brain and Language*, 17, pp. 73–91.

ARENDT, T., BIGL, V., ARENDT, A. and TENNSTEDT, A. (1983) 'Loss of neurons in the nucleus basalis of Meynert in Alzheimer's disease, paralysis agitans and Korsakoff's disease,' *Acta Neuropathologica*, 61, pp. 101–8.

ARENDT, T., BIGL, V., TENNSTEDT, A. and ARENDT, A. (1985) 'Neuronal loss in different parts of the nucleus basalis is related to neuritic plaque formation in cortical target areas in Alzheimer's disease,' *Neuroscience*, 14, pp. 1–14.

ARMSTRONG, D. M., BRUCE, G., HERSH, L. B. and TERRY, R. D. (1986) 'Choline acetyl-transferase immunoreactivity in neuritic plaques of Alzheimer brain,' *Neuroscience Letters*, 71, pp. 229–34.

ARMSTRONG, D. M., LEROY, S., SHIELDS, D. and TERRY, R. D. (1985) 'Somatostatin-like immunoreactivity within neuritic plaques,' *Brain Research*, 338, pp. 71–80.

ARONYK, K., PETITO, F. and SOLOMON, G. E. (1984) 'Partial elementary motor seizures as the first symptom of Creutzfeldt–Jakob disease,' *Annals of Neurology*, 15, pp.210–11.

ASHFORD, J. W., SOLDINGER, S., SCHAEFFER, J., COCHRAN, L. and JARVIK, L. F. (1981) 'Physostigmine and its effect on six patients with dementia,' *American Journal of Psychiatry*, 138, pp. 829–30.

AU, R., ALBERT, M. L. and OBLER, L. K. (1988) 'The relation of aphasia to dementia,' *Aphasiology*, 2, pp. 161–73.

BACKLUND, E. O., GRANBERG, P. O., HAMBERGER, B., KNUTSSON, E., MARTENSSON, A., SEDVALL, G., SEIGER, A. and OLSON, L. (1985) 'Transplantation of adrenal medullary tissue to striatum in parkinsonism. First clinical trials,' *Journal of Neurosurgery*, 62, pp. 169–73.

BADDELEY, A. D. (1978) 'The trouble with levels: a re-examination of Craik and Lockhart's framework for memory research, *Psychological Review*, 85, pp. 139–52.

BADDELEY, A. D. (1982a) 'Implications of neuropsychological evidence for theories of normal memory,' *Philosophical Transactions of the Royal Society London*, B298, pp. 59–72.

BADDELEY, A. D. (1982b) 'Amnesia: a minimal model and an interpretation', in Cermak, L. S. (Ed.) *Human Memory and Amnesia*, Hillsdale, N. J., Lawrence Erlbaum Associates, pp. 305–36.

BADDELEY, A. D. (1986) *The Psychology of Memory*, New York, Harper & Row.

BADDELEY, A. D. (1987) *Working Memory*, Oxford, Oxford University Press.

BADDELEY, A. D. and HITCH, G. J. (1977) 'Recency re-examined,' in Dornic, S. (Ed.) *Attention and Performance VI*, Hillsdale, N.J., Lawrence Erlbaum Associates, pp. 647–67.

BADDELEY, A. D., LOGIE, R., BRESI, S., DELLA SALA, S. and SPINNLER, H. (1986) 'Dementia and working memory,' *Quarterly Journal of Experimental Psychology*, 38, pp. 603–18.

BADDELEY, A. D. and WARRINGTON, E. K. (1970) 'Amnesia and the distinction between long- and short-term memory,' *Journal of Verbal Learning and Verbal Behaviour*, 9, pp. 176–89.

BAGNE, C. A., POMARA, N., CROOK, T. and GERSHON, S. H. (1986) 'Alzheimer's disease: strategies for treatment and research,' in Crook, T., Bartus, R., Ferris, S. and Gershon, S. (Eds) *Treatment Development Strategies for Alzheimer's Disease*, Madison, Mark Powley Associates, pp. 585–638.

BAINES, S., SAXBY, P. and EHLERT, K. (1987) 'Reality orientation and reminiscence therapy: a controlled cross-over study of elderly confused people,' *British Journal of Psychiatry*, 151, pp. 222–31.

BAJADA, S. (1982) 'A trial of choline chloride and physostigmine in Alzheimer's disease,' in Corkin, S., Davis, K. L., Growdon, J. H., Usdin, E. and Wurtman, R. J. (Eds) *Alzheimer's Disease; A report of Progress in Research, Aging*, Vol. 19, New York, Raven Press, pp. 427–32.

BAJALAN, A. A., WRIGHT, C. E. and VAN DER VLIET, V. J. (1986) 'Changes in the human visual evoked potential caused by the anticholinergic agent hyosine hydrobromide: comparison of results with Alzheimer's disease,' *Journal of Neurology, Neurosurgery and Psychiatry*, 49, 175–82.

BALL, M. J. (1976) 'Neurofibrillary tangles and the pathogenesis of dementia; a quantitative study,' *Neuropathology and Applied Neurobiology*, 2, pp. 395–410.

BALL, M. J. (1977) 'Neuronal loss, neurofibrillary tangles and granulo-vacuolar degeneration in the hippocampus with ageing and dementia,' *Acta Neuropathologica (Berlin)*, 37, pp. 111–18.

BALL, M. J., HACHINSKI, V., FOX, A., KIRSHNER, A. J., FISHMAN, M., BLUME, W., KRAL, V. A., FOX, H. and MERSKEY, H. (1985) 'A new definition of Alzheimer's disease: a hippocampal dementia,' *Lancet*, i, pp. 14–16.

BALL, M. J. and LO, P. (1977) 'Granulovacuolar degeneration in the ageing brain and in dementia,' *Journal of Neuropathology and Experimental Neurology*, 36, 474–87.

BANKS, W. P. (1970) 'Signal detection theory and human memory,' *Psychological Bulletin*, 74, pp. 81–99.

BARKER, M. G. and LAWSON, J. S. (1968) 'Nominal aphasia in dementia,' *British Journal of Psychiatry*, 114, pp. 1351–6.

BARLOW, D. H. and HERSEN, M. (1984) *Single Case Designs: Strategies for Studying Behaviour Change*, London, Pergamon Press.

BARTOL, M. A. (1979) 'Nonverbal communication in patients with Alzheimer's disease,' *Journal of Gerontological Nursing*, 5, pp. 21–31.

BAUER, R. M. and RUBENS, A. B. (1985) 'Agnosia,' in Heilman, K. M. and Valenstein, E. (Eds) *Clinical Neuropsychology*, Oxford, Oxford University Press, pp. 187–241.

BAYLES, K. A. (1982) 'Language function in senile dementia,' *Brain and Language*, 16, pp. 265–80.

BAYLES, K. A. and BOONE, D. R. (1982) 'The potential of language tasks for identifying senile dementia,' *Journal of Speech and Hearing Disorders*, 47, 210–17.

BAYLES, K. A. and KASZNIAK, A. W. (1987) *Communication and cognition in normal ageing and dementia*, Boston, Little, Brown and Company.

BAYLES, K. A. and TOMOEDA, C. K (1983) 'Confrontation naming impairment in dementia,' *Brain and Language*, 19, pp. 98–114.

BAYLES, K. A., TOMOEDA, C. K. and CAFFREY, J. T. (1982) 'Language and dementia-producing conditions,' *Communicative Disorders*, 7, pp. 131–46.

BEAL, M. F., GROWDON, J. H., MAZUREK., M. F. and MARTIN, J. B. (1986b) 'CSF somatostatin-like immunoreactivity in dementia,' *Neurology*, 36, pp. 294–7.

BEAL, M. F. and MARTIN, J. B. (1986) 'Neuropeptides in neurological disease,' *Annals of Neurology*, 20, pp. 547–65.

BEAL, M. F., MAZUREK, M. F., CHATTHA, G., SVENDSEN, C. N., BIRD, E. D. and MARTIN, J. B. (1986a) 'Widespread reduction of somatostatin-like immunoreactivity in the cerebral cortex in Alzheimer's disease,' *Annals of Neurology*, 20, pp.489–95.

BEAL, M. F., MAZUREK, M. F., TRAN, V. T., CHATTHA, G., BIRD, E. D. and MARTIN, J. B. (1985) 'Reduced numbers of somatostatin receptors in the cerebral cortex in Alzheimer's disease,' *Science*, 229, pp. 289–291.

BEATTY, W. W. and BUTTERS, N. (1986) 'Further analysis of encoding in patients with Huntington's disease,' *Brain and Cognition*, 5, pp. 387–98.

BEATTY, W. W., BUTTERS, N. and JANOWSKY, D. S. (1986) 'Patterns of memory failure after scopolamine treatment: implications for cholinergic hypotheses of dementia,' *Behavioural Neural Biology*, 45, pp. 196–211.

BEATTY, W. W., SALMON, D. P., BUTTERS, N., HEINDEL, W. C. and GRANHOLM, E. L. (1988) 'Retrograde amnesia in patients with Alzheimer's disease or Huntington's disease,' *Neurobiology of Aging*, 9, pp. 181–6.

BECKER, J. T., BOLLER, F., SAXTON, J. and MCGONIGLE-GIBSON, K. L. (1987) 'Normal rates of forgetting of verbal and non-verbal material in Alzheimer's disease,' *Cortex*, 23, pp. 59–72.

BEGLEITER, H., PORJESZ, B. and TENNER, M. (1980) 'Neuroradiological and neurophysio-logical evidence of brain deficits in chronic alcoholics,' *Acta Psychiatrica Scandinavica*, 62, Suppl. 286, pp. 3–13.

BEHRENDT, J. E. (1984) 'Alzheimer's disease and its effects on handwriting,' *Journal of Forensic Sciences*, 29, pp. 87–91.

BELLER, S. A., OVERALL, J. E. and SWANN, A. C. (1985) 'Efficacy of oral physostigmine in primary degenerative dementia. A double-blind study of response to different dose level,' *Psychopharmacology*, 87, pp. 147–51.

BENECKE, R., ROTHWELL, J. C., DICK, J. P. R., DAY, B. L. and MARSDEN, C. D. (1987) 'Disturbance of sequential movements in patients with Parkinson's disease, *Brain*, 110, pp. 361–79.

BENSON, D. F. (1975) 'Disorders of verbal expression,' in Benson, D. F. and Blumer, D. (Eds) *Psychiatric Aspects of Neurological Disease*, New York, Grune & Stratton, pp. 121–35.

BENSON, D. F. (1979) 'Neurologic correlates of anomia,' in Whitaker H. and Whitaker, H. A. (Eds) *Studies in Neurolinguistics*, Vol. 4, New York, Academic Press, pp. 293–328.

BENSON, D. F. (1982) 'The use of positron emission scanning techniques in the diagnosis of Alzheimer's disease,' in Corkin, S., Davis, K. L. Growdon, J. H., Usdin, E. and Wurtman, R. J. (Eds) *Alzheimer's Disease: A Report of Progress in Research, Ageing*, Vol. 19, New York, Raven Press, pp. 79–82.

BENSON, D. F. (1988) 'PET/dementia: an update,' *Neurobiology of Ageing*, 9, pp. 87–8.

BENSON, D. F., CUMMINGS, J. L. and TSAI, S. Y. (1982) 'Angular gyrus syndrome simulating Alzheimer's disease,' *Archives of Neurology*, 39, pp. 16–20.

BENTON, A. L. (1959) *Right-Left Discrimination and Finger Localization: Development and Pathology*, New York, Hoeber-Harper.

BENTON, A. L. (1969) 'Constructional apraxia: some unanswered questions,' in Benton, A. L. (Ed.) *Contributions to Clinical Neuropsychology*, Chicago, Aldine Publishing Company, pp. 129–41.

BERG, L. (1984) 'Clinical dementia rating,' *British Journal of Psychiatry*, 145, p. 339.

BERG, L. (1985) 'Does Alzheimer's disease constitute an exaggeration of normal ageing?' *Archives of Neurology*, 37, pp. 447–52.

BERG, L., MILLER, J. P., STORANDT, M., DUCHEK, J., MORRIS, J. C., RUBIN, E. H., BURKE, W. J. and COBEN, L. A. (1988) 'Mild senile dementia of the Alzheimer type: 2. Longitudinal assessment,' *Annals of Neurology*, 23, pp. 477–84.

BERGMANN, K. (1979) 'The problem of early diagnosis,' in Glen, A. I. M. and Whalley, L. J. (Eds) *Alzheimer's Disease: Early Recognition of Potentially Reversible Deficits*, Edinburgh, Churchill Livingstone, pp. 68–77.

BERGMANN, K. (1985) 'Epidemiological aspects of dementia and considerations in planning services,' *Danish Medical Bulletin*, 32, Suppl. 1, pp. 84–91.

BERNOUILLI, C., SIEGFRIED, J., BAUMGARTNER, G., REGLI, F., RABINOWICZ, T., GAJDUSEK, D. C. and GIBBS, C. J. (1977) 'Danger of accidental person-to-person infection of Creutzfeldt–Jakob disease by surgery,' *Lancet*, i, pp. 478–9.

BIBER, C., BUTTERS, N., ROSEN, J., GERSTMAN, L. and MATTIS, S. (1981) 'Encoding strategies and recognition of faces by alcoholic Korsakoff and other brain-damaged patients,' *Journal of Clinical Neuropsychology*, 3, pp. 315–30.

BIELIAUSKAS, L. A. and FOX, J. H. (1987) 'Early cognitive data in a case of Creutzfeldt–Jakob disease,' *Neuropsychology*, 1: 2, pp. 49–50.

BIELIAUSKAS, L. A. and MATTHEWS, C. G. (1987) 'American Board of Clinical Neuropsychology: policies and procedures,' *Clinical Neuropsychologist*, 1, pp. 21–8.

BINNS, J. K. and ROBERTSON, E. E. (1962) 'Pick's disease in old age,' *Journal of Mental Science*, 108, pp. 804–10.

BIRD, E. D. (1978) 'The brain in Huntington's chorea,' *Psychological Medicine*, 8, pp. 357–60.

BIRREN, J. E. and SCHAIE, K. W. (1985) *Handbook of the Psychology of Aging*, New York, Van Nostrand Reinhold.

BIRREN, J. E., WOODS, A. M. and WILLIAMS, M. V. (1980) 'Behavioural slowing with age: causes, organization, and consequences,' in Poon, L. W. (Ed.) *Aging in the 1980s: Psychological Issues*, Washington, D. C., American Psychological Association, pp. 293–308.

BISIACH, E. and VALLAR, G. (1988) 'Hemineglect in humans,' in Boller, F. and Grafman, J. (Eds) *Handbook of Neuropsychology*, Vol. I, New York, Elsevier Science Publishers, (Biomedical Division), pp. 195–222.

BLACKWOOD, D. H. R. and CHRISTIE, J. E. (1986) 'The effects of physostigmine on memory and auditory P300 in Alzheimer-type dementia,' *Biological Psychiatry*, 21, pp. 557–60.

BLACKWOOD, D. H. R., ST. CLAIR, D. M., BLACKBURN, I. M. and TYRER, M. B. (1987) 'Cognitive brain potentials in Alzheimer's dementia and Korsakoff amnesic syndrome,' *Psychological Medicine*, 17, pp. 349–58.

BLANEY, P. H. (1986) 'Affect and memory: a review,' *Psychological Bulletin*, 99, pp. 299–346.

BLAZER, D. and WILLIAMS, C. (1980) 'Epidemiology of dysphoria and depression in an elderly population,' *American Journal of Psychiatry*, 137, pp. 439–44.

BLESSED, G., TOMLINSON, B. E. and ROTH, M. (1968) 'The association between quantitative measures of dementia and of senile change in the cerebral grey matter of elderly subjects,' *British Journal of Psychiatry*, 114, pp. 797–811.

BLOXHAM, C. A., DICK, D. J. and MOORE, M. (1987) 'Reaction times and attention in Parkinson's disease,' *Journal of Neurology, Neurosurgery and Psychiatry*, 50, pp. 1178–83.

BODIS-WOLLNER, I., MARX, M. S., MITRA, S., BOBAK, P., MYLIN, L. and YAHR, M. (1987) 'Visual dysfunction in Parkinson's disease. Loss in spatiotemporal contrast sensitivity,' *Brain*, 110, pp. 1675–98.

BODIS-WOLLNER, I. and ONOFRJ, M. (1986) 'The visual system in Parkinson's disease,' in Yahr, M. D. and Bergmann, K. J. (Eds) *Advances in Neurology*, Vol. 45, New York, Raven Press.

BOLLEN, E., ARTS, R. J., ROOS, R. A., V AN DER VELDE, E. A. and BURUMA, O. J. (1986) 'Brainstem reflexes and brainstem auditory evoked responses in Huntington's chorea,' *Journal of Neurology, Neurosurgery and Psychiatry*, 49, pp. 313–315.

BOLLER, F. and DENNIS, M. (1979) *Auditory Comprehension: Clinical and Experimental Studies with the Token Test*, New York, Academic Press.

BOLLER, F. and GRAFMAN, J. (1988) *Handbook of Neuropsychology*, Vol. I, New York, Elsevier Science Publishers (Biomedical Division).

BOLLER, F., MIZUTANI, T., ROESSMANN, U. and GAMBETTI, P. (1980) 'Parkinson disease, dementia and Alzheimer disease: clinicopathological correlations,' *Annals of Neurology*, 7, pp. 329–35.

BOLLER, F., PASSAFIUME, D., KEEFE, N., ROGERS, K., MORROW, L. and KIM, Y. (1984) 'Visuo-spatial impairment in Parkinson's disease: role of perceptual and motor factors,' *Archives of Neurology*, 41, pp. 485–90.

BOLT, J. M. W. (1970) 'Huntington's chorea in the west of Scotland,' *British Journal of Psychiatry*, 116, pp. 259–70.

BONDAREFF, W., BALDY, R. and LEVY, R. (1981) 'Quantitative computed tomogrpahy in senile dementia,' *Archives of General Psychiatry*, 34, pp. 1365–8.

BOTWINICK, J., STORANDT, M. and BERG, L. (1986) 'A longitudinal study of senile dementia of the Alzheimer type,' *Archives of Neurology*, 43, pp. 1124–7.

BOWEN, D. M. (1980) 'Biochemical evidence for nerve cell changes in senile dementia,' in Amaducci, L., Davison, A. N. and Antuono, P. (Eds) *Aging of the Brain and Dementia, Aging*, Vol. 13, New York, Raven Press, pp. 127–38.

BOWEN, D. M. (1983) 'Biochemical assessment of neurotransmitter and metabolic dysfunction and cerebral atrophy in Alzheimer's disease,' in Katzman, R. (Ed.) *Banbury Report 15: Biological Aspects of Alzheimer's Disease*, Cold Spring Harbor Laboratory, pp. 219–30.

BOWEN, D. M. and DAVISON, A. N. (1986) 'Can the pathophysiology of dementia lead to rational therapy?' in Crook, T., Bartus, R., Ferris, S. and Gershon, S. (Eds) *Treatment Development Strategies for Alzheimer's Disease*, Madison, Mark Powley Associates, pp. 35–66.

BOWEN, D. M., SMITH, C. B., WHITE, P. and DAVISON, A. N. (1976) 'Neuro-transmitter-related enzymes and indices of hypoxia in senile dementia and other abiotrophies,' *Brain*, 99, pp. 459–96.

BOWEN, D. M., WHITE, P., SPILLANE, J. A., GOODHARDT, M. J., CURZON, G., IWANGOFF, P., MEIER-RUGE, W. and DAVISON, A. N. (1979) 'Accelerated ageing or selective neuronal loss as an improtant cause of dementia?' *Lancet*, i, pp. 11–14.

BOWEN, F. P. (1976) 'Behavioural alterations in patients with basal ganglia lesions,' in Yahr, M. D. (Ed.) *The Basal Ganglia*, New York, Raven Press, pp. 169–80.

BOWEN, F. P., BURNS, M., BRADY, E. M. and YAHR, M. D. (1976) 'A note on alterations of personal orientation in Parkinsonism,' *Neuropsychologia*, 14, pp. 425–9.

BOWER, G. H. (1981) 'Mood and memory,' *American Psychologist*, 36, pp. 129–48.

BOWER, G. H. (1983) 'Affect and cognition,' *Philosophical Transactions of the Royal Society London Series B*, 302, pp. 387–402.

BOYD, W. D., GRAHAM-WHITE, J., BLACKWOOD, G., GLEN, I. and McQUEEN, J. (1977) 'Clinical effects of choline in Alzheimer senile dementia,' *Lancet*, ii, p. 711.

BRACKENRIDGE, C. J. (1971) 'The relation of type of initial symptoms and line of transmission to ages at onset and death in Huntington's disease,' *Clinical Genetics*, 2, pp. 287–97.

BRADSHAW, J. R., THOMSON, J. L. G. and CAMPBELL, M. J. (1983) 'Computed tomography in the investigation of dementia,' *British Medical Journal*, 286, pp. 277–80.

BRANCONNIER, R. J. (1982) 'Predictive value of intrusion errors as a differential diagnostic sign of Alzheimer disease,' *Annals of Neurology*, 12, p. 317.

BREITNER, J. C. S. and FOLSTEIN, M. F. (1984) 'Familial Alzheimer's dementia: a prevalent disorder with specific clinical features,' *Psychological Medicine*, 14, pp. 63–80.

BRIERLEY, J. B. (1961) 'Clinico-pathological correlations in amnesia,' *Gerontologia Clinica*, 3, pp. 97–109.

BRINKMAN, S. D. and BRAUN, P. (1984) 'Classification of dementia patients by a WAIS profile related to central cholinergic deficiencies,' *Journal of Clinical Neuropsychology*, 6, pp. 393–400.

BRINKMAN, S. D. and GERSHON, S. (1983) 'Measurement of cholinergic drug effects on memory in Alzheimer's disease,' *Neurobiology of Aging*, 4, pp. 139–45.

BRINKMAN, S. D., LARGEN, L. W., CUSHMAN, L. and SARWAR, M. (1986) 'Anatomical validators: progressive changes in dementia,' in Poon, L. W. (Ed.) *Handbook of Clinical*

Memory Assessment of Older Adults, Washington, American Psychological Association, pp. 359–66.

BRINKMAN, S. D., SMITH, R. C., MEYER, J. S., VROULIS, G., SHAW, T., GORDON, J. R. and ALLEN, R. H. (1982) 'Lecithin and memory training in suspected Alzheimer's disease,' *Journal of Gerontology*, 37, pp. 4–9.

BROADBENT, D. E. (1958) *Perception and Communication*, London, Pergamon Press.

BROCK, D. J., MENNIE, M., CURTIS, A., MILLAN, F. A., BARRON, L., RAEBURN, J. A. DINWOODIE, D., HOLLOWAY, S., CROSBIE, A., WRIGHT, A. and PULLEN, I. (1989) 'Predictive testing for Huntington's disease with linked DNA markers,' *Lancet* ii, pp. 463–6.

BROOKS, N. (editor) (1984) *Closed Head Injury: Psychological, Social and Family Consequences*, Oxford, Oxford University Press.

BROOKSHIRE, R. H. and MANTHIE, M. A. (1980) 'Speech and language disturbances in the elderly,' in Maletta, G. J. and Pirozzolo, F. J. (Eds) *The Aging Nervous System*, Basel, Praeger, pp. 241–63.

BROSGOLE, L., KURUCZ, J., PLAHOVINSAK, T. J. and GUMIELA, E. (1981) 'On the mechanisms underlying facial-affective disorder in senile demented patients,' *International Journal of Neuroscience*, 15, pp. 207–15.

BROUWERS, P., COX, C., MARTIN, A., CHASE, T. and FEDIO, P. (1984) 'Differential perceptual-spatial impairment in Huntington's and Alzheimer's dementias,' *Archives of Neurology*, 41, pp. 1073–8.

BROWN, P., CATHALA, F., CASTAIGNE, P. and GAJDUSEK, D. C. (1986) 'Creutzfeldt–Jakob disease: clinical analysis of a consecutive series of 230 neuropathologically verified cases,' *Annals of Neurology*, 20, pp. 597–602.

BROWN, P., CATHALA, F. and GAJDUSEK, D. C. (1979a) 'Creutzfeldt–Jakob disease in France: III. Epidemiological study of 170 patients dying during the decade 1968–1977,' *Annals of Neurology*, 6, pp. 438–46.

BROWN, P., CATHALA, F., SADOWSKI, D. and GAJDUSEK, D. C. (1979b) 'Creutzfeldt–Jakob disease in France: II. Clinical characteristics of 124 consecutively verified cases during the decade 1968–1977,' *Annals of Neurology*, 6, pp. 430–7.

BROWN, R. G. and MARSDEN, C. D. (1984) 'How common is dementia in Parkinson's disease,' *Lancet*, ii, pp. 1262–5.

BROWN, R. G. and MARSDEN, C. D. (1986) 'Visuospatial function in Parkinson's disease,' *Brain*, 109, pp. 987–1002.

BROWN, R. G. and MARSDEN, C. D. (1988) 'Internal *versus* external cues and the control of attention in Parkinson's disease,' *Brain*, 111, pp. 323–47.

BRUN, A. and GUSTAFSON, L. (1976) 'Distribution of cerebral degeneration in Alzheimer's disease: a clinico-pathological study,' *Archives of Psychiatry and Neurological Sciences*, 223, pp. 15–33.

BRUN, A. and GUSTAFSON, L. (1978) 'Limbic lobe involvement in presenile dementia,' *Archives of Psychiatry and Neurological Sciences*, 226, pp. 79–93.

BRUNO, G., MOHR, E., GILLESPIE, M., FEDIO, P. and CHASE, T. N. (1986) 'Muscarinic agonist therapy of Alzheimer's disease: a clinical trial of RS86,' *Archives of Neurology*, 43, pp. 659–61.

BRUST, J. C. M. (1983) 'Vascular dementia – still overdiagnosed,' *Stroke*, 14, pp. 298–300.

BUELL, S. J. and COLEMAN, P. O. (1981) 'Quantitative evidence for selective dendritic growth in normal human aging but not in senile dementia,' *Brain Research*, 214, pp. 23–41.

BUFFERY, A. W. H. (1977) 'Clinical neuropsychology: a review and preview', in Rachman, S. (Ed.) *Contributions to Medical Psychology*, Vol. 1, Oxford, Pergamon Press, pp. 115–36.

BULENS, C., MEERWALDT, J. D. and VAN DER WILDT, G. J. (1988) 'Effect of stimulus orientation on contrast sensitivity in Parkinson's disease,' *Neurology*, 380, pp. 76–81.

BULENS, C., MEERWALDT, J. D., VAN DER WILDT, G. J. and KEEMINK, C. J. (1986) 'Contrast sensitivity in Parkinson's disease,' *Neurology*, 36, pp. 1121–5.

BURNS, A. and PHILPOT, M. (1987) 'Capgras' syndrome in a patient with dementia,' *British Journal of Psychiatry*, 150, pp. 876–7.

BURNSIDE, I. M. (1973) 'Touching is talking,' *American Journal of Nursing*, 73, pp. 2060–3.

BUSCHKE, H. (1973) 'Selective reminding for analysis of memory and learning,' *Journal of Verbal Learning and Verbal Behaviour*, 12, pp. 543–50.

BUTCHER, L. L. and WOOLF, N. J. (1989) 'Neurotrophic agents may exacerbate the pathological cascade of Alzheimer's disease,' *Neurobiology of Ageing*, 10, pp. 557–70.

BUTTERS, N., ALBERT, M. S., and SAX, D. (1979) 'Investigations of the memory disorders of patients with Huntington's disease,' in Chase, T., Wexler, N. and Barbeau, A. (Eds) *Huntington's Disease: Advances in Neurology*, Vol. 23, New York, Raven Press, pp. 203–14.

BUTTERS, N. and CERMAK, L. S. (1980) *Alcoholic Korsakoff's syndrome: An information processing approach to amnesia*, New York, Academic Press.

BUTTERS, N., MARTONE, M., WHITE, B., GRANHOLM, E. and WOLFE, J. (1986) 'Clinical validators: comparisons of demented and amnesic patients,' in Poon, L. W. (Ed.) *Handbook of Clinical Memory Assessment of Older Adults*, Washington, American Psychological Association, pp. 337–52.

BUTTERS, N., SALMON, D. P., GRANHOLM, E., HEINDEL, W. and LYON, L. (1987) 'Neuropsychological differentiation of amnesic and dementing states,' in Stahl, S. M., Iversen, S. D. and Goodman, E. C. (Eds) *Cognitive Neurochemistry*, Oxford, Oxford University Press, pp. 3–20.

BUTTERS, N., SAX, D., MONTGOMERY, K. and TARLOW, S. (1978) 'Comparison of the neuropsychological deficits associated with early and advanced Huntington's disease,' *Archives of Neurology*, 35, pp. 585–9.

CAINE, E. D. (1980) 'Cholinomimetic treatment fails to improve memory disorders,' *New England Medical Journal*, 303, pp. 585–6.

CAINE, E. D. (1981) 'Pseudodementia: current concepts and future directions,' *Archives of General Psychiatry*, 38, pp. 1359–64.

CAINE, E. D., EBERT, M. H. and WEINGARTNER, H. (1977) 'An outline for the analysis of dementia: the memory disorder of Huntington's disease,' *Neurology*, 27, pp. 1087–92.

CAINE, E. D., WEINGARTNER, H., LUDLOW, C. L., CUDAHY, E. A. and WEHRY, S. (1981) 'Qualitative analysis of scopalamine-induced amnesia,' *Psychopharmacology*, 74, pp. 74–80.

CAIRD, W. K. and HANNAH, F. (1964) 'Short-term memory disorder in elderly psychiatraic patients,' *Diseases of the Nervous System*, 25, pp. 564–8.

CALTAGIRONE, C., ALBANESE, A., GAINOTTI, G. and MASULLO, C. (1983) 'Acute administration of individual optimal dose of physostigmine fails to improve performances in Alzheimer's presenile dementia,' *International Journal of Neuroscience*, 18, pp. 143–8.

CALTAGIRONE, C., GAINOTTI, G. and MASULLO, C. (1982) 'Oral administration of chronic physostigmine does not improve cognitive or mnesic performances in Alzheimer's presenile dementia,' *International Journal of Neuroscience*, 16, pp. 247–9.

CANDY, J. M., GASCOIGNE, A. D., BIGGINS, J. A., SMITH, I., PERRY, R. H., PERRY, E. K., MCDERMOT, J. R. and EDWARDSON, J. A. (1985) 'Somatostatin immunoreactivity in cortical and some subcortical regions in Alzheimer's disease,' *Journal of the Neurological Sciences*, 71, pp. 315–23.

CANDY, J. M., KLINOWSKI, J., PERRY, R. H., PERRY, E. K., FAIRBAIRN, A., OAKLEY, A., CARPENTER, J., ATACK, J., BLESSED, G. and EDWARDSON, J. (1986) 'Alumino-silicates and senile plaque formation in Alzheimer's disease,' *Lancet*, i, pp. 354–6.

CANDY, J. M., PERRY, R. H., PERRY, E. K., IRVING, D., BLESSED, G., FAIRBAIRN, A. F. and TOMLINSON, B. E. (1983) 'Pathological changes in the nucleus of Meynert in Alzheimer's and Parkinson's diseases,' *Journal of the Neurological Sciences*, 59, pp. 277–89.

CANTONE, G., ORSINI, A., GROSSI, D. and DE MICHELE, G. (1978) 'Verbal and spatial memory span in dementia (an experimental study of 185 subjects), *Acta Neurologica*, 33, pp. 175–83.

CAPITANI, E. DELLA SALA, S., LUCCHELLI, F., SOAVE, P. and SPINNLER, H. (1988) 'Gottschaldt's hidden figure test: sensitivity of perceptual attention to ageing and dementia,' *Journal of Gerontology*, 43, pp. 157–63.

CARANASOS, G. J., FENNELL, E. B., BELLES, D. R. and KRISCHNER, J. P. (1985) 'Caregivers of the dementing elderly,' *Journal of the Florida Medical Association*, 72, pp. 266–70.

CARLSON, R. J. (1976) 'Pre-senile dementia presenting as a depressive illness: a case report,' *Canadian Psychiatric Association Journal*, 21, pp. 527–31.

CARROLL, B. J., FEINBERG, M., GREDEN, J. F., TARIKA, J., ALBALA, A. A., HASKETT, R. F., JAMES, N. MCI., KRONFOL, Z., LOHR, N., STEINER, M., DEVIGNE, J. P. and YOUNG, E. (1981) 'A specific laboratory test for the diagnosis of melancholia: standardization, validation, and clinical utility,' *Archives of General Psychiatry*, 38, pp. 15–22.

CATHALA, F., CHATELAIN, J., BROWN, P., DUMAS, M. and GAJDUSEK, D. C. (1980) 'Familial Creutzfeldt–Jakob disease: autosomal dominance in 14 members over three generations,' *Journal of the Neurological Sciences*, 47, pp. 343–51.

CATONA, M. C., LAZZARINI, A. M. and MCCORMACK, M. K. (1985) 'A psychometric study of children at-risk for Huntington's disease,' *Clinical Genetics*, 28, pp. 307–16.

CELESIA, G. G. and WANAMAKER, W. M. (1972) 'Psychiatric disturbances in Parkinson's disease,' *Diseases of the Nervous: System*, 33, pp. 557–83.

CENTRAL STATISTICAL OFFICE (1984) *Social Trends*, London, HMSO.

CERELLA, J., POON, L. W. and WILLIAMS, D. M. (1980) 'Age and the complexity hypothesis,' in Poon, L. W. (Ed.) *Aging in the 1980s: Psychological Issues*, Washington, D. C., American Psychological Association, pp. 332–40.

CERMAK, L. S. (1979) 'Amnesic patients' level of processing,' in Cermak, L. S. and Craik, F. I. M. (Eds) *Levels of Processing in Human Memory*, Hillsdale, N. J., Lawrence Erlbaum Associates, pp. 119–39.

CERMAK, L. S. (1982) 'The long and short of it in amnesia,' in Cermak, L. S. (Ed.) *Human Memory and Amnesia*, Hillsdale, N. J., Lawrence Erlbaum Associates, pp. 43–59.

CERMAK, L. S., NAUS, M. J. and REALE, L. (1976) 'Rehearsal and organizational strategies of alcoholic Korksakoff patients,' *Brain and Language*, 3, pp. 375–85.

CHAN, Y. W., McLEOD, J. G., TUCK, R. R., and FEARY, P. A. (1985) 'Brain stem auditory evoked responses in chronic alcoholics,' *Journal of Neurology, Neurosurgery and Psychiatry*, 48, pp. 1107–12.

CHANG, T. M. (1986) 'Semantic memory: facts and models', *Psychological Bulletin*, 99, pp. 199–220.

CHAPMAN, L. J. and CHAPMAN, J. P. (1973) 'Problems in the measurement of cognitive deficit,' *Psychological Bulletin*, 79, pp. 380–5.

CHAPMAN, L. J. and CHAPMAN, J. P. (1978) 'The measurement of differential deficit,' *Journal of Psychiatric Research*, 14, pp. 303–11.

CHAWLUK, J. B., MESULAM, M. M., HURTIZ, H., KUSHNER, M., WEINTRAUB, S., SAYKIN, A., RUBIN, N., ALAVI, A. and REIVICH, M. (1986) 'Slowly progressive aphasia without generalized dementia: studies with positron emission tomography,' *Annals of Neurology*, 19, pp. 68–74.

CHIAPPA, K. H. (1983) *Evoked Potentials in Clinical Medicine*, New York, Raven Press.

CHIBA, K., TREVOR, A. and CASTAGNOLI, N. (1984) 'Metabolism of the neurotoxic amine MPTP by brain monoamine oxidase,' *Biochemical Biophysical Research Communications*, 120, pp. 574–8.

CHRISTIE, J. E. (1982) 'Physostigmine and arecoline infusions in Alzheimer's disease,' in Corkin, S., Davis, K. L., Growdon, J. H., Usdin, E. and Wurtman, R. J. (Eds) *Alzheimer's Disease: A Report of Progress in Research, Aging*, Vol. 19, New York, Raven Press, pp. 413–20.

CHRISTIE, J. E., GLEN, A. I. M., YATES, C. M., BLACKBURN, I. M., SHERING, A., JELLINEK, E. M. and ZEISEL, S. (1979) 'Choline and lecithin effects on CSF choline levels and on cognitive function in Alzheimer presenile dementia', in Glen, A. I. M. and Whalley, L. J. (Eds) *Alzheimer's Disease: Early Recognition of Potentially Reversible Deficits*, Edinburgh, Churchill Livingstone, pp. 163–8.

CHRISTIE, J. E., KEAN, D. M., DOUGLAS, R. H. B., ENGELMAN, H. M., ST. CLAIR, D. and BLACKBURN, I. M. (1988) 'Magnetic imaging in pre-senile dementia of the Alzheimer-type, multi-infarct dementia and Korsakoff's syndrome,' *Psychological Medicine*, 18, pp. 319–29.

CHRISTIE, J. E., SHERING, A., FERGUSON, J. and GLEN, A. I. M. (1981) 'Physostigmine and arecoline: effects of intravenous infusions in Alzheimer presenile dementia,' *British Journal of Psychiatry*, 138, pp. 46–50.

CHUI, H. C., MORTIMER, J. A., SLAGER, U., ZAROW, C., BONDAREFF, W. and WEBSTER, D. D. (1986) 'Pathologic correlates of dementia in Parkinson's disease,' *Archives of Neurology*, 43, pp. 991–5.

CHUI, H. C., TENG, E. L., HENDERSON, V. W. and MOY, A. C. (1985) 'Clinical subtypes of dementia of the Alzheimer type,' *Neurology*, 35, pp. 1544–50.

CLARFIELD, A. M. (1988) 'The reversible dementias: do they reverse?' *Annals of Internal Medicine*, 109, pp. 476–86.

CLARK, A. W., PARHAD, I. M., CURRY, B., WHITE, C. L., MANZ, H. J., WHITEHOUSE, P. J., LEHMANN, J. and COYLE, J. T. (1986) 'Primary degenerative dementia, without Alzheimer pathology,' *Canadian Journal of Neurological Sciences*, 13, pp. 462–70.

CLARK, C. R., GEFFIN, G. M. and GEFFIN, L. B. (1986a) 'Role of monoamine pathways in the control of attention: effets of droperidol and methylphenidate in normal adult humans,' *Psychopharmacologia*, 90, pp. 28–34.

CLARK, C. R., GEFFIN, G. M. and GEFFIN, L. B. (1986b) 'Role of monoamine pathways in attention and effort: effects of clonidine and methylphenidate in normal adult humans,' *Psychopharmacology*, 90, pp. 34–9.

CLARK, N. M. and RAKOWSKI, W. (1983) 'Family caregivers of older adults: improving helping skills,' *Gerontologist*, 23, pp. 637–42.

COBLENTZ, J. M., MATTHIS, S., ZINGESSER, L. M., KASOFF, S. S., WISNIEWSKI, H. M. and KATZMAN, R. (1973) 'Presenile dementia; clinical aspects and evaluation of cerebrospinal fluid dynamics,' *Archives of Neurology*, 29, pp. 299–308.

CODE, C. and LODGE, B. (1987) 'Language in dementia of recent referral,' *Age and Ageing*, 16, pp. 366–72.

COGAN, D. G. (1985) 'Visual disturbances with focal progressive dementing disease,' *American Journal of Ophthalmology*, 100, pp. 68–72.

COHEN, E. L. and WURTMAN, R. J. (1976) 'Brain acetycholine: control by dietary choline,' *Science*, 191, pp. 561–2.

COHEN, G. and MARTIN, M. (1975) 'Hemisphere differences in an auditory Stroop test,' *Perception and Psychophysics*, 17, pp. 79–83.

COHEN, N. J. and SQUIRE, L. R. (1981) 'Retrograde amnesia and remote memory impairment,' *Neuropsychologia*, 19, pp. 337–56.

COLGAN, J., NAGUIB, M. and LEVY, R. (1986) 'Computed tomographic density numbers: a comparative study of patients with senile dementia and normal elderly controls,' *British Journal of Psychiatry*, 149, pp. 716–19.

COLTHEART, M. (1982) 'Psycholinguistic analysis of acquired dyslexias: some illustrations,' *Philosophical Transactions of the Royal Society, London*, B298, pp. 151–64.

COLQUHOUN, W. P. (1962) 'Effects of hyoscine and meclozine on vigilance and short-term memory,' *British Journal of Industrial Medicine*, 19, pp. 287–96.

CONGRESS OF THE UNITED STATES OFFICE OF TECHNOLOGY ASSESSMENT (1987) 'Losing a million minds: confronting the tragedy of Alzheimer's disease and other dementias,' Washington, U.S. Government Printing Office.

CONSTANTINIDIS, J . (1978) 'Is Alzheimer's disease a major form of senile dementia? Clinical, anatomical and genetic data,' in Katzman, R., Terry, R. D. and Bick, K. L. (Eds) *Alzheimer's Disease: Senile Dementia and Related Disorders, Aging*, Vol. 7, New York, Raven Press, pp. 15–25.

CONSTANTINIDIS, J., RICHARD, J. and DE AJURIAGUERRA, J. (1978) 'Dementias with senile plaques and neurofibrillary changes,' in Isaacs, A. D. and Post, F. (Eds) *Studies in Geriatric Psychiatry*, London, Wiley, pp. 119–52.

COOK, R. H., WARD, B. E. and AUSTIN, J. E. (1979) 'Studies in ageing of the brain: IV. Familial Alzheimer's disease: relation to transmissible dementia, aneuploidy and microtubular defects,' *Neurology*, 29, pp. 1402–9.

COOLS, A. R., BERCKEN, J. H. L., HORSTINK, M. W., SPAENDONCK, K. P. and BERGER, H. J. (1984) 'Cognitive and motor shifting aptitude disorder in Parkinson's disease,' *Journal of Neurology, Neurosurgery and Psychiatry*, 47, pp. 443–53.

CORBIN, S., REED, M., NOBBS, H., EASTWOOD, K. and EASTWOOD, M. R. (1984) 'Hearing assessment in homes for the aged: a comparison of audiometric and self-report methods,' *Journal of the American Geriatrics Society*, 32, pp. 396–400.

CORKIN, S. (1982) 'Some relationships between global amnesias and the memory impairments in Alzheimer's disease,' in Corkin, S., Davis, K. L., Growdon, J. H., Usdin, E. and Wurtman, R. J. (Eds) *Alzheimer's Disease: A Report of Progress in Research, Aging*, Vol. 19, New York, Raven Press, pp. 149–64.

CORKIN, S., GROWDON, J. H., NISSEN, M. J., HUFF, F. J., FREED, D. M. and SAGAR, H. J. (1984) 'Recent advances in the neuropsychological study of Alzheimer's disease,' in Wurtman, R. J., Corkin, S. and Growdon, J. H. (Eds) *Alzheimer's Disease: Advances in Basic Research and Therapies*, Cambridge, Mass., Centre for Brain Sciences Charitable Trust, pp. 75–93.

CORKIN, S., GROWDON, J. H., SULLIVAN, E. V., NISSEN, M. J. and HUFF, F. J. (1986) 'Assessing treatment effects: a neuropsychological battery,' in Poon, L. W. (Ed.) *Handbook of Clinical Memory Assessment of Older Adults*, Washington, American Psychological Association, pp. 156–67.

CORSELLIS, J. A. N. (1962) *Mental Illness and the Ageing Brain*, London, Oxford University Press.

CORSELLIS J. A. N. (1976) 'Ageing and the dementias,' in Blackwood, W. and Corsellis, J. A. N. (Eds) *Greenfield's Neuropathology*, 3rd ed., London, Edward Arnold, pp. 796–848.

CORSER, C. M., BAIKIE, E. and BROWN, E. (1979) 'Effect of lecithin in senile dementia: a report of four cases,' in Glen, A. I. M. and Whalley, L. J. (Eds) *Alzheimer's Disease: Early Recognition of Potentially Reversible Deficits*, Edinburgh, Churchill Livingstone, pp. 169–172.

COWAN, N. (1988) 'Evolving conceptions of memory storage, selective attention, and their mutual-constraints within the human information-processing system,' *Psychological Bulletin*, 104, pp. 163–191.

CRAIK, F. I. M. (1977) 'Age differences in human memory,' in Birren, J. E. and Schaie, K. W. (Eds) *Handbook of the Psychology of Aging*, New York, Van Nostrand Reinhold Company, pp. 384–420.

CRAIK, F. I. M. (1979) 'Levels of processing: overview and closing comments,' in Cermak, L. S. and Craik, F. I. M. (Eds) *Levels of Processing in Human Memory*, Hillsdale, N.J., Lawrence Erlbaum Associates, pp. 447–461.

CRAIK, F. I. M. and BYRD, M. (1982) 'Aging and cognitive deficits: the role of attentional resources,' in Craik, F. I. M. and Trehub, S. (Eds) *Aging and Cognitive Processes*, New York, Plenum Press, pp. 191–211.

CRAIK, F. I. M. and LOCKHART, R. S. (1972) 'Levels of processing: A framework for memory research,' *Journal of Verbal Learning and Verbal Behaviour*, 11, pp. 671–684.

CRAIK, F. I. M. and SIMON, E. (1980) 'Age differences in memory: the role of attention and depth of processing,' in Poon, L. W., Fozard, J. L., Cermak, L. S. Arenberg, D. and Thompson, L. W. (Eds) *New Directions in Memory and Ageing*, Hillsdale, N.J., Lawrence Erlbaum, pp. 95–112.

CRAMER, H., SCHAUNDT, D., RISSLER, K., STRUBEL, D., WARTER, J. M. and KUNTZMANN, F. (1985) 'Somatostatin-like immunoreactivity and substance-P-like immunoreactivity in the CSF of patients with senile dementia of Alzheimer type, multi-infarct syndrome and communicating hydrocephalus,' *Journal of Neurology*, 232, pp. 346–51.

CRAPPER MCLACHLAN, D. R. (1986) 'Aluminium and Alzheimer's disease,' *Neurobiology of Ageing*, 7, pp. 525–32.

CRAWFORD, J. R., STEWART, L. E., COCHRANE, R. H. B., FOULDS, J. A., BESSON, J. A. and PARKER, B. M. (1989) 'Estimating premorbid IQ from demographic variables: regression equations derived from a U.K. sample,' *British Journal of Clinical Psychology*, 28, pp. 275–8.

CRAWFORD, J. R., STEWART, L. E., GARTHWAITE, P. H., PARKER, B . M. and BESSON, J. A. (1988) 'The relationship between demographic variables and NART performance in normal subjects,' *British Journal of Clinical Psychology*, 27, pp. 181–2.

CRITCHLEY, M. (1964) 'The neurology of psychotic speech,' *British Journal of Psychiatry*, 110, pp. 353–64.

CROOK, T., FERRIS, S., MCCARTHY, M. and RAE, D. (1980) 'Utility of digit recall tasks for assessing memory in the aged,' *Journal of Consulting and Clinical Psychology*, 48, pp. 228–33.

CROSS, A. J., CROW, T. J., JOHNSON, J. A., JOSEPH, M. H., PERRY, E. K., PERRY, R. H., BLESSED, G. and TOMLINSON, B. E. (1983) 'Monoamine metabolism in senile dementia of Alzheimer type,' *Journal of the Neurological Sciences*, 60, pp. 383–92.

CROSS, A. J., CROW, T. J. and PETERS, T. J. (1986) 'Cortical neurochemistry in Alzheimer-type dementia,' *Progress in Brain Research*, 70, pp. 153–69.

CROSS, A. J., SLATER, P., CANDY, J. M., PERRY, E. K. and PERRY, R. H. (1987) 'Glutamate deficits in Alzheimer's disease,' *Journal of Neurology Neurosurgery and Psychiatry*, 50, pp. 357–8.

CROW, T. J. and GROVE-WHITE, I. G. (1973) 'An analysis of the learning deficit following hyoscine administration to man,' *British Journal of Pharmacology*, 49, pp. 322–7.

CRYSTAL, H. A., HOROUPIAN, D. S., KATZMAN, R. and JOTKOWITZ, S. (1982) 'Biopsy-proved Alzheimer disease presenting as a right parietal lobe syndrome,' *Annals of Neurology*, 12, pp. 186–8.

CUMMINGS, J. L. (1986) 'Subcortical dementia: neuropsychology, neuropsychiatry and pathophysiology,' *British Journal of Psychiatry*, 149, pp. 682–97.

CUMMINGS, J. L. and BENSON, D. F. (1983) *Dementia: A Clinical Approach*, Boston, Butterworths.

CUMMINGS, J. L. and BENSON, D. F. (1984) 'Subcortical dementia: review of an emerging concept,' *Archives of Neurology*, 41, pp. 874–9.

CUMMINGS, J. L., BENSON, D. F. and LOVERME, S. (1980) 'Reversible dementia: illustrative cases, definition, and review,' *Journal of the American Medical Association*, 243, pp. 2434–9.

CUMMINGS, J. L., BENSON, D. F., HILL, M. A. and READ, S. (1985) 'Aphasia in dementia of the Alzheimer type,' *Neurology*, 35, pp. 394–7.

CUMMINGS, J. L., DARKINS, A., MANDEZ, M., HILL, M. A. and BENSON, D. F. (1988) 'Alzheimer's disease and Parkinson's disease: comparison of speech and language alterations,' *Neurology*, 38, pp. 680–4.

CUMMINGS, J. L. and DUCHEN, L. W. (1981) 'Kluver-Bucy syndrome in Pick's disease: clinical and pathologic correlations,' *Neurology*, 31, pp. 1415–22.

CUMMINGS, J. L., HOULIHAN, J. P., and HILL, M. A. (1986) 'The pattern of reading deterioration in dementia of the Alzheimer-type: observations and implications,' *Brain and Language*, 29, pp. 315–23.

CURRAN, D. (1930) 'Huntington's chorea without choreiform movements,' *Journal of Neurology and Psychopathology*, 10, pp. 305–10.

CUTTING, J. (1978) 'Specific psychological deficits in alcoholism,' *British Journal of Psychiatry*, 133, pp. 119–22.

DARLEY, F., ARONSON, A. and BROWN, J. (1975) *Motor Speech Disorders*, Philadelphia, Lea & Fibiger.

DAVIDSON, M., ZEMISHLANY, Z., MOHS, R. C., HORVATH, T. B., POWCHICK, P., BLASS, J. P. and DAVIS, K. L. (1988) '4-Aminopyridine in the treatment of Alzheimer's disease,' *Biological Psychiatry*, 23, pp. 485–90.

DAVIES, P. (1979) 'Neurotransmitter-related enzymes in senile dementia of the Alzheimer type,' *Brain Research*, 171, pp. 319–27.

DAVIES, P. (1986) 'Cholinergic and somatostatin deficits in the Alzheimer brain,' in Crook, T., Bartus, R., Ferris, S and Gershon, S. (Eds) *Treatment Development Strategies for Alzheimer's Disease*, Madison, Mark Powley Associates, pp. 473–82.

DAVIES, P., KATZ, D. A., and CRYSTAL, H. A. (1982) 'Choline acetyltransferase, somatostatin and substance P in selected cases of Alzheimer's disease', in Corkin, S., Davis, K. L., Growdon, J. H., Usdin, E. and Wurtman, R. J. (Eds) *Alzheimer's Disease: A Report of Progress in Research, Aging*, Vol. 19, New York, Raven Press, pp. 385–92.

DAVIES, P., KATZMAN, R. and TERRY, R. D. (1980) 'Reduced somatostatin – like immunoreactivity in cerebral cortex from Alzheimer's disease and Alzheimer senile dementia,' *Nature*, 288, pp. 279–80.

DAVIES, P., MALONEY, A. F. J. (1976) 'Selective loss of central cholinergic neurons in Alzheimer's disease,' *Lancet*, ii, p. 1403.

DAVIES, P. and VERTH, A. H. (1978) 'Regional distribution of muscarinic acetycholine receptor in normal and Alzheimer's-type dementia brains,' *Brain Research*, 138, pp. 385–92.

DAVIS, K.L., HOLLANDER, E., DAVIDSON, M., DAVIS, B.M., MOHS, R.C. and HORVATH, T.B. (1987) 'Induction of depression with oxotremorine in patients with Alzheimer's disease,' *American Journal of Psychiatry*, 144, pp. 468–71.

DAVIS, K.L. and MOHS, R.C. (1982) 'Enhancement of memory processes in Alzheimer's disease with multiple-dose intravenous physostigmine,' *American Journal of Psychiatry*, 139, pp. 1421–4.

DAVIS, K.L., MOHS, R.C. and TINKLENBERG, J.R. (1976) 'Enhancement of memory by physostigmine,' *New England Journal of Medicine*, 301, p. 946.

DAVIS, K.L., MOHS, R.C., TINKLENBERG, J.R., HOLLISTER, L.E., PFEFFERBAUM, A. and KOPELL, B.S. (1980) 'Cholinomimetics and Memory: the effect of choline chloride,' *Archives of Neurology*, 37, pp. 49–52.

DAVIS, K.L., MOHS, R. and TINKLENBERG, J.R. (1979) 'Enhancement of memory by physostigmine,' *New England Journal of Medicine*, 301, p. 946.

DAVIS, K.L., MOHS, R., TINKLENBERG, J.R., PFEFFERBAUM, A., HOLLISTER, L.E. and KOPELL, B.S. (1978) 'Physostigmine: improvement of long-term memory processes in normal humans,' *Science*, 201, pp. 272–4.

DAVIS, P.E. and MUMFORD, S.J. (1984) 'Cued recall and the nature of the memory disorder in dementia,' *British Journal of Psychiatry*, 144, pp. 383–6.

DAVISON, L.A. (1974) 'Introduction,' in Reitan, R.M. and Davison, L.A. (Eds) *Clinical Neuropsychology: Current status and applications*, New York, Wiley, pp. 1–18.

DAVOUS, P. and LAMOUR, Y. (1986) 'Bethaniecol decreases reaction time in patients with senile dementia of the Alzheimer type,' *Journal of Neurology, Neurosurgery and Psychiatry*, 48, pp. 1297–9.

DAWBURN, D., ROSSOR, M.N., MOUNTJOY, C.Q., ROTH, M. and EMSON, P.C. (1986) 'Decreased somatostatin immunoreactivity but not neuropeptide Y immunoreactivity in cerebral cortex in senile dementia of Alzheimer type,' *Neuroscience Letters*, 70, pp. 154–9.

DELLA SALA, S., DI LORENZO, G., GIORDANO, A. and SPINNLER, H. (1986) 'Is there a specific visuo-spatial impairment in Parkinsonians?' *Journal of Neurology, Neurosurgery and Psychiatry*, 49, pp. 1258–65.

DELLA SALA, S., LUCCHELLI, F. and SPINNLER, H. (1987b) 'Ideomotor apraxia in patients with dementia of Alzheimer type,' *Neurology*, 234, pp. 91–3.

DELLA SALA, S., PASETTI, C., SEMPIO, P. (1987a) 'Deficit in the "primacy effect" in parkinsonians interpreted by means of the working memory model,' *Archives of Neurology and Psychiatry*, 138 pp. 5–14.

DELWAIDE, P.J., DEVOITILLE, J.M. and YLIEFF, M. (1980) 'Acute effects of drugs upon memory of patients with senile dementia,' *Acta Psychiatrica Belgica*, 80, pp. 748–54.

DEMUTH, G.W., and RAND, B.S. (1980) 'A typical major depression in a patient with severe primary degenerative dementia,' *American Journal of Psychiatry*, 137, pp. 1609–10.

DePAULO, J.R. and FOLSTEIN, M.F. (1978) 'Psychiatric disturbance in neurological patients: detection, recognition and hospital course,' *Annals of Neurology*, 4, pp. 225–8.

DE RENZI, E. (1985) 'Apraxia,' in Adelman, G. (Ed.) *Encyclopedia of Neuroscience*, Vol. 1, Boston, Birkhauser, pp. 73–4.

DE RENZI, E. and FAGLIONI, P. (1978) 'Normative data and screening power of a shortened version of the Token Test,' *Cortex*, 14, pp. 41–9.

DE RENZI, E. and FERRARI, C. (1978) 'The Reporter's Test: a sensitive test to detect expressive disturbances in aphasics,' *Cortex*, 14, pp. 279–93.

DE RENZI, E., MOTTI, F. and NICHELLI, P. (1980) 'Imitating gestures: a quantitative approach to ideomotor apraxia,' *Archives of Neurology*, 37, pp. 6–10.

DEUTSCH, J. A. (1971) 'The cholinergic synapse and the site of memory,' *Science*, 174, pp. 788–94.

DEWHURST, K., OLIVER, J., TRICK, K. L. K. and MCKNIGHT, A. L. (1969) 'Neuropsychiatric aspects of Huntington's disease,' *Confines Neurologica*, 31, pp. 258–68.

DI CHIRO, G. (1987) 'Neuroimaging,' in Adelman, G. (Ed.) *Encyclopedia of Neuroscience*, Vol. 1, Boston, Birkhauser, pp. 795–8.

DIESFELDT, H. F. A. (1984) 'The importance of encoding instructions and retrieval cues in the assessment of memory in senile dementia,' *Archives of Gerontology and Geriatrics*, 3, pp. 51–7.

DIESFELDT, H. F. A. (1985) 'Verbal fluency in senile dementia: an analysis of search and knowledge,' *Archives of Gerontology and Geriatrics*, 4 pp. 231–9.

DINNERSTEIN, A. J., FRIGYESI, T. and LOWENTHAL, M. (1962) 'Delayed feedback as a possible mechanism in parkinsonism,' *Perceptual and Motor Skills*, 15, pp. 667–80.

DINNERSTEIN, A. J., LOWENTHAL, M., BLAKE, G. (1964) 'Tactile delay in parkinsonism,' *Journal of Mental and Nervous Diseases*, 139, pp. 521–4.

DOHN, H. H. and CREWS, E. L. (1986) 'Capgras syndrome: a literature review and case series,' *Hillside Journal of Clinical Psychiatry*, 8, pp. 56–74.

DOTY, R. L., REYES, P. F. and GREGOR, T. (1987) 'Presence of both odour identification and detection deficits in Alzheimer's disease,' *Brain Research Bulletin*, 18, pp. 597–600.

DRACHMAN, D. A. (1977) 'Memory and cognitive function in man: does the cholinergic system have a specific role?' *Neurology*, 27, pp. 783–90.

DRACHMAN, D. A. (1978) 'Memory, dementia, and the cholinergic system,' in Katzman, R., Terry, R. D. and Bick, K. L. (Eds) *Alzheimer's Disease: Senile Dementia and Related Disorders, Aging*, Vol. 7, New York, Raven Press, pp. 141–8.

DRACHMAN, D. A. (1983) 'How normal aging relates to dementia: a critique and classification,' in Samuel, D., Algeri, S., Gershon, S., Grimm, V. E. and Toffano, G. (Eds) *Aging of the Brain, Aging*, Vol. 22, New York, Raven Press, pp. 19–31.

DRACHMAN, D. A. and LEAVITT, J. (1974) 'Human memory and the cholinergic system: a relationship to aging?' *Archives of Neurology*, 30, pp. 113–21.

DRACHMAN, D. A., NOFFSINGER, D., SAHAKIAN, B. J., KURDZIEL, S. and FLEMING, P. (1980) 'Aging, memory, and the cholinergic system: a study of dichotic listening,' *Neurobiology of Aging*, 1, pp. 39–43.

DRACHMAN, D. A. and SAHAKIAN, B. J. (1979) 'Effects of cholinergic agents on human learning and memory,' in Barbeau, A., Growdon, J. H. and Wurtman, R. J. (Eds) *Nutrition and the Brain*, Vol. 5, New York, Raven Press, pp. 351–66.

DRACHMAN, D. A. and SAHAKIAN, B. J. (1980) 'Memory and cognitive function in the elderly: a preliminary trial of physostigmine,' *Archives of Neurology*, 37, pp. 674–5.

DRACHMAN, D. A. and STAHL, S. (1975) 'Extrapyramidal dementia and levodopa,' *Lancet*, i, p. 809.

DUBOIS, B., PILLON, B., LEGAULT, F., AGID, Y. and LHERMITTE, F. (1988) 'Slowing of cognitive processing in progressive supranuclear palsy. A comparison with Parkinson's disease,' *Archives of Neurology*, 45, pp. 1194–9.

DUCKWORTH, G. S. and ROSS, H. (1975) 'Diagnostic diffrences in psychogeriatric patients in Toronto, New York & London, England,' *Canadian Medical Association Journal*, 112, pp. 847–51.

DUFFY, P., WOLF, J., COLLINS, G., DEVOE, A. G., STREETEN, B. and COHEN, D. (1974) 'Possible person-to-person transmission of Creutzfeldt–Jakob disease,' *New England Journal of Medicine*, 290, pp. 692–3.

DUNDEE, J. W. and PANDIT, S. K. (1972) 'Anterograde amnesic effects of pethidine, hyosine and diazepam in adults,' *British Journal of Pharmacology*, 44, pp. 140–4.

DUNNE, M. P., and HARTLEY, L. R. (1985) 'The effects of scopolamine on verbal memory: evidence for an attentional hypothesis,' *Acta Psychologia*, 58, pp. 205–17.

DUNNE, M. P. and HARTLEY, L. R. (1986) 'Scopolamine and the control of attention in humans,' *Psychopharmacology*, 89, pp. 94–7.

DUNNETT, S. B. (1989) 'Neural transplantation: normal brain function and repair after damage,' *The Psychologist: Bulletin of the British Psychological Society*, 1, pp. 4–8.

DYER, F. N. (1973) 'The Stroop phenomenon and its use in the study of perceptual, cognitive, and response processes,' *Memory and Cognition*, 1, pp. 106–20.

DYSKEN, M. W., FOVALL, P., HARRIS, C. M., NORONHA, A., BERGEN, D., HOEPPNER, T. and DAVIS, J. M. (1982) 'Lecithin administration in patients with primary degenerative dementia and in normal volunteers,' in Corkin, S., Davis, K. L., Growdon, J. H., Usdin, E. and Wurtman, R. J. (Eds) *Alzheimer's Disease: A Report of Progress in Research, Aging*, Vol. 19, New York, Raven Press, pp. 385–392.

EBINGER, G., BRUYLAND, M., MARTIN, J. J., HERREGODTA, P., CRAS, P., MICHOTTE, Y. and GOMME, L. (1987) 'Distribution of biogenic amines and their catabolites in brains from patients with Alzheimer's disease,' *Journal of the Neurological Sciences*, 77, pp. 267–83.

ECKERNAS, S.-A., SAHLSTROM, L. and AQUILONIUS, S.-M. (1977) '*In vivo* turnover rate of acetylcholine in rat brain parts at elevated steady-state concentration of plasma choline,' *Acta Physiologica Scandinavica*, 101, pp. 404–10.

EDITORIAL (1978) 'Dementia – the quiet epidemic,' *British Medical Journal*, 1, pp. 1–2.

EDITORIAL (1980) 'Cerebral atrophy or hydrocephalus?' *British Medical Journal*, 280, pp. 348–9.

EICHENBAUM, H., MORTON, T. H., POTTER, H. and CORKIN, S. (1983) 'Selective olfactory deficits in case H.M.,' *Brain*, 106, pp. 459–72.

EISDORFER, C. (1981) 'Biobehavioural approaches to dementia,' *Mount Sinai Journal of Medicine*, 48, pp. 500–6.

EISDORFER, C. and COHEN, D. (1980) 'Diagnostic criteria for primary degeneration of the Alzheimer's type,' *Journal of Family Practice*, 11, pp. 553–7.

EISDORFER, C. and COHEN, D. (1981) 'Management of the patient and family coping with dementing illness,' *Journal of Family Practice*, 12, pp. 831–7.

ELIZAN, T. S., YAHR, M. D., MOROS, D. A., MENDOZA, M. R., PANG, S. and BODIAN, C. A. (1989) 'Selegiline use to prevent progression of Parkinson's disease: experience with 22 *de novo* patients,' *Archives of Neurology*, 46, pp. 1275–9.

ELLISON, D. W., BEAL, M. F., MAZUREK, M. F., BIRD, E. D. and MARTIN, J. B. (1986) 'A postmortem study of amino acid neurotransmitters in Alzheimer's disease,' *Archives of Neurology*, 20, pp. 616–21.

EMERY, O. D. and EMERY, P. E. (1983) 'Language in senile dementia of the Alzheimer type,' *Psychiatric Journal University of Ottawa*, 8, pp. 169–78.

ENGEN, T. (1977) 'Taste and Smell,' in Birren, J. E. and Schaie, K. W. (Eds) *Handbook of the Psychology of Aging*, 1st ed., New York, Van Nostrand, pp. 554–61.

ERBER, J. T. (1981) 'Remote memory and age: a review,' *Experimental Ageing Research*, 7, pp. 189–99.

ERKINJUNTTI, T., LARSEN, T., SULKAVA, R., KETONEN, L., LAAKSONEN, R. and PALO, J. (1988) 'EEG in the differential diagnosis between Alzheimer's disease and vascular dementia,' *Acta Neurologica Scandinavica*, 77, pp. 36–43.

ERKINJUNTTI, T., SIPPONEN, J. T., IVANAINEN, M., KETONEN, L., SULKAVA, R. and SEPPONEN, R. E. (1984) 'Cerebral NMR and CT imaging in dementia,' *Journal of Computer Assisted Tomography*, 8, pp. 614–18.

ERMINI-FUENFSCHILLING, D. E., MONSCH, A. U. and STAEHELIN, H. B. (1989) 'Neuropsychological tests as a means of correcting inappropriate behaviour of caregivers,' paper presented at the Fifth International Conference of Alzheimer's Disease International, Dublin.

ERNST, B., DALBY, M. A. and DALBY, A. (1970) 'Aphasic disturbances in presenile dementia,' *Acta Neurologica Scandinavica*, Supplement, 43, pp. 99–100.

ESIRI, M. and WILCOCK, G. K. (1984) 'The olfactory bulbs in Alzheimer's disease,' *Journal of Neurology, Neurosurgery and Psychiatry*, 47, pp. 56–69.

ESLINGER, P. J. and DAMASIO, A. R. (1986) 'Preserved motor learning in Alzheimer's disease: implications for anatomy and behaviour,' *Journal of Neuroscience*, 6, pp. 3006–9.

ESLINGER, P. J., DAMASIO, A. R. BENTON, A. L. and VAN ALLEN, M. (1985) 'Neuropsychologic detection of abnormal mental decline in older persons,' *Journal of the American Medical Association*, 253, pp. 670–4.

ESLINGER, P. J., DAMASIO, A. R., and VAN HOESEN, G. W. (1982) 'Olfactory dysfunction in man: anatomical and behavioural aspects,' *Brain and Cognition*, 1, pp. 259–85.

ETIENNE, P., DASTOOR, D., GAUTHIER, S., LUDWICK, R. and COLLIER, B. (1982) 'Lecithin in the treatment of Alzheimer's disease,' in Corkin, S., Davis, K. L., Growdon, J. H., Usdin, E. and Wurtman, R. J. (Eds) *Alzheimer's Disease: A Report of Progress in Research, Aging*, Vol. 19, New York, Raven Press, pp. 369–72.

ETIENNE, P., GAUTHIER, S., DASTOOR, D., COLLIER, B. and RATNER, J. (1978b) 'Lecithin in Alzheimer's disease,' *Lancet*, ii, p. 1286.

ETIENNE, P., GAUTHIER, S., JOHNSON, G., COLLIER, B., MENDIS, T., DASTOOR, D., COLE, M. and MULLER, H. F. (1978a) 'Clinical effects of choline in Alzheimer's disease,' *Lancet*, i, pp. 508–9.

EVARTS, E. V., TEAVAINEN, J. and CALNE, D. B. (1981) 'Reaction time in Parkinson's disease,' *Brain*, 104, pp. 167–86.

267

EYSENCK, M. W. and EYSENCK, M. C. (1979) 'Processing depth, elaboration of encoding, memory stores, and expanded processing capacity,' *Journal of Experimental Psychology: Human Learning and Memory*, 5, pp. 472–84.

FADEN, A. I. and TOWNSEND, J. J. (1976) 'Myoclonus in Alzheimer disease: a confusing sign,' *Archives of Neurology*, 33, pp. 278–80.

FELDMAN, R. G., CHANDLER, K. A., LEVY, L. L. and GLASER, G. H. (1963) 'Familial Alzheimer's disease,' *Neurology*, 13, pp. 811–24.

FELDON, S. E. and LANGSTON, J. W. (1977) 'Square-wave jerks; a disease of microsaccades?' *Neurology*, 27, pp. 278–81.

FERRIS, S. H., CROOK, T., CLARK, E., MCCARTHY, M. and RAE, D. (1980) Facial recognition memory deficits in normal ageing and senile dementia, *Journal of Gerontology*, 35, pp. 707–14.

FERRIS, S. H., CROOK, T., SATHANANTHAN, G. and GERSHON, S. (1976) 'Reaction time as a diagnostic measure in senility,' *Journal of The American Geriatrics Society*, 24, pp. 529–33.

FERRIS, S. H., REISBERG, B., CROOK, T., FRIEDMAN, E., SCHNECK, M. K., MIR, P., SHERMAN, K. A., CORWIN, J., GERSHON, S. and BARTUS, R. T. (1982) 'Pharmacological treatment of senile dementia: Choline, L-DOPA, piracetam and choline plus piracetam,' in Corkin, S., Davis, K. L., Growdon, J. H., Usdin, E. and Wurtman, R. J. (Eds) *Alzheimer's Disease: A Report of Progress in Research, Aging*, Vol. 19, New York, Raven Press, pp. 475–81.

FERRIS, S. H., SATHANANTHAN, G., REISBERG, B. and GERSHON, S. (1979) 'Long-term choline treatment of memory-impaired elderly patients,' *Science*, 205, pp. 1039–40.

FILLEY, C. M., KOBAYASHI, J. and HEATON, R. K. (1987) 'Weschler Intelligence scales profiles, the cholinergic system and Alzheimer's disease,' *Journal of Clinical and Experimental Neuropsychology*, 9, pp. 180–6.

FINK, M., GREEN, M. and BENDER, M. B. (1952) 'The face-hand test as a diagnostic sign of organic mental syndrome,' *Neurology*, 2, pp. 46–58.

FISHER, J. M., KENNEDY, J. L., CAINE, E. D. and SHOULSON, I. (1983) 'Dementia in Huntington's disease: a cross-sectional analysis of intellectual decline,' in Mayeux R. and Rosen, W. G. (Eds) *The Dementias*, New York, Raven Press, pp. 229–38.

FISHER, R. P. and CRAIK, F. I. M. (1977) 'The interaction between encoding and retrieval operations in cued recall,' *Journal of Experimental Psychology: Human Learning and Memory*, 3, pp. 701–11.

FISK, J. D., GOODALE, M. A., BURKHART, G. and BARNETT, H. J. M. (1982) 'Progressive supranuclear palsy: the relationship between ocular motor dysfunction and psychological test performance,' *Neurology*, 32, pp. 698–705.

FISMAN, M., MERSKEY, H., HELMES, E., MCCREADY, J., COLHOUN, E. H. and RYLETT, B. J. (1981) 'Double blind study of lecithin in patients with Alzheimer's disease,' *Canadian Journal of Psychiatry*, 26, pp. 426–8.

FITZGERALD, M. J. T. (1985) *Neuroanatomy Basic and Applied*, Eastbourne, Bailliere Tindall.

FLETCHER, W. A. and SHARPE, J. A. (1988) 'Smooth pursuit dysfunction in Alzheimer's disease,' *Neurology*, 38, pp. 272–7.

FLICKER, C., BARTUS, R. T., CROOK, T. and FERRIS, S. H. (1984) 'Effects of ageing and dementia upon recent visuospatial memory,' *Neurobiology of Ageing*, 5, pp. 275–83.

FLICKER, C., FERRIS, S. H., CROOK, T. and BARTUS, R. T. (1987) 'Implications of memory and language dysfunction in the naming deficit of senile dementia,' *Brain and Language*, 31, pp. 187–200.

FLOWERS, K. A. (1975) 'Ballistic and corrective movements on an aiming task: intention tremor and parkinsonian movement disorders compared,' *Neurology*, 25, pp. 413–21.

FLOWERS, K. A. (1976) 'Visual "closed-loop" and "open-loop" characteristics of voluntary movement in patients with parkinsonism and tremor,' *Brain*, 99, pp. 269–310.

FLOWERS, K. A. (1978) 'Lack of prediction in the motor behaviour of parkinsonism,' *Brain*, 101, pp. 35–52.

FLOWERS, K. A., PEARCE, I., and PEARCE, J. M. (1984) 'Recognition memory in Parkinson's disease,' *Journal of Neurology, Neurosurgery and Psychiatry*, 47, pp. 1174–81.

FLOWERS, K. A. and ROBERTSON, C. (1985) 'The effect of Parkinson's disease on the ability to maintain a mental set,' *Journal of Neurology, Neurosurgery and Psychiatry*, 48, pp. 517–29.

FLYNN, D. D. and MASH, D. C. (1986) 'Characterization of L-[3H]nicotine binding in human cerebral cortex: comparision between Alzheimer's disease and the normal,' *Journal of Neurochemistry*, 47, pp. 1948–53.

FOLSTEIN, M. F. and BREITNER, J. C. S. (1981) 'Language disorder predicts familial Alzheimer's disease,' *Johns Hopkin Medical Journal*, 149, pp. 145–7.

FOLSTEIN, M. F., FOLSTEIN, S. E. and McHUGH, P. R. (1975) ' "Mini-Mental State", A practical method for grading the cognitive state for the clinician,' *Journal of Psychiatric Research*, 12, pp. 189–198.

FOSTER, N. L., CHASE, T. N., PATRONAS, N. J., GILLESPIE, M. M. and FEDIO, P. (1986) 'Cerebral mapping of apraxia in Alzheimer's disease by positron emission tomography,' *Annals of Neurology*, 19, pp. 139–43.

FOVALL, P., DYSKEN, M. W., LAZARUS, L. W., DAVIS, J. M., KAHN, R. L., JOPE, R., FINKEL, S. and RATTAN, P. (1980) 'Choline bitartrate treatment of Alzheimer-type dementias,' *Communications in Psychopharmacology*, 4, pp. 141–5.

FRANCIS, P. T., BOWEN, D. M., LOWE, S. L., NEARY, D., MANN, D. M. A. and SNOWDON, J. S. (1987) 'Somatostatin content and release measured in cerebral biopsies from demented patients,' *Journal of the Neurological Sciences*, 78, pp. 1–16.

FREDERIKS, J. A. M. (1969) 'Disorders of attention in neurological syndromes,' in Vinken, P. J. and Bruyn, G. W. (Eds) *Disorders of Higher Nervous Activity, Handbook of Clinical Neurology*, Vol. 3, Amsterdam, North Holland, pp. 187–201.

FREEDMAN, M. and OSCAR-BERMAN, M. (1986) 'Selective delayed response deficits in Parkinson's and Alzheimer's disease,' *Archives of Neurology*, 43, pp. 886–90.

FREEDMAN, M. and OSCAR-BERMAN, M. (1987) 'Tactile discrimination learning defects in Alzheimer's and Parkinson's diseases,' *Archives of Neurology*, 44, pp. 394–8.

FREEMAN, T. and GATHERCOLE, C. E. (1966) 'Perseveration – the clinical symptoms – in chronic schizophrenia and organic dementia,' *British Journal of Psychiatry*, 112, pp. 27–32.

FREEMON, F. R. (1976) 'Evaluation of patients with progressive intellectual deterioration,' *Archives of Neurology*, 33 pp. 658–9.

FRITH, C. D., RICHARDSON, J. T. E., SAMUEL, M., CROW, T. J. and MCKENNA, P. J. (1984) 'The effects of intravenous diazepam and hyosine upon human memory,' *Quarterly Journal of Experimental Psychology*, 36A, pp. 133–44.

FULD, P. A. (1982) 'Behavioural signs of cholinergic deficiency in Alzheimer dementia,' in Corkin, S., Davis, K. L., Growdon, J. H., Usdin, E. and Wurtman, R. J. (Eds) *Alzheimer's Disease: A Report of Progress in Research, Aging*, Vol. 19, New York, Raven Press, pp. 193–6.

FULD, P. A. (1984) 'Test profile of cholinergic dysfunction and of Alzheimer-type dementia,' *Journal of Clinical Neuropsychology*, 6, pp. 380–92.

FULD, P. A., KATZMAN, R., DAVIES, P. and TERRY, R. D. (1982) 'Intrusions as a sign of Alzheimer dementia: chemical and pathological verification,' *Annals of Neurology*, 11, pp. 155–9.

FUNKENSTEIN, H. H., HICKS, R., DYSKEN, M. W., and DAVIS, J. M. (1981) 'Drug treatment of cognitive impairment in Alzheimer's disease and the late life dementias,' in Miller, N. E. and Cohen, G. D. (Eds) *Clinical Aspects of Alzheimer's Disease and Senile Dementia, Aging*, Vol. 15, New York, Raven Press, pp. 139–58.

GADO, M., DANZIGER, W., CHI, D., HUGHES, C. P. and COBEN, L. A. (1983) 'Brain parenchymal density measurements by CT in demented subjects and normal controls,' *Radiology*, 147, pp. 703–10.

GANDOLFO, C., VECCHIA, R., MORETTI, C., BRUSA, G. and SCOTTO, P. A. (1986) 'WAIS testing in degenerative and multi-infarct dementia,' *Acta Neurologica*, 8, pp. 45–50.

GARCIA, C. A., REDING, M. J. and BLASS, J. P. (1981) 'Over-diagnosis of dementia,' *Journal of the American Geriatrics Society*, 29, pp. 407–10.

GAWEL, M. J., DAS, P., VINCENT, S. and CLIFFORD ROSE, F. (1981) 'Visual and auditory evoked responses in patients with Parkinson's disease,' *Journal of Neurology, Neurosurgery and Psychiatry*, 44, pp. 227–32.

GEDDES, J. W., CHANG-CHUI, H., COOPER, S. M., LOTT, I. T. and COTMAN, C. W. (1986) 'Density and distribution of NMDA receptors in the human hippocampus in Alzheimer's disease,' *Brain Research*, 399, pp. 156–61.

GENDRON, C. E., POITRAS, L. R., ENGELS, M. L., DASTOOR, D. P., SIROTA, S. E., BARZA, S. L., DAVIS, J. C., and LEVINE, N. B. (1986) 'Skills training with supporters of the demented,' *Journal of the American Geriatrics Society*, 34, pp. 875–80.

GEORGE, A., DE LEON, M., FERRIS, S. and KRICHEFF, I. I. (1981) 'Parenchymal CT correlates of senile dementia (Alzheimer's disease) loss of grey-white matter discriminability,' *American Journal of Neuroradiology*, 2, pp. 205–13.

GESCHWIND, N. (1982) 'Disorders of attention: a frontier in neuropsychology,' *Philosophical Transactions of the Royal Society, London*, B298, pp. 173–85.

GEVINS, A. S. (1986) 'Quantitative human neurophysiology,' in Hannay, H. J. (Ed.) *Experimental Techniques in Human Neuropsychology*, Oxford, Oxford University Press, pp. 419–56.

GEWIRTH, L. R., SHINDLER, A. G. and HIER, D. B. (1984) 'Altered patterns of word associations in dementia and aphasia,' *Brain and Language*, 21, pp. 307–17.

GHONEIM, M. M. and MEWALDT, S. P. (1975) 'Effects of diazepam and scopolamine on storage, retrieval and organizational processes in memory,' *Psychopharmacologica (Berlin)*, 44, pp. 257–62.

GHONEIM, M. M. and MEWALDT, S. P. (1977) 'Studies on human memory: the interactions of diazepam, scopolamine, and physostigmine,' *Psychopharmacology*, 52, pp. 1–6.

GIANUTSOS, R. and GIANUTSOS, J. (1979) 'Rehabilitating the verbal recall of brain-injured patients by mnemonic training: an experimental demonstration using single-case methodology,' *Journal of Clinical Neuropsychology*, 1, pp. 117–35.

GIBSON, A. J. (1981) 'A further analysis of memory loss in dementia and depression in the elderly,' *British Journal of Clinical Psychology*, 20, pp. 179–85.

GIBSON, A. J. and KENDRICK, D. C. (1979) *The Kendrick Battery for the Detection of Dementia in the Elderly*, Windsor, NFER Publishing Company.

GILHOME-HERBST, K. and HUMPHREY, C. (1980) 'Hearing impairment and mental state in the elderly living at home,' *British Medical Journal*, 281, pp. 903–5.

GILHOOLY, M. L. M. (1984) 'The impact of caregiving on caregivers: factors associated with the psychological wellbeing of people supporting a dementing relative in the community,' *British Journal of Medical Psychology*, 57, pp. 35–44.

GILHOOLY, M. L. M. (1986) 'Legal and ethical issues in the management of the dementing elderly,' in Gilhooly, M. L. M., Zarit, S. H. and Birren, J. E. (Eds) *The Dementias: Policy and Management*, Englewood Cliffs, Prentice Hall, pp. 131–60.

GILLEARD, C. J. (1984) 'Living with dementia: community care of the elderly mentally infirm,' London, Crom Helm.

GIMENEZ-ROLDAN, S., PERAITA, P., LOPEZ AGREDA, J. M., ABAD, J. M. and ESTEBAN, A. (1971) 'Myoclonus and photic-induced seizures in Alzheimer's disease,' *European Neurology*, 5, pp. 215–24.

GLANZER, M. and CUNITZ, A. R. (1966) 'Two storage mechanisms in free recall,' *Journal of Verbal Learning and Verbal Behaviour*, 5, pp. 351–60.

GLENNER, G. G., (1989) 'The pathobiology of Alzheimer's disease', *Annual Review of Medicine*, 40, pp. 45–51.

GLOBUS, M., MILDWORF, B. and MALAMED, E. (1985) 'Cerebral blood flow and cognitive impairment in Parkinson's disease,' *Neurology*, 35, pp. 1135–9.

GLOOR, P. (1980) 'EEG characteristics in Creutzfeldt–Jakob disease,' *Annals of Neurology*, 8, p. 341.

GOLDENBERG, G., WIMMER, A., AUFF, E. and SCHNABERTH, G. (1986) 'Impairment of motor planning in patients with Parkinson's disease: evidence from ideomotor apraxia testing,' *Journal of Neurology, Neurosurgery and Psychiatry*, 49, pp. 1266–72.

GOMEZ, S., UUYMIRAT, J., VALADE, P., DAVOUS, P., RONDOT, P. and COHEN, P. (1986) 'Patients with Alzheimer's disease show an increased content of 15 Kdalton somatostatin precursor and a lowered level of tetradecapeptide in their cerebrospinal fluid,' *Life Sciences*, 39, pp. 623–37.

GOODGLASS, H. and KAPLAN, E. (1976) *The Assessment of Aphasia and Related Disorders*, Philadelphia, Lea & Fibiger.

GOODIN, D. S. (1985) 'Electrophysiologic evaluation of dementia,' *Neurological Clinics*, 3, pp. 633–47.

GOODIN, D. S. (1986) 'P300 latency as a biological marker of dementia,' *Biological Psychiatry*, 21, pp. 1111–13.

GOODIN, D. S. and AMINOFF, M. J. (1987) 'The distinction between different types of dementia using evoked potentials,' in Rohrbaugh, J. W. and Parasuraman, R. (Eds) *Current trends in event-related potential research*, New York, Elsevier Science Publishers (Biomedical Division), pp. 695–8.

GOODIN, D. S., SQUIRES, K. C. and STARR, A. (1978) 'Long latency event-related components of the auditory evoked potential in dementia,' *Brain*, 191, pp. 635–48.

GOODMAN, L. (1953) 'Alzheimer's disease: a clinicopathologic analysis of twenty-three cases with a theory on pathogenesis,' *Journal of Nervous and Mental Disease*, 117, pp. 97–138.

GORDON, E. B. and SIM, M. (1967) 'The E.E.G. in presenile dementia,' *Journal of Neurology, Neurosurgery and Psychiatry*, 30, pp. 285–91.

GOTTFRIES, C. G. and WINBLAD, B. (1980) 'Neurotransmitters and related enzymes in normal aging and in dementia of Alzheimer type (DAT)', in Gurski, G. E. (Ed) *Determining the Effects of Aging on the Central Nervous System*, Berlin, Schering, pp. 7–18.

GOTTLOB, I., SCHNEIDER, E., HEIDER, W. and SKRANDIES, W. (1987) 'Alteration of the evoked potentals and electroretinograms in Parkinson's disease,' *Electroencephalography and Clinical Neurophysiology*, 66, pp. 349–57.

GOTTSDANKER, R. (1982) 'Age and simple reaction time,' *Journal of Gerontology*, 37, pp. 342–8.

GRAY, J. A. (1977) 'Drug effects on fear and frustration: possible limbic site of action of minor tranquilizers,' in Iversen, L. L., Iversen, S. D. and Snyder, S. H. (Eds) *Handbook of Psychopharmacology*, Vol. 7, *Drugs, Neurotransmitters and Behaviour*, New York, Plenum Press, pp. 433–529.

GRAY, J. A. (1985) 'A whole and its parts: behaviour, the brain, cognition and emotion', *Bulletin of the British Psychological Society*, 38, pp. 99–112.

GREENAMYRE, J. T. (1986) 'The role of gluamate in neurotransmission and in neurologic disease,' *Archives of Neurology*, 43, pp. 1058–63.

GRIFFITH, D. (1976) 'The attentional demands of mnemonic control processes,' *Memory and Cognition*, 4, pp. 103–8.

GRIMES, A. M., GRADY, C. L. and PIKUS, A. (1987) 'Auditory evoked responses in patients with dementia of the Alzheimer type,' *Ear and Hearing*, 8, pp. 157–61.

GROBER, E., BUSCHKE, H., KAWAS, C. and FULD, P. (1985) 'Impaired ranking of semantic attributes in dementia,' *Brain and Language*, 26, pp. 276–86.

GROWDON, J. H., CORKIN, S., HUFF, F. J. and ROSEN, T. J. (1986) 'Piracetam combined with lecithin in the treatment of Alzheimer's disease,' *Neurobiology of Ageing*, 7, pp. 269–76.

GRUNHAUS, L., DILSAVER, S., GREDEN, J. F. and CARROLL, B. J. (1983) 'Depressive pseudodementia: a suggested diagnostic profile,' *Biological Psychiatry*, 18, pp. 215–25.

GRZEGORCZYK, P. B., JONES, S. W. and MISTRETTA, C. M. (1979) 'Age related differences in salt taste acuity,' *Journal of Gerontology*, 34, pp. 834–40.

GURLAND, B.J. (1976) 'The comparative frequency of depression in various adult age groups,' *Journal of Gerontology*, 31, pp. 283–92.

GURLAND, B.J. (1981) 'The borderlands of dementia: the influence of sociocultural characteristics on rates of dementia occurring in the senium,' in Miller, N.E. and Cohen, G.D. (Eds) *Clinical Aspects of Alzheimer's Disease and Senile Dementia, Aging*, Vol. 15, New York, Raven Press, pp. 61–8.

GUSTAFSON, L. (1979) 'Regional cerebral blood flow in Alzheimer's disease – differential diagnosis, the possibility of early recognition and evaluation of treatment,' in Glen, A.I.M. and Whalley, L.J. (Eds) *Alzheimer's Disease: Early Recognition of Potentially Reversible Deficits*, Edinburgh, Churchill Livingstone, pp. 102–7.

GUSTAFSON, L., EDVINSON, L., DAHLGREN, N., HAGBERG, B., RISBERG, B., ROSEN, I. and FERNO, H. (1987) 'Intravenous treatment of Alzheimer's disease evaluated by psychometric testing, regional blood flow (rCBF) measurement, and by EEG,' *Psychopharmacology*, 93, pp. 31–5.

GUSTAFSON, L. and NILSSON, L. (1982) 'Differential diagnosis of pre-senile dementia on clinical grounds,' *Acta Psychiatrica Scandinavica*, 65, pp. 194–209.

GUSTAFSON, L. and RISBERG, J. (1979) 'Regional cerebral blood flow measurements by the ^{133}Xe inhalation technique in differential diagnosis of dementia,' *Acta Neurologica Scandinavica*, 60, Supplement 72, pp. 546–7.

HACHINSKI, V. (1979) 'Relevance of cerebrovascular changes to mental function,' *Mechanisms of Ageing and Development*, 9, pp. 173–83.

HACHINSKI, V.C., ILIFF, L.D., ZILHKA, E., DUBOULAY, G.H., MCALLISTER, V.L., MARSHALL, J., RUSSELL, R.W.R. and SYMON, L. (1975) 'Cerebral blood flow in dementia,' *Archives of Neurology*, 32, pp. 632–7.

HACHINSKI, V.C., LASSEN, N.A. and MARSHALL, J. (1974) 'Multi-infarct dementia: a cause of mental deterioration in the elderly,' *Lancet*, ii, pp. 207–10.

HACHINSKI, V.C., POTTER, P. and MERSKEY, H. (1986) 'Leuko-araiosis: an ancient term for a new problem,' *Canadian Journal of Neuroscience*, 13, pp. 533–4.

HAKIM, A.M. and MATHIESON, G. (1978) 'Basis of dementia in Parkinson's disease,' *Lancet*, ii, p. 729.

HAKIM, A.M. and MATHIESON, G. (1979) 'Dementia in Parkinson's disease: a neuropathologic study,' *Neurology*, 29, pp. 1209–14.

HALASZ, N. and SHEPHERD, G.M. (1983) 'Neurochemistry of the olfactory bulb,' *Neuroscience*, 10, pp. 579–619.

HAMMOND, E.J., MEADOR, K.J., AUNG-DIN, R. and WILDER, B.J. (1987) 'Cholinergic modulation of human P3 event-related potentials,' *Neurology*, 37, pp. 346–50.

HAMSHER, K. (1981) 'Intelligence and aphasia,' in Sarno, M.T. (Ed.) *Acquired Aphasia*, New York, Academic Press, pp. 327–59.

HANLEY, I.G. (1981) 'The use of signposts and active training to modify ward disorientation in elderly patients,' *Journal of Behaviour Therapy and Experimental Psychiatry*, 12, pp. 241–7.

HANLEY, I.G. (1984) 'Theoretical and practical considerations in reality orientation therapy with the elderly,' in Hanley, I. and Hodge, J. (Eds) *Psychological Approaches to Care of the Elderly*, London, Croom Helm, pp. 164–91.

HANSCH, E. C., SYNDULKO, K., COHEN, S. N., GOLDBERG, Z. I., POTVIN, A. R. and TOURTELLOTTE, W. W. (1982) 'Cognition in Parkinson's disease: an event-related potential perspective,' *Annals of Neurology*, 11, pp. 599–607.

HARBAUGH, R. E., ROBERTS,. D. W., COOMBS, D. W., SAUNDERS, R. L. and REEDER, T. M. (1984) 'Preliminary report: Intracranial cholinergic drug infusion in patients with Alzheimer's disease,' *Neurosurgery*, 15, pp. 514–18.

HARDING, G. F. A., WRIGHT, C. E. and ORWIN, A. (1985) 'Primary presenile dementia: the use of the visual evoked potential as a diagnostic indicator,' *British Journal of Psychiatry*, 147, pp. 532–9.

HARDY, J. A., COWBURN, R., BARTON, A., REYNOLDS, G. P., DODD, P., WESTER, P., O'CARROLL, A. M., LOFDAHL, E. and WINBLAD, B. (1987a) 'A disorder of GABAergic innervation in Alzheimer's disease,' *Neuroscience Letters*, 73, pp. 192–6.

HARDY, J. A., COWBURN, R., BARTON, A., REYNOLDS, G. P., LOFDAHL, E., O'CARROLL, A. M. and WESTER, P. (1987b) 'Glutamate deficits in Alzheimer's disease,' *Journal of Neurology, Neurosurgery and Psychiatry*, 50, pp. 356–7.

HARNER, R. N. (1975) 'EEG evaluation of the patient with dementia,' in Benson, D. F., and Blumer, D. (Eds) *Psychiatric Aspects of Neurological Disease*, New York, Grune & Stratton, pp. 63–82.

HARPER, C. G. and KRIL, J. J. (1985) 'Brain atrophy in chronic alcoholic patients: a quantitative pathological study,' *Journal of Neurology, Neurosurgery and Psychiatry*, 48, pp. 211–17.

HARPER, C. G., KRIL, J. J. and HOLLOWAY, R. L. (1985) 'Brain shrinkage in chronic alcoholics: a pathological study,' *British Medical Journal*, 290, pp. 501–4.

HARPER, P. S. and MORRIS, M. J. (1989) 'Predictive testing for Huntington's disease,' *British Medical Journal*, 298, pp. 404–5.

HARRELL, L. E., CALLAWAY, R., and SEKAR, B. C. (1987) 'Magnetic resonance imaging and the diagnosis of dementia,' *Neurology*, 37, pp. 540–3.

HARRIS, J. (1984) 'Methods of improving memory,' in Wilson, B. A. and Moffat, N. (Eds) *Clinical Management of Memory Problems*, London, Croom Helm, pp. 46–62.

HARRIS, S. J. and DOWSON, J. H. (1982) 'Recall of a 10-word list in the assessment of dementia in the elderly,' *British Journal of Psychiatry*, 141, pp. 524–7.

HART, R. P., KWENTUS, J. A., HARKINS, S. W., and TAYLOR, J. R. (1988) 'Rate of forgetting in mild Alzheimer's-type dementia,' *Brain and Cognition*, 7, pp. 31–8.

HART, S. (1985) *Explorations of Cognitive Dysfunction in Dementia of Alzheimer Type*, unpublished PhD Thesis, University of London.

HART, S. (1988a) 'Language and dementia: a review,' *Psychological Medicine*, 18, pp. 99–112.

HART, S. (1988b) 'Aphasia and dementia: steps towards a new era in neuropsychology,' *Aphasiology*, 2, pp. 195–7.

HART, S., SMITH, C. M. and SWASH, M. (1985) 'Recognition memory in Alzheimer's disease,' *Neurobiology of Aging*, 6, pp. 287–92.

HART, S., SMITH, C. M. and SWASH, M. (1986a) 'Assessing intellectual deterioration,' *British Journal of Clinical Psychology*, 25, pp. 119–24.

HART, S., SMITH, C. M. and SWASH, M. (1986b) 'Intrusion errors in Alzheimer's disease,' *British Journal of Clinical Psychology*, 25, pp. 149–50.

HART, S., SMITH, C. M. and SWASH, M. (1988) 'Word fluency in patients with early dementia of Alzheimer type,' *British Journal of Clinical Psychology*, 27, pp. 115–24.

HAUBRICH, D. R. and CHIPPENDALE, T. J. (1977) 'Regulation of acetycholine synthesis in nervous tissue,' *Life Sciences*, 20, pp. 1465–78.

HAUBRICH, D. R., WANG, P. F. L., CLODY, D. E. and WEDEKING, P. W. (1975) 'Increase in rat brain acteylcholine induced by choline or deanol,' *Life Sciences*, 17, pp. 975–80.

HASHER, L. and ZACKS, R. T. (1979) 'Automatic and effortful processes in memory,' *Journal of Experimental Psychology: General*, 108, pp. 356–88.

HAY, J. W. and ERNST, R. L. (1987) 'The economic costs of Alzheimer's disease,' *American Journal of Public Health*, 77, pp. 1169–75.

HEATH, P. D., KENNEDY, P. and KAPUR, N. (1983) 'Slowly progressive aphasia without generalized dementia,' *Annals of Neurology*, 13, pp. 687–8.

HEBB, D. O. (1949) *The Organization of Behaviour: A Neuropsychological Theory*, New York, Wiley.

HECAEN, H. and ALBERT, M. L. (1978) *Human Neuropsychology*, New York, John Wiley.

HEFTER, H., HOMBERG, V., LANGE, H. W. and FREUND, H. J. (1987) 'Impaired rapid movement in Huntington's disease,' *Brain*, 110, pp. 585–612.

HEFTI, F. (1983) 'Is Alzheimer disease caused by lack of nerve growth factor?' *Annals of Neurology*, 13, pp. 109–10.

HEFTI, F., HARTIKKA, J. and KNUSEL, B. (1989) 'Function of neurotrophic factors in the adult and ageing brain and their possible use in treatment of neurodegenerative diseases,' *Neurobiology of Aging*, 10, pp. 515–33.

HEILMAN, K. M. and ROTHI, L. J. G. (1985) 'Apraxia,' in Heilman, K. M. and Valenstein, E. (Eds) *Clinical Neuropsychology*, Oxford, Oxford University Press, pp. 131–50.

HEILMAN, K. M. and VALENSTEIN, E. (1985) *Clinical Neuropsychology*, Oxford, Oxford University Press.

HEINDEL, W. C., BUTTERS, N. and SALMON, D. P. (1988) 'Impaired learning of a motor skill in patients with Huntington's disease,' *Behavioural Neuroscience*, 102, pp. 141–7.

HEISS, W. D., HERHOLTZ, K., PAWLIK, G., WAGNER, R. and WIENHARD, K. (1986) 'Positron emission tomography in neuropsychology,' *Neuropsychologia*, 24, pp. 141–9.

HENDERSON, A.S. and HUPPERT, F. A. (1984) 'The problem of mild dementia,' *Psychological Medicine*, 14, pp. 5–11.

HENKE, H. and LANG, W. (1983) 'Cholinergic enzymes in neocortex, hippocampus and basal forebrain of non-neurological and senile dementia of Alzheimer-type patients,' *Brain Research*, 267, pp. 281—91.

HEPBURN, K. and WASOW, M. (1986) 'Support groups for family caregivers of dementia victims: questions, directions and future research,' in Abrahamson, N. S., Quam, J. K. and Wasow, M. (Eds) *The Elderly and Chronic Mental Illness*, San Francisco, Jossey-Boss, pp. 83–92.

HERZOG, A. G. and KEMPER, T. L. (1980) 'Amygdaloid changes in ageing and dementia,' *Archives of Neurology*, 37, pp. 625–9.

HESTON, L. L., LOWTHER, D. L. W. and LEVENTHAL, C. M. (1966) 'Alzheimer's Disease: a family study,' *Archives of Neurology*, 15, pp. 225–33.

HESTON, L. L., MASTRI, A. R., ANDERSON, E. and WHITE, J. (1981) 'Dementia of the Alzheimer type: clinical genetics, natural history and associated conditions,' *Archives of General Psychiatry*, 38, pp. 1085–90.

HEYMAN, A., LOGUE, P., WILKINSON, W., HOLLOWAY, D. and HURWITZ, B. (1982) 'Lecithin therapy of Alzheimer's disease: a preliminary report,' in Corkin, S., Davis, K. L., Growdon, J. H., Usdin, E. and Wurtman, R. J. (Eds) *Alzheimer's Disease: A Report of Progress in Research, Aging*, Vol. 19, New York, Raven Press, pp. 373–8.

HEYMAN, A., WILKINSON, W. E., HURWITZ, B. J., SCHMECHEL, D., SIGMON, A. H., WEINBERG, T., HELMS, M. J. and SWIFT, M. (1983) 'Alzheimer's disease: genetic aspects and associated clinical disorders,' *Annals of Neurology*, 14, pp. 507–15.

HIER, D. B., HAGENLOCKER, K. and SHINDLER, A. G. (1985) 'Language disintegration in dementia: effects of etiology and severity,' *Brain and Language*, 25, pp. 117–33.

HILL, R. D., EVANKOVICH, K. D., SHEIKH, J. I. YESAVAGE, J. A. (1987) 'Imagery mnemonic training in a patient with primary degenerative dementia,' *Psychology and Aging*, 2, pp. 204–5.

HINES, T. M. and VOLPE, B. T. (1985) 'Semantic activation in patients with Parkinson's disease,' *Experimental Aging Research*, 11, pp. 105–7.

HINTON, D. R., SADUN, A. A., BLANKS, J. C. and MILLER, C. A. (1986) 'Optic-nerve degeneration in Alzheimer's disease,' *New England Journal of Medicine*, 315, pp. 485–7.

HIRST, W. (1982) 'The amnesic syndrome: descriptions and explanations,' *Psychological Bulletin*, 91, pp. 435–68.

HITCHCOCK, E. R., CLOUGH, C., HUGHES, R. and KENNY, B. (1988) 'Embryos and Parkinson's disease,' *Lancet*, i, p. 1274.

HODKINSON, H. M. (1973) 'Mental impairment in the elderly,' *Journal of the Royal College of Physicians, London*, 7, pp. 305–17.

HOFFMAN, S. B ., PLATT, C. A., BARRY, K. E., and HAMILL, L. A. (1985) 'When language fails: nonverbal communication abilities of the demented,' in Hutton, J. T. and Kenny, A. D. (Eds) *Senile Dementia of the Alzheimer type*, New York, Alan R. Liss, pp. 49–64.

HOLDEN, U. P. (1988) *Neuropsychology and Ageing*, London, Croom Helm.

HOLDEN, U. P. and WOODS, R. T. (1988) *Reality Orientation: Psychological Approaches to the 'Confused' Elderly*, 2nd ed., Edinburgh, Churchill Livingstone.

HOLLAND, A. L., MCBURNEY, D. H., MOSSY, J. and REINMUTH, O. M. (1985) The dissolution of language in Pick's disease with neurofibrillary tangles: a case study,' *Brain and Language*, 24 pp. 36–58.

HOLLANDER, E., MOHS, R. C. and DAVIS, K. L. (1986) 'Antemortem markers of Alzheimer's disease,' *Neurobiology of Ageing*, 7, pp. 367–87.

HOLLANDER, E., DAVIDSON, M., MOHS, R. C., HORVATH, T. B., DAVIS, B. T., ZEMISHLANY, Z. and DAVIS, K. L. (1987) 'RS86 in the treatment of Alzheimer's disease: a clinical trial of RS86: cognitive and biological effects,' *Biological Psychiatry*, 22, pp. 1067–78.

HOMBERG, V., HEFTER, H., GRANSEYER, G., STRAUSS, W., LANGE, H. and HENNERICI, M. (1986) 'Event-related potentials in patients with Huntington's disease and relatives at risk in relation to detailed psychometry,' *Electroencephalography and Clinical Neurophysiology*, 63, pp. 552–69.

HOMER, A.C., HONAVER, M., LANTOS, P.L., HASTIE, I.R., KELLETT, J.M. and MILLARD, P.H. (1988) 'Diagnosing dementia: do we get it right?' *British Medical Journal*, 297, pp. 894–6.

HORNYKIEWICZ, O. and KISH, S.J. (1986) 'Biochemical pathophysiology of Parkinson's disease,' in Yahr, M.D. and Bergman, K.J. (Eds) *Advances in Neurology*, Vol. 45, New York, Raven Press, pp. 19–34.

HORTON, A.M. (1979) 'Behavioural Neuropsychology: rationale and research,' *Clinical Neuropsychology*, 1 (2), pp. 20–3.

HUBBARD, B.M. and ANDERSON, J.M. (1981) 'A quantitative study of cerebral atrophy in old age and senile dementia,' *Journal of the Neurological Sciences*, 50, pp. 135–45.

HUBER, S.J., SHUTTLEWORTH, E.C., PAULSON, G.W., (1986) 'Dementia in Parkinson's disease,' *Archives of Neurology*, 43, pp. 987–90.

HUFF, F.J., BOLLER, F., LUCCHELLI, F., QUERRIERA, R., BEYER, J. and BELLE, S. (1987) 'The neurologic examination in patients with probable Alzheimer's disease,' *Archives of Neurology*, 44, pp. 929–32.

HUFF, F.J., CORKIN, S. and GROWDON, J. (1986) 'Semantic impairment and anomia in Alzheimer's disease,' *Brain and Language*, 280, pp. 235–49.

HUFF, F.J., MACK, L., MAHLMANN, J. and GREENBERG, S. (1988) 'A comparison of lexical-semantic impairment in left hemisphere stroke and Alzheimer's disease,' *Brain and Language*, 43, pp. 262–78.

HUGHES, C.P., BERG, L., DANZIGER, W.L., COBEN, L.A. and MARTIN, R.L. (1982) 'A new clinical scale for the staging of dementia,' *British Journal of Psychiatry*, 140, pp. 566–72.

HUGHES, W. (1970) 'Alzheimer's disease,' *Gerontologica Clinica*, 12, pp. 129–48.

HUISMAN, U.W., POSTHUMA, J., VISSER, S.L., JONKER, C. and DE RIJKE, W. (1987) 'The influence of attention on visual evoked potentials in normal adults and dementias,' *Clinical Neurology and Neurosurgery*, 89, pp. 151–6.

HUPPERT, F.A., and PIERCY, M. (1978) 'Dissociation between learning and remembering in organic amnesia,' *Nature*, 275, pp. 317–18.

HUPPERT, F.A., and PIERCY, M. (1979) 'Normal and abnormal forgetting in organic amnesia: effect of locus of lesion,' *Cortex*, 15, pp. 385–90.

HUTTON, J.T. (1985) 'Eye movements and Alzheimer's disease: significance and relationship to visuospatial confusion,' in Hutton, J.T. and Kenny, A.D. (Eds) *Senile Dementia of the Alzheimer Type*, New York, Alan R. Liss, pp. 3–33.

HUTTON, J.T., NAGAL, J.A. and LOEWENSON, R.B. (1984) 'Eye tracking dysfunction in Alzheimer-type dementia,' *Neurology*, 34, pp. 99–102.

HYMAN, B.T., VAN-HOESEN, G.W. and DAMASIO, A.R. (1987) 'Alzheimer's disease: glutamate depletion in the hippocampal perforant pathway zone,' *Annals of Neurology*, 22, pp. 37–40.

INGLIS, J. (1958) 'Psychological investigations of cognitive deficit in elderly psychiatric patients,' *Psychological Bulletin*, 55, pp. 197–214.

INGLIS, J. (1970) 'Memory disorder,' in Costello, C.G. (Ed.) *Symptoms of Psychopathology*, London, Wiley, pp. 95–133.

IRLE, E., KESSLER, J., MARKOWITSCH, H.J. and HOFFMANN, W. (1987) 'Primate learning tasks reveal strong impairments in patients with presenile or senile dementia of the Alzheimer-type,' *Brain and Cognition*, 6, pp. 429–49.

IRVING, G., ROBINSON, R.A., and MCADAM, W. (1970) 'The validity of some cognitive tests in the diagnosis of dementia,' *British Journal of Psychiatry*, 117, pp. 149–56.

ISAACS, B. (1983) 'The dementia syndrome,' *Lancet*, i, p. 187.

ISAACS, B. and KENNIE, A.T. (1973) 'The Set Test as an aid to the detection of dementia in old people,' *British Journal of Psychiatry*, 123, pp. 467–70.

ISRAEL, L., KOZAREVIC, D. and SARTORIUS, N. (1984a) *Source Book of Geriatric Assessment*, Vol. 1, *Evaluations in Gerontology*, Basel, S. Karger.

ISRAEL, L., KOZAREVIC, D. and SARTORIUS, N. (1984b) *Source Book of Geriatric Assessment*, Vol. 2, *Review of Analysed Instruments*, Basel, S. Karger.

IVERSEN, L.L., IVERSEN, S.D. and SNYDER, S.H. (editors) (1988) *Handbook of Psychopharmacology*, Vol. 20, *Psychopharmacology of the Ageing Nervous System*, New York, Plenum Press.

IVERSEN, S.D. (1977)'Brain dopamine systems and behaviour', in Iversen, L.L., Iversen, S.D. and Snyder, S.H. (Eds) *Handbook of Psychopharmacology*, Vol. 7, *Drugs, Neurotransmitters and Behaviour*, New York, Plenum Press, pp. 333–84.

JACOB, M. (1970) 'Muscular twitchings in Alzheimer's disease,' in Wolstenholme, G.E.W. and O'Connor, M. (Eds) *Alzheimer's Disease and Related Conditions*, London, Church Livingstone, pp. 75–93.

JACOBS, J.W., BERNHARD, M.R., DELGADO, A. and STRAIN, J.J. (1977) 'Screening for organic mental syndromes in the medically ill,' *Annals of Internal Medicine*, 86, pp. 40–6.

JACOBY, R.J. and LEVY, R. (1980) 'Computed tomography in the elderly: 2. Senile dementia: diagnosis and functional impairment,' *British Journal of Psychiatry*, 136, pp. 256–69.

JAGUST, W.J., BUDINGER, T.F. and REED, B.R. (1987) 'The diagnosis of dementia with single photon emission computed tomography,' *Archives of Neurology*, 44, pp. 258–62.

JANOWSKY, D.S. (1982) 'Pseudodementia in the elderly: differential diagnosis and treatment,' *Journal of Clinical Psychiatry*, 43, pp. 19–25.

JEEVES, M.A. and BAUMGARTNER, G. (1986) 'Methods of investigation in neuropsychology,' *Neuropsychologia*, 24, pp. 1–4.

JELLINGER, K. (1976) 'Neuropathological aspects of dementias resulting from abnormal blood and cerebrospinal fluid dynamics,' *Acta Neurologica Belgica*, 76, pp. 83–102.

JENSEN, A.R. and ROHWER, W.D. (1966) 'The Stroop Color-Word Test: a review,' *Acta Psychologica*, 25, pp. 36–93.

JOHNS, C.A., HAROUTINIAN, V., GREENWALD, B.S., MOHS, R.C., DAVIS, B.M., KANOF, P., HORVATH, T.B. and DAVIS, K.L. (1985) 'Development of cholinergic drugs for the treatment of Alzheimer's disease,' *Drug Development Research*, 5, pp. 77–96.

JOHNSON, K.A., DAVIS, K.R., BUONANNO, F.S., BRADY, T.J., ROSEN, J. and GROWDON, J.H. (1987) 'Comparison of magnetic resonance and Roentgen ray computed tomography in dementia,' *Archives of Neurology*, 44, pp. 1075–80.

JOHNSON, R. (1984) 'P300: a model of the variables controlling its amplitude,' *Annals of the New York Academy of Sciences*, 425, pp. 223–9.

JOLKKONEN, J., SOININEN, H., HALONEN, T., YLINEN, A., LAULUMAA, V., LAAKSO, M. and RIEKKINEN, P. (1986) 'Somatostatin-like immunoreactivity in the cerebrospinal fluid of patients with Parkinson's disease and its relation to dementia,' *Journal of Neurology, Neurosurgery and Psychiatry*, 49, pp. 1374–7.

JONES, A., FRIEDLAND, R. P., KOSS, B., STARK, L. and THOMPKINS-OBER, B.A. (1983) 'Saccadic intrusions in Alzheimer-type dementia,' *Neurology*, 229, pp. 189–94.

JONES, D.A., VICTOR, C.R. and VETTER, N.J. (1984) 'Hearing difficulty and its psychological implications for the elderly,' *Journal of Epidemiology and Community Health*, 38, pp. 75–8.

JONES, D.M., JONES, M.E.L., LEWIS, M.J. and SPRIGGS, T.L.B. (1979) 'Drugs and human memory: effects of low doses of Nitrazepam and hyoscine on retention,' *British Journal of Clinical Pharmacology*, 7, pp. 479–83.

JONES-GOTMAN, M. and ZATORRE, R.J. (1988) 'Olfactory identification deficits in patients with focal cerebral excision,' *Neuropsychologia*, 26, pp. 387–400.

JORG, J. and GERHARD, H. (1987) 'Somatosensory, motor and special visual evoked potentials to single and double stimulation in "Parkinson's disease" an early diagnostic test?' *Journal of Neural Transmission*, 25 (Suppl.), pp. 81–8.

JORM, A.F. (1985) 'Subtypes of Alzheimer's disease: a conceptual analysis and critical review,' *Psychological Medicine*, 15, pp. 543–53.

JORM, A.F. (1986) 'Controlled and automatic information processing in senile dementia: a review,' *Psychological Medicine*, 16, pp. 77–88.

JORM, A.F. and HENDERSON, A.S. (1985) 'Possible improvements to the diagnostic criteria for dementia in DSM-III,' *British Journal of Psychiatry*, 147, pp. 394–9.

JOSEPH, M.H., FRITH, C.D. and WADDINGTON, J.L. (1979) 'Dopaminergic mechanisms and cognitive deficit in schizophrenia: a neurobiological model,' *Psychopharmacology*, 63, pp. 273–80.

JOSEPHY, H. (1953) 'Pick's disease,' *Archives of Neurology and Psychiatry*, 69, pp. 637–8.

JOTKOWITZ, S. (1983) 'Lack of clinical efficacy of chronic oral physostigmine in Alzheimer's disease,' *Annals of Neurology*, 14, pp. 690–1.

KAHAN, J., KEMP, B., STAPLES, F.R. and BRUMMEL-SMITH, K. (1985) 'Decreasing the burden in families caring for a relative with a dementing illness: a controlled study,' *Journal of the American Geriatrics Society*, 33, pp. 664–70.

KAHN, R.L., GOLDFARB, A.I., POLACK, M. and PECK, A. (1960) 'Brief objective measures for the determination of mental status in the aged,' *American Journal of Psychiatry*, 117, pp. 326–8.

KAHN, R.L., ZARIT, S.H., HILBERT, N.M. and NIEDEREHE, G. (1975) 'Memory complaint and impairment in the aged: the effect of depression and altered brain function,' *Archives of General Psychiatry*, 32, pp. 1569–73.

KAHNEMAN, D. (1973) *Attention and Effort*, Englewood Cliffs, N.J., Prentice-Hall.

KARLINSKY, H. (1986) 'Alzheimer's disease and Down's syndrome: a review,' *Journal of the American Geriatric Society*, 34, pp. 728–34.

KASZNIAK, A.W., FOX, J., GANDELL, D.L., GARRON, D.C., HUCKMAN, M.S. and RAMSEY, R.G. (1978) 'Predictors of mortality in presenile and senile dementia,' *Annals of Neurology*, 3, pp. 246–52.

KASZNIAK, A. W., GARRON, D. C. and FOX, J. (1979) 'Differential effects of age and cerebral atrophy upon span of immediate recall and paired-associate learning in older patients suspected of dementia,' *Cortex*, 15, pp. 285–95.

KATZMAN, R. (1976) 'The prevalence and malignancy of Alzheimer disease: a major killer,' *Archives of Neurology*, 33, pp. 217–18.

KAUSLER, D. H. (1982) *Experimental Psychology and Human Aging*, New York, John Wiley.

KAY, D. W. K. (1962) 'Outcome and cause of death in mental disorders of old age: a long-term follow-up of functional and organic psychoses,' *Acta Psychiatrica Scandinavica*, 38, pp. 249–76.

KAY, D. W. K. (1972) 'Epidemiological aspects of organic brain disease in the aged,' in Gaitz, C. M. (Ed.) *Aging and the Brain*, New York, Plenum Press, pp. 15–27.

KAY, D. W. K., BEAMISH, P. and ROTH, M. (1964) 'Old age mental disorders in Newcastle upon Tyne. Part 1: A study of prevalence,' *British Journal of Psychiatry*, 110, pp. 146–58.

KAY, D. W. K., BERGMANN, K., FOSTER, E. M., MCKECHNIE, A. A. and ROTH, M. (1970) 'Mental illness and hospital usage in the elderly: a random sample follow-up,' *Comprehensive Psychiatry*, 11, pp. 26–35.

KAYE, W. H., SITARAM, N., WEINGARTNER, H., EBERT, M. H., SMALLBERG, S. and GILLIN, J. C. (1982) 'Modest facilitation of memory in dementia with combined lecithin and anti-cholinesterase treatment,' *Biological Psychiatry*, 17, pp. 275–80.

KEMPLER, D. (1988) 'Lexical and pantomime abilities in Alzheimer's disease,' *Aphasiology*, 2, pp. 147–59.

KEMPLER, D., CURTIS, S. and JACKSON, C. (1987) 'Syntactic preservation in Alzheimer's disease,' *Journal of Speech and Hearing Research*, 30, pp. 343–50.

KENDALL, E. R. and SCHWARTZ, J. A. (Editors) (1985) *Principles of Neuroscience*, London, Edward Arnold.

KENDELL, R. E. (1974) 'The stability of psychiatric diagnoses,' *British Journal of Psychiatry*, 124, pp. 352–6.

KENDRICK, D. C. (1972) 'The Kendrick Battery of tests: theoretical assumptions and clinical uses,' *British Journal of Social and Clinical Psychology*, 11, pp. 373–86.

KENDRICK, D. C., GIBSON, A. J. and MOYES, I. C. A. (1979) 'The revised Kendrick Battery: clinical studies,' *British Journal of Social and Clinical Psychology*, 18, pp. 329–40.

KENDRICK, D. C. and MOYES, I. C. A. (1979) 'Activity, depression, medication and performance on the Revised Kendrick Battery,' *British Journal of Social and Clinical Psychology*, 18, pp. 341–50.

KERTESZ, A. (1980) *Western Aphasia Battery*, London, Canada, University of Western Ontario.

KESNER, R. P., ADELSTEIN, T. and CRUTCHER, K. A. (1987) 'Rats with nucleus basalis magnocellularis lesions mimic mnemonic symptomatology observed in patients with dementia of the Alzheimer's type,' *Behavioural Neuroscience*, 101, pp. 451–6.

KESSLAK, J. P., COTMAN, C. W., CHUI, H. C., VAN DE NOORT, S., FANG, H., PFEFFER, R. and LYNCH, G. (1988) 'Olfactory tests as possible probes for detecting and monitoring Alzheimer's disease,' *Neurobiology of Ageing*, 9 pp. 399–403.

KESSLER, J., IRLE, E. and MARKOWITSCH, H. J. (1986) 'Korsakoff and alcholic subjects are severely impaired in animal tests of associative memory,' *Neuropsychologia*, 24, pp. 671–80.

KHACHATURIAN, Z. S., (1985) 'Diagnosis of Alzheimer's disease,' *Archives of Neurology*, 42, pp. 1097–105.

KILOH, L. G. (1961) 'Pseudo-dementia,' *Acta Psychiatrica Scandinavica*, 37, pp. 336–51.

KILPATRICK, C., BURNS, R. and BLUMBERGS, P. (1983) 'Identical twins with Alzheimer's disease,' *Journal of Neurology, Neurosurgery and Psychiatry*, 46, pp. 421–5.

KIMBRELL, G. MCA. and FURCHTGOTT, E. (1963) 'The effects of ageing on olfactory threshold,' *Journal of Gerontology*, 18, pp. 364–5.

KIMURA, D., BARNETT, H. J. M. and BURKHART, G. (1981) 'The psychological test pattern in progressive supranuclear palsy,' *Neuropsychologia*, 19, pp. 301–6.

KINSBOURNE, M. (1980) 'Attentional dysfunction and the elderly: theoretical models and research perspectives,' in Poon, L. W., Fozard, J. L., Cormak, L. S., Arenberg, D. and Thompson, L. M. (Eds) *New Directions in Memory and Aging*, Hillsdale, N.J., Lawrence Erlbaum Associates, pp. 113–29.

KINSBOURNE, M. and WARRINGTON, E. K. (1962) 'A disorder of simultaneous form perception,' *Brain*, 85, pp. 461–86.

KIRCHENBAUM, W. R. (1968) *Creutzfeldt–Jakob Disease*, New York, Elsevier.

KIRSHNER, H. S., TANRIDAY, O., THURMAN, L. and WHETSELL, W. O. (1987) 'Progressive aphasia without dementia: two cases with focal spongiform degeneration,' *Annals of Neurology*, 22, pp. 527–32.

KIRSHNER, H. S., WEBB, W. G. and KELLY, M. P. (1984) 'The naming disorder of dementia,' *Neuropsychologica*, 22, pp. 23–38.

KISH, S. J., CHANG, L. J., MIRCHANDANI, L., SHANNAK, K. and HORNYKIEWICZ, O. (1985) 'Progressive supranuclear palsy: relationship between extrapyramidal disturbances, dementia and brain neurotransmitter markers,' *Annals of Neurology*, 18, pp. 530–6.

KITTNER, S. J., WHITE, L. R., FARMER, M. E., WOLZ, M., KAPLAN, E., MOES, E., BRODY, J. A. and FEINLEIB, M. (1986) 'Methodological issues in screening for dementia: the problem of education adjustment,' *Journal of Chronic Diseases*, 39, pp. 163–70.

KLEIN, G. S. (1964) 'Semantic power measured through the interference of words with color-naming,' *American Journal of Psychology*, 77, pp. 576–88

KLINE, D. W. and SCHIEBER, F. (1985) 'Vision and aging,' in Birren, J. E. and Schaie, K. W. (Eds) *Handbook of the Psychology of Aging*, New York, Van Nostrand Reinhold Company, pp. 296–331.

KLUVER, H. and BUCY, P. L. (1939) 'Preliminary analysis of functions of the temporal lobes in monkeys,' *Archives of Neurology and Psychiatry*, 42, pp. 979–1000.

KNIGHTS, E. B., and FOLSTEIN, M. F. (1977) 'Unsuspected emotional and cognitive disturbance in medical patients,' *Annals of Internal Medicine*, 87, pp. 723–4.

KNOPMAN, D. S. and NISSEN, M. J. (1987) 'Implicit learning in patients with probable Alzheimer's disease,' *Neurology*, 37, pp. 784–8.

KNUPFER, L. and SPIEGEL, R. (1986) 'Differences in olfactoray test performance between normal aged, Alzheimer and vascular type dementia individuals,' *International Journal of Geriatric Psychiatry*, 1, pp. 3–14.

KOLB, B. and WISHAW, I. Q. (1980) *Fundamentals of Human Neuropsychology*, New York, W. H. Freeman.

KOLERS, P. A. (1973) 'Remembering operations,' *Memory and Cognition*, 1, pp. 347–55.

KOLLER, W. C. (1984) 'Sensory symptoms in Parkinson's disease,' *Neurology*, 34, pp. 957–9.

KONORSKI, J. (1959) 'A new method of physiological investigation of recent memory in animals,' *Bulletin de L'Academie Polonaise de Sciences*, 7, pp. 115–17.

KOPELMAN, M. D. (1985) 'Multiple memory deficits in Alzheimer type dementia: implications for pharmacotherapy,' *Psychological Medicine*, 15, pp. 527–41.

KOPELMAN, M. D. (1986) 'Recall of anomalous sentences in dementia and amnesia,' *Brain and Language*, 29, pp. 154–70.

KOPELMAN, M. D. (1989) 'Remote and autobiographical memory, temporal context memory and frontal atrophy in Korsakoff and Alzheimer patients,' *Neuropsychologica*, 27, pp. 437–60.

KOPELMAN, M. D. and CORN, T. H. (1988) 'Cholinergic "blockade" as a model for cholinergic depletion. A comparison of the memory deficits with those of Alzheimer-type dementia and the alcoholic Korsakoff syndrome,' *Brain*, 111, pp. 1079–110.

KOPELMAN, M. D., WILSON, B. A. and BADDELEY, A. D. (1989) 'The autobiographical memory interview: a new assessment of autobiographical and personal semantic memory in amnesic patients,' *Journal of Clinical and Experimental Neuropsychology*, 11, pp. 724–44.

KOSS, E., WEIFFENBACH, J. M., HAXBY, J. V. and FRIEDLAND, R. P. (1988) 'Olfactory detection and identification are dissociated in early Alzheimer's disease,' *Neurology*, 38, pp. 1228–32.

KRAL, V. A. (1962) 'Senescent forgetfulness: benign and malignant,' *Canadian Medical Association Journal*, 86, pp. 257–68.

KRAL, V. A. (1978) 'Benign senescent forgetfulness,' in Katzman, R., Terry, R. D. and Bick, K. L. (Eds) *Alzheimer's Disease: Senile Dementia and Related Disorders, Aging*, Vol. 7, New York, Raven Press, pp. 47–51.

KUMAR, V. (1987) 'Capgras syndrome in a patient with dementia,' *British Journal of Psychiatry*, 150, p. 251.

KURIANSKY, J. and GURLAND, B. (1976) 'The performance test of activities of daily living,' *International Journal of Aging and Human Development*, 7, pp. 343–52.

KURUCZ, J. and FELDMAR, G. (1979) 'Prosopo-affective agnosia as a symptom of cerebral organic disease,' *Journal of the American Geriatrics Society*, 27, pp. 225–30.

KURUCZ, J., FELDMAR, G. and WERNER, W. (1979) 'Prosopo-affective agnosia associated with chronic organic brain syndrome,' *Journal of the American Geriatrics Society*, 27, pp. 91–5.

LANGLAND, R. M. and PANICUCCI, C. L. (1982) 'Effects of touch on communication with elderly confused clients,' *Journal of Gerontological Nursing*, 8, pp. 152–5.

LANGSTON, J. W., BALLARD, P., TETRUD, J. W. and IRWIN, I. (1983) 'Chronic Parkinsonism in humans due to a product of meperidine synthesis,' *Science*, 219, pp. 979–80.

LANGSTON, J. W., IRWIN, I., LANGSTON, E. B. and FORNO, L. S. (1984) '1-Methyl-4-phenylpyridinium ion (MPP+): identification of a metabolite of MPTP, a toxin selective for the substantia nigra,' *Neuroscience Letters*, 48, pp. 87–92.

LARNER, S. (1977) 'Encoding in senile dementia and elderly depressives: a preliminary study', *British Journal of Social and Clinical Psychology*, 16, pp. 379–90.

LARSSON, T., SJOGREN, T. and JACOBSON, G. (1963) 'Senile dementia: a clinical, sociomedical and genetic study,' *Acta Psychiatrica Scandinavica*, 39, Suppl., p. 167.

LASHLEY, K. S. (1929) *Brain Mechanisms and Intelligence*, Chicago, University of Chicago Press.

LASHLEY, K. S. (1960) The Neuropsychology of Lashley, Beach, F. (Ed.), New York, McGraw Hill.

LASKER, Q. G., ZEE, D.S., HAIN, T.C., FOLSTEIN, S.E. and SINGER, H.S. (1988) 'Saccades in Huntington's disease: slowing and dysmetria,' *Neurology*, 38, pp. 427–31.

LAURIAN, S., GAILLARD, J.-M. and WERTHEIMER, J. (1982) 'Evoked potentials in the assessment of brain function in senile dementia,' in Courjon, J., Mauguiere, F. and Revol, M. (Eds) *Clinical Applications of Evoked Potentials in Neurology*, New York, Raven Press, pp. 287–93.

LAWSON, J. S. and BARKER, M. G. (1968) 'The assessment of nominal dysphasia in dementia; the use of reaction-time measures,' *British Journal of Medical Psychology*, 41, pp. 411–14.

LAWTON, M. P. and BRODY, E. M. (1969) 'Assessment of older people: self-maintaining and instrumental activities of daily living,' *Gerontologist*, 9, pp. 179–86.

LEBRUN, Y., DEVREUX, F. and ROUSSEAU, J.J. (1986) 'Language and speech in a patient with a clinical diagnosis of progessive supranuclear palsy,' *Brain and Language*, 27, pp. 247–56.

LEES, A. J. and SMITH, E. (1983) 'Cognitive deficits in the early stages of Parkinson's disease,' *Brain*, 106, pp. 257–70.

LEIBOWITZ, S. F. (1987) 'Appetite regulation and eating disorders in relation to brain neurotransmitter systems,' in Adelman, G. (Ed.) *Encyclopedia of Neuroscience*, Vol. 1, Boston, Birkhauser, pp. 71–2.

LEIGHT, K. A., and ELLIS, H. C. (1981) 'Emotional mood states, strategies and state-dependency in memory,' *Journal of Verbal Learning and Verbal Behaviour*, 20, pp. 251–66.

LESSER, R. (1976) 'Verbal and non-verbal memory components in the Token Test,' *Neuropsychologia*, 14, pp. 79–85.

LEVIN, H. S. and PETERS, B. H. (1982) 'Long-term administration of oral physostigmine and lecithin improve memory in Alzheimer's disease,' in Corkin, S., Davis, K. L., Growdon, J. H., Usdin, E. and Wurtman, R. J. (Eds) *Alzheimer's Disease: A Report of Progress in Research*, New York, Raven Press, pp. 373–8.

LEVY, R., LITTLE, A., CHUAQUI, P. and REITH, M. (1983) 'Early results from double blind placebo controlled trial of high dose phosphatidyl choline in Alzheimer's disease,' *Lancet*, i, pp. 987–8.

LEWIS, D. A., CAMPBELL, M.J., TERRY, R. D. and MORRISON, J. H. (1987) 'Laminar distribution of neurofibrillary tangles and neuritic plaques in Alzheimer's disease: a quantitative study of visual and auditory cortices,' *Journal of Neuroscience*, 7, pp. 1799–808.

LEWIS, P. R. and SHUTE, C. C. D. (1978) 'Cholinergic pathways in CNS', in Iversen, L. L., Iversen, S. D. and Snyder, S. H. (Eds) *Chemical Pathways in the Brain*, (Handbook of Psychopharmacology, Vol. 9), New York, Plenum Press, pp. 315–55.

LEWIS, S. W. (1987) 'Brain imaging in a case of Capgras' syndrome,' *British Journal of Psychiatry*, 150, pp. 117–21.

LEZAK, M. D. (1983) *Neuropsychological Assessment*, 2nd ed., New York, Oxford University Press.

LIEBERMAN, A., DZIATOLOWSKI, M., KUPERSMITH, M., SERBY, M., GOODGOLD, A., KOREIN, J. and GOLDSTEIN, M. (1979) 'Dementia in Parkinson disease,' *Annals of Neurology*, 6, pp. 355–9.

LILJEQUIST, R. and MATTILA, M. J. (1979) 'Effect of physostigmine and scopolamine on the memory functions of chess players,' *Medical Biology*, 57, pp. 402–5.

LINDSAY, P. H. and NORMAN, D. A. (1972) *Human Information Processing: an Introduction to Psychology*, New York, Academic Press.

LINDVALL, O., BRUNDIN, P., WIDNER, H., REHNCRONA, S., GUSTAVII, B., FRACKOWIAK, R., LEENDERS, K.L., SAWLE, G., ROTHWELL, J.C., MARSDEN, C.D and BJORKLUND, A., (1990) 'Grafts of foetal dopamine neurons survive and improve motor function in Parkinson's disease,' *Science*, 247, pp. 547–77.

LINDVALL, O., REHNCRONA, S., BRUNDIN, P., GUSTAVII, B., ASTEDT, B., WIDNER, H., LINDHOLM, T., BJORKLUND, A., LEENDERS, K.L., ROTHWELL, J.C., FRACKOWIAK, R., MARSDEN, C.D., JOHNELS, B., STEG, G., FREEDMAN, R., HOFFER, B.J., SEIGER, A., BYGDEMAN, M., STROMBERG, I. and OLSON, L. (1989) 'Human fetal dopamine neurons grafted into the striatum in two patients with severe Parkinson's disease. A detailed account of methodology and a 6-month follow-up,' *Archives of Neurology*, 46, pp. 615–31.

LIPOWSKI, Z. J. (1982) 'Differentiating delirium from dementia in the elderly', *Clinical Gerontology*, 1, pp.3–10.

LISHMAN, W. A. (1978) 'Research into the dementias,' *Psychological Medicine*, 8, pp. 353–6.

LISHMAN, W. A. (1986) 'Alcoholic dementia: a hypothesis,' *Lancet*, i, pp. 1184–6.

LISHMAN, W. A. (1987) *Organic Psychiatry: The Psychological Consequences of Cerebral Disorder*, 2nd ed., Oxford, Blackwell Scientific Publications.

LISTON, E. H. (1977) 'Occult presenile dementia,' *Journal of Nervous and Mental Disease*, 164, pp. 263–7.

LISTON, E. H. (1978) 'Diagnostic delay in presenile dementia,' *Journal of Clinical Psychiatry*, 39, pp. 599–603.

LISTON, E. H. and LARUE, A. (1983a) 'Clinical differentiation of primary degenerative and multi-infarct dementia: a clinical review of the evidence. Part 1: Clincial studies,' *Biological Psychiatry*, 18, 1451–65.

LISTON, E. H. and LARUE, A. (1983b) 'Clinical differentiation of primary degenerative and multi-infarct dementia: a critical review of the evidence. Part 2: Pathological studies,' *Biological Psychiatry*, 18, pp.1467–84.

LITTLE, A., LEVY, R., CHUAQUI-KIDD, P. and HAND, D. (1985) 'A double-blind, placebo controlled trial of high dose lecithin in Alzheimer's disease,' *Journal of Neurology, Neurosurgery and Psychiatry*, 48, pp. 736–42.

LITVAN, I., GRAFMAN, J., VENDRELL, P., MARTINEZ, J.M., JUNIQUE, C., VENDRELL, J.M. and BARRAQUER-BORDAS, J.L. (1988) 'Multiple memory deficits in patients with multiple sclerosis. Exploring the working memory system,' *Archives of Neurology*, 45, pp. 607–10.

LOCKHART, R.S. and MURDOCK, B.B. (1970) 'Memory and the theory of signal detection,' *Psychological Bulletin*, 74, pp. 100–9.

LOEB, C. (1980) 'Clinical diagnosis of multi-infarct dementia,' in Amaducci, L., Davison, A.N. and Antuono, P. (Eds) *Aging of the Brain and Dementia, Aging*, Vol. 13, New York, Raven Press, pp. 251–60.

MCALLISTER, T.W. (1981) 'Cognitive functioning in affective disorders,' *Comprehensive Psychiatry*, 22, pp. 572–86.

MCALLISTER, T.W., FERRELL, R.B., PRICE, T.R.P. and NEVILLE, M.B. (1982) 'The dexamethasone suppression test in two patients with severe depressive pseudo-dementia,' *American Journal of Psychiatry*, 139, pp. 479–81.

MCALLISTER, T.W., and PRICE, T.R.P. (1982) 'Severe depressive pseudodementia with and without dementia,' *American Journal of Psychiatry*, 139, pp. 626–9.

MCDONALD, C. (1969) 'Clinical heterogeneity in senile dementia,' *British Journal of Psychiatry*, 115, pp. 267–71.

MCDONALD, R.J. (1982) 'Drug treatment of senile dementia,' in Wheatley, D. (Ed.) *Psychopharmacology of Old Age*, Oxford, Oxford University Press, pp. 113–38.

MCHUGH, P.R. and FOLSTEIN, M.F. (1975) 'Psychiatric syndromes of Huntington's chorea: a clinical and phenomenological study,' in Benson, D.F. and Blumer, D. (Eds) *Psychiatric Aspects of Neurologic Disease*, New York, Grune & Stratton, pp. 267–86.

MCKEEVER, W.F. (1986) 'Tachistoscopic methods in neuropsychology,' in Hannay, H.J. (Ed.) *Experimental Techniques in Human Neuropsychology*, Oxford, Oxford University Press, pp. 167–211.

MCKHANN, G., DRACHMAN, D., FOLSTEIN, M., KATZMAN, R., PRICE, D. and STADLAN, E.M. (1984) 'Clinical diagnosis of Alzheimer's disease: report of the NINCDS-ADRDA work group under the auspicies of Department of Health and Human Services task force on Alzheimer's disease,' *Neurology* 34, pp. 939–44.

MACE, N. (1987) 'The family,' in *Losing a million minds: confronting the tragedy of Alzheimer's disease and other dementias*, Congress of the United States Office of Technology Assessment (1987), Washington, U.S. Government Printing Office, pp. 135–65.

MADRAZO, I., DRUCHER-COLIN, R., LEON, V. and TORRES, C. (1987) 'Adrenal medulla transplanted to caudate nucleus for treatment of Parkinson's disease,' *Surgical Forum*, 38, pp. 510–11.

MADRAZO, I., LEON, V., TORRES, C., DEL CARMEN AGUILERA, M., VARELA, G., ALVAREZ, F., FRAGA, A., DRUCHER-COLIN, R., OSTROGOSKY, F., SKUROVICH, M. and FRANCO, R. (1988) 'Transplantation of foetal substantia nigra and adrenal medulla to the caudate nucleus in two patients with Parkinson's disease,' *New England Journal of Medicine*, 318, p. 51.

MAHENDRA, B. (1984) *Dementia*, London, MTP Press.

MAHER, E.R., SMITH, E.M. and LEES, A.J. (1985) 'Cognitive deficits in the Steele–Richardson–Olszewski syndrome (progressive supranuclear palsy),' *Journal of Neurology, Neurosurgery and Psychiatry*, 48, pp. 1234–9.

MAIR, R.G., DOTY, R.L., KELLY, K.M., WILSON, C.S., LANGLAIS, P.J., MCENTEE, W.J. and VOLLMECKE, T.A. (1986) 'Multimodal sensory discrimination deficits in Korsakoff's psychosis, *Neuropsychologia*, 24, pp. 831–9.

MALAMUD, N. (1972) 'Neuropathology of organic brain syndromes associated with aging,' in Gaitz, C. M. (Ed.) *Aging and the Brain*, New York, Plenum Press, pp. 63–87.

MANN, D. M. A. and YATES, P. O. (1986) 'Neurotransmitter deficits in Alzheimer's disease and in other dementing disorders,' *Human Neurobiology*, 5, pp. 147–58.

MANN, D. M. A., YATES, P. O. and MARCYNUIK, B. (1984) 'Age and Alzheimer's disease,' *Lancet*, i, pp. 281–2.

MARAGOS, W. F., GREENAMYRE, J. T., PENNEY, J. B. and YOUNG, A. B. (1987) 'Glutamate dysfunction in Alzheimer's disease: an hypothesis,' *Trends in Neurosciences*, 10, pp. 65–8.

MAREK, K. L., BOWEN, D. M., SIMS, N. R. and DAVISON, A. N. (1982) 'Stimulation of acetylcholine synthesis by blockade of pre-synaptic muscarinic inhibitory autoreceptors: observations in rat and human brain preparations and comparison with the effect of choline,' *Life Sciences*, 30, pp. 1517–24.

MARKOWITSCH, H. J. and PRITZEL, M. (1985) 'The neuropathology of amnesia,' *Progress in Neurobiology*, 25, pp. 189–287.

MARSDEN, C. D. (1978) 'The diagnosis of dementia,' in Isaacs, A. D. and Post, F. (Eds) *Studies in Geriatric Psychiatry*, London, Wiley, pp. 95–118.

MARSDEN, C. D. (1982) 'The mysterious motor function of the basal ganglia: the Robert Wartenberg lecture,' *Neurology*, 32, pp. 514–39.

MARSDEN, C. D. and HARRISON, M. J. G. (1972) 'Outcome of investigation of patients with presenile dementia,' *British Medical Journal*, 2, pp. 249–52.

MARSHALL, J. C. (1986) 'The description and interpretation of aphasic language disorder,' *Neuropsychologia*, 28, pp. 5–24.

MARTIN, A. (1987) 'Representation of semantic and spatial knowledge in Alzheimer's patients: implications for models of preserved learning in amnesia,' *Journal of Clinical and Experimental Neuropsychology*, 9, pp. 191–224.

MARTIN, A., BROUWERS, P., COX, C. and FEDIO, P. (1985) 'On the nature of the verbal memory deficit in Alzheimer's disease,' *Brain and Language*, 25, pp. 323–41.

MARTIN, A., BROUWERS, P., LALONDE, F., COX, C., TELESKA, P., FEDIO, P., FOSTER, N. L. and CHASE, T. N. (1986) 'Towards a behavioural typology of Alzheimer's patients,' *Journal of Clinical and Experimental Neuropsychology*, 8, pp. 594–610.

MARTIN, A. and FEDIO, P. (1983) 'Word production and comprehension in Alzheimer's disease; the breakdown of semantic knowledge,' *Brain and Language*, 19, pp. 124–41.

MARTIN, J. B. and GUSELLA, J. F. (1986) 'Huntington's disease. Pathogenesis and management,' *New England Journal of Medicine*, 315, pp. 1267–76.

MARTIN, W. E., LOEWENSON, R. B., RESCH, J. A. and BAKAR, A. B. (1973) 'Parkinson's disease: clinical analysis of 100 cases,' *Neurology*, 23, pp. 783–90.

MARTONE, M., BUTTERS, N., PAYNE, M., BECKER, J. T. and SAX, D. S. (1984) 'Dissociations between skill learning and verbal recognition in amnesia and dementia,' *Archives of Neurology*, 41, pp. 965–70.

MARTONE, M., BUTTERS, N. and TRAUNER, D. (1986) 'Some analyses of forgetting of pictorial material in amnesic and demented patients,' *Journal of Experimental and Clinical Neuropsychology*, 8, pp. 161–78.

MARTTILA, R. J. and RINNE, U. K. (1976) 'Dementia in Parkinson's disease,' *Acta Neurologica Scandinavica*, 54, pp. 431–41.

MARX, M., BODIS-WOLLNER, I., BOBAK, P., HARNOIS, C., MYLIN, L. and YAHR, M. (1986) 'Temporal frequency dependent VEP changes in Parkinson's disease,' *Vision Research*, 26, pp. 185–93.

MASH, D. C., FLYNN, D. D. and POTTER, L. T. (1985) 'Loss of M2 muscarinic receptors in the cerebral cortex of Alzheimer's disease and experimental cholinergic denervation,' *Science*, 238, pp. 115–17.

MASON, S. T. (1980) 'Noradrenaline and selective attention: a review of the model and the evidence,' *Life Sciences*, 27, pp. 617–31.

MASTERS, C. L., SIMMS, G., WEINMAN, N. A., MULTHAUP, G., McDONALD, B. L. and BEYREUTHER, K. (1985) 'Amyloid plaque core proteins in Alzheimer's disease and Down's syndrome,' *Proceedings of the National Academy of Sciences of the U.S.A.*, 82, pp. 4245–54.

MATARAZZO, R. G., WIENS, A. N., MATARAZZO, J. D. and MANAUGH, T. S. (1973) 'Test-retest reliability of the WAIS in a normal population,' *Journal of Clinical Psychology*, 29, pp. 194–7.

MATISON, R., MAYEUX, R., ROSEN, J. and FAHN, S. (1982) '"Tip-of-the-tongue" phenomena in Parkinson's disease,' *Neurology*, 32, pp. 567–70.

MATTIS, S. (1976) 'Mental status examination for organic mental syndromes in the elderly patient,' in Bellak, L. and Karasu, T. E. (Eds) *Geriatric Psychiatry*, New York, Grune & Stratton, pp. 77–121.

MATTIS, S., KOVNER, R., GARTNER, J. and GOLDMEIER, E. (1981) 'Deficits in retrieval of category exemplars in alcoholic Korsakoff patients,' *Neuropsychologia*, 19, pp. 357–63.

MAUGUIERE, F., DESMEDT, J. E. and COURJON, J. (1983) 'Astereognosis and dissociated loss of frontal or parietal components of somatosensory evoked potentials: detailed correlations with clinical signs and computerized tomographic scanning,' *Brain*, 106, pp. 271–313.

MAY, W. W. (1968) 'Creutzfeldt–Jakob disease: 1. Survey of the literature and clinical diagnosis,' *Acta Neurologica Scandinavica*, 44, pp. 1–32.

MAYER-GROSS, W., SLATER, E. and ROTH, M. (1969) *Clinical Psychiatry*, 3rd ed., London, Bailliere Tindall.

MAYEUX, R., HUNTER, S. and FAHN, S. (1980) 'More on myoclonus in Alzheimer's disease,' *Annals of Neurology*, 8, p. 200.

MAYEUX, R. and STERN, Y. (1983) 'Intellectual dysfunction and dementia in Parkinson's disease,' in Mayeux, R. and Rosen, W. G. (Eds) *The Dementias: Advances in Neurology*, Vol. 38, New York, Raven Press, pp. 211–27.

MAYEUX, R., STERN, Y., ROSEN, J. and BENSON, D. F. (1983) 'Is "subcortical dementia" a recognizable clinical entity?' *Annals of Neurology*, 14, pp. 278–83.

MAYEUX, R., STERN, Y., SANO, M., COTE, L. and WILLIAMS, J. B. W. (1987) 'Clinical and biochemical correlates of bradyphrenia in Parkinson's disease,' *Neurology*, 37, pp. 1130–4.

MAYEUX, R., STERN, Y., WILLIAMS, J. B. W., SANO, M. and COTE, L. (1986) 'Depression in Parkinson's disease,' in Yahr, M. D. and Bergman, K. J. (Eds) *Advances in Neurology*, Vol. 45, New York, Raven Press, pp. 191–206.

MAZZUCCHI, A., CAPITANI, E., POLETTI, A., POSTERARO, L., BOCELLI, G., CAMPARI, F. and PARMA, M. (1987) 'Discriminant analysis of WAIS results in different types of dementia and depressed patients,' *Functional Neurology*, 2, pp. 156–63.

MEADOR, K.J., LORING, D.W., ADAMS, R.J., PATEL, B.R., DAVIS, H.C. and HAMMOND, E.J. (1987) 'Central cholinergic systems and the P3 evoked response,' *International Journal of Neuroscience*, 33, pp. 199–205.

MEIER, M., BENTON, A. and DILLER, L. (1987) *Neuropsychological Rehabiliation*, London, Churchill Livingstone.

MELDMAN, M.J. (1970) *Diseases of Attention and Perception*, Oxford, Pergamon Press.

MELTZER, H.Y. (1987) *Psychopharmacology: the Third Generation of Progress*, New York, Raven Press.

MERSKEY, H., BLUME, W.T., COLHOUN, E.H., FISMAN, M., FOX, A.J., FOX, H., HACHINSKI, V.C., KRAL, V.A., RYLETT, R.J. and SMITH, R. (1985) 'Correlative studies in Alzheimer's disease,' *Progress in Neuropsychopharmacology and Biological Psychiatry*, 9, pp. 509–14.

MESULAM, M.M. (1981) 'A cortical network for directed attention and unilateral neglect,' *Annals of Neurology*, 10, 309–25.

MESULAM, M.M. (1982) 'Slowly progressive aphasia without generalized dementia,' *Annals of Neurology*, 11, pp. 592–8.

MESULAM, M.M. (1985) 'Attention, confusional states and neglect,' in Mesulam, M.M. (Ed.) *Principles of Behavioural Neurology*, Philadelphia, F.A. Davis, pp. 125–68.

MESULAM, M.M. (1987) 'Primary progressive aphasia: differentiation from Alzheimer's disease,' *Annals of Neurology*, 22, pp. 533–4.

MEYER, J.S., JUDD, B.W., TAWAKINA, T., ROGERS, R.L. and MORTEL, K.F. (1986) 'Improved cognition after control of risk factors for multi-infarct dementia,' *Journal of the American Medical Association*, 256, pp. 2203–9.

MEYER, J.S., ROGERS, R.L., MCCLINTIC, K., MORTEL, K.F. and LOFTI, J. (1989) 'Randomized clinical trial of daily aspirin therapy in multi-infarct dementia: a pilot study,' *Journal of the American Geriatrics Society*, 37, pp. 549–55.

MILLER, E. (1971) 'On the nature of the memory disorder in presenile dementia,' *Neuropsychologia*, 9, pp. 75–81.

MILLER, E. (1972) 'Efficiency of coding and the short-term memory defect in presenile dementia,' *Neuropsychologia*, 10, pp. 133–6.

MILLER, E. (1973) 'Short- and long-term memory in patients with presenile dementia (Alzheimer's disease),' *Psychological Medicine*, 3, pp. 221–4.

MILLER, E. (1974) 'Psychomotor performance in presenile dementia,' *Psychological Medicine*, 4, pp. 65–8.

MILLER, E. (1975) 'Impaired recall and the memory disturbance in presenile dementia,' *British Journal of Social and Clinical Psychology*, 14, pp. 73–9.

MILLER, E. (1977a) *Abnormal Ageing*, London, Wiley.

MILLER, E. (1977b) 'A note on visual information processing in presenile dementia: A preliminary report,' *British Journal of Social and Clinical Psychology*, 16, pp. 99–100.

MILLER, E. (1978) 'Retrieval from long-term memory in presenile dementia; two tests of an hypothesis,' *British Journal of Social and Clinical Psychology*, 17, pp. 143–8.

MILLER, E. (1980) 'Cognitive assessment of the older adult,' in Birren, J. E. and Sloane, R. B. (Eds) *Handbook of Mental Health and Aging*, Englewood Cliffs, N.J., Prentice-Hall, p. 520–36.

MILLER, E. (1981a) 'The nature of the cognitive deficit in senile dementia,' in Miller, N. E. and Cohen, G. D. (Eds) *Clinical Aspects of Alzheimer's Disease and Senile Dementia, Aging*, Vol. 15, New York, Raven Press, pp. 103–20.

MILLER, E. (1984a) *Recovery and Management of Neuropsychologial Impairments*, London, Wiley.

MILLER, E. (1984b) 'Verbal fluency as a function of a measure of verbal intelligence and in relation to different types of cerebral pathology,' *British Journal of Clinical Psychology*, 23, pp. 53–7.

MILLER, E. and HAGUE, F. (1975) 'Some characteristics of verbal behaviour in presenile dementia,' *Psychological Medicine*, 5, pp. 255–9.

MILLER, E. and LEWIS, P. (1977) 'Recognition memory in elderly patients with depression and dementia: a signal detection analysis,' *Journal of Abnormal Psychology*, 86, pp. 84–6.

MILLER, N. (1986) *Dyspraxia and its Management*, London, Croom Helm.

MILLER, N. E. (1980) 'The measurement of mood in senile brain disease; examiner ratings and self-reports,' in Cole, J. O. and Barrett, J. E. (Eds) *Psychology in the Aged*, New York, Raven Press, pp. 97–118.

MILNER, B. (1964) 'Some effects of frontal lobectomy in man,' in Warren, J. M. and Alert, K. (Eds) *The Frontal Granular Cortex and Behaviour*, New York, McGraw Hill, pp. 313–477.

MILNER, B. (1966) 'Amnesia following operation on the temporal lobes,' in Whitty, C. M. W. and Zangwill, O. L. (Eds) *Amnesia*, London, Butterworths, pp. 109–33.

MILNER, B., CORKIN, S. and TEUBER, H. L. (1968) 'Further analysis of the hippocampal amnesia syndrome: 14 year follow-up study of HM,' *Neuropsychologia*, 6, pp. 215–34.

MOBERG, P. J., PEARLSON, G.D., SPEEDIE, L. J., LIPSEY, J. R., STRAUSS, M. E. and FOLSTEIN, S. E. (1987) 'Olfactory recognition: differential impairments in early and late Huntington's and Alzheimer's diseases,' *Journal of Clinical and Experimental Neuropsychology*, 9, pp. 650–64.

MOFFAT, N. (1984) 'Strategies of memory therapy,' in Wilson, B. A. and Moffat, N. (Eds) *Clinical Management of Memory Problems*, London, Croom Helm, pp. 63–88.

MOHS, R. C. and DAVIS, K. L. (1980) 'Choline chloride effects on memory: correlation with the effects of physostigmine,' *Psychiatry Research*, 2, pp. 149–56.

MOHS, R. C. and DAVIS, K. L. (1982) 'A signal detectability analysis of the effect of physostigmine on memory in patients with Alzheimer's disease,' *Neurobiology of Aging*, 3, pp. 105–10.

MOHS, R. C., DAVIS, K. L. and LEVY, M. I. (1981) 'Partial reversal of anti-cholinergic amnesia by choline chloride,' *Life Sciences*, 29, pp. 1317–23.

MOHS, R. C., DAVIS, K. L., TINKLENBERG, J. R. and HOLLISTER, L. E. (1980) 'Choline chloride effects on memory in the elderly,' *Neurobiology of Aging*, 1, pp. 21–5.

MOHS, R. C., DAVIS, K. L., TINKLENBERG, J. R., HOLLISTER, L. E., YESAVAGE, J. A. and KOPELL, B. S. (1979) 'Choline chloride treatment of memory deficits in the elderly,' *American Journal of Psychiatry*, 136, pp. 1275–7.

MOORE, R. G., WATTS, F. N. and WILLIAMS, J. M. G. (1988) 'The specificity of personal memories in depression,' *British Journal of Clinical Psychology*, 27, pp. 275–6.

MOORE, V., and WYKE, M. A. (1984) 'Drawing disability in patients with senile dementia,' *Psychological Medicine*, 14, pp. 97–105.

MORAY, N. (1969) *Listening and Attention*, London, Penguin.

MORRIS, C. H., HOPE, R. A. and FAIRBURN, C. G. (1989) 'Eating habits in dementia: a descriptive study,' *British Journal of Psychiatry*, 154, pp. 801–6.

MORRIS, J. C., COLE, M., BANKER, B. Q., and WRIGHT, D. (1984) 'Hereditary dysphasic dementia and the Pick-Alzheimer spectrum,' *Annals of Neurology*, 16, pp. 455–66.

MORRIS, P. (1978) 'Task and material variables,' in Gruneberg, M. M. and Morris, P. (Eds) *Aspects of memory*, London, Methuen, pp. 26–39.

MORRIS, R. G., ANDERSON, E., LYNCH, G. S. and BAUDRY, M. (1986) 'Selective impairment of learning and blockade of long-term potentiation by an N-methyl-D-aspartate receptor antagonist, AP5,' *Nature*, 319, pp. 774–6.

MORRIS, R. G. (1984) 'Dementia and the functioning of the articulatory loop system,' *Cognitive Neuropsychology*, 1, pp. 143–57.

MORRIS, R. G. (1986) 'Short-term forgetting in senile dementia of the Alzheimer type,' *Cognitive Neuropsychology*, 3, pp. 77–97.

MORRIS, R. G. (1987a) 'Identity matching and oddity learning in patients with moderate to severe Alzheimer-type dementia,' *Quarterly Journal of Experimental Psychology*, 39B, pp. 215–27.

MORRIS, R. G. (1987b) 'The effect of concurrent articulation on memory span in Alzheimer type dementia,' *British Journal of Clinical Psychology*, 26, pp. 233–4.

MORRIS, R. G. (1987c) 'Articulatory rehearsal in Alzheimer type dementia,' *Brain and Language*, 30, pp. 351–62.

MORRIS, R. G., DOWNES, J.J., SAHAKIAN, B.J., EVENDEN, J.L., HEALD, A. and ROBBINS, T. W. (1988a) 'Planning and spatial working memory in Parkinson's disease,' *Journal of Neurology, Neurosurgery and Psychiatry*, 51, pp. 757–66.

MORRIS, R. G., MORRIS, L. W. and BRITTON, P. (1988b) 'Factors affecting the wellbeing of the caregivers of dementia sufferers,' *British Journal of Psychiatry*, 155, pp. 147–56.

MORRIS, R. G., WHEATLEY, J. and BRITTON, P. (1983) 'Retrieval from long-term memory in senile dementia: cued recall revisited, *British Journal of Clinical Psychology*, 22, pp. 141–2.

MORTIMER, J. A. (1980) 'Epidemiological aspects of Alzheimer's disease,' in Maletta, G. J. and Pirozzolo, F. J. (Eds) *The Aging Nervous System*, New York, Praeger, pp. 307–32.

MORTON, J. (1969) 'Categories of interference: verbal mediation and conflict in card sorting,' *British Journal of Psychology*, 60, pp. 329–46.

MOSCOVITCH, M. (1982) 'Multiple dissociations of function in amnesia,' in Cermak, L. (Ed.) *Human Memory and Amnesia*, Hillsdale, N.J., Lawrence Erlbaum, pp. 337–70.

MOSCOVITCH, M., WINOCUR, G. and MCLACHLAN, D. (1986) 'Memory as assessed by recognition and reading time in normal and memory-impaired people with Alzheimer's disease and other neurological disorders,' *Journal of Experimental Psychology: General*, 115, pp. 331–47.

MOSS, M. B., ALBERT, M. S., BUTTERS, N. and PAYNE, M. (1986) 'Differential patterns of memory loss among patients with Alzheimer's disease, Huntington's disease, and alcoholic Korsakoff's syndrome,' *Archives of Neurology*, 43, pp. 239–46.

MRC (1977) *Senile and Presenile Dementia*, A Report of the MRC Subcommittee, compiled by Lishman, W. A., London, Medical Research Council.

MULLER-HILL, B. and BEYREUTHER, K. (1989) 'Molecular biology of Alzheimer's disease,' *Annual Review of Biochemistry*, 58, pp. 287–307.

MUNOZ-GARCIA, D. and LUDWIN, S. K. (1984) 'Classic and generalized variants of Pick's disease: a clinicopathological, ultrastructural and immunocytochemical comparative study,' *Annals of Neurology*, 16, pp. 237–54.

MURAMOTO, O., SUGISHITA, M. and ANDO, K. (1984) 'Cholinergic system and constructional praxis: a further study of physostigmine in Alzheimer's disease,' *Journal of Neurology, Neurosurgery and Psychiatry*, 47, pp. 485–91.

MURAMOTO, O., SUGISHITA, M., SUGITA, H. and TOYOKURA, Y. (1979) 'Effect of physostigmine on constructional and memory tasks in Alzheimer's disease,' *Archives of Neurology*, 36, pp. 501–3.

MURDOCH, B. E., CHANEY, H. J., WILKS, V. and BOYLE, R. S. (1987) 'Language disorders in dementia of the Alzheimer type,' *Brain and Language*, 31, pp. 122–37.

MURPHY, C. (1979) 'The effect of age on taste sensitivity, in Han, S. S. and Coons, D. H. (Eds) *Special Senses in Aging*, Ann Arbor, University of Michigan, pp. 21–33.

MURPHY, C. (1983) Age-related effects on the threshold, psychophysical function and pleasantness of methanol, *Journal of Gerontology*, 38, pp. 217–22.

NAESER, M. A., ALBERT, M. S. and KLEEFIELD, J. (1982) 'New methods in the CT scan diagnosis of Alzheimer's disease: examination of white and gray matter mean CT density numbers,' in Corkin, S., Davis, K. L., Growdon, J. H., Usdin, E. and Wurtman, R. J. (Eds) *Alzheimer's Disease: A Report of Progress in Research*, Aging, Vol. 19, New York, Raven Press, pp. 63–78.

NAGUIB, M. and LEVY, R. (1982) 'Prediction of outcome in senile dementia: a computed tomographic study,' *British Journal of Psychiatry*, 140, pp. 263–7.

NAKAMURA, S. and VINCENT, S. R. (1986) 'Somatostatin and neuropeptide Y immunoreactive neurons in the neocortex in senile dementia of Alzheimer type,' *Brain Research*, 370, pp. 11–20.

NEARY, D., SNOWDEN, J. S., BOWEN, D. M., SIMS, N. R., MANN, D. M. A., BENTON, J. S., NORTHERN, B., YATES, P. O. and DAVISON, A. D. (1986) 'Neuropsychological syndromes in presenile dementia,' *Journal of Neurology, Neurosurgery and Psychiatry*, 49, pp. 163–74.

NEARY, D., SNOWDEN, J. S., SHIELDS, R. A., BURJAN, A. W. I., NORTHERN, B., MACDERMOTT, N., PRESCOTT, M. C. and TESTA, H. J. (1987) 'Single photon emission tomography using 99m-Tc-HM-PAO in the investigation of dementia,' *Journal of Neurology, Neurosurgery and Psychiatry*, 50, pp. 1101–9.

NEBES, R. D. (1978) 'Vocal *versus* manual response as a determinant of age difference in simple raction time,' *Journal of Gerontology*, 33, pp. 884–9.

NEBES, R. D., BOLLER, F. and HOLLAND, A. (1986) 'Use of semantic context by patients with Alzheimer's disease,' *Psychology and Aging*, 1, pp. 261–9.

NEBES, R. D. and BRADY, C. B. (1988) 'Integrity of semantic fields in Alzheimer's disease,' *Cortex*, 24, pp. 291–9.

NEBES, R. D., MARTIN, D. C. and HORN, L. C. (1984) 'Sparing of semantic memory in Alzheimer's disease,' *Journal of Abnormal Psychology*, 93, pp. 321–30.

NELSON, A., FOGEL, B. S. and FAUST, D. (1986) 'Bedside cognitive screening instruments: a critical assessment,' *Journal of Nervous and Mental Disease*, 174, pp. 73–83.

NELSON, H. E. (1982) *National Adult Reading Test (NART): Test Manual*, Windsor, NFER-Nelson.

NELSON, H. E. and McKENNA, P. (1975) 'The use of current reading ability in the assessment of dementia,' *British Journal of Social and Clinical Psychology*, 14, pp. 259–67.

NELSON, H. E. and O'CONNELL, A. (1978) 'Dementia: the estimation of premorbid intelligence levels using the New Adult Reading Test,' *Cortex*, 14, pp. 234–44.

NESHIGE, R., BARRETT, G. and SHIBASAKI, H. (1988) 'Auditory long latency event-related potentials in Alzheimer's disease and multi-infarct dementia,' *Journal of Neurology, Neurosurgery and Psychiatry*, 51, pp. 1120–5.

NEUMANN, M. A. (1947) 'Chronic progressive subcortical encephalopathy – report of a case,' *Journal of Gerontology*, 2, pp. 57–64.

NEUMANN, M. A. and COHN, R. (1953) 'Incidence of Alzheimer's disease in a large mental hospital: relation to senile psychosis with cerebral arteriosclerosis,' *Archives of Neurology and Psychiatry*, 69, pp. 615–36.

NEUMANN, M. A. and COHN, R. (1978) 'Epidemiological approach to questions of identity of Alzheimer's and senile brain disease: a proposal,' in Katzman, R., Terry, R. D. and Bick, K. L. (Eds) *Alzheimer's Disease: Senile Dementia and Related Disorders*, Aging, Vol. 7, New York, Raven Press, pp. 27–34.

NEWHOUSE, P. A., SUNDERLAND, T., TARIOT, P. N., BLEMHARD, C. L., WEINGARTNER, H. and MELLOW, A. (1988) 'Intravenous nicotine in Alzheimer's disease: a pilot study,' *Psychopharmacology*, 95, pp. 171–5.

NEWTON, R. D. (1948) 'The identity of Alzheimer's disease and senile dementia and their relationship to senility,' *Journal of Mental Science*, 94, pp. 225–49.

NICHOLAS, M., OBLER, L. K., ALBERT, M. L. and HELM-EASTABROOK, N. (1985) 'Empty speech in Alzheimer's disease,' *Journal of Speech and Hearing Research*, 28, pp. 405–10.

NICHOLSON, C. D. (1990) 'Pharmacology of nootropics and metabolically active compounds in relation to their use in dementia,' *Psychopharmacology*, 101, pp. 147–59.

NIELSEN, J., HOMMA, A. and BIORN-HENDRIKSEN, T. (1977) 'Follow-up 15 years after a geronto-psychiatric prevalence study: conditions concerning death, and life expectancy in relation to psychiatric diagnosis,' *Journal of Gerontology*, 32, pp. 554–61.

NIGHTINGALE, S., MITCHELL, K. W. and HOWE, J. W. (1986) 'Visual evoked cortical potentials and pattern electroretinograms in Parkinson's disease and control subjects,' *Journal of Neurology, Neurosurgery and Psychiatry*, 49, pp. 1280–7.

NISSEN, M. J., CORKIN, S., BUONANNO, F. S., GROWDON, J. H., WRAY, S. H. and BAUER, J. (1985) 'Spatial vision in Alzheimer's disease: general findings and a case report,' *Archives of Neurology*, 42, pp. 667–71.

NISSEN, M. J., KNOPMAN, D. S. and SCHACTER, D. L. (1987) 'Neurochemical dissociation of memory systems,' *Neurology*, 37, pp. 789–94.

NOONBERG, A. R. and PAGE, H. A. (1982) 'Graduate neuropsychology training: a later look,' *Professional Psychology*, 13, pp. 252–7.

NORDBERG, A. and WINBLAD, B. (1986) 'Reduced numbers of [3H] nicotinic and [3H] acetylcholine binding sites in the frontal cortex of Alzheimer brains,' *Neuroscience Letters*, 72, pp. 115–19.

NORMAN, D. A. and BOBROW, D. G. (1975) 'On data-limited and resource-limited processes,' *Cognitive Psychology*, 7, pp. 44–64.

NOTT, P. N. and FLEMINGER, J. J. (1975) 'Presenile dementia: the difficulties of early diagnosis,' *Acta Psychiatrica Scandinavica*, 51, pp. 210–17.

NYBERG, P., ALMAY, B. G., CARLSON, A., MASTERS, C. and WINBLAD, B. (1982) 'Brain monoamine abnormalities in the two types of Creutzfeldt–Jakob disease,' *Acta Neurologica Scandinavica*, 66, pp. 16–24.

OBER, B. A., DRONKERS, N. F., KOSS, E., DELIS, D. C. and FRIEDLAND, R. P., (1986) 'Retrieval from semantic memory in Alzheimer type dementia,' *Journal of Clinical and Experimental Neuropsychology*, 8, pp. 75–92.

OBER, B. A. and SHENAUT, G. K. (1988) 'Lexical decision and priming in Alzheimer's disease,' *Neuropsychologia*, 26, pp. 273–86.

OBLER, L. (1981) 'Review: Le langage des dements,' by L. Irigaray, 1973, *Brain and Language*, 12, pp. 375–86.

OBLER, L. K. (1983) 'Language and brain dysfunction in dementia,' in Segalowitz, S. J. (Ed.) *Language Functions and Brain Organization*, New York, Academic Press, pp. 267–82.

OBLER, L. K. and ALBERT, M. L. (1981) 'Language in the elderly aphasic and in the dementing patient,' in Sarno, M. T. (Ed.) *Acquired Aphasia*, New York, Academic Press, pp. 385–98.

O'CONNOR, K. (1981) 'Post-imperative negativity and prognosis in senile dementia,' *Perceptual and Motor Skills*, 52, p. 234.

O'DONNELL, B. F., SQUIRES, N. K., MARTZ, M. J., CHEN, J.-R. and PHAY, A. J. (1987) 'Evoked potential changes and neuropsychological performance in Parkinson's disease,' *Biological Psychology*, 24, pp. 23–37.

OHM, T. G. and BRAAK, H. (1989) 'Auditory brainstem nuclei in Alzheimer's disease,' *Neuroscience Letters*, 96, pp. 60–3.

OLDFIELD, R. C. and WINGFIELD, A. (1965) 'Response latencies in naming objects,' *Quarterly Journal of Experimental Psychology*, 17, pp. 273–81.

OLIVER, C. and HOLLAND, A. J. (1986) 'Down's syndrome and Alzheimer's disease: a review,' *Psychological Medicine*, 16, pp. 307–22.

OLSHO, L. W., HARKINS, S. W. and LENHART, M. L. (1985) 'Aging and the auditory system,' in Birren, J. E. and Schaie, K. W. (Eds) *Handbook of the Psychology of Aging*, New York, Van Nostrand Reinhold, pp. 332–77.

OLSON, C. M. (1989) 'Vision-related problems may offer clues for earlier diagnosis of Alzheimer's disease,' *Journal of the American Medical Association*, 261, p. 1259.

ORSINI, A., FRAGASSI, N. A., CHIACCHO, L., FALANGA, A. M., COCCHIARO, C. and GROSSI, D. (1987) 'Verbal and spatial memory in patients with extrapyramidal disease,' *Perception and Motor Skills*, 65, pp. 555–8.

ORWIN, A., WRIGHT, C. E., HARDING, G. F. A., ROWAN, D. C. and ROLFE, E. B. (1986) 'Serial visual evoked potential recordings in a case of Alzheimer's disease,' *British Medical Journal*, 293, pp. 9–10.

OSTFELD, A. M. and ARUGUETE, A. (1962) 'Central nervous system effects of hyoscine in man,' *Journal of Pharmacology and Experimental Therapeutics*, 137, pp. 133–4.

PALMER, A. M., FRANCIS, P. T., BENTON, J. S., SIMS, N. R., MANN, D. M. A., NEARY, D. and BOWEN, D. M. (1987b) 'Presynaptic serotonergic dysfunction in patients with Alzheimer's disease,' *Journal of Neurochemistry*, 48, pp. 8–15.

PALMER, A. M., FRANCIS, P. T., BOWEN, D. M., BENTON, J. S., NEARY, D., MANN, D. M. and SNOWDEN, J. S. (1987a) 'Catecholaminergic neurons assessed ante-mortem in Alzheimer's disease,' *Brain Research*, 414, pp. 365–75.

PARASURAMAN, R. and DAVIES, D. R. (1984) *Varieties of Attention*, Orlando, Academic Press.

PARR, D. (1955) 'Diagnostic problems in pre-senile dementia illustrated by a case of Alzheimer's disease proven histologically during life,' *Journal of Mental Science*, 101, pp. 387–90.

PARROTT, A. C. (1986) 'The effects of transdermal scopolamine and four dose levels of oral scopolamine (0.15, 0.3, 0.6 and 1.2 mg) on psychological performance,' *Psychopharmacology*, 89, pp. 347–54.

PARROTT, A. C. (1987) 'Transdermal scopolamine: effects of single and repeated patches upon psychological task performance,' *Neuropsychobiology*, 17, pp. 53–9.

PARSONS, O. A. (1970) 'Clinical neuropsychology,' in Spielberger, C. D. (Ed.) *Current Topics in Clinical and Community Psychology*, Vol. 2, New York, Academic Press, pp. 1–60.

PATTIE, A. M. and GILLEARD, C. J. (1979) *Manual of the Clifton Assessment Procedures for the Elderly*, Sevenoaks, Kent, Hodder & Stoughton Educational.

PAULSON, G. and GOTTLIEB, G. (1968) 'Development reflexes: the reappearance of foetal and neonatal reflexes in aged patients,' *Brain*, 91, pp. 37–52.

PEABODY, C. A. and TINKLENBERG, J. R. (1985) 'Olfactory deficits and primary degenerative dementia,' *American Journal of Psychiatry*, 142, pp. 524–5.

PEARCE, J. and MILLER, E. (1973) *Clinical Aspects of Dementia*, London, Bailliere Tindall.

PEARSON, R. C. A., ESIRI, M. M., HIORNS, R. W., WILCOCK, G. K. and POWELL, T. P. S. (1985) 'Anatomical correlates of the distribution of the pathological changes within neocortex in Alzheimer's disease,' *Proceedings of the National Academy of Sciences U.S.A.*, 82, pp. 4531–4.

PENN, R. D., MARTIN, E. M., WILSON, R. S., FOX, J. H. and SAVOY, S. M. (1988) 'Intraventricular bethanecol infusion for Alzheimer's disease: results of double-blind and escalating-dose trials,' *Neurology*, 38, pp. 19–22.

PENFIELD, W. and MATHIESON, G. (1974) 'Memory: autopsy findings and comments on the role of hippocampus in experimental, recall,' *Archives of Neurology*, 31, pp. 145–54.

PEREZ, F. I., GAY, J. R. A. and COOKE, N. A. (1978) 'Neuropsychological aspects of Alzheimer's disease and multi-infarct dementia,' in Nandy, K. (Ed.) *Senile Dementia: A Biomedical Approach*, New York, Elsevier North-Holland Biomedical Press, pp. 185–99.

PEREZ, F. I., GAY, J. R. A., TAYLOR, R. L. and RIVERA, V. M. (1976) 'Patterns of memory performance in the neurologically impaired aged,' *Canadian Journal of Neurological Sciences*, 2, pp. 347–55.

PEREZ, F. I., RIVERA, V. M., MEYER, J. S., GAY, J. R. A., TAYLOR, R. L. and MATHEW, N. T. (1975) 'Analysis of intellectual and cognitive performance in patients with multi-infarct dementia, vertebrobasilar insufficiency with dementia, and Alzheimer's disease', *Journal of Neurology, Neurosurgery and Psychiatry*, 38, pp. 533–40.

PERRY, E. K., BLESSED, G., TOMLINSON, B. E., PERRY, R. H., CROW, T. J., CROSS, A. J., DOCKRAY, G. J., DIMALINE, R. and ARREGUI, A. (1981a) 'Neurochemical activities in human temporal lobe related to aging and Alzheimer-type changes,' *Neurobiology of Aging*, 2, pp. 251–6.

PERRY, E. K., GIBSON, P. H., BLESSED, G., PERRY, R. H., TOMLINSON, B. E. (1977a) 'Neurotransmitter enzyme abnormalities in senile dementia,' *Journal of the Neurological Sciences*, 34, pp. 247–65.

PERRY, E. K., PERRY, R. H., BLESSED, G. and TOMLINSON, B. E. (1977b) 'Necropsy evidence of central cholinergic deficits in senile dementia,' *Lancet*, i, p. 189.

PERRY, E. K., PERRY, R. H., BLESSED, G. and TOMLINSON, B. E. (1978a) 'Changes in brain cholinesterases in senile dementia of Alzheimer type,' *Neuropathology and Applied Neurobiology*, 4, pp. 273–7.

PERRY, E. K., PERRY, R. H., GIBSON, P. H., BLESSED, G. and TOMLINSON, B. E. (1977c) 'A cholinergic connection between normal aging and senile dementia in the human hippocampus,' *Neuroscience Letters*, 6, pp. 85–9.

PERRY, E. K., PERRY, R. H., SMITH, C. J., PUROHIT, D., BONHAM, J., DICK, D. J., CANDY, J. M., EDWARDSON, J. A. and FAIRBAIRN, A. (1986) 'Cholinergic receptors and cognitive disorders,' *Canadian Journal of Neurological Sciences*, 13, pp. 521–7.

PERRY, E. K., TOMLINSON, B. E., BLESSED, G., BERGMANN, K., GIBSON, P. H. and PERRY, R. H. (1978b) 'Correlation of cholinergic abnormalities with senile plaques and mental test scores in senile dementia,' *British Medical Journal*, 2, pp. 1457–9.

PERRY, E. K., TOMLINSON, B. E., BLESSED, G., PERRY, R. H., CROSS, A. J. and CROW, T. J. (1981b) 'Neuropathological and biochemical observations on the noradrenergic system in Alzheimer's disease,' *Journal of the Neurological Sciences*, 51, pp. 279–87.

PERRY, R. H., CANDY, J. M., PERRY, E. K., IRVING, D., BLESSED, G., FAIRBAIRN, A. F. and TOMLINSON, B. E. (1982) 'Extensive loss of choline acetyltransferase activity is not reflected by neuronal loss in the nucleus of Meynert in Alzheimer's disease,' *Neuroscience Letters*, 33, pp. 311–15.

PETERS, B. H. and LEVIN, H. S. (1977) 'Memory enhancement after physostigmine treatment in the amnesic syndrome,' *Archives of Neurology*, 34, pp. 216–19.

PETERS, B. H. and LEVIN, H. S. (1979) 'Effects of physostigmine and lecithin on memory in Alzheimer disease,' *Annals of Neurology*, 6, pp. 219–21.

PETERS, B. H. and LEVIN, H. S. (1982) 'Chronic oral physostigmine and lecithin administration in memory disorders of aging,' in Corkin, S., Davis, K. L., Growdon, J. H., Usdin, E. and Wurtman, R. J. (Eds) *Alzheimer's Disease: A Report of Progress in Research, Aging*, Vol. 19, New York, Raven Press, pp. 421–6.

PETERS, C. A., POTTER, J. F. and SCHOLER, S. G. (1988) 'Hearing impairment as a predictor of cognitive decline in dementia,' *Journal of the American Geriatrics Society*, 36, pp. 981–6.

PETERSEN, R. C. (1977) 'Scopolamine-induced learning failures in man,' *Pscychopharmacology*, 52, pp. 283–9.

PETERSEN, R. C. (1979) 'Scopolamine state-dependent memory processes in man,' *Psychopharmacology*, 64, pp. 309–14.

PETIT, T. L. (1982) 'Neuroanatomical and clinical neuropsychological changes in aging and senile dementia,' in Craik, F. I. M. and Trehub, S. (Eds) *Aging and Cognitive Processes*, New York, Plenum Press, pp. 1–21.

PFEFFERBAUM, A., HORVATH, T. B., ROTH, W. T. and KOPELL, B. S. (1979) 'Event-related potential changes in chronic alcoholics,' *Electroencephalography and Clinical Neurophysiology*, 47, pp. 637–47.

PFEFFERBAUM, A., WENEGART, B. G., FORD, J. M., ROTH, W. T. and KOPELL, B. S. (1984) 'Clinical application of the P3 component of event-related potentials. II. Dementia, depression and schizophrenia,' *Electroencephalography and Clinical Neurophysiology*, 59, pp. 104–24.

PFEIFFER, E. (1975) 'A short portable mental status questionnaire for the assessment of organic brain deficit in elderly patients,' *Journal of the American Geriatric Society*, 23, pp. 433–41.

PFEIFFER, E. and BUSSE, E. W. (1973) 'Affective disorders,' in Busse, E. W. and Pfeiffer, E. (Eds) *Mental Illness in Later Life*, Washington, D.C., American Psychiatric Association, pp. 109–44.

PILLON, B., DUBOIS, B., LHERMITTE, F. and AGID, Y. (1986) 'Heterogeneity of cognitive impairment in progressive supranuclear palsy, Parkinson's disease and Alzheimer's disease,' *Neurology*, 36, pp. 1179–85.

PIROZZOLO, F. J., CHRISTENSEN, K. J., OGLE, K. M., HANSCH, E. C. and THOMPSON, W. G. (1981) 'Simple and choice reaction time in dementia: clinical implications.' *Neurobiology of Aging*, 2, pp. 113–17.

PIROZZOLO, F. J., HANSCH, E. C., MORTIMER, J. A., WEBSTER, D. D. and KUSKOWSKI, M. A. (1982) 'Dementia in Parkinson's disease: a neuropsychological analysis,' *Brain and Cognition*, 1, pp. 78–83.

PITT, B. (1982) *Psychogeriatrics: An Introduction to the Psychiatry of Old Age*, Edinburgh, Churchill Livingstone.

POGACAR, S. and WILLIAMS, R. S. (1984) 'Alzheimer's disease presenting as a slowly progressive aphasia,' *Rhode Island Medical Journal*, 67, pp. 181–5.

POLLOCK, M. and HORNABROOK, R. W. (1966) 'The prevalence, natural history and dementia of Parkinson's disease,' *Brain*, 89, pp. 429–48.

POMARA, N., DOMINO, E. F., YOON, H., BRINKMAN, S., TAMMINGA, C. A. and GERSHON, S. (1983) 'Failure of single-dose lecithin to alter aspects of central cholinergic activity in Alzheimer's disease,' *Journal of Clinical Psychiatry*, 44, pp. 293–5.

PORSCHE-WIEBKING, E. (1989) 'New N-methyl-D-aspartate antagonists for the treatment of stroke,' *Drug Development Research*, 17, pp. 367–75.

POSNER, M. I. and BOIES, S. J. (1971) 'Components of attention,' *Psychological Review*, 78, pp. 391–408.

POSNER, M. I., COHEN, Y. and RAFAL, R. D. (1982) 'Neural systems control of spatial orienting,' *Philosophical Transactions of the Royal Society of London*, Series B, 298, pp. 187–98.

POST, F. (1975) 'Dementia, depression, and pseudodementia,' in Benson, D. F. and Blumer, D. (Eds) *Psychiatric Aspects of Neurological Disease*, New York, Grune & Stratton, pp. 99–120.

POWELL, G. E. (1981) *Brain Function Therapy*, Aldershot, Gower Publishing.

PREECE, M. A. (1986) 'Creutzfeldt–Jakob disease: implication for growth hormone deficient children,' *Neurophathology and Applied Neurobiology*, 12, pp. 509–15.

PRIBRAM, K. M. and McGUINNESS, D. (1975) 'Arousal, activation, and effort in the control of attention,' *Psychological Review*, 82, pp. 116–49.

QUINN, N. P., KOLLER, W. C., LONG, A. E. and MARSDEN, C. D. (1986) 'Painful Parkinson's disease,' *Lancet*, i, pp. 1366–9.

QUINN, N. P., ROSSOR, M. N. and MARSDEN, C. D. (1987) 'Olfactory threshold in Parkinson's disease,' *Journal of Neurology, Neurosurgery and Psychiatry*, 50, pp. 88–9.

QUIRION, R., MARTEL, J. C., ROBITAILLE, Y., ETIENNE, P., WOOD, P., NAIR, N. V. P. and GAUTHIER, S. (1986) 'Neurotransmitter and receptor deficits in senile dementia of the Alzheimer type,' *Canadian Journal of Neurological Sciences*, 13, pp. 503–10.

RABBITT, P. M. A. (1979) 'Some experiments and a model for changes in attentional selectivity with old age,' in Hoffmeister, F. and Muller, C. (Eds) *Brain Function in Old Age: Evaluation of Changes and Disorders*, Berlin, Springer-Verlag, pp. 82–94.

RABBITT, P. M. A. (1980) 'A fresh look at changes in reaction times in old age,' in Stein, D. G. (Ed.) *The Psychobiology of Aging: Problems and Perspectives*, New York, Elsevier North-Holland, pp. 425–42.

RABBITT, P. M. A. (1988) 'Social psychology, neurosciences and cognitive psychology need each other; (and gerontology needs all three of them),' *The Psychologist: Bulletin of the British Psychological Society*, 12, pp. 500–6.

RABINOWITZ, J. C., CRAIK, F. I. M. and ACKERMAN, B. P. (1982) 'A processing resource account of age differences in recall,' *Canadian Journal of Psychology*, 36, pp. 325–44.

RAE-GRANT, A., BLUME, W., LAU, C., HACHINSKI, V. C., FISMAN, M. and MERSKEY, H. (1987) 'The electroencephalogram in Alzheimer-type dementia: a sequential study correlating the electroencephalogram with psychometric and quantitative pathologic data,' *Archives of Neurology*, 44, pp. 50–4.

RAFAL, R. D., POSNER, M. I., FRIEDMAN, J. H., INHOFF, A. W. and BERNSTEIN, E. (1988) 'Orienting of visual attention in progressive supranuclear palsy,' *Brain*, 111, pp. 267–80.

RAFAL, R. D., POSNER, M. I., WALKER, J. A. and FRIEDRICH, F. J. (1984) 'Cognition and the basal ganglia: separating mental and motor components of performance in Parkinson's disease,' *Brain*, 107, pp. 1083–94.

RAISMAN, R., CASH, R. and AGID, Y. (1986) 'Decreased density of [3H]-imipramine and [3H]-paroxetine binding sites in the putamen of parkinsonian patients,' *Neurology*, 36, pp. 556–60.

RANSMAYR, G., SCHMIDHUBER-EILER, B., KARAMAT, E., ENGLER-PLORER, S., POEWE, W. and LEIDLMAIR, K. (1987) 'Visuoperception and visuospatial and visuorotational performance in Parkinson's disease', *Journal of Neurology*, 235, pp. 99–101.

REGAN, D. and MAXNER, C. (1987) 'Orientation-selective visual loss in patients with Parkinson's disease,' *Brain*, 118, pp. 415–32.

REIFLER, B. V., LARSON, E. and HANLEY, R. (1982) 'Coexistence of cognitive impairment and depression in geriatric outpatients,' *American Journal of Psychiatry*, 139, pp. 623–6.

REISBERG, B., FERRIS, S. H. and GERSHON, S. (1980) 'Pharmacotherapy of senile dementia,' in Cole, J. O. and Barrett, J. E. (Eds) *Psychopathology in the Aged*, New York, Raven Press, pp. 233–61.

REISBERG, B., FERRIS, S. H. and GERSHON, S. (1981) 'An overview of pharmacologic treatment of cognitive decline in old age,' *American Journal, of Psychiatry*, 138, pp. 593–600.

REISINE, T. D., YAMAMURA, H. I., BIRD, E. D., SPOKES, E. and ENNA, S. J. (1978) 'Pre- and post-synaptic neurochemical alterations in Alzheimer's disease,' *Brain Research*, 159, pp. 477–81.

RENVOIZE, E. B. and JERRAM, T. (1979) 'Choline in Alzheimer's disease,' *New England Journal of Medicine*, 301, p. 330.

REZEK, D. L. (1987) 'Olfactory deficits as a neurological sign in dementia of the Alzheimer type,' *Archives of Neurology*, 44, pp. 1030–2.

RIBOT, T. (1882) *Diseases of Memory*, New York, Appleton.

RICHTER, J. A., PERRY, E. K. and TOMLINSON, B. E. (1980) 'Acetylcholine and choline levels in post-mortem human brain tissue: preliminary observations in Alzheimer's disease,' *Life Sciences*, 26, pp. 1683–9.

RIEGE, W. H. and METTER, E. J. (1988) 'Cognitive and brain imaging measures of Alzheimer's disease,' *Neurobiology of Ageing*, 9, pp. 69–86.

RINNE, J. O., RINNE, J. K., LAAKSO, K., PALJARVI, L. and RINNE, U. K. (1984) 'Reduction in muscarinic receptor binding in limbic areas of Alzheimer brain,' *Journal of Neurology, Neurosurgery and Psychiatry*, 47, pp. 651–3.

RINNE, J. O., SAKO, E., PALJARVI, L., MOLSA, P. K. and RINNE, U. K. (1986a) 'Brain dopamine D1 receptors in senile dementia,' *Journal of the Neurological Sciences*, 73, pp. 219–30.

RINNE, J. O., SAKO, E. PALJARVI, L., MOLSA, P. K. and RINNE, U. K. (1986b) 'Brain dopamine D2 receptors in senile dementia,' *Journal of Neurotransmission*, 65, pp. 51–62.

RIPICH, D. N. and TERRELL, B. Y. (1988) 'Patterns of discourse cohesion and coherence in Alzheimer's disease,' *Journal of Speech and Hearing Disorders*, 53, pp. 8–15.

RISSENBERG, M. and GLANZER, M. (1986) 'Picture superiority in free recall: the effects of ageing and primary degenerative dementia,' *Journal of Gerontology*, 41, pp. 64–71.

RISSENBERG, M. and GLANZER, M. (1987) 'Free recall and word finding ability in normal ageing and senile dementia of the Alzheimer type: the effect of item concreteness,' *Journal of Gerontology*, 42, pp. 318–22.

RITCHIE, K. (1988) 'The screening of cognitive impairment in the elderly: a critical review of current methods,' *Journal of Clinical Epidemiology*, 41, pp. 635–43.

RIZZOLATTI, G. and GALLESE, V. (1988) 'Mechanisms and theories of spatial neglect,' in Boller, F. and Grafman, J. (Eds) *Handbook of Neuropsychology*, Vol. I, New York, Elsevier Science Publishers (Biomedical Division), pp. 223–46.

ROBBINS, T. W. and EVERITT, B. (1987) 'Psychopharmacological nature of arousal and attention,' in Stahl, S. M., Iversen, S. D. and Goodman, E. C. (Eds) *Cognitive Neurochemistry*, Oxford, Oxford University Press, pp. 135–70.

ROBERTS, E. (1986) 'Alzheimer's disease may begin in the nose and may be caused by aluminosilicates,' *Neurobiology of Ageing*, 7, pp. 561–7.

ROBERTS, G. W., CROW, T. J. and POLAK, J. M. (1985) 'Localization of neuronal tangles in somatostatin neurons in Alzheimer's disease,' *Nature* 314, pp. 92–4.

ROBERTSON, E. E. (1978) 'Organic disorders', in Forrest, A., Affleck, J., and Zealley, A. (Eds.) *Companion to Psychiatric Studies*, 2nd ed., Edinburgh, Churchill Livingstone, pp. 459–98.

ROBERTSON, E. E., LE ROUX, A. and BROWN, J. H. (1958) 'The clinical differentiation of Pick's disease,' *Journal of Mental Science*, 104, pp. 1000–24.

ROCHFORD, G. (1971) 'A study of naming errors in dysphasic and in demented patients,' *Neuropsychologia*, 9, pp. 437–43.

ROGERS, J. D., BROGAN, D. and MIRRA, S. S. (1985) 'The nucleus basalis of Meynert in neurological disease: a quantitative morphological study,' *Annals of Neurology*, 17, pp. 163–70.

ROMAN, C. G. (1987) 'Lacunar dementia: a form of vascular dementia,' *Texas Medicine*, 83, pp. 37–9.

RON, M. A. (1983) 'The alcoholic brain: CT scan and psychological findings,' *Psychological Medicine* (Monograph Supplement) Supplement 3, pp. 1–33.

RON, M. A., TOONE, B. K., GARRALOA, M. E. and LISHMAN, W. A. (1979) 'Diagnostic accuracy in presenile dementia,' *British Journal of Psychiatry*, 134, pp. 161–8.

ROSE, R. P. and MOULTHROP, M. A. (1986) 'Differential responsivity of verbal and visual recognition memory to physostigmine and ACTH,' *Biological Psychiatry*, 21, pp. 538–42.

ROSEN, W. G. (1980) 'Verbal fluency in aging and dementia,' *Journal of Clinical Neuropsychology*, 2, pp. 135–46.

ROSEN, W. G. (1983) 'Neuropsychological investigation of memory, visuoconstructional, visuoperceptual and language abilities in senile dementia of the Alzheimer type,' in Mayeux, R. and Rosen, W. G. (Eds.), *The Dementias*, New York, Raven Press, pp. 65–73.

ROSEN, W. G., TERRY, R. D., FULD, P. A., KATZMAN, R. and PECK, A. (1980) 'Pathological verification of ischemic score in differentiation of dementias,' *Annals of Neurology*, 7, pp. 486–8.

ROSENBERG, M. B., FRIEDMAN, T., ROBERTSON, R. C. TUSZYNSKI, M. WOLFF, J. A., BREAKFILED, X. O. and GAGE, F. H. (1988) 'Grafting genetically modified cells to the damaged brain; restorative effects of NGF expression,' *Science* 242, pp. 1575–8.

ROSENSTOCK, H. A. (1970) 'Alzheimer's presenile dementia: a review of 11 clinically diagnosed cases,' *Diseases of the Nervous System*, 31, pp. 826–9.

ROSS, E. D. (1980) 'Sensory-specific and fractional disorders of recent memory,' *Archives of Neurology*, 37, pp. 193–200.

ROSS, E. D. (1981) 'The aprosodias: functional organization of the affective components of language in the right hemisphere,' *Archives of Neurology*, 38, pp. 561–9.

ROSS, E. D. (1982) 'Disorders of recent memory in humans,' *Trends in Neurosciences*, 5, pp. 170–2.

ROSSI, L., BENVENUTI, F., PANTALEO, T., BINDI, A., COSTANTINI, S., DE SCISCIOLO, G. and ZAPPOLI, R. (1985) 'Auditory and somatosensory evoked responses (AEPs and SEPs) and ballistic movements in Parkinson's disease,' *Italian Journal of Neurological Science*, 6, pp. 329–37.

ROSSOR, M. N. (1981) 'Parkinson's disease and Alzheimer's disease as disorders of the isodendritic core,' *British Medical Journal*, 283, pp. 1588–90.

ROSSOR, M. N., EMSON, P. C., MOUNTJOY, C. Q., ROTH, M. and IVERSEN, L. L. (1980b) 'Reduced amounts of immunoreactive somatostatin in the temporal cortex in senile dementia of Alzheimer type,' *Neuroscience Letters*, 20, pp. 373–7.

ROSSOR, M. N., FAHRENKRUG, J., EMSON, P., MOUNTJOY, C. Q., IVERSEN, L. and ROTH, M. (1980a) 'Reduced cortical choline acetyltransferase activity in senile dementia of Alzheimer type is not accompanied by changes in vasoactive intestinal polypeptide,' *Brain Research*, 201, pp. 249–53.

ROSSOR, M. N., GARRETT, N. J., JOHNSON, A. L., MOUNTJOY, C. Q., ROTH, M. and IVERSEN, L. (1982a) 'A post-mortem study of cholinergic and GABA systems in senile dementia,' *Brain*, 105, pp. 313–30.

ROSSOR, M. N., IVERSEN, L. L., JOHNSON, A. L., MOUNTJOY, C. Q. and ROTH, M. (1981) 'Cholinergic deficit in frontal cerebral cortex in Alzheimer's disease is age dependent,' *Lancet*, ii, p. 1422.

ROSSOR, M. N., IVERSEN, L. L., REYNOLDS, G. P., MOUNTJOY, C. Q. and ROTH, M. (1984) 'Neurochemical characteristics of early and late onset types of Alzheimer's disease,' *British Medical Journal*, 288, pp. 961–4.

ROSSOR, M. N. and MOUNTJOY, C. Q. (1986) 'Post-mortem neurochemical changes in Alzheimer's disease compared with normal ageing,' *Canadian Journal of the Neurological Sciences*, 13, pp. 499–502.

ROSSOR, M. N., SVENDSEN, C., HUNT, S. P., MOUNTJOY, C. Q., ROTH, M. and IVERSEN, L. L. (1982b) 'The substantia innominata in Alzheimer's disease: an histochemical and biochemical study of cholinergic marker enzymes,' *Neuroscience Letters*, 28, pp. 217–22.

ROSVOLD, H. E., MIRSKY, A. F., SARASON, I., BRANSOME, E. D. and BECK, L. H. (1956) 'A continuous performance test of brain damage,' *Journal of Consulting Psychology*, 20, pp. 343–50.

ROTH, M. (1955) 'The natural history of mental disorder in old age,' *Journal of Mental Science*, 101, pp. 281–301.

ROTH, M. (1978) 'Diagnosis of senile and related forms of dementia, in Katzman, R., Terry, R. D. and Bick, K. L. (Eds) *Alzheimer's Disease: Senile Dementia and Related Disorders, Aging*, Vol. 7, New York, Raven Press, pp. 71–85.

ROTH, M. (1979) 'The early diagnosis of Alzheimer's disease: an introduction,' in Glen, A. I. M. and Whalley, L. J. (Eds) *Alzheimer's Disease: Early Recognition of Potentially Reversible Deficits*, Edinburgh, Churchill Livingstone, pp. 65–7.

ROTH, M. (1980a) 'The diagnosis of dementia in late and middle life,' in Mortimer, J. A. (Ed.) *The Epidemiology of Dementia*, Oxford, Oxford University Press, pp. 24–61.

ROTH, M. (1980b) 'Senile dementia and its borderlands,' in Cole, J. O. and Barrett, J. E. (Eds) *Psychopathology in the Aged*, New York, Raven Press, pp. 205–32.

ROTH, M. (1986) 'The association of clinical and neurological findings and its bearing to the classification and aetiology of Alzheimer's disease,' *British Medical Bulletin*, 42, pp. 42–50.

ROTH, M. and MYERS, D. H. (1975) 'The diagnosis of dementia,' *British Journal of Psychiatry*, Special Publication No. 9, pp. 87–99.

ROTH, M., TYM, E., MOUNTJOY, C. Q. HUPPERT, F. A., HENDRIE, H., VERMA, S. and GODDARD, R. (1986) 'CAMDEX: a standarized instrument for the diagnosis of mental disorder in the elderly with special reference to the early detection of dementia,' *British Journal of Psychiatry*, 149, pp. 698–709.

ROTHSCHILD, D. (1937) 'Pathologic changes in senile psychoses and their psychobiologic significance,' *American Journal of Psychiatry*, 93, pp. 757–88.

ROTHSCHILD, D. (1942) 'Neuropathologic changes in arteriosclerotic psychoses and their psychiatric significance,' *Archives of Neurology and Psychiatry*, 48, pp. 417–36.

ROTHSCHILD, D. and SHARP, M. L. (1941) 'The origin of senile psychoses: neuopathologic factors and factors of a more personal nature,' *Diseases of the Nervous System*, 2, pp. 49–54.

ROY, E. A. (1985) *Neuropsychological Studies of Apraxia and Related Disorders*, New York, Elsevier Science Publishers.

ROYAL COLLEGE OF PHYSICIANS COMMITTEE ON GERIATRICS (1981) 'Organic mental impairment in the elderly,' *Journal of the Royal College of Physicians*, 15, pp. 142–67.

RUBERG, M. and AGID, Y. (1988) 'Dementia in Parkinson's disease,' in Iversen, L. L., Iversen, S. D. and Snyder, S. H. (Eds) *Handbook of Psychopharmacology, Volume 20: Psychopharmacology of the Ageing Nervous System*, New York, Plenum Press, pp. 157–206.

RUDORFER, M. V., and CLAYTON, P. J. (1981) 'Depression, dementia, and dexamethasone suppression,' *American Journal of Psychiatry*, 138, p. 701.

SADUN, A. A., BORCHERT, M., DE VITA, E., HINTON, D. R. and BASSI, C. J. (1987) 'Assessment of visual impairment in patients with Alzheimer's disease,' *American Journal of Ophthalmology*, 104, pp. 113–20.

SAFER, D. J. and ALLEN, R. P. (1971) 'The central effects of scopolamine in man,' *Biological Psychiatry*, 3, pp. 347–55.

SAGAR, H., COHEN, N. J., SULLIVAN, E. V., CORKIN, S. and GROWDON, J. H. (1988) 'Remote memory function in Alzheimer's and Parkinson's disease,' *Brain*, 111, pp. 185–206.

SAGAR, H., SULLIVAN, E. V., COHEN, N. J., GABRIELI, J. D. E., CORKIN, S. and GROWDON, J. H. (1985) 'Specific cognitive deficit in Parkinson's disease,' *Journal of Experimental and Clinical Neuropsychology*, 7, p. 158.

SAHAKIAN, B. J., JONES, G., LEVY, R., GRAY, J. and WARBURTON, D. (1989) 'The effects of nicotine on attention, information processing and short-term memory in patients with dementia of the Alzheimer type,' *British Journal of Psychiatry*, 154, pp. 797–800.

SAHAKIAN, B.J., JOYCE, E. and LISHMAN, W.A. (1987) 'Cholinergic effects on constructional abilities and on mnemonic processes: a case report,' *Psychological Medicine*, 17, pp. 329–33.

SAHAKIAN, B.J., MORRIS, R.G., EVENDEN, J.L., HEALD, A., LEVY, R., PHILPOT, M. and ROBBINS, T.W. (1988) 'A comparative study of visuospatial memory and learning in Alzheimer-type dementia and Parkinson's disease,' *Brain*, 111, pp. 695–718.

ST. CLAIR, D.M., BLACKBURN, I., BLACKWOOD, D.H.R. and TYRER, G. (1988) 'Measuring the course of Alzheimer's disease: a longitudinal study of neuropsychological function and changes in P3 event-related potential,' *British Journal of Psychiatry*, 152, pp. 48–54.

ST. CLAIR, D.M., BLACKWOOD, D.H.R. and CHRISTIE, J.E. (1985) 'P300 and other long latency auditory evoked potentials in presenile dementia Alzheimer type and alcoholic Korsakoff syndrome,' *British Journal of Psychiatry*, 147, pp. 702–6.

SALMON, D.P., SHIMAMURA, A.P., BUTTERS, N. and SMITH, S.M. (1988) 'Lexical and priming deficits in patients with Alzheimer's disease,' *Journal of Experimental and Clinical Neuropsychology*, 10, pp. 377–394.

SALTHOUSE, T.A. (1980) 'Age and memory: strategies for localizing the loss,' in Poon, L.W., Fozard, J.L., Cermak, L.S., Arenberg, D. and Thompson, L.W. (Eds) *New Directions in Memory and Aging*, Hillsdale, N.J., Lawrence Erlbaum Associates, pp. 47–65.

SANDYK, R. (1986) 'Anticholinergic-induced analgesia: possible role for the cholinergic system in abnormal sensory systems in Parkinson's disease,' *Postgraduate Medical Journal*, 62, pp. 749–51.

SANTO PIETRO, M.J. and GOLDFARB, R. (1985) 'Characteristic patterns of word association responses in institutionalized elderly with and without dementia,' *Brain and Language*, 26, pp. 230–43.

SAPIR, S. and ARONSON, A. (1985) 'Aphasia after closed head injury,' *British Journal of Disorders of Communication*, 20, pp. 289–96.

SASAKI, H., MURAMOTO, O., MANAZAWA, I., ARAI, H., KOSAKA, K. and IIZUKA, R. (1986) 'Regional distribution of amino acid transmitters in post-mortem brains of presenile and senile dementia of the Alzheimer type,' *Annals of Neurology*, 19, pp. 263–9.

SATZ, P., VAN GORP, W.S., SOPER, H.V. and MITRUSHINA, M. (1987) 'WAIS-R marker for dementia of the Alzheimer type? An empirical and statistical induction test,' *Journal of Experimental and Clinical Neuropsychology*, 9, pp. 767–74.

SCHIFFMAN, S.S. (1983a) 'Taste and smell in disease,' (First of two parts), *New England Journal of Medicine*, 308, pp. 1275–9.

SCHIFFMAN, S.S. (1983b) 'Taste and smell in disease,' (Second of two parts), *New England Journal of Medicine*, 308, pp. 1337–43.

SCHIFFMAN, S.S., HORNACK, K. and REILLY, D. (1979) 'Increased taste thresholds of amino acids with age,' *American Journal of Clinical Nutrition*, 32, pp. 1622–7.

SCHIFFMAN, S.S., MOSS, J. and ERICKSON, R.P. (1976) 'Thresholds of food odours in the elderly,' *Experimental Ageing Research*, 2, pp. 389–98.

SCHLOTTERER, G., MOSCOVITCH, M. and CRAPPER-MCLACHLAN, D. (1984) 'Visual processing deficits as assessed by spatial frequency contrast sensitivity and backward masking in normal ageing and Alzheimer's disease,' *Brain*, 107, pp. 309–25.

SCHNEIDER, W. and SHIFFRIN, R. M. (1977) 'Controlled and automatic human information processing: 1. Detection, search and attention,' *Psychological Review*, 84, pp. 1–66.

SCHOLTZ, C. L., SWETTENHAM, K., BROWN, A. and MANN, D. M. A. (1981) 'A histoquantitative study of the striate cortex and lateral geniculate body in normal, blind and demented subjects' *Neuropathology and Applied Neurobiology*, 7, pp. 103–14.

SCHWARTZ, A. S. and KOHLSTAEDT, E. V. (1986) 'Physostigmine and Alzheimer's disease: relationship to dementia severity,' *Life Sciences*, 38, pp. 1021–8.

SCHWARTZ, M. F., MARIN, O. S. M. and SAFFRAN, E. M. (1979) 'Dissociations of language function in dementia: a case study,' *Brain and Language*, 7, pp. 277–306.

SCOTT, D. F., HEATHFIELD, K. W. TOONE, B., and MARGERISON, J. H. (1972) 'The EEG in Huntington's Chorea: a clinical and neuropathological study,' *Journal of Neurology, Neurosurgery and Psychiatry*, 35, pp. 97–102.

SCOTT, S., CAIRD, F. C. and WILLIAMS, B. O. (1984) 'Evidence for an apparent sensory speech disorder in Parkinson's disease,' *Journal of Neurology, Neurosurgery and Psychiatry*, 47, pp. 840–3.

SELKOE, D. J. (1989) 'Molecular pathology of amyloidogenic proteins and the role of vascular amyloidosis in Alzheimer's disease,' *Neurobiology of Aging*, 10, pp. 387–95.

SELTZER, B. and SHERWIN, I. (1978) '"Organic brain syndromes": an empirical study and critical review,' *American Journal of Psychiatry*, 135, pp. 13–21.

SELTZER, B. and SHERWIN, I. (1983) 'A comparison of clinical features in early- and late-onset primary degenerative dementia: one entity or two?' *Archives of Neurology*, 40, pp. 143–6.

SEMPLE, S. A., SMITH, C. M. and SWASH, M. (1982) 'The Alzheimer disease syndrome,' in Corkin, S., Davis, K. L., Growdon, J. H., Usdin, E. and Wurtman, R. J. (Eds) *Alzheimer's Disease: A Report of Progress in Research, Aging*, Vol 19, New York, Raven Press, pp. 93–107.

SERBY, M. (1987) 'Olfactory deficits in Alzheimer's disease,' *Journal of Neural Transmission* (Suppl) 24, pp. 69–77.

SERBY, M., CORWIN, J., ROTROSEN, J., FERRIS, S. H., REISBERG, B., FRIEDMAN, E., SHERMAN, K., BARTUS, R. T. and JORDAN, B. (1983) 'Lecithin and piracetam in Alzheimer's disease,' *Psychopharmacological Bulletin*, 19, pp. 126–9.

SHAH, K. V., BANKS, G. D. and MERSKEY, H. (1969) 'Survival in atherosclerotic and senile dementia,' *British Journal of Psychiatry*, 115, pp. 1283–6.

SHALLICE, T. (1979) 'Case study approach in neuropsychological research,' *Journal of Clinical Neuropsychology*, 1, pp. 183–211.

SHALLICE, T. and WARRINGTON, E. K. (1970) 'Independent functioning of verbal memory stores, a neuropsychological study,' *Quarterly Journal of Experimental Psychology*, 22, pp. 261–73.

SHEER, D. E. (1984) 'Focused arousal, 40-Hz EEG and dysfunction,' in Elbert, T. (Ed.) *Self-regulation of the brain and behaviour*, New York, Springer-Verlag, pp. 64–84.

SHERIDAN, M. R., FLOWERS, K. A. and HURRELL, J. (1987) 'Programming and execution of movement in Parkinson's disease,' *Brain*, 110, pp. 1247–71.

SHIFFRIN, R. M. and SCHNEIDER, W. (1977) 'Controlled and automatic human information processing: 2. Perceptual learning, automatic attending, and a general theory,' *Psychological Review*, 84, pp. 127–90.

SHIMAMURA, A. P., (1986) 'Priming effects in amnesia: Evidence for a dissociable memory function,' *Quarterly Journal of Experimental Psychology*, 38A, pp. 619–44.

SHIMAMURA, A. P., SALMON, D. P., SQUIRE, L. R. and BUTTERS, N. (1987) 'Memory dysfunction and word priming in dementia and amnesia,' *Behavioural Neuroscience*, 101, pp. 347–51.

SHIMAMURA, A. P., and SQUIRE, L. R. (1986) 'Korsakoff's syndrome: a study of the relationship between anterograde amnesia and remote memory impairment,' *Behavioural Neuroscience*, 100, pp. 165–70.

SHINDLER, A. G., CAPLAN, L. B., and HIER, D. B. (1984) 'Intrusions and perseverations,' *Brain and Language*, 23, pp. 148–58.

SHIRAKI, H. and MIZUTANI, T. (1983) 'Neuropathologic characteristics of types of Creutzfeldt–Jakob disease with special reference to the panencephalitic type prevalent among Japanese,' in Hirano, A. and Miyoshi, K. (Eds) *Neuropsychiatric Disorders in the Elderly*, Tokyo, Igaku-Shoin, pp. 139–88.

SHRABERG, D. (1978) 'The myth of pseudodementia: depression and the aging brain,' *American Journal of Psychiatry*, 135, pp. 601–3.

SHUTTLEWORTH, E. C. and HUBER, S. J. (1988) 'The naming disorder of dementia of Alzheimer type,' *Brain and Language*, 34, pp. 222–34.

SIGNORET, J. L., WHITELEY, A. and LHERMITTE, F. (1978) 'Influence of choline on amnesia in early Alzheimer's disease,' *Lancet*, ii, p. 837.

SIM, M. (1965) 'Alzheimer's disease: a forgotten entity,' *Geriatrics*, 20, pp. 668–74.

SIM, M. (1979) 'Early diagnosis of Alzheimer's disease,' in Glen, A. I. M. and Whalley, L. J. (Eds) *Alzheimer's Disease: Early recognition of Potentially Reversible Deficits*, Edinburgh, Churchill Livingstone, pp. 78–85.

SIM, M. and SUSSMAN, I. (1962) 'Alzheimer's disease: its natural history and differential diagnosis,' *Journal of Nervous and Mental Disease*, 135, pp. 489–99.

SIM, M., TURNER, E. and SMITH, W. T. (1966) 'Cerebral biopsy in the investigation of presenile dementia,' *British Journal of Psychiatry*, 112, pp. 119–25.

SIMPSON, L., YATES, C. M., GORDON, A. and ST. CLAIR, D. M. (1984) 'Olfactory tubercle choline acetyltransferase activity in Alzheimer-type dementia Down's syndrome and Huntington's disease,' *Journal of Neurology, Neurosurgery and Psychiatry*, 47, pp. 1138–40.

SIMS, N. R., BOWEN, D. M. and ALLEN, S. J. (1983) 'Presynaptic cholinergic dysfunction in patients with dementia,' *Journal of Neurochemistry*, 40, pp. 503–9.

SINGER, J. A. and SALOVEY, P. (1988) 'Mood and memory: evaluating the network theory of affect,' *Clinical Psychology Review*, 8, pp. 211–51.

SITARAM, N., WEINGARTNER, H., CAINE, E. D. and GILLIN, J. C. (1978b) 'Choline: selective enhancement of serial learning and encoding of low imagery words in man,' *Life Sciences*, 22, pp. 1555–60.

SITARAM, N., WEINGARTNER, H. and GILLIN, J. C. (1978a) 'Human serial learning: enhancement with arecholine and choline and impairment with scopolamine,' *Science*, 201, pp. 274–6.

SJOGREN, H. (1952) 'Clinical analysis of Morbus Alzheimer and Morbus Pick,' *Acta Psychiatrica et Neurologica Scandinavica*, Suppl 82, pp. 67–115.

SKELTON-ROBINSON, M. and JONES, S. (1984) 'Nominal dysphasia and the severity of senile dementia,' *British Journal of Psychiatry*, 145, pp. 168–71.

SKRANDIES, W. and GOTTLOB, I. (1986) 'Alterations of visual contrast sensitivity in Parkinson's disease,' *Human Neurobiology*, 5, pp. 255–9.

SLATER, E. and ROTH, M. (1969) *Clinical Psychiatry*, 3rd Ed., Baltimore, Williams & Wilkins.

SMIRNE, S., FRANCESCHI, M., TRUCI, G., CAMERLINGO, M., PIROLA, R., FERINI-STRAMBI, L. and BAREGGI, S. R. (1985) 'Homovanillic acid and 5-hydroxyindoleacetic acid modifications in the CSF of patients with stroke and multi-infarct dementia,' *Stroke*, 16, pp. 1003–6.

SMITH, C. C. T., BOWEN, D. M., FRANCIS, P. T., SNOWDON, J. S. and NEARY, D. (1985) 'Putative amino acid transmitters in lumbar cerebrospinal fluid of patients with histologically verified Alzheimer's dementia,' *Journal of Neurology, Neurosurgery and Psychiatry*, 48, pp. 469–71.

SMITH, C. C. T., BOWEN, D. M., SIMS, N. R., DEARY, D. and DAVISON, A. N. (1983) 'Amino acid release from biopsy samples of temporal neocortex from patients with Alzheimer's disease,' *Brain Research*, 264, pp. 138–41.

SMITH, C. M. and SWASH, M. (1979) 'Physostigmine in Alzheimer's disease,' *Lancet*, i, p. 42.

SMITH, C. M., SWASH, M., EXTON-SMITH, A. N., PHILLIPS, M. J., OVERSTALL, P. W., PIPER, M. E. and BAILEY, M. R. (1978) 'Choline therapy in Alzheimer's disease,' *Lancet*, ii, p. 318.

SMITH, J. S. and KILOH, L. G. (1981) 'The investigation of dementia: results in 200 consecutive admissions,' *Lancet*, i, pp. 824–7.

SMITH, R. C., VROULIS, G., JOHNSON, R. and MORGAN, R. (1984) 'Comparison of the therapeutic response to long-term treatment with lecithin *versus* piracetam plus lecithin in patients with Alzheimer's disease,' *Psychopharmacological Bulletin*, 20, pp. 542–5.

SMITH, S., BUTTERS, N., WHITE, R., LYON, L. and GRANHOLM, E. (1988) 'Priming semantic relations in patients with Huntington's disease,' *Brain and Language*, 33, pp. 27–40.

SNIDER, S. R., FAHN, S., ISGREEN, W. P. and COTE, L. J. (1976) 'Primary sensory symptoms in parkinsonism,' *Neurology*, 26, pp. 423–9.

SOININEN, H., RIEKKINEN, P. J., PARTANEN, J., HELKALA, E. L., LAULUMAA, V., JOLKKONEN, J. and REINIKAINEN, K. (1988) 'Cerebrospinal fluid somatostatin correlates with spectral EEG variables and with parietotemporal cognitive dysfunction in Alzheimer patients,' *Neuroscience Letters*, 85, pp. 131–6.

SPARKS, D. L., MARKESBERY, W. R. and SLEVIA, J. T. (1986) 'Alzheimer's disease: monoamines and spiperone binding in the nucleus basalis,' *Annals of Neurology*, 19, pp. 602–4.

SPIRDUSO, W. W. (1975) 'Reaction and movement time as a function of age and physical activity level,' *Journal of Gerontology*, 30, pp. 435–40.

SPRING, B. J. (1980) 'Shift of attention in schizophrenia, siblings of schizophrenics, and depressed patients,' *Journal of Nervous and Mental Disease*, 168, pp. 133–40.

SPRINGER, S. P. (1986) 'Dichotic listening,' in Hannay, H. J., (Ed.) *Experimental Techniques in Human Neuropsychology*, Oxford, Oxford University Press, pp. 138–66.

SQUIRE, L. R. (1980) 'Specifying the defect in human amnesia: storage, retrieval and semantics,' *Neuropsychologia*, 18, pp. 369–72.

SQUIRE, L. R. (1981) 'Two forms of human amnesia: an analysis of forgetting,' *Journal of Neuroscience*, 1, pp. 635–40.

SQUIRE, L. R. (1986) 'Mechanisms of memory,' *Science*, 232, pp. 1612–19.

SQUIRE, L. R. (1987) *Memory and the Brain*, Oxford, Oxford University Press.

SQUIRES, K. C., CHIPPENDALE, T. J., GOODIN, D. and STARR, A. (1980) 'Electrophysiological assessment of mental function in ageing and dementia,' in Poon, L. W. (Ed.) *Aging in the 1980s: Psychological Issues*, Washington DC., American Psychological Association, pp. 125–34.

SROKA, H., ELIZAN, T. S., YAHR, M. D., BURGER, A. and MENDOZA, M. R. (1981) 'Organic mental syndrome and confusional states in Parkinson's disease: relationship to computerized tomographic signs of cerebral atrophy,' *Archives of Neurology*, 38, pp. 339–42.

STEEL, K. and FELDMAN, R. G. (1979) 'Diagnosing dementia and its treatable causes,' *Geriatrics*, 34, pp. 79–88.

STEELE, J. C., RICHARDSON, J. C. and OLSZEWSKI, J. (1964) 'Progressive supranuclear palsy,' *Archives of Neurology*, 10, pp. 333–59.

STEFFES, R. and THRALOW, J. (1987) 'Visual field limitations in the patient with dementia of Alzheimer's type,' *Journal of the American Geriatrics Society*, 35, pp. 198–204.

STEIN, L., WISE, D. and BELLUZZI, J. D. (1977) 'Neuropharmacology of reward and punishment,' in Iversen, L. L., Iversen, S. D. and Snyder, S. H. (Eds) *Handbook of Psychopharmacology*, Vol 7. *Drugs, Neurotransmitters and Behaviour*, New York, Plenum Press, pp. 25–53.

STENGEL, E. (1943) 'A study on the symptomatology and differential diagnosis of Alzheimer's disease and Pick's disease,' *Journal of Mental Science*, 89, pp. 1–20.

STENGEL, E. (1964a) 'Speech disorders and mental disorders,' in DeReuck, A. V. S. and O'Connor, M. (Eds) *Disorders of Language*, London, Churchill Livingstone, pp. 285–92.

STENGEL, E. (1964b) 'Psychopathology of dementia,' *Proceedings of the Royal Society of Medicine*, 57, pp. 911–14.

STEPHENS, L. P. (Editor) (1969) 'Reality Orientation: a technique to rehabilitate elderly and brain damaged patients with moderate to severe degree of disorientation,' Washington D.C., American Psychiatric Association Hospital and Community Psychiatric Service.

STERN, Y., MAYEUX, R. and ROSEN, J. (1984) 'Contribution of perceptual motor dysfunction to construction and tracing disturbances in Parkinson's disease,' *Journal of Neurology, Neurosurgery and Psychiatry*, 47, pp. 983–9.

STERN, Y., MAYEUX, R., ROSEN, J. and ILSON, J. (1983) 'Perceptual motor dysfunction in Parkinson's disease: a deficit in sequential and predictive voluntary movement,' *Journal of Neurology, Neurosurgery and Psychiatry*, 46, pp. 145–51.

STERN, Y., SANO, M. and MAYEUX, R. (1987) 'Effects of oral physostigmine in Alzheimer's disease,' *Annals of Neurology*, 22, pp. 306–10.

STEVENS, S. (1985) 'The language of dementia in the elderly: a pilot study,' *British Journal of Disorders of Communication*, 20, pp. 181–90.

STORANDT, M., BOTWINICK, J., DANZIGER, W. L., BERG, L. and HUGHES, C. P. (1984) 'Psychometric differentiation of mild senile dementia of the Alzheimer type,' *Archives of Neurology*, 41, pp. 497–9.

STOUDEMIRE, A. and THOMPSON, T. L. (1981) 'Recognizing and treating dementia,' *Geriatrics*, 36, pp. 112–20.

SULKAVA, R. (1982) 'Alzheimer's disease and senile dementia of Alzheimer type: a comparative study,' *Acta Neurologica Scandinavica*, 65, pp. 636–50.

SULKAVA, R. MALTIA, M., PAETAU, A., WIKSTROM, J. and PALO, J. (1983) 'Accuracy of clinical diagnosis in primary degenerative dementia: correlation with neuropathological findings,' *Journal of Neurology, Neurosurgery and Psychiatry*, 46, pp. 9–13.

SULLIVAN, E. V., SHEDLACK, K. J., CORKIN, S. and GROWDON, J. H. (1982) 'Physostigmine and lecithin in Alzheimer's disease,' in Corkin, S., Davis, K. L., Growdon, J. H., Usdin, E. and Wurtman, R. J. (Eds) *Alzheimer's Disease: A Report of Progress in Research, Aging*, Vol. 19, New York, Raven Press, pp. 361–7.

SUMMERS, W. K., MAJOVSKI, L. V., MARSH, G. M., TACHIKI, K. and KLING, A. (1986) 'Oral tetrahydroaminoacridine in long-term treatment of senile dementia, *New England Journal of Medicine*, 315, pp. 1241–5.

SUMMERS, W. K., VIESSELMAN, J. D., MARSH, G. M. and CANDELORA, K. (1981) 'Use of THA in treatment of Alzheimer-like dementia: pilot study in twelve patients,' *Biological Psychiatry*, 16, pp. 145–53.

SUNDERLAND, A., HARRIS, J. E. and BADDELEY, A. D. (1983) 'Do laboratory tests predict everyday memory? A neuropsychological study,' *Journal of Verbal Learning and Verbal Behaviour*, 22, pp. 341–57.

SUNDERLAND, T., RUBINOW, D. R., TARIOT, P. N., COHEN, R. M., NEWHOUSE, P. A., MELLOW, A. M., MEULLER, E. A. and MURPHY, D. L. (1987) 'CSF somatostatin in patients with Alzheimer's disease, older depressed patients and age-matched control subjects,' *American Journal of Psychiatry*, 144, pp. 1313–16.

SUNDERLAND, T., TARIOT, P., MURPHY, D. L., WEINGARTNER, H., MEULLER, E. A. and COHEN, R. M. (1985) 'Scopolamine challenges in Alzheimer's disease,' *Psychopharmacology*, 87, pp. 247–9.

SWEET, R. D., McDOWELL, F. H., FEIGENSON, J. S., LORANGER, A. W. and GOODELL, M. (1976) 'Mental symptoms in Parkinson's disease during chronic treatment with levodopa,' *Neurology*, 26, pp. 305–10.

SYNDULKO, K., HANSCH, E. C., COHEN, S. N., PEARCE, J. W., GOLDBERG, Z., MONTANA, B., TOURTELLOTTE, W. W. and POTVIN, A. (1982) 'Long-latency event related potentials in normal ageing and dementia, in Courjon, J., Mauguiere, F. and Revol, M. (Eds) *Clinical Applications of Evoked Potentials in Neurology*, New York, Raven Press, pp. 279–86.

TACHIBANA, H., MEYER, J.S., KITAGAWA, Y., ROGERS, R.L., OKAYASU, H. and
MORTEL, K.F. (1984) 'Effects of aging on cerebral blood flow in dementia,' *Journal of
the American Geriatrics Society*, 32, pp. 114–20.

TAGLIAVINI, F. and PILLERI, G. (1983) 'Neuronal counts in basal nucleus of Meynert in
Alzheimer disease and in simple senile dementia,' *Lancet*, i, pp. 469–70.

TALAMO, B.R., RUDEL, R.A., KOSIK, K.S., LEE, V.M.-Y., NEFF, S., ADELMAN, L. and
KAUER, J.S. (1989) 'Pathological changes in olfactory neurons in patients with
Alzheimer's disease,' *Nature*, 337, pp. 736–9.

TAMMINGA, C.A., FOSTER, N.L., FEDIO, P., BIRD, E.D. and CHASE, T.N. (1987)
'Alzheimer's disease: low cerebral somatostatin levels correlate with impaired cognitive
function and cortical metabolism,' *Neurology*, 37, pp. 161–5.

TANZI, R.E., ST. GEORGE-HYSLOP, P.H. and GEUSELLA, J.F. (1989) 'Molecular genetic
approaches to Alzheimer's disease,' *Trends in Neurosciences*, 12, pp. 152–8.

TARISKA, I. (1970) 'Circumscribed cerebral atrophy in Alzheimer's disease: a pathological
study,' in Wolstenholme, G.EW. and O'Connor, M. (Eds) *Alzheimer's Disease and
Related Conditions*, London, Churchill Livingstone, pp. 51–73.

TEASDALE, J.D. (1983) 'Affect and accessability,' *Philosophical Transactions of the Royal Society
London*, Series B, 302, pp. 403–12.

TECCE, J. (1983) 'C.N.V. Rebound in Ageing and Hydergine,' paper delivered at the
Conference on Research Progress in Dementia, Charing Cross Hospital Medical School.

TERRY, R.D. (1976) 'Dementia: a brief and selective review,' *Archives of Neurology*, 33,
pp. 1–4.

TERRY, R.D. (1978) 'Senile dementia,' *Federation Proceedings*, 37, pp. 2837–40.

TERRY, R.D., GONTAS, N.K. and WEISS, M. (1964) 'Ultrastructural studies in
Alzheimer's presenile dementia,' *American Journal of Pathology*, 44, pp. 269–97.

TERRY, R.D., HANSEN, L.A., DETERESA, R., DAVIES, P., TOBIAS, H. and KATZMAN,
R. (1987) 'Senile dementia of the Alzheimer type without neocortical neurofibrillary
tangles,' *Journal of Neuropathology and Experimental Neurology*, 46, pp. 262–8.

TERRY, R.D. and KATZMAN, R. (1983) 'Senile dementia of the Alzheimer type: defining a
disease,' in Katzman, R. and Terry, R.D. (Eds) *The Neurology of Aging*, Philadelphia,
F.A. Davis, pp. 51–84.

TERRY, R.D., PECK, A., DETERESA, R., SCHECHTER, R. and HOROUPIAN, D.S. (1981)
'Some morphometric aspects of the brain in senile dementia of the Alzheimer type,'
Annals of Neurology, 10, pp. 184–92.

TETRUD, J.W. and LANGSTON, J.W. (1989) 'The effect deprenyl (Selegiline) on the natural
history of Parkinson's disease,' *Science*, 245, pp. 519–22.

TEUBER, H.L. (1968) 'Perception,' in Weiskrantz, L. (Ed.) *Analysis of Behavioural Change*,
New York, Harper & Row, pp. 274–328.

THAL, L.J. and FULD, P.A. (1983) 'Memory enhancement with oral physostigmine in
Alzheimer's disease,' *New England Journal of Medicine*, 308, pp. 720–1.

THAL, L.J., FULD, P.A., MASUR, D.M. and SHARPLESS, N.S. (1983) 'Oral,
physostigmine and lecithin improve memory in Alzheimer disease,' *Annals of
Neurology*, 13, pp. 491–6.

THAL, L. J., FULD, P. A., MASUR, D. M. and SHARPLESS, N. S. (1984) 'Letter on long-term administration of oral physostigmine and lecithin in Alzheimer's disease,' *Annals of Neurology*, 15, p. 210.

THAL, L. J., ROSEN, W., SHARPLESS, N. S. and CRYSTAL, H. (1981) 'Choline chloride fails to improve cognition in Alzheimer's disease,' *Neurobiology of Aging*, 2, pp. 205-8.

THE PARKINSON STUDY GROUP (1989) 'The effect of deprenyl on the progression of disability in early Parkinson's disease,' *New England Journal of Medicine*, 321, pp. 1364-71.

THOMAS, L. (1981) 'The problem of dementia,' *Discovery*, August, pp. 34-6.

THOMAS, P. D., HUNT, W. C., GARRY, P. J., HOOD, R. B., GOODWIN, J. M., and GOODWIN, J. S. (1983) 'Hearing acuity in a healthy elderly population: effects of emotional, cognitive and social status,' *Journal of Gerontology*, 38, pp. 321-5.

TIERNEY, M. C., FISHER, R. H., LEWIS, A. J., ZORZITTO, M. L., SNOW, W. G., REID, D. W. and NIEUWETRATEN, P. (1988) 'The NINCDS-ADRDA Work Group criteria for the clinical diagnosis of probable Alzheimer's disease: a clinicopathologic study of 57 cases,' *Neurology*, 38, pp. 359-64.

TODOROV, A. B., GO, R. C.P., CONSTANTINIDIS, J. and ELSTON, R. C. (1975) 'Specificity of the clinical diagnosis of dementia,' *Journal of the Neurological Sciences*, 26, pp. 81-98.

TOMLIINSON, B. E. (1980) 'The structural and quantitative aspects of the dementias,' in Roberts, P. (Ed.) *Biochemistry of Dementia*, London, Wiley, pp. 15-52.

TOMLINSON, B. E. (1982) 'Plaques, tangles and Alzheimer's disease,' *Psychological Medicine*, 12, pp. 449-59.

TOMLINSON, B. E., BLESSED, G. and ROTH, M. (1968) 'Observations on the brains of non-demented old people,' *Journal of the Neurological Sciences*, 7, pp. 331-56.

TOMLINSON, B. E., BLESSED, G. and ROTH, M. (1970) 'Observations on the brains of demented old people,' *Journal of the Neurological Sciences*, 11, pp. 205-42.

TOMLINSON, B. E. and HENDERSEN, G. (1976) 'Some quantitative cerebral findings in normal and demented old people,' in Terry, R. D. and Gershon, S. (Eds) *Neurobiology of Aging, Aging*, Vol. 3, New York, Raven Press, pp. 183-204.

TORRES, F. and HUTTON, J. T. (1986) 'Clinical neurophysiology of dementia,' *Neurological Clinics*, 4, pp. 369-86.

TORVIK, A., LINDBOE, C. F. and ROGDE, S. (1982) 'Brain lesions in alcoholics. A neuropathological study with clinical correlations,' *Journal of the Neurological Sciences*, 56, pp. 233-48.

TULVING, E. (1972) 'Episodic and semantic memory,' in Tulving, E. and Donaldson, W. (Eds) *Organization of Memory*, New York, Academic Press, pp. 381-403.

TULVING, E. (1979) 'Relation between encoding specificity and levels of processing,' in Cermak, L. S. and Craik, F. I. M. (Eds) *Levels of Processing in Human Memory*, Hillsdale, N.J., Lawrence Erlbaum Associates, pp. 405-28.

TULVING, E. (1987) 'Multiple memory systems and consciousness,' *Human Neurobiology*, 6, pp. 67-80.

TULVING, E. and COLOTLA, V. A. (1970) 'Free recall of trilingual lists,' *Cognitive Psychology*, 1, pp. 86-98.

TULVING, E. and THOMPSON, D. M. (1973) 'Encoding specificity and retrieval processes in episodic memory,' *Psychological review*, 88, pp. 352–73.

TUOKKO, H. and CROCKETT, D. (1987) 'Clinical cholinergic deficiency WAIS profiles in a nondemented aged sample,' *Journal of Clinical and Experimental Neuropsychology*, 9, pp. 225–7.

TURVEY, M. (1973) 'On peripheral and central processes in vision: inferences from an information-processing analysis with pattern masking stimuli,' *Psychological Review*, 80, pp. 1–50.

TWEEDY, J. R., LANGER, K. G., and MCDOWELL, F. H. (1982) 'The effect of semantic relations on the memory deficit associated with Parkinson's disease,' *Journal of Clinical and Experimental Neuropsychology*, 4, pp. 235–47.

UHLMANN, R. F., LARSON, E. B. and KOEPSELL, T. D. (1986) 'Hearing impairment and cognitive decline in senile dementia of the Alzheimer's type,' *Journal of the American Geriatrics Society*, 34, pp. 207–10.

UHLMANN, R. F., LARSON, E. B., REES, T. S., KOEPSELL, T. D. and DUCKERT, L. G. (1989) 'Relationship of hearing impairment to dementia and cognitive dysfunction in older adults,' *Journal of the American Medical Association*, 261, pp. 1916–19.

ULATOWSKA, H. K., CANNITO, M. P., HAYASHI, M. M. and FLEMMING, S. G. (1985) 'Language abilities in the elderly,' in Ulatowska, H. K. (Ed.) *The Aging Brain: Communication in the Elderly*, London, Taylor and Francis, pp. 125–39.

UZZELL, B. P. and GROSS, Y. (1986) *Clinical Neuropsychology of Intervention*, Boston, Martinus Nijhoff.

VIGNOLO, L. A. (1969) 'Auditory agnosia' in Benton, A. L. (Ed.) *Contributions to Clinical Neuropsychology*, Chicago, Aldane, pp. 172–208.

VILLARDITA, C., SMIRNI, P., LE PIRA, F., ZAPPALA, G., and NICOLETTI, F. (1982) 'Mental deterioration, visuoperceptive disabilities and constuctional apraxia in Parkinson's disease,' *Acta Neurologica Scandinavica*, 66, pp. 112–20.

VROULIS, G. A., SMITH, R. C., BRINKMAN, S., SCHOOLAR, J. and GORDON, J. (1981) 'The effects of lecithin on memory in patients with senile dementia of the Alzheimer's type,' *Psychopharmacology Bulletin*, 17, pp. 127–8.

WAGNER, H. N. (1986) 'Quantitative imaging of neuroreceptors in the living human brain,' *Seminars in Nuclear Medicine*, 16, pp. 51–62.

WALSH, K. (1978) *Neuropsychology: a Clinical Approach*, Edinburgh, Churchill Livingstone.

WANG, H. S. (1978) 'Prognosis in dementia and related disorders in the aged,' in Katzman, R., Terry, R. D. and Bick, K. L. (Eds) *Alzheimer's Disease: Senile Dementia and Related Disorders, Aging*, Vol. 7, New York, Raven Press, pp. 309–13.

WANG, H. S. (1981) 'Neuropsychiatric procedures for the assessment of Alzheimer's disease, senile dementia, and related disorders,' in Miller, N. E. and Cohen, G. D. (Eds) *Clinical Aspects of Alzheimer's Disease and Senile Dementia, Aging*, Vol. 15, New York, Raven Press, pp. 85–100.

WARBURTON, D. M. (1979) 'Neurochemical basis of consciousness,' in Brown, K. and Cooper, S. J. (Eds) *Chemical Influences on Behaviour*, London, Academic Press, pp. 421–62.

WARBURTON, D. M. and WESNES, K. (1984) 'Drugs as research tools in psychology: cholinergic drugs and information processing, *Neuropsychobiology*, 11, pp. 121–32.

WARBURTON, J. W. (1967) 'Depressive symptoms in Parkinson's disease,' *Journal of Neurology, Neurosurgery and Psychiatry*, 30, pp. 368–70.

WARD, C. D., HESS, W. A. and CALNE, D. B. (1983) 'Olfactory impairment in Parkinson's disease', *Neurology*, 33, pp. 943–6.

WARNER, M. D., PEABODY, C. A., FLATTERY, J. L. and TINKLENBERG, J. R. (1986) 'Olfactory deficits and Alzheimer's disease,' *Biological Psychiatry*, 21, pp. 116–18.

WARREN, R. E. (1972) 'Stimulus encoding and memory,' *Journal of Experimental Psychology*, 94, pp. 90–100.

WARRINGTON, E. K. (1975) 'The selective impairment of semantic memory,' *Quarterly Journal of Experimental Psychology*, 27, pp. 635–57.

WARRINGTON, E. K. (1981) 'Neuropsychological evidence for mulitple memory systems,' *Acta Neurologica Scandinavica*, 64, Suppl 89, pp. 13–19.

WARRINGTON, E. K. and SHALLICE, T. (1969) 'The selective impairment of auditory short-term memory,' *Brain*, 92, pp. 885–96.

WARRINGTON, E. K. and WEISKRANTZ, L. (1970) 'Amnesic syndrome: consolidation or retrieval,' *Nature*, 228, pp. 628–30.

WASYLENKI, D. (1980) 'Depression in the elderly,' *Canadian Medical Association Journal*, 122, pp. 525–40.

WATSON, C. P. (1979) 'Clinical similarity of Alzhiemer and Creutzfeldt–Jakob disease,' *Annals of Neurology*, 6, pp. 368–9.

WECHSLER, A. F. (1977) 'Presenile dementia presenting as aphasia,' *Journal of Neurology. Neurosurgery and Psychiatry*, 40, pp. 303–5.

WECHSLER, A. F., VERITY, M. A., ROSENSCHEIN, S., FRIED, I. and SCHEIBEL, A. B. (1982) 'Pick's disease: a clinical, computed tomographic, and histologic study with golgi impregnation observations,' *Archives of Neurology*, 39, pp. 287–290.

WECHSLER, D. (1955), 'Wechsler Adult Intelligence Test (WAIS) Manual,' New York, The Psychological Test Corporation.

WECHSLER, D. (1958) 'The Measurement and Appraisal of Adult Intelligence,' Baltimore, Williams & Wilkins Co.

WECHSLER, D. (1981) 'Wechsler Adult Intelligence Test Revised (WAIS–R) Manual', Cleveland, The Psychological Test Corporation.

WEEKS, D. (1988) 'The Anomalous Sentences Repetition Test,' Windsor, NFER-Nelson.

WEINGARTNER, H. (1986) 'Automatic and effort-demanding cognitive processes in depression,' in Poon, L. W. (Ed.) *Handbook of Clinical Memory Assessment of Older Adults*, Washington, American Psychological Association, pp. 218–225.

WEINGARTNER, H., KAYE, W., SMALLBERG, S. A., EBERT, M. H., GILLIN, J. C. and SITARAM, N. (1981) 'Memory failure in progressive idiopathic dementia,' *Journal of Abnormal Psychology*, 90, pp. 187–96.

WEINGARTNER, H., SITARAM, N. and GILLIN, J. C. (1979) 'The role of the cholinergic nervous system in memory consolidation,' *Bulletin of the Psychonomic Society*, 13, pp. 9–11.

WEINTRAUB, S., MESULAM, M. M., AUTRY, R., BARATZ, R., CHOLAKOS, B. N., KAPUST, L., RANSIL, B., TELLERS, J. G., ALBERT, M. S., LoCASTRO, S. and MOSS, M. (1983) 'Lecithin in the treatment of Alzheimer's disease,' *Archives of Neurology*, 40, pp. 527–8.

WEINSTEIN, E. A. and KAHN, R. L. (1952) 'Nonaphasic misnaming (paraphasia) in organic brain syndrome', *Archives of Neurology and Psychiatry*, 67, pp. 72–9.

WEISKRANTZ, L. (1987) 'Neuroanatomy of memory and amnesia: a case for multiple memory systems,' *Human Neurobiology*, 6, pp. 93–105.

WEISSMAN, M. M. and MYERS, J. K. (1978) 'Affective disorders in a US urban community,' *Archives of General Psychiatry*, 35, pp. 1304–11.

WELFORD, A. T. (1977) 'Motor performance,' in Birren, J. E. and Schaie, K. W., (Eds) *Handbook of the Psychology of Aging*, New York, Van Nostrand Reinhold Company, pp. 450–96.

WELFORD, A. T. (1980a) 'Relationship between reaction time and fatigue, stress, age and sex,' in Welford, A. T. (Eds) *Reaction Times*, New York, Academic Press, pp. 321–54.

WELFORD, A. T. (1980b) 'Memory and age: a perspective view,' in Poon, L. W., Fozard, J. L., Cermak, L. S., Arenberg, D. and Thompson, L. W. (Eds) *New Directions in Memory and Aging*, Hillsdale, N.J., Lawrence Erlbaum Associates, pp. 1–17.

WELLS, C. E. (1978) 'Chronic brain disease: an overview,' *American Journal of Psychiatry*, 135, pp. 1–12.

WELLS, C. E. (1979) 'Pseudodementia,' *American Journal of Psychiatry*, 136, pp. 895–900.

WELLS, C. E. (1980) 'The differential diagnosis of psychiatric disorders in the elderly,' In Cole, J. O. and Barrett, J. E. (Eds) *Psychopathology in the Aged*, New York, Raven Press, pp. 19–31.

WELLS, N. E. J. (1979) 'Dementia in Old Age,' London, Office of Health Economics.

WESNES, K. and REVELL, A. (1984) 'The separate and combined effects of scopolamine and nicotine on human information processing,' *Psychopharmacology*, 84, pp. 5–11

WESNES, K. and WARBURTON, D. M. (1983a) 'Effects of scopolamine on stimulus sensitivity and response bias in a visual vigilance task,' *Neuropsychobiology*, 9, pp. 154–7.

WESNES, K. and WARBURTON, D. M. (1983b) 'Effects of smoking on rapid visual information processing performance,' *Neuropsychobiology*, 9, pp. 223–9.

WESSELING, H., AGOSTON, S., VAN DAM, G. B., PASMA, J., DEWITT, D. J. and HAVINGA, H. (1984) 'Effects of 4-aminopyridine in elderly patients with Alzheimer's disease,' *New England Journal of Medicine*, 310, pp. 988–9.

WETTSTEIN, A. (1983) 'No effect from double-blind trial of physostigmine and lecithin in Alzheimer disease,' *Annals of Neurology*, 13, pp. 210–2.

WETTSTEIN, A. and SPIEGEL, R. (1984) 'Clinical trials with the drug RS86 in Alzheimer's disease (AD) and senile dementia of the Alzheimer type (SDAT)', *Psychopharmacology*, 84, pp. 572–3.

WHITAKER, H. (1976) 'A case of the isolation of the language function,' in Whitaker, H. and Whitaker, H. A., (Eds) *Studies in Neurolinguistics*, Vol. 2, New York, Academic Press, pp. 1–58.

WHITE, O. B., SAINT-CYR, J. A. and SHARPE, J. A. (1983a) 'Ocular motor deficits in Parkinson's disease. I. The horizontal vestibulo-ocular reflex and its regulation,' *Brain*, 106, pp. 355–70.

WHITE, O. B., SAINT-CYR, J. A., TOMLINSON, R. D. and SHARPE, J. A. (1983b) 'Ocular motor deficits in Parkinsons disease. II. Control of the saccadic and smooth pursuit systems,' *Brain*, 106, pp. 371–87.

WHITE, P., HILEY, C. R., GOODHARDT, M. J., CARRASCO, L. M., KEET, J. P., WILLIAMS, I. E. I. and BOWEN, D. M. (1977) 'Neocortical cholinergic neurons in elderly people,' *Lancet*, i, pp. 668–71.

WHITEHEAD, A. (1973a) 'The pattern of WAIS performance in elderly psychiatric patients,' *British Journal of Social and Clinical Psychology*, 12, pp. 435–6.

WHITEHEAD, A. (1973b) 'Verbal learning and memory in elderly depressives,' *British Journal of Psychiatry*, 123, pp. 203–8.

WHITEHEAD, A. (1975) 'Recognition memory in dementia,' *British Journal of Social and Clinical Psychology*, 14, pp. 191–4.

WHITEHEAD, A. and HUNT, A. (1982) 'Elderly psychiatric patients: a five-year prospective study,' *Psychological Medicine*, 12, pp. 149–57.

WHITEHOUSE, P. J. (1986) 'The concept of subcortical and cortical dementia: another look,' *Annals of Neurology*, 19, pp. 1–6.

WHITEHOUSE, P. J., PRICE, D. L., CLARK, A. W., COYLE, J. T. and DeLONG, M. R. (1981) 'Alzheimer disease: evidence for selective loss of cholinergic neurons in the nucleus basalis,' *Annals of Neurology*, 10, pp. 122–6.

WHITEHOUSE, P. J. PRICE, D. L., STRUBBLE, R. G., CLARK, A. W., COYLE, J. T. and DeLONG, M. R. (1982) 'Alzheimer's disease and senile dementia: loss of neurons in the basal forebrain,' *Science*, 215, pp. 1237–9.

WHITFORD, G. M. (1986) 'Alzheimer's disease and serotonin: a review,' *Neuropsychobiology*, 15, pp. 133–42.

WHURR, R. (1974) *The Aphasia Screening Test*, London, published by the author.

WILCOCK, G. K. and ESIRI, M.M. (1982) 'Plaques, tangles and dementia: a quantitative study,' *Journal of the Neurological Sciences*, 56, pp. 343–56.

WILCOCK, G. K., ESIRI, M. M., BOWEN, D. M., and SMITH, C. C. T. (1982) 'Alzheimer's disease: correlation of cortical choline acetyltransferase activity with the severity of dementia and hisitological abnormalities,' *Journal of the Neurological Sciences*, 57, pp. 407–17.

WILKINS, R. M. and BRODY, I. A. (1969) 'Neurological Classics 20: Alzheimer's disease,' *Archives of Neurology*, 21, pp. 109–10.

WILL, R. G. and MATTHEWS, W. B. (1984) 'A retrospective study of Creutzfeld–Jakob disease in England and Wales, 1970–1979. I Clinical features,' *Journal of Neurology, Neurosurgery and Psychiatry*, 47, pp. 134–40.

WILLIAMS, J. M. G. and BROADBENT, K. (1986) 'Autobiographical memory in suicide attempts,' *Journal of Abnormal Psychology*, 95, pp. 144–9.

WILLIAMS, M. (1956) 'Studies of perception in senile dementia: cue-selection as a function of intelligence,' *British Journal of Medical Psychology*, 29, pp. 270–9.

WILLIAMSON, J. (1978) 'Depression in the elderly,' *Age and Ageing*, 7, Suppl, pp. 35–40.

WILLIAMSON, J., STOKOE, I. H., GRAY, S., FISHER, M., SMITH, A., McGHEE, A. and STEPHENSON, E. (1964) 'Old people at home: their unsupported needs,' *Lancet*, i, pp. 117–20.

WILMOT, C. A. (1989) 'Excitatory amino acid antagonists: behavioural and biochemical approaches for the development of new central nervous system therapeutic agents,' *Drug Development Research*, 17, pp. 339–65.

WILLNER, P. (1989) *Depression: a Psychobiological Synthesis*, New York, John Wiley.

WILSON, B. A. (1987a) 'Single case experimental designs in neuropsychological rehabilitation,' *Journal of Clinical and Experimental Neuropsychology*, 9, pp. 527–44.

WILSON, B. A. (1987b) *Rehabilitation of Memory*, New York, Guilford Press.

WILSON, B. A. (1988) 'Models of cognitive rehabilitation,' in Wood, R. LL. and Eames, P. (Eds) *Models of brain injury rehabilitation*, London, Chapman & Hall, pp. 117–41.

WILSON, R. S., BACON, L. D., FOX, J. H. and KASZNIAK, A. W. (1983) 'Primary memory and secondary memory in dementia of the Alzheimer type,' *Journal of Clinical Neuropsychology*, 5, pp. 337–44.

WILSON, R. S., FOX, J. H., HUCKMAN, M. S., BACON, L. D. and LOBICK, J. J. (1982a) 'Computed tomography in dementia,' *Neurology*, 32, pp. 1054–7.

WILSON, R. S., KASZNIAK, A. W., BACON, L. D., FOX, J. H. and KELLY, M. P. (1982b) 'Facial recognition memory in dementia,' *Cortex*, 18, pp. 329–36.

WILSON, R. S., KASZNIAK, A. W. and FOX, J. H. (1981) 'Remote memory in senile dementia,' *Cortex*, 17, pp. 41–8.

WILSON, R. S., KASZNIAK, A. W., KLAWANS, H. L. and GARRON, D. C. (1980) 'High speed memory scanning in Parkinsonism,' *Cortex*, 16, pp. 67–72.

WILSON, R. S., ROSENBAUM, G., BROWN, G., ROUKE, D., WHITMAN, D. and GRISELL, J. (1978) 'An index of premorbid intelligence,' *Journal of Consulting and Clinical Psychology*, 46, pp. 1554–5.

WILSON, S. A. K. (1912) 'Progressive lenticular degeneration: a familial nervous disease associated with cirrhosis of the liver,' *Brain*, 34, pp. 295–509.

WINBLAD, B., BUCHT, G., FOWLER, C. J. and WALLACE, W. (1986) 'Beyond the transmitter-based approach to Alzheimer's disease,' in Crook, T., Bartus, R., Ferris, S. and Gershon, S. (Eds) *Treatment Development Strategies for Alzheimer's Disease*, Madison, Mark Powley Associates, pp. 35–66.

WINGFIELD, A. (1980) 'Attention, levels of processing and state-dependent recall,' in Poon, L. W., Fozard, J. L., Cermak, L. S., Arenberg, D. and Thompson, L. W. *New Directions in Memory and Ageing*, Hillsdale, N.J., Lawrence Erlbaum, pp. 135–41.

WISNIEWSKI, H. M., MORETZ, R. C. and IQBAL, K. (1986) 'No evidence for aluminium in etiology and pathogenesis of Alzheimer's disease,' *Neurobiology of Ageing*, 7, pp. 532–3.

WOOD, P. L., NAIR, N. P., ETIENNE, P., LAL, S., GAUTHIER, S., ROBITAILLE, Y., BIRD, E. D., PALO, J., HALTIA, M. and PAETAU, A. (1983) 'Lack of cholinergic deficit in the neocortex in Pick's disease,' *Progress in Neuropsychopharmacology and Biological Psychiatry*, 7, pp. 725–7.

WOODS, R. T. and BRITTON, P. G. (1985) *Clinical Psychology with the Elderly*, London, Croom Helm.

WOODS, R. T. and PIERCY, M. (1974) 'A similarity between amnesic memory and normal forgetting,' *Neuropsychologia*, 12, pp. 437–45.

WOODWORTH, R. S. and SCHLOSBERG, H. (1954) *Experimental Psychology*, New York, Holt.

WRIGHT, A. F. and WHALLEY, L. J. (1984) 'Genetics, ageing and dementia,' *British Journal of Psychiatry*, 145, pp. 20–38.

WRIGHT, C. E., BRASDA, N. and HARDING, G. F. A. (1987) 'Pathology of the optic nerve and visual association areas. Information given by the flash and pattern visual evoked potential, and the temporal and spatial contrast sensitivity function,' *Brain*, 110, pp. 107–20.

WRIGHT, C. E. and FURLONG, P. L. (1988) 'Visual evoked potentials in elderly patients with primary or multi-infarct dementia,' *British Journal of Psychiatry*, 152, pp. 679–82.

WRIGHT, C. E., HARDING, G. F. A. and ORWIN, A. (1984) 'Presenile dementia – the use of the flash and pattern VEP in diagnosis, *Electroencephalography and Clinical Neurophysiology*, 57, pp. 405–15.

WRIGHT, C. E., HARDING, G. F. A. and ORWIN, A. (1986) 'The flash and pattern VEP as a diagnostic indicator of dementia,' *Documenta Opthalmologica*, 62, pp. 89–96.

WRIGLEY, M. (1987) 'Capgras' syndrome in a patient with dementia,' *British Journal of Psychiatry*, 151, pp. 273–4.

WURTMAN, R. J. (1985) 'Alzheimer's disease,' *Scientific American*, 252, pp. 62–66, 71–4.

YATES, A. J. (1956) 'The use of vocabulary in the measurement of intellectual deterioration – a review,' *Journal of Mental Science*, 102, pp. 409–40.

YATES, C. M., ALLISON, Y., SIMPSON, J., MALONEY, A. F. J. and GORDON, A. (1979) 'Dopamine in Alzheimer's disease and senile dementia,' *Lancet*, ii, pp. 851–2.

YATES, C. M., SIMPSON, J., MALONEY, A. F. J. and GORDON, A. (1980a) 'Neurochemical observations in a case of Pick's disease,' *Journal of Neurological Sciences*, 48, pp. 257–63.

YATES, C. M., SIMPSON, J., MALONEY, A. F. J., GORDON, A. and REID, A. H. (1980b) 'Alzheimer-like cholinergic deficiency in Down's syndrome,' *Lancet*, ii, p. 979.

YESAVAGE, J. (1979) 'Dementia: differential diagnosis and treatment,' *Geriatrics*, 34, pp. 51–9.

ZANGWILL, O. L. (1964) 'Intelligence in aphasia,' in De Reuck, A. V. S. and O'Connor, M. (Eds) *Disorders of Language*, London, Churchill Livingstone, pp. 261–84.

ZARIT, S. H. (1986) 'Issues and directions in family intervention research,' in Light, E. and Lebowitz, B. (Eds) *Alzheimer's Disease, Treatment and Family Stress: Directions for Research*, DHSS Publication number (ADM) 89–1569, Washington, D.C., U.S. Government Printing Office.

ZARIT, S. H., MILLER, N. E. and KAHN, R. L. (1978) 'Brain fucntion, intellectual impairment and education in the aged,' *Journal of the American Geriatrics Society*, 26, pp. 58–67.

ZIEGLER, D. K. (1954) 'Cerebral atrophy in psychiatric patients,' *American Journal of Psychiatry*, 111, pp. 454–8.

ZUBIN, J. (1975) 'Problem of attention in schizophrenia,' in Kietzman, M. L., Sutton, S. and Zubin, J. (Eds) *Experimental Approaches to Psychopathology*, New York, Academic Press, pp. 139–66.

Author Index

Subject Index

acetylcholine (ACh), 46–51, 61, 66, 69, 188
  enhancing release of, 74
  increasing synthesis of, 71–3
  preventing breakdown of, 73–4
  acelycholinesterase (AChE) 47, 48
achromatopsia, 210
ageing, accelerated, 44, 64–5, 236
aggression, 76
agnosia, 85, 200–1, 217
  auditory sound, 201
  prosopagnosia, 201–2, 210, 211
  visual, 201, 202, 210
    apperceptive, 201
    associative, 201
agraphia, 85, 90, 179–82
AIDS, 25
akinesia, 96
alcoholism 41, 42
  see also dementia, alcoholic
aluminium toxicity, 33
Alzheimer's disease (AD), 23–4
  attentional impairment in, 189, 191, 194, 195,
    197, 198
  clinical features of, 83–92
    agnosia, 85, 92, 111
    aphasia, 85, 92, 164
    apraxia, 85, 92, 224, 228, 230
    decreased life expectancy, 91
    disorientation, spatial, 84, 111
    disorientation, temporal, 84
    dyspasia, 86
    dyspraxia, 111
    emotional changes, 86
    extrapyramidal features, 87

    incontinence, 88, 111
    language disturbance, 89, 90, 169–82
    memory disturbance, 84, 88
    personality changes, 86
    psychotic features, 87
  diagnosis of, 107–9, 114
    DEFINITE, 107, 109
    POSSIBLE, 107, 108–9
    PROBABLE, 107, 108
  discourse impairment in, 175–7
  DNA markers for, 247
  gustatory impairment in, 205
  hearing impairment in, 217
  lexicon impairment in, 173, 174
  memory impairment in
    implicit, 159, 160
    intrusion errors, 150, 151
    long-term, 144, 145, 146, 147, 148, 149
    recognition, 153–4
    remote, 155, 156, 157
    retrieval cues to combat, 151–2
    semantic, 157, 158, 182–3
    short-term, 139, 140, 141, 142, 143
  naming impairment in, 169–71
  neurochemistry of, 48–9, 52–3, 54, 55, 59,
    60–1, 61–2, 64–5
  neuropathology of, 29–34, 44–5
  olfactory impairment in, 203, 204, 205, 206
  reading impairment in, 167–8, 179
  somatosensory impairment in, 208, 209
  visual impairment in, 171, 211, 212, 213, 214
  word fluency impairment in, 172, 173–4, 182
  writing impairment in, 179–82
  see also DAT; SDAT

Neuropsychology and the dementias

amnesia
  anterograde, 42
  retrograde, 42
amygdala, 31, 203
amyloid, 246, 247
angular gyrus syndrome, 37
animal neuropsychology, 3–5, 104
anticholinergics
  effects of, in normal subjects, 66–9
  see also atropine; scopolamine
anticholinesterases, 67, 69, 73
  see also physostigmine and THA
antidepressants, 102
apathy, 94, 96
aphasia, 85, 90, 164, 165
  tests for, 176
  types of, 176, 178
apraxia, 221, 222
  buccofacial, 230
  constructional, 222–7
  dressing, 222–3
  ideational, 229
  ideomotor, 227–9
arecholine, 70, 77
arousal disturbances, 187
aspirin, 243
assessment procedures, 5
astereognosis, 208
astrocytes, 38, 40
ataxia, 94
attention, 68, 69, 162–3, 187–99
  intensive aspects of, 193–8
  selective aspects of, 188–93
atrophy, 110, 116
  circumscribed lobar, 110
  cortical, 29–30, 37
  subcortical, 37
atropine, 67

BAEP (brainstem auditory evoked potential), 115
BAERs (brainstem auditory evoked response),
    218
Binswanger's disease, 35, 37
Boston Naming Test, 171
bradykinesia, 96, 196, 198
bradyphrenia, 196, 198
Brown-Peterson distractor paradigm, 67, 140,
    141, 142

Capgras syndrome, 211
caudate nucleus, 38
ChAT (choline acetyltransferase), 47, 48, 49, 50,
    64, 203

choline, 46, 47, 70
cholinomimetics
  clinical studies using, 70–5
  effects of, in normal subjects, 69–71
  side-effects of, 77
chorea, 97
cognitive assessment, 120–31
communication
  non-verbal, 183–5
  optimization of, 241–2
community care, 15, 16
Continuous Performance Test, 196–7, 198
core, isodendritic, 31, 42
cortex, cerebral, 31
Creutzfeldt-Jakob disease, 25, 35
  clinical features of, 87, 93
  diagnosis of, 109, 114
  memory impairment in, 158
  neurochemistry of, 54, 55
  neuropathology of, 38–41
  reading impairment in, 168
  somatosensory impairment in, 209
  visual impairment in, 211
CT (computed tomography), 116–17

DAT (dementia of Alzheimer's type), 24, 43
  depletion of ACh in, 69
  treatment of, 72, 76, 77
  see also Alzheimer's disease; SDAT
degeneration
  granulovacuolar, 34, 38
  neurofibrillary, 38
dementia
  alcoholic 25
    clinical features of, 98
    neurochemistry of, 51, 55, 58
    neuropathology of, 41–2
    see also Korsakoff's syndrome
  Alzheimer's presenile, 85
  conditions causing, 22–3
  cortical, 24, 25, 43, 98–9
  definition of, 17–20
  differential diagnosis of
    between DAT and multi-infarct, 111–13, 118
    between DAT and other degenerative,
      106–11, 118
    and functional psychiatric disorders, 101–6
  DSM III-R criteria for diagnosis of, 18–19
  economic costs of, 14–15
  epidemiology of, 20–1
  'functional', 101, 102
  human costs of, 15–17
  lacunar, 35